THE BUDTENDER'S GUIDE TO THE GALAXY

CANADIAN CANNABIS FIRST IMPRESSIONS

DYLAN BRUCK

~ A WEALTH OF CANNABIS KNOWLEDGE ~

~ A RECORD OF DAYS SPENT IN THE HAZE ~

~ A TESTAMENT TO STONER INGENUITY ~

~ ENJOY THE TRIP ~

The Budtender's Guide to the Galaxy
Canadian Cannabis First Impressions
By Dylan Bruck

Published by Dylan Bruck

ISBN: 978-1-7781755-0-3

Revised Edition

THE BUDTENDER'S GUIDE TO THE GALAXY

CANADIAN CANNABIS FIRST IMPRESSIONS

DYLAN BRUCK

"Many but not all my cannabis trips have somewhere in them a symbolism significant to me, which…. has produced a very rich array of insights….

….Some of the hardest work I've ever done has been to put such insights down on tape or in writing"

- Mr. X (Dr. Carl Sagan)
"Acute Intoxication: Literary Reports" (1969)
Essay Written for "Marijuana Reconsidered" (1971)

Dedication

In Loving Memory of Jeff Horan

A Friend with Weed is a Friend Indeed - I'll Never Forget Our Sessions Together

Foreword

Pot Jesus and The Bible: The Dylan Bruck Saga

Standing on the doorstep of our newly built shop was Dylan Bruck - or "Pot Jesus," as early coworkers would come to refer to him. He was now on the front line of Canada's cannabis legalization workforce, where he immediately impacted the people around him, flaunting his infectious passion for removing the stigma around cannabis. My relationship with Dylan was simple: he wanted to write a book about cannabis, a "Bible" of sorts, and I wanted to give him the nurturing environment and culture to do precisely that. Dylan is not the Mr. Miyagi of cannabis knowledge, nor is he the crane kick that took down the Cobra Kai dojo and its menacing delinquents - he is Karate.

Before opening my eyes and learning about cannabis, I had a negative opinion about it and its consumers. Hypothetically speaking, my quality of life could have been higher had I tried cannabis sooner, which is pun intended. Misinformation will forever be the Achilles heel of the cannabis industry; in a world plagued by "Reefer Madness," we have become a product of our own naive bias towards this beautiful plant.

Cannabis is not what you think it is. You deserve to appreciate cannabis how Dylan does, break free from the misinformation, and learn to love the cannabis you consume and cultivate. I invite you to journey through these pages and observe this tome stripping away the stigma and planting the seeds of inspiration, enlightenment, and a passion for higher learning.

- Tyler Steiger

Operations Manager
Plantlife Cannabis

Thanks

My Family and Friends

Without the love and support of my dearest family and friends, I wouldn't have come so far as to be able to write this book. I thank you all: my family in Ontario, my friends in the cannabis industry, the Edmonton area MTG community, and everyone else I've momentarily forgotten due to stoned-ness.

For your support and assistance with proofreading the book, thank you Melissa and Wesley.

Thank you, Jourdan and Hayle, for always being there, even when we never see each other.

Grandma and Grandpa, for always being there, even when we never see each other, and for lending me used car money, thank you.

Thank you to my family for putting up with the dankness of my room leaching out into the house and supporting me in countless ways throughout this writing process and in my life.

Mom, for believing in me since the very beginning back in '96, and for being my mom, turned friend, turned stoner pal, thank you.

Sarah, my sister, the most positive memories of my childhood are those of you. Ever since, you have grown yourself into an increasingly wonderful and impressive person - something that I now admire and look up to. Thank you for setting the bar so high.

Finally, Kelsie, without your support throughout this experience, I do not know that I would have had the motivation to continue at various points where I struggled - thank you.

Thanks

The Plantlife Team

Without the fine folks at Plantlife, who've supported my project since its inception, I may have never found the confidence to pursue this book to completion. To them, I owe immense gratitude.

Ian, for hiring me, listening to me passionately ramble on about the Volcano for a half-hour during training, and knowing who The Dillinger Escape Plan is, thank you. Tyler, for recognizing my potential and for laying the groundwork for my path forward, thank you. Vanessa, thank you for the endless support of my work and the constant problem-solving at work. Thank you, Coleman, for re-igniting the creative spark within me during our mid-shift "nonsense" chats (what IS a sandwich?) and co-envisioning a future with me where my work is a success. Bret, Ashton and Chris, thank you for giving me motivation during the final year of writing and for all of the stoned sessions along the way.

I'd like to thank the Plantlife staff who have assisted me throughout my reviews: your efforts helped make this entire project possible. Gaige, Travis, Myron, Connor, Ash, Lisa, Kalli, Brent, Matthew, Trevor, Wesley, AJ, Sarah, Ria, Haley, Shaan, Steph and everyone else that provided support, without you, I simply would not have been able to try all of the cannabis that I did in such a short time.

A special thanks is also owed to supporters of my pre-order for the book at Plantlife - you all made this book a reality instead of just a PDF.

Lastly, to the entire Plantlife team: thank you. I appreciate you all, but I'm certainly too stoned to start naming everyone, let's face it.

Thanks

The Cannabis Industry

Without this industry, my book would serve no purpose and never have been created.

Thank you to all budtenders who make sincere and meaningful recommendations. Thank you to all brand representatives equipped with cultivar cards and terpene percentages.

Thank you to every advocate who has believed in cannabis and fought, suffered, and persevered to ensure its eventual legalization.

To the consumers: the occasional tokers, the weekend weed enthusiasts, the sincere stoners out there, however much and however you consume, thank you for not buying into the stigma, the misinformation, the "reefer madness."

To those who have inspired me along the way within the realm of cannabis: Tommy Chong and Cheech Marin, Seth Rogen and James Franco, Bob Marley and the Wailers, Sublime and Lou Dog, Hermes Conrad and "The Omichronic," Little Jacob and Niko Bellic… the list goes on, thank you.

For providing the soundtrack for much of my writing process, a big thank you to Stoner Doom Metal. From Black Sabbath's "Master of Reality", to Sleep's "Holy Mountain", to Electric Wizard's "Dopethrone", and everything else within that hazy realm of sound, it all got the creative juices flowing.

A special thanks is also due for Randy Daigneau, Casey Hiltemann and Shahbaaz Kara-Virani, for their contributions to the back cover.

Table of Contents

Dedication ...II

Foreword ...III

Thanks ...IV

Introduction ...1

Cannabis 101 ...2

Cannabis Species ...2

Cannabinoids ...4

Terpenes ...7

Flower ...11

Higher Learning ...16

Making a First Impression ...20

A Planned Procedure ...20

The Right Tool for the Job ...26

My Main Insights and Takeaways ...29

Brand Bios and Cultivar Reviews ...40

Brand Score Ranking ...40

18Twelve ...42
- 8 Ball Kush

48North ...44
- Granddaddy Purple
- Green Cush
- Paris OG
- Strain Hunters' Franco's Lemon Cheese
- Strain Hunters' Holy Punch

7Acres ...50
- Ice Cream Cake
- Island Pink Kush
- Jack Haze
- Jean Guy
- Sensi Star
- White Widow

Abba Medix ...57
- Critical Orange Punch
- Purple Bud
- Sage 'n Sour

Acreage Pharms ...61
- All Kush
- CBD Kush
- Mazar
- OA

Acreage Pharms ...61
- Rewind
- Scentimental
- Sensi Star
- Star Banner

AltaVie ...70
- Airplane Mode
- Cabaret
- Campfire
- Harmonic

Ankr Organics ...75
- Siren

Artisan Batch ...77
- Meat Breath
- Original Glue

Aurora ...80
- Banana Split
- Blue Dream
- Ghost Train Haze
- LA Confidential
- MK Ultra
- OG Melon
- Summer Fling
- Temple

Blissco ...89
- Green Cush

Boaz ...91
- CBD Skunk Haze
- Crescendo
- Green Kraken
- Mandarin Cookies
- Platinum Gelato
- Wedding Cake
- White Russian
- Zour Apples

Broken Coast ...100
- Denman
- Gabriola
- Galiano
- Keats
- Moresby
- Quadra
- Ruxton
- Saturna
- Savary
- Sonora
- Stryker

Caliber ...112
- Berry White
- Koffee
- Lemon Z

Canaca ...116
- Alien Dawg
- Citrus Tangerine
- Ghost Train Haze
- Glue
- Glueberry
- Great North CBD
- Green Cush
- GSC
- Hash Plant
- Jean Guy
- Mango
- OG Kush
- Oregon Golden Goat
- Sensi Star
- Shishkaberry
- White Widow
- White Widow Haze

Canna Farms ...134
- Blue Dream
- Bubba Kush
- CBD Critical Mass
- Critical Silver Super Haze
- GSC
- Hash Plant
- Pink Kush
- Tangerine Dream

Citizen Stash ...143
- MAC1
- Sage 'n Sour
- Stonewall
- Sunset Sherbet

Color ...148
- Blueberry Seagal
- Ghost Train Haze
- Mango Haze
- Pedro's Sweet Sativa
- White Shark

Cove ...154
- Reflect
- Rest
- Revive
- Rise

Delta 9 ...159
- Afghani Kush
- Apple Fritter
- Blue Venom
- CBD Skunk Haze
- Electric Punch
- GGIV
- Headbanger
- Jack Herer

Delta 9 ...159
- Kali Mist
- Lava Cake
- Lemon Meringue
- Lemon Skunk
- OG Kush
- Sinaloa Gold
- Space Cake
- Stargazer
- Super Lemon Haze
- White Out
- White Russian
- White Widow

DNA Genetics ...180
- Chocolate Fondue
- Kosher Kush
- Lemon Skunk
- Sour Kush
- Sour Tangie

Edison ...186
- Black Cherry Punch
- Blue Velvet
- Casa Blanca
- Chemdog
- City Lights
- El Dorado
- Ice Cream Cake
- La Strada
- Limelight
- Lola Montes
- Rio Bravo
- Samurai Spy
- Slurricane
- The General

Emerald Health ...201
- Afghani Kush
- Black Widow
- Chemdog
- Durga Mata
- Hash Plant
- Jack the Ripper
- Timewarp A3
- White Rhino

Farmstead ...210
- Colada

FIGR ...212
- No. 7
- No. 8
- No. 14

Fireside ...216
- Sensi Star
- Wappa

Flowr ...219
- Atomical Haze
- Delahaze
- Diesel
- Durga Mata
- Durga Mata 2 CBD
- Intergalactic Princess
- Pink Kush
- Sensi Star
- Tahoe OG

Good Buds ...229
- Mango Taffie
- Salty God
- Sapphire OG

Good Supply ...233
- Jean Guy
- Monkey Glue
- Royal Highness

Grail ...237
- Headband
- Pink Kush
- Rockstar

Habitat ...241
- Cake

Haven St. ...243
- Beach Hammock
- Big Dipper
- Blue Comet
- Blueberry Kush
- Cosmic Thunder
- Couch Surf
- Indigo Daze
- Midnight Jam
- Napali CBD
- Noisy Neighbour
- Sonic Express
- Twilight

Hexo ...256
- Atlantis
- Bayou
- Helios
- Horizon
- Lagoon
- Nebula
- Sierra
- Terra
- Tsunami

High Tide ...266
- A. Haze
- Ghost Train Haze
- Headband

High Tide ...266
- Kade's Kush

Highland Grow ...271
- Cherry Burst
- White Lightning

Houseplant ...274
- Hybrid
- Indica
- Sativa

Ignite ...278
- Crescendo
- GG4
- Tropicana Cookies

Joi Botanicals ...282
- Cake Crasher #1

Kingsway ...284
- Dayshift
- Nightshift

Kiwi ...287
- Cali-O
- Mango Haze
- San Fernando Valley

Kolab ...291
- Ice Cream Cake
- Kalifornia

LBS ...294
- Moonbeam
- Ocean View
- Palm Tree CBD
- Sunset

Marley Natural ...299
- Berry Lights
- Blue Dream
- Cannatonic
- Island Sweet Skunk

Namaste ...304
- Citrique
- Death Bubba
- Durga Mata 2
- MK Ultra
- Sensi Star
- Shishkaberry
- Ultra Sour
- Wappa

Natural History ...313
- ACDC Cookies
- Crescendo
- Fruit Cake
- LA Kush Cake
- Mandarin Cookies
- Melon Cookies
- Zour Apples

Ness ...321
- Lemon Berry
- Mint Sour

Northern Harvest ...324
- Blue Haze
- Strawberry Ice

Ogen ...327
- Early Glue RBx1
- Gas Berries
- Lemon Z

Palmetto ...331
- Chemdog
- Headband

Palmetto ...331
- Nuken

Poolboy ...335
- Bruce
- Chemdog
- King T
- Raspberry Cough

Pure Sunfarms ...340
- Afghan Kush
- Critical Kali Mist
- D. Bubba
- Headband
- Island Honey
- Pink Kush
- Pure Sun CBD
- Purple Sun God
- White Rhino

Qwest ...350
- Black Lime Reserve
- Death Bubba
- Ex-Wife
- Forbidden Fruit
- Gelato 33
- Gelato 41
- Goji OG
- Ice Cream Cake
- JB Cookies
- Kalifornia
- Kush Mints
- MAC1
- OG Kush 25
- Oregon Lemons
- Original Glue
- Phenome OG Spike
- Pineapple Upside Down Cake

Qwest ...350
- Point Break
- Strawberry Cough
- Super Silver Skunk
- Wedding Breath
- Wedding Cake

Redecan ...373
- Charlees
- Cold Creek Kush
- God Bud
- Outlaw
- Wappa

Reef ...379
- Coastal Kush
- High Seas

Riff ...382
- Blue Ninety Eight
- DT81
- Hawaii Heartbreak
- Raider Kush
- Subway Scientist
- Sunday Special
- Sweet Jersey 3
- Two-Tone Ban

Robinsons ...391
- GG#4
- Lemon Garlic OG

Royal City Cannabis Co. ...394
- Dreamzicle
- Dukem
- Orange Hill Special

Royal City Cannabis Co. ...394
- Rockstar Tuna
- Royal Goddess

Royal High ...400
- Liberty Haze
- Super Skunk

San Rafael '71 ...403
- Delahaze
- Great White Shark
- Island Sweet Skunk
- Pink Kush
- Purple Chitral
- Tangerine Dream

Simply Bare ...410
- Apple Toffee
- Blue Dream
- Creek Congo
- SFV OG Kush
- Sour Cookies

Skosha ...416
- Lemon Dory
- Mirage
- Nor'Easter

Solei ...420
- Balance
- Free
- Gather
- Renew
- Sense
- Unplug

Spinach ...427
- Blueberry
- Blue Dream
- Dancehall

Spinach ...427
- Diesel
- Rockstar Kush
- Sensi Star
- White Widow

Strain Rec ...435
- 24K Gold
- 8 Ball Kush
- Candy Kush
- CVK Cookie
- Ice Cream Cake
- Raspberry Cough
- Strawberry Magic

Sundial ...443
- Berry Bliss
- Blue Nova
- Citrus Punch
- Daydream
- Lemon Riot
- Strawberry Twist
- Twilight
- Wild Indigo
- Zen Berry

Symbl ...453
- Bella Luna
- Daily Rind
- Dreamweaver
- Grape Royale
- Hoverboard
- Solar Power
- Wave Runner

Tantalus Labs ...461
- Blue Dream
- Harlequin
- LA Kush Cake
- Pacific OG
- Serratus

Tantalus Labs ...461
- Sky Pilot

The Green Organic Dutchman ...468
- GG#4
- Harmony
- Rockstar Tuna
- Unite

Thumbs Up ...473
- Amnesia x Super Haze
- Garlic Z
- Strain Hunters' Lemon Skunk
- Strain Hunters' White Lemon

Tokyo Smoke ...478
- Ease
- Go
- Pause
- Rise

Top Leaf ...483
- Blue Dream
- Bubba
- GSC
- Jager OG
- Northern Lights
- Oregon Golden Goat
- Pink Kush
- Purple Clementine
- Strawberry Cream
- Super Skunk

Tweed ...494
- Argyle
- Bakerstreet

Tweed ...494
- Balmoral
- Boaty McBoatface
- Donegal
- Herringbone
- Highlands
- Houndstooth
- Penelope

Up ...504
- Cold Creek Kush
- Ghost Train Haze
- Northern Berry

Van Der Pop ...508
- Cloudburst
- Eclipse

Vertical ...511
- Banana Split
- Blissberry
- Cold Creek Kush
- Hifi 4G
- Kent County Kush
- Longwoods Leaf
- Maple City Monster
- Shishkaberry

Viridis ...520
- Blue Dream
- Durban Spice
- Northern Lights
- White Widow

Weed Me ...525
- Blackberry Gum
- Cindy Jack
- Grandpa's Stash
- Melon Gum

Weed Me ...525
- Tutti Frutti

Whistler Cannabis Company ...531
- Bubba Kush
- Chocolope
- Rockstar
- SSC

Wink ...536
- Mmmosa
- Strain Hunters' Super Lemon Haze
- Wedding Cake

Cultivar Rankings ...540

Top 50 Overall Score ...540

Top 20 Bud Quality ...542

Top 20 High Potency ...542

Top 20 Aroma ...542

Top 20 Flavour ...543

Top 20 Appearance ...543

Top 20 High Quality ...544

My Top 10 THC Sativas ...544

My Top 10 THC Sativa Hybrids ...544

My Top 10 THC Hybrids ...544

My Top 10 THC Indica Hybrids ...545

My Top 10 THC Indicas ...545

My Top 10 THC Cultivars ...545

My Top 5 THC:CBD Balanced Cultivars ...545

My Top 3 CBD Cultivars ...545

The Budtender's Cannabis Dictionary ...546

A - Ca ...546

Ca - Co ...547

Cr - F ...548

G - La ...549

Le - Pr ...550

Pr - St ...551

Su - Z ...552

About the Author ...554

Dylan Bruck ...554

Introduction

As a Beginner's Guide to Cannabis

Legalization has brought education to the forefront of the cannabis community in Canada. Complete with everything you'll need to know to start your cannabis journey, The Budtender's Guide to the Galaxy is the perfect introduction to cannabis consumption. This book will teach you about cannabis, and it will prepare you to teach others as well.

As a Product Catalogue of Cannabis

The Budtender's Guide to the Galaxy comes with reviews on (damn near) everything you'll have seen on the Alberta cannabis market for flower products between April 2019 and February 2021. Filled with all of the information required to get a decent historical look at the cannabis market and get a clear vision of where we may be heading in the future, this is the ultimate cannabis catalogue and buyer's guide for the savvy cannaisseur.

As a Journal of Experiences with Cannabis

Creative, informative, and full of metal and cartoon references, The Budtender's Guide to the Galaxy is a testament to stoner ingenuity. Completely spaced-out (hence the book title) when writing every review in this book, Dylan Bruck has experienced cannabis throughout his review journey in an unprecedented fashion and via an unbelievable amount of the "meditation medication" - as an Old Rasta once put it. 420 one gram cannabis reviews, ~4500 Volcano bags, ~13500 human lung capacities, and all of the thoughts, emotions, and perceptions they inspired in one book. Enjoy the trip.

Cannabis 101

Cannabis Species

What Cannabis Species Exist?

When we refer to cannabis species, the two that come to mind for most people are cannabis indica and cannabis sativa. Beyond these two more common species, we also have cannabis ruderalis, which is much less commonly represented on the consumer market - while there may be ruderalis genetics in many recreational market products, it is not often labelled.

Combining any of these cannabis species will produce a sort of "hybrid" offspring species; we commonly refer to these cultivars as "hybrids" (I wonder where we got that name…).

Hybrid cultivars will often bear characteristics of both of their parent cultivars, just as we see in human children to their parents.

Most cannabis cultivars on the market today are a hybrid of some sort; the availability of indica/sativa/ruderalis landrace cultivars is very little compared to hybrids. This is partially due to the rarity of landraces and the benefits gained from cross-breeding cannabis varieties.

On the Origin of Species

What is a landrace, you ask? A landrace typically refers to a ~100% indica or sativa native to a specific region of the world and grows exceptionally well in that region and environments mimicking that region. All of the cannabis cultivars we see today originate in their genetics from landraces of some kind. However, due to high levels of cross-breeding in some cultivars, they may be far removed from their ancestors genetically.

Differences Between Species

Sativa cannabis plants were initially discovered in Asia, although sativa landraces are found on several other continents, including Africa and South America.

Sativa cultivars are typically generalized as having uplifting, euphoric, and light effects.

Indica cannabis plants were initially discovered in India but are found in other regions, including the Middle East and northern Africa.

Indica cultivars are generally associated with relaxing, calming, and heavy effects.

Many differences between sativa and indica cannabis plants are observable when the plant is growing:

- Branch Density: sativa plants are sparsely branched compared to densely branched indica plants
- Flower Density: sativa buds are typically less dense than indica buds
- Height: sativas grow taller, whereas indicas grow shorter
- Leaf Shape: sativa leaf shape is thinner and taller than the short and broad shape of an indica leaf

Dense Indica Flower
(DJ Short Blueberry)

Sparse Sativa Flower
(Up Eldo)

Ruderalis cannabis plants were initially discovered in Asia and Russia and differ from sativa and indica plants.

Ruderalis is typically much shorter and smaller than indicas or sativas, but it is also naturally autoflowering. When growing, rather than requiring a change in the light cycle to begin the flowering stage of growth, flowering starts due to the age of the plant. When ruderalis genetics are bred with indica or sativa genetics, their hybrid offspring may bear this autoflowering trait.

Cannabis Species Misconceptions

Cannabis is an exceptionally complex plant, especially when considering its effect when consumed. Often, the features of a cannabis flower's effect profile are associated simply with whether it is a sativa or an indica. However, this is not always accurate; there are always exceptions to the rule of thumb effects for the species.

In other words, it is not necessarily as simple as "sativa = daytime; indica = nighttime." In reality, there are several compounds present within cannabis responsible for the characteristics of its flowers and the effects they give us. They are classified into a few different types, the most important two being "cannabinoids" and "terpenes."

These compounds all have distinct characteristics and effects, and when combined, they produce effects that we experience as "the entourage effect." This just refers to the combined total effect of cannabinoids and terpenes, and with this effect, the whole is greater than the sum of its parts.

Cannabinoids

What are Cannabinoids?

Cannabinoids are a group of compounds found naturally in cannabis.

They are responsible for the effects we experience when consuming cannabis, as well as another group of compounds called terpenes.

While there are many other cannabinoids present in smaller quantities (minor cannabinoids) in cannabis flowers, there are two that are the most well known and most abundant in comparison: tetrahydrocannabinol (THC) and cannabidiol (CBD). These are the two most commonly labelled on consumer packaging and most well understood by consumers and budtenders alike.

Tetrahydrocannabinol (THC)

THC: the favourite cannabinoid of most recreational consumers of cannabis. Given its psychoactive properties, it is the main reason cannabis consumers experience a "high". In our endocannabinoid system, THC will bind to receptor sites in the brain and body, altering our perception, cognition and motor function.

A Pure THCa Diamond (Greybeard Diamonds)

While there are many medical applications for THC, most commonly it is consumed for its recreational effects. Effects of consuming THC will vary from person to person, and if there are other cannabinoids or terpenes consumed with it.

When consumed in isolation, THC will typically induce a relatively clean and clear head high, coupled with mild physical sensations in the body and more intense physical feelings in the head and face - particularly in the forehead (this is referred to as the "headband effect").

Depending on the amount of THC consumed in a given session, assuming no other cannabinoids or terpenes are present, the effects of THC can be perceived as being either motivational, sedating, or anywhere in between. Typically, lower doses of THC are more functional, whereas higher doses are more stupefying.

To a limited extent, mood, perspective, and energy before THC intake may also impact the high you experience and how you perceive its effects. For example, if one is already exhausted, an uplifting cultivar may have a reduced effect compared to well-rested consumption.

Cannabidiol (CBD)

Renowned mainly for its medical applications, CBD, a non-intoxicating cannabinoid, is used for many reasons across a wide variety of consumers.

CBD interacts with the body's cannabinoid receptors and provides calming, relieving, and overall quite "zen" effects.

A Jar of CBD Isolate Powder

Likening the effects of CBD to meditation, it is also very grounding and aids in feeling present. It also has a very mild headband effect relative to that of THC.

CBD will have differing effects if taken in with other cannabinoids or terpenes due to the resultant entourage effect.

CBD offers increased comfort and a sense of calm (relative to a THC-only high) when consumed with THC, particularly in high doses. However, more research must be done into the interactions between these two cannabinoids before drawing conclusions.

Cannabinoid Content Product Labelling

THC and CBD content on cannabis products (and most recently, some terpenes) are typically labelled with a mg/g number and may also have a weight % to represent the overall content. Both units are a reflection of cannabinoids to total cannabis.

In the case of a mg/g number, this is read as "milligrams of cannabinoid per gram of total flower weight." In the case of a weight percentage, this number represents the total milligrams of cannabinoids to the total mass of cannabis in a given jar. Both values essentially provide the same information. Percentages just tend to be more intuitive.

It is as simple as moving a decimal point to convert between the two. For example, 15% THC, regardless of the overall weight of the jar, can also be represented as 150mg/g. Mathematically, with units, the conversion is:

mg/g to %:

(X mg/g)*(1g/1000mg)*(100%)= %

% to mg/g:

(X%)*(1/100%)*(1000mg/1g)= mg/g

Terpenes

What Are Terpenes?

Terpenes are a group of naturally occurring compounds - organic aromatic molecules, to be specific - that are produced (mainly) by plants. Terpenes are the primary component of the essential oils of many plants and are responsible for much of their aroma and flavour. Cannabis produces various terpenes, differing from cannabis plant to cannabis plant, based on genetics and several growing condition factors.

In nature, terpenes are produced by plant species to improve survival rates, such as by attracting pollinators or by repelling pests.

During cannabis cultivation, specific cannabis genetics are selected and then placed in particular environments to produce a desired "terpene profile" in the flowers grown. This allows producers to "design" their cannabis to create it for specific markets and achieve specific effects that address various problems consumers may face (such as mood, perspective, energy, etc.).

The Entourage Effect

As is typical with cannabinoids, all terpenes have distinct effects that differentiate them from each other. Just as with combining cannabinoids, their effects will combine and change to produce a resultant effect when combining terpenes. When consumed together, the total combined effects of cannabinoids and terpenes are called "The Entourage Effect."

Given that every cannabis plant will produce flowers with different cannabinoid and terpene profiles - although this can be somewhat predicted and controlled via genetic selection and environment control - much like snowflakes, no cannabis flower is truly the same.

A Variety of Cannabis Flowers

Not only is cannabis a special plant, but each cultivar is unique in its own way as well. Different terpene profiles in cannabis are suited to different consumers, including a preference for certain aromas, flavours, and effects. Preferences for cannabis can be rooted in individual biases. However, body chemistry, metabolism, weight, personality, mood, energy, perspective, and tons of other factors also affect what will work for an individual and inform those preferences.

Common Cannabis Terpenes

Understanding the effects of individual cannabinoids and terpenes can aid in deciphering the entourage effect of a given high and is crucial to truly understand the effects of different cultivars and who they are grown for. The following is a list of the most common terpenes consumed during my reviews:

- Bisabolol:

- Found In: Chamomile, sage
- Aroma/Flavour: Floral, light
- Effects: Calming, relaxing, relieving, sedating

- Camphene:

- Found In: Dill, fennel, nutmeg, sage, thyme
- Aroma/Flavour: Citrusy, minty, spicy
- Effects: Relaxing, relieving

- Carene:

- Found In: Basil, kumquat, lime
- Aroma/Flavour: Citrusy, piney, sweet
- Effects: Focusing, relieving

- Caryophyllene:

- Found In: Black pepper, cloves, oregano
- Aroma/Flavour: Pungent, spicy
- Effects: Calming, relaxing, relieving

- Cymene:

- Found In: Cumin, thyme
- Aroma/Flavour: Citrusy, fresh, spicy, woody
- Effects: Calming, relieving

- Farnesene:

- Found In: Apple, ginger, jasmine, lemon, lime
- Aroma/Flavour: Citrusy, floral, fruity, herbal
- Effects: Calming, relaxing, relieving, sedating

- **Guaiol:**

- Found In: Cypress pine, guaicum wood
- Aroma/Flavour: Floral, fresh, piney, woody
- Effects: Relieving

- **Geraniol:**

- Found In: Citronella oil, geranium, rose oil
- Aroma/Flavour: Floral, fruity
- Effects: Calming, relaxing

- **Humulene:**

- Found In: Hops
- Aroma/Flavour: Floral, herbal, piney, woody
- Effects: Appetite reduction, calming, relaxing, relieving

- **Limonene:**

- Found In: Grapefruit, lemon, lime, orange
- Aroma/Flavour: Citrusy, pungent, sweet
- Effects: Calming, energizing, euphoric, uplifting

- **Linalool:**

- Found In: Lavender, lemon, mint, orange, rose
- Aroma/Flavour: Floral, fresh
- Effects: Calming, relaxing, relieving, sedating

- **Myrcene:**

- Found In: Hops, lemongrass, mango
- Aroma/Flavour: Earthy, herbal, spicy, sweet, woody
- Effects: Increased THC intensity, relaxing, sedating

- **Nerolidol:**

- Found In: Ginger, jasmine, neroli
- Aroma/Flavour: Earthy, floral, fresh, herbal, woody
- Effects: Calming, relaxing, relieving, sedating

- **Ocimene:**

- Found In: Guava, kumquat, mango
- Aroma/Flavour: Floral, fruity, fresh, herbal, sweet, woody
- Effects: Relieving

- <u>Phytol:</u>

- Found In: Green tea
- Aroma/Flavour: Floral, grassy, herbal
- Effects: Calming, relaxing, relieving, sedating

- <u>Pinene:</u>

- Found In: Dill, orange, pine needles, rosemary
- Aroma/Flavour: Piney, pungent, spicy, woody
- Effects: Focusing, relaxing, relieving, sedating, uplifting

- <u>Santalene:</u>

- Found In: Black pepper, carrot, sandalwood, star anise
- Aroma/Flavour: Woody
- Effects: Relieving

- <u>Terpinene:</u>

- Found In: Cardamom, juniper, lime, marjoram
- Aroma/Flavour: Citrusy, pungent, sweet, spicy, woody
- Effects: Relaxing, sedating

- <u>Terpineol:</u>

- Found In: Eucalyptus, lilac, lime, pine
- Aroma/Flavour: Floral, piney
- Effects: Relaxing, relieving

- <u>Terpinolene:</u>

- Found In: Apple, cumin, lilac, pine, rosemary, sage
- Aroma/Flavour: Floral, fresh, pungent, spicy, woody
- Effects: Calming, energizing, relaxing, relieving

Flower

Cannabis Flower Anatomy

Cannabis flowers can vary a great deal in appearance from cultivar to cultivar, even more so when considering aroma, flavour, potency, and tons of other factors. Still, all of them can be described similarly in the parts that make them up. Apart from the stem, all cannabis flowers consist of 4 main parts: sugar leaves, calyxes, pistils, and trichomes.

- **Sugar Leaves:**

- Small leaves that extend out of the flower itself
- Often have a healthy coating of trichomes, just as the calyxes do
- Serve the cannabis plant by performing photosynthesis and creating food for the plant to grow and further develop flowers
- Often are removed from the flower during the trimming process

- **Calyxes:**

- Teardrop-shaped structure
- Make up the bulk of a cannabis flower
- A significant source of trichome production in the cannabis flower
- Biologically, it serves the purpose of protecting the female reproductive parts of the cannabis flower

- **Pistils:**

- Tiny "hairs" that extend out of the cannabis flower
- Can vary in colour from orange to brown, to purple or red, depending on the grow and cultivar
- Act as a reproductive organ of the flower by collecting pollen

- **Trichomes:**

- Tiny resin glands found throughout the cannabis flower
- Consisting of cannabinoids and terpenes, these are responsible for the psychoactive and medicinal properties of cannabis
- Exist to protect the plant from pests, predators, disease and excess radiation from the sun

In the flower photo on the next page, examples of all four parts can be seen. The flower is covered in a thick layer of trichomes, with orange pistils extending out from a surface of calyxes, with dark purple sugar leaves sticking out.

Citizen Stash
MAC1 Flower

Another critical thing to consider when talking about cannabis flower anatomy is how the anatomy of the entire plant affects flower development. No one flower on a given plant will be precisely the same as the next.

One thing primarily responsible for this is the different positions of flowers on the plant. Lower flowers on the plant will typically have less access to light than those at the top of the plant.

This affects their access to nutrients and energy, producing a flower with less potency potential due to reduced trichome production.

This is why the top flowers, or "cola flowers," nearest to the center stem are the most coveted flowers on the cannabis plant. Given their access to light and nutrients, they will typically be larger and more potent than the other flowers on the plant.

What Makes a Cultivar?

A lot of work and decision-making goes into creating a cannabis flower product for the recreational market. One early step involves selecting the cannabis genotype. Let's say we pick Jean Guy for our genotype. Assuming the same environmental conditions and genetically identical Jean Guy seeds, all cannabis plants produced by these seeds would be the same phenotype and bear the same expressed traits.

Now consider the same cultivar produced by two different producers: Jean Guy from 7Acres, and Jean Guy from Good Supply. These products are undoubtedly different phenotypes, as they smell, look, taste, and feel different from one another; their traits are different, so their phenotype is not the same.

By selecting particular genotypes that typically yield specific phenotypes and modifying environmental conditions to ensure the desired phenotype, licensed producers can produce products with goals in mind.

Whether it be an energetic sativa, a sedating indica, or a mellow hybrid, producers can choose and hone in on what they want to be growing through genetic selection and environment control.

Quality and Potency

Two concepts that tend to be confused by some cannabis consumers are flower quality and flower potency.

Often in this market, there is an emphasis from producers and consumers on potency first and quality second.

For the sake of this topic, potency is just cannabinoid potency. Given that terpene percentages are less frequently on consumer packaging, THC and CBD are what consumers are hunting for these days. Given this, producers have emphasized producing high THC cannabis products. However, time and time again, some of these producers neglect product quality and focus too much on cannabinoid content. It isn't too difficult to find products boasting +20% THC; however, they often lack the quality to back up that percentage.

In this case, quality refers to moisture content, density, terpene content and profile, appearance, trimming, drying, and curing. Cutting corners in any of these areas will decrease the value and enjoyability of a given cannabis product.

Without quality, a 20% THC cannabis flower can offer a poor consumption experience, and effects and potency are often underwhelming. When quality and potency come together in a well-rounded cannabis product, the improvement over potency-focused flower is huge. That same 20% THC cannabis flower with improved moisture and terpene content and added care in growing and processing can last longer and feel substantially stronger than an average 20% flower product that lacks significant terpene content and appropriate moisture.

Product Types and Varieties

Since legalization day, tons of different flower products have hit the market, split between two main SKU types: flower and pre-rolls. Both formats have seen different preparations, and many sizes, so here is a breakdown of what we have seen so far:

- Pre-Rolls:

- Single and multi-unit packs from 1 to 80 units
- Pre-roll sizes from 0.25g glass bats to 0.3g-1g traditional rolls
- Mostly cone rolls, or straight rolls in the case of Redecan / Back Forty / etc.
- Pre-rolls are available in both flower-only and flower infused with concentrates, including hash and resin

- Flower:

- 1g, 3.5g, 5g, 7g, 10g, 14g, 15g, 21g, and 28g unit sizes have been used for flower products
- Both whole flower and milled flower products have been released
- A mix of single-cultivar, unlabelled-cultivar, and mixed-cultivar flower SKUs are available
- In one case, from the AHLOT brand, a 5 pack of 1g units of assorted flower was tested out

Higher Learning

Cannabis Tolerance

Why don't I get as high as I did when I first started consuming cannabis? Why does the first session of the day always hit a little harder? Why doesn't a cultivar feel as intense after smoking it exclusively for a while?

Most frequent consumers of cannabis have probably asked these questions, and the answer to all of them is cannabis tolerance.

Over time, with repeated frequent exposure to cannabis, consumers tend to find that they will need to consume more to achieve the same effects and intensity of high.

Tolerance to cannabis is often no cause for great concern unless budgeting comes into play. Cannabis costs money, and unless you're growing your own, eventually, it can get expensive.

There is a way to lower your cannabis tolerance; this is often referred to as a "tolerance break". Abstaining from cannabis for a few days can reduce cannabis tolerance significantly, though for a short time if the pace of consumption before the break is resumed. A complete tolerance break, which rids your body of any lingering THC stored in the body's fat cells, can take weeks or months but will produce an even greater outcome in tolerance reduction.

Why Are There Two THC Values?

You can find two THC percentages on a jar of recreational cannabis: a THC percentage and a Total THC percentage. Both numbers represent different amounts of THC at different times, and it is essential to know which one is relevant.

The THC percentage represents the amount of THC found on the plant before decarboxylation.

So, before smoking or vaporizing your cannabis, it is the amount of THC just naturally present in the flower, and typically a minimal amount.

The Total THC percentage represents the total amount of THC found in the flower after a complete decarboxylation. At that point, all of the THCa (THC's cannabinoid acid) present in the flower has been converted to THC and has become "activated" and turned into a more useful form for consumption. Simply smoking or vaporizing your cannabis flower will decarboxylate it and give you access to the full THC potential of the flower.

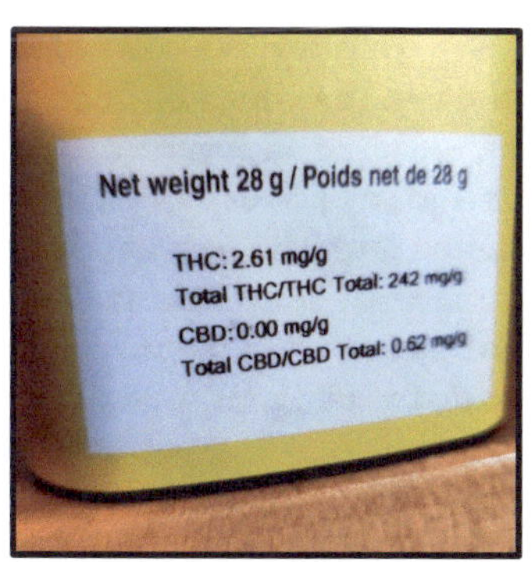

THC and Total THC Values on a Cannabis Jar

An essential note for understanding the difference between THC and Total THC: Total THC is the sum of the THC value and all of the THCa that is converted into THC during decarboxylation, where the THC value is just representing any THC present on the flower due to naturally occurring decarboxylation (due to light and air exposure over time).

Minor Cannabinoids

While THC and CBD are the most well-known cannabinoids, it is also important to note the many minor cannabinoids present in cannabis. Two of the most common are cannabigerol (CBG) and cannabinol (CBN).

CBG, the mother of all cannabinoids, is referred to as such because CBGa (cannabigerolic acid) is a precursor to both THCa and CBDa, the acid compounds that form THC and CBD when decarboxylated. Most CBGa present in a given cannabis plant will convert into THCa or CBDa during growth.

As such, it is uncommon to find more significant amounts of CBG in dried flower products.

Through cross-breeding and early harvesting, higher CBGa yields can be achieved to reap the benefits of CBG. Beyond strictly medical applications, CBG has effects that are blissful and appetite-increasing.

CBN, a slightly intoxicating, more relaxing cannabinoid, can be formed when THCa degrades into CBNa (cannabinolic acid). When CBNa is decarboxylated, it turns into CBN, which the body can then consume and utilize.

Given that most CBN is produced from THC degradation in the presence of air, light, or heat, this means that poorly stored cannabis and older cannabis are likely to have higher levels of CBN.

CBN, like CBG and CBD, has many medical applications.

Cannabis and Humidity

Adequately dried, cured, and stored cannabis shouldn't be bone dry, and it shouldn't be reduced to dust if you try to squeeze the buds. Appropriate moisture content is essential for any cannabis product to maintain its quality over time and be fully enjoyable. Even just for ease of handling milled cannabis, it is crucial - no one wants to roll joints with something the consistency of fine sand. Just as well, a smoother smoke is typically the case when cannabis is moist compared to dry.

Many producers have added humidity packs to their products to maintain a higher moisture content as the product ages. In a pinch, this can be done at home with everyday household food items, such as a piece of apple, bread or carrot. Humidity stones also exist for a more reusable moisture option.

A Boveda Humidity Pack for Cannabis

Drying and Curing

Essential to any cannabis production process is drying and curing the buds after harvest. The care put into the post-grow processes is part of what separates the top premium cannabis producers from more midrange producers and products. When shortcuts are taken here, it shows.

Cannabis is quite wet when first cut (it is a plant, after all) and must be dried out before being consumed. This is typically done via rack-drying or hang-drying for 1-2 weeks. Better product smoothness and flavour are found with hang-drying rather than rack-drying.

A good test for properly dried cannabis is that the stems will snap rather than bend.

After drying, comes curing, an essential part of post-grow care that allows the cannabis to develop its true character. Slow curing cannabis in sealed jars is the best means of curing. A slower cure will yield a product with less chlorophyll and sugar content than a faster cure, improving the smoke's flavour, aroma, and smoothness.

Due to variation in procedures between different licensed producers and different levels of quality assurance, these essential steps can be overlooked at times. This was a more common practice during early legalization days when producers struggled to feed a starving market. Unfortunately for the consumer, this meant that corners were cut during drying, curing and other post-grow steps, as these processes were seen as less essential than the growing process by some LPs.

Making a First Impression

A Planned Procedure

The Toker's Tenets

At the beginning of my journey down the path of cannabis reviews, I thought to myself: what are the principles on which my work will stand? Without a guiding philosophy, my project would have no foundation, no stability, and may be a failure. After much deliberation, I arrived at the first destination on my journey and a core set of beliefs in cannabis reviewing: The Toker's Tenets.

1. Accuracy:

- Record all product information for review cultivar before the review date to avoid losing data
- Source information from industry contacts, LP websites, and legacy market resources to maintain the validity of the project
- Assess my emotions, perceptions, and thoughts correctly to deliver a proper representation of my experiences

2. Advocacy:

- Respect the plant, respect the cultivators, respect the industry
- Focus on the positive aspects of any given flower and the high it provides
- Erase the stigma surrounding cannabis through education and access to information

3. Consistency:

- Set review size of a single gram in the Volcano vaporizer, to be consumed under sober conditions (minimum 4 hours since previous cannabis intake)
- Standard scoring system and review criteria

- A standardized, procedural, and measured approach to consuming cannabis

4. Honesty:

- Practicing self-reflection and mindfulness while consuming cannabis regularly (being honest with myself, about myself, to ensure the accuracy of my work)
- Transparent in my process, my scoring, and my perception of cannabis
- Delivering cannabis assessments with integrity in both writing and researching

5. Objectivity:

- Eliminate personal biases and opinions of cannabis from the review perspective
- Focus on what is being experienced, rather than preconceived notions about the potential experience
- Develop and reflect on the mindset of a typical cannabis consumer

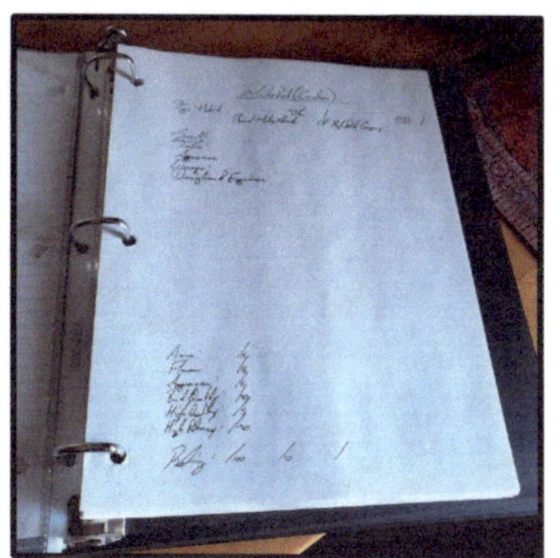

A Prepared Review Template for Recording Product Details

Gotta Vape 'Em All

Much like the fabled "Ash Ketchum," when I set out on my journey, I sought to become a "master" of sorts in my field, feeling as though it were my "destiny." To fulfill this destiny, I decided that I must try every single flower product available to me in Alberta.

Little did I know that during the 22 months to follow, I would try and review over 90% of the flower varieties available in 1g, 3.5g and pre-roll format.

I began my official review-writing process in April 2019.

August 2019 Reviews in Waiting

I reviewed over 120 different cultivars from the Alberta market in my first four months and assembled them into my first binder of reviews. Due to the important teachings held within, this binder was dubbed "The Bible" by various Plantlife staff during training sessions.

By the end of 2019, I had managed to cover over 200 products. At this point, I was determined to create a book, but it would require more. At that moment, I decided that 420 was the essential number, and my 2020 journey on the road to 420 began.

When 2020 ended, I had well over 420 reviews done, but there were many cuts to be made, which meant my reviews would continue into the new year.

Finally, on February 28th, 2021, my official 420 reviews were complete. "Professor Oak" (more like "Professor Toke," am I right?) would be proud.

Anatomy of a First Impression

Given that my reviews were my introduction to most of the products within this book, I have called them "First Impressions." To offer more clarity and transparency in my process, the following is a breakdown of my reviews:

A. First Impression:

- This portion of the review reflects on the overall experience that I am going through, considering both pre-consumption and post-consumption experience.

- The effects associated with the high I am experiencing are expressed here. For every "First Impression" in the book, I was high on the cultivar I was reviewing at the time of writing (you have been warned…), so even the effects on my writing process are documented.

B. <u>Cultivar/Product Information:</u>

- Type: The type represents which cannabis species the product belongs to. Among the reviews I've completed, there are sativas, sativa hybrids, hybrids, indica hybrids, and indicas.

- Effect: The effect of a given cultivar is judged on the overall lightness or heaviness of the effects. Effect profiles vary depending on terpene and cannabinoid content.

- Effect profiles can loosely be categorized into: super heavy, heavy, medium heavy, neutral, medium light, light, and super light.

- Legacy Name: This is either a confirmed legacy market name matched to the recreational product or, in some cases, an alternate name for the recreational product given to it by the producer.

- Lineage: The genetics of the associated legacy market cultivar, or the lineage provided by the producer for the product - this is represented through crosses of various parent cultivars for the products in the book.

- Cannabinoids: This section displays the cannabinoid content of the cultivar as a THC and CBD percentage.

- Terpenes: A list of the top three most abundant terpenes in the reviewed products will be given in this section, provided I could source accurate terpene information for the product from the producers.

C. Observations:

- Aroma/Flavour: A list of adjectives that describe the smell and taste of the cultivar reviewed. While some other descriptors are used, the core list I always considered for reviews were: berry, citrusy, earthy, floral, fresh, fruity, funky, grassy, herbal, piney, pungent, sour, spicy, sweet, and woody. Others range from minty to diesel, chocolate, cheese, and so on.

- Bud/Pistil Colour: A colour description of the bud and pistils of the cultivar.

- Trichome Density: A rating from low, low-medium, medium, medium-high, to high, describing the overall "frostiness" (thickness/opacity) of the surface trichome layer.

D. Score Details:

- Appearance: How does the bud look? Out of five possible points. Trichome density, colour, pistil abundance, and size are relevant details. I usually give 4 points, 3 if below average, 5 if above average, 0-2 if poor appearance.

- High Quality: The quality of the high. Out of five possible points. Think about what you don't want in a high, is it there? If not, I typically give 5 points. Point reductions are based on the severity of undesirable feelings.

- Aroma/Flavour: How pleasant/strong does it smell/taste? Out of 15 possible points each. Typically I consider 14-15 to be amazing, 12-13 to be great, 10-11 to be good, 8-9 to be okay, and 0-7 to be bad. Usually, I average 10-12 points here when scoring.

- Bud Quality: How good is the bud? Out of 30 possible points. Consider the density, squish, size, trim, seed/stem/leaf content, and moisture content. Is it substantial or underwhelming to the visual/tactile senses? 27-30 points is amazing, 23-26 is great, 19-22 is good, 15-18 is okay, 0-14 is bad, depending on the degree of awfulness.

- High Potency: How GOOD is the bud? Out of 30 possible points. I fill this in after finishing my consumption and the First Impression notes.

- I start my score at the THC % on the package and reduce or increase it based on intensity and effect potency. This often leads to a score 0-6 points above the THC potency. For balanced/CBD-only cultivars, I take the combined % of THC and CBD into account and start from there for scoring. Notably, THC cultivars and balanced or CBD cultivars are judged on different scales for potency and will feel different, even with the same potency score.

- Overall Score and Cultivar Ranking: The total sum of each section in the score details, as a percentage score, and where the cultivar ranks among those in the book.

E. <u>Other Information:</u>

- Product Name: Located at the top of the review in large bold text.

- Product Photo: A photograph of a flower of the reviewed cultivar.
- Review Order/Date: A value for the order in which the reviews were completed and the date the review was completed.

The Tools of the Trade

Review Requirements

Given the consistency with which I wanted to review cannabis, I knew that selecting my consumption method and sticking to it would be crucial. I would also have to choose a consumption method that allowed for minimal losses and maximum flavour while offering an experience most authentic to the flower.

Fortunately, I had experience with several different consumption methods and could weigh the pros and cons of each method. It was time to start making my decision…

Smoking vs. Vaporizing

Potentially the most important choice to make for my reviews was the choice between smoking and vaporization. Smoking would offer readers a more relatable consumption method, but its positives end there.

Whether bong, pipe, or joint, most smoking methods are inefficient. Excusing the inefficiencies of the process of smoking or vaporizing (they both have inefficiencies related to temperature and some other factors), what I'm talking about here is vapour losses.

Think about a joint, in your hand, outside… it's not done in one draw, and there's plenty of time where it's being held there, burning without you consuming anything. With the right vaporizer, I could significantly reduce the losses associated with joint smoking.

Bongs and pipes lack the losses of joints, but where they fail to meet my criteria is flavour.

Pipes, well, to me, they taste terrible. Bongs taste okay at first, but bongwater doesn't take long to get nasty. Vaporizers, however, taste fantastic and offer an unambiguous representation of the flower's authentic flavour - undisguised by the flavour of smoke, I might add.

In addition to these considerations, vaporizing also offers a much less harmful means of intaking cannabis. Given that vaporizers do not produce smoke and all of the awfulness that comes along with it, I would remain as healthy as possible while reviewing.

It seemed the choice between smoking and vaporizing was obvious; now, I just needed the right piece of hardware.

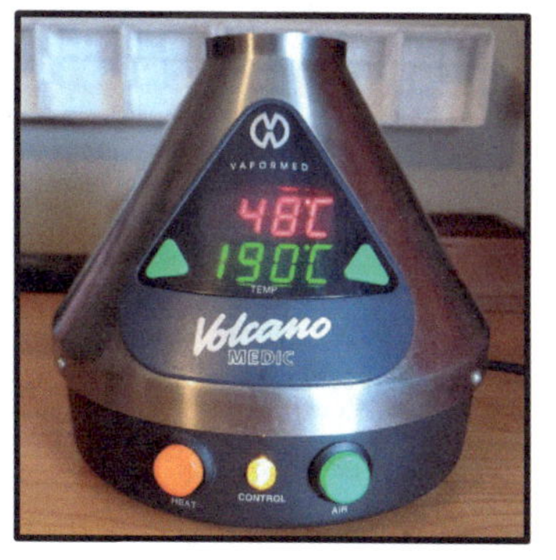

A Volcano Warming Up

Fortunately, I already owned the device I had in mind as the "ideal vaporizer."

The Storz and Bickel Volcano

Ah, the Volcano, perhaps the most excellent cannabis-related purchase I've ever made. It offers smooth, flavourful draws and long-lasting sessions to make for a gratifying consumption experience. It also stretches a gram further than any other consumption method, in my experience, and the vaporized flower can be used for edibles.

The setup consists of 3 main components: the Volcano vaporizer base, the Volcano bowl, and the easy-valve bag.

The Volcano base consists of a pump, a heating chamber, and some electronics (including a temperature control system) enclosed within a metal housing. As well: yes, it is indeed shaped like a Volcano.

Four buttons control it, two for increasing or decreasing the temperature setpoint, one for warming up, and one for running the unit.

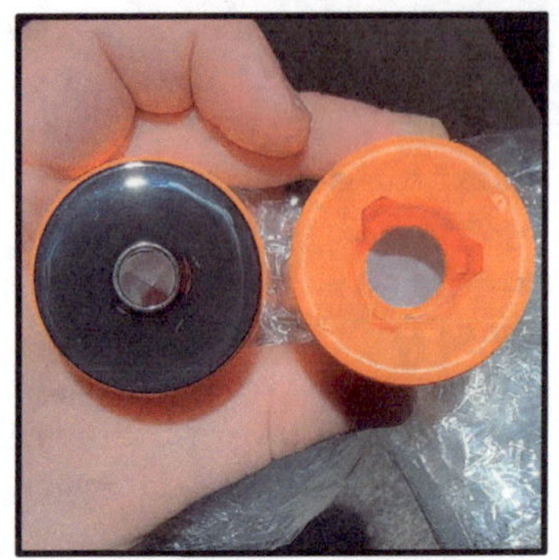

The Easy-Valve, with and without a Mouthpiece

A Warmed-Up Volcano with a Full Bowl and Filled Bag

What is the easy-valve bag, you ask? Well, it's a bag with a simple plastic valve that opens when the bowl piece is inserted (to fill) and when the mouthpiece is inserted and pushed in (to inhale). The valve limits losses and contamination.

As for the bowl, it's a two-piece metal and plastic bowl with a screen on the top and bottom and an elongated tip for fitting into the valve on the bag. It opens by twisting the top and bottom bowl pieces apart and can be filled with up to a gram (or more) of milled flower, depending on bud density and fineness of the grind.

One Sealed and One Opened Volcano Bowl

The Volcano vaporizer itself operates by heating up air taken in from the environment around the unit. The air then passes through the pre-loaded bowl on top of the unit, creating vapour inside the bag placed on the bowl. When the bag is full of vapour, turn the fan off, remove the bag, insert the mouthpiece, and start inhaling. Not the typical "spark a lighter and you're done" setup, but super simple and easy to learn.

On average, when filled with a gram of milled flower, the Volcano usually produces around 7-12 standard-size vapour bags if run at a consistent 190 degrees celsius. Per bag, that's around 18000 cubic centimetres, or about three full human lung capacities - though you'll likely take more than three complete draws to finish the bag; the vapour isn't as hard to inhale as smoke, but it isn't quite fresh air either.

The vapour is hot air and gaseous cannabinoids and terpenes: all of the components of cannabis flower that give you the experience without anything else getting in the way of flavour or effect. This is precisely what I was looking for in my reviews.

My Main Insights and Takeaways

The Average Cannabis Consumer

When I started as a budtender, I regularly asked myself: what is the average cannabis consumer looking for? Given the complexity of interactions between different cultivars of cannabis and different consumers, it almost seemed like an unanswerable question.

The answer wouldn't be as simple as "Girl Scout Cookies" or "to get f***ed up." Not every consumer will be able to appreciate every cultivar to the same extent, nor is every consumer looking for the absolute highest THC potency they can find.

After all, there are many different types of cannabis consumer out there: serious stoners, occasional tokers, wake n' bake-ers, nightly ritualists, THC fiends, CBD chronics, the list goes on…

Eventually I settled on three key things that define what the average consumer is looking for:

- <u>Intensity to Match the Tolerance Level of the Consumer</u>

- <u>Effects to Match the Needs and Wants of the Consumer</u>

- <u>Quality to Match or Exceed the Minimum Standards of the Consumer</u>

With intensity, what to consider is the overall strength of the high due to THC. In general, this intensity increases with THC content, and is changed a bit as well by terpenes and other cannabinoids. The reason the intensity must match the tolerance level of the consumer is simple: they won't feel sufficiently high otherwise.

While many things contribute to an individual's tolerance level, two major contributing factors are frequency of consumption and experience level - how often do you consume, and how long have you been consuming at that level? In a budtending scenario, asking both of these questions should ensure you get an accurate picture of an individual's tolerance level and will inform what THC percentage range is most appropriate for them.

An analogy: a cannabis high is a lot like a musical performance. THC is the master volume control (the intensity) of the music at the concert, and the terpenes are all of the mixers that the DJ is playing around with to change the sound you are experiencing (the effects).

Where the intensity of a high must line up with consumer tolerance level, the effects that define the profile of a high must line up with the individual needs and wants of the consumer.

It's all about providing the right tool for the job when it comes to budtending, and you wouldn't give someone a screwdriver to hammer a nail. The effect profile of every cultivar is unique, and each one is suited to a different potential need or want of a consumer.

By getting to know that consumer, you can provide the right cannabis for the right experience, but it takes asking the crucial questions:

- Who are you consuming with?
- What are you doing after consuming?
- When are you consuming?
- Where are you consuming?
- Why are you consuming?
- How are you consuming?

These questions are relevant and can provide you with the critical information necessary to suggest the appropriate cannabis.

The last key to suggesting the correct cultivar is ensuring the quality of the cannabis meets or exceeds the minimum standard of that consumer. Everyone has a different idea of "the worst flower in the world" and "the dopest dope I've ever smoked"; finding out what an individual is used to smoking on that spectrum can help in recommending cannabis.

First, it helps to ensure you don't recommend something way below an individual's standard for cannabis quality. Personally, if I open a 3.5g jar below my standard for quality, I'll try it, but typically, I won't touch it again afterward.

This is the result of recommending the wrong product. As the industry standards for minimum quality at various price points have become less variable (and have been increasing actually), it has become much easier to infer the quality of a product based on price. A great way to get an idea of someone's standard for cannabis is to ask what they typically spend on 3.5g.

Given this, avoiding products below one's typical price range is a decent way to avoid disappointing cannabis experiences due to quality.

In addition, knowing someone's minimum standard for quality, and being aware of products that are aggressively priced for their quality, allows a budtender to save someone money or increase value - a huge bonus.

In summary, an average consumer of cannabis is looking for the appropriate intensity, effects, and quality, all for a reasonable price. As far as what defines a reasonable price, that is left up to the budtender. If proper suggestions are made and expectations of the products are kept realistic with the consumer, price is less of a conversation.

Trends and Patterns

Over the years, many trends emerged within the cannabis industry. The following is some of what I was able to observe during that time:

- 2018:
- Limited product availability and variety characterized much of late 2018. There were only a few products from only a few brands.
- Overall product quality was very low relative to current standards, and flower was overpriced.
- 2019:
- Early 2019 was much like 2018, but product availability and variety were of no concern by the second half of the year.
- In 2019 there was a large variety of balanced flower options relative to current market presence and relative to demand at the time. Every brand had to have its take on a THC:CBD flower option.

- THC was king in 2019, and the other factors contributing to a high were rarely discussed. More often than not, THC was the sole deciding factor on whether something would sell, especially so with overpriced products.

- Broken Coast launches in Alberta as the first premium flower option in early 2019, offering consumers a look at quality cannabis. Formerly, quality was rarely part of the cannabis conversation in stores, but it became more commonplace in the latter half of the year.

- Flower was sold almost exclusively in 1g to 7g during 2019; small formats were a focus for companies while they tested out which genetics would work. Consumers seemed focused on shopping for variety, made easy with small formats.

- <u>2020:</u>

- Early 2020 was spring cleaning for AGLC, which meant that a TON of products from 2019 had to go on sale. Cheaper flower was easy to come by in the first few months of the year, and following that, prices of the average 3.5g were starting to drop as companies like Redecan began producing at aggressive potencies and prices.

- By 2020, the flower quality was a common talking point for budtenders and consumers, and there was much more competition on the market, forcing producers to raise the bar. The quality of the average 3.5g increased dramatically across 2020, and there was a greater focus on producing a premium flower. By the end of 2020, the price point of premium flower saw a significant drop.

- **THC was still king in 2020, but quality was no longer an afterthought for the average consumer. Terpene-centric conversations started becoming more and more common by the year's end.**

- **For premium 3.5g, there was a significant focus on glass during 2020. Packaging moved away from plastic jars for average products and toward bags. Across the year, humidity packs were beginning to become more and more a standard as well - even some non-premium 3.5g were starting to follow Edison's long-running example and include humidity packs.**

- **In 2020 there were only a handful of balanced flower products available on the market. Producers saw limited success with these SKUs in 2019 and drove innovation toward high THC flower.**

- **Bulk flower products emerged in 2020 as producers ramped up their production capabilities, and many more entered the market. 7g formats became much more popular in the first half of the year, and by the end of 2020, half and whole ounces of flower were the standard purchase for the average cannabis consumer. Flower for less than $5/gram was available legally at last - even sometimes in the 3.5g format.**

- **2021:**

- **In early 2021, Ogen began hitting the Alberta market with their premium ounces, raising the bar for quality in bulk flower.**

- **Prices continued dropping on all flower products during the early part of 2021; ounces for less than $100 were a common sight, as were eighths for less than $25.**

- Through the previous years, flower had three distinct price and quality groupings: value, mid-range and premium. However, by 2021, much of this dynamic had shifted toward either value or premium. As premium flower became priced the same as mid-range flower, and quality of value products became the same as mid-range products, the mid-range product category was phased out. Emerging in 2021 was a new dynamic: premium, value, and bulk.

- Terpenes had finally arrived in 2021: they were a more common topic of conversation. Many brands began to label their products with terpene percentages, typically with the total percentage and top three terpenes.

- Broken Coast's 28g units were released in late 2021, setting a high bar for premium ounces.

- 2022:

- Prices on bulk and value flower continue to fall in early 2022, with many ounces falling below $100 and eights falling below $20

- Selling cannabis products on effect profile and terpene profile/content is a more common practice as consumers realize that THC isn't everything cannabis has to offer them.

- Alberta Cannabis shuts down its public-facing consumer website for online ordering and delivery launches in Alberta for recreational dispensaries.

- Alberta Cannabis increases the cost of cannabis products by 6%, reducing retailer margins across the board and shaking up the cannabis market in the province.

Apart from the trends specific to each year, several patterns have presented themselves throughout the lifespan of the market:

- Fad Cultivars: Every 3-6 months, a new cultivar comes to the market that every brand seems to jump on and produce. 2019 had Blue Dream, 2020 had Glue and Cake cultivars, and BCP and GMO dominated 2021.

- Discounted Flower: Given the nature of cannabis as a product that will only get drier, less fragrant, and lower quality over time, price reductions on older flower options are a common practice, and not just for retailers. Much like the spring cleaning at AGLC in 2020, this occurred again in 2021 and one last time in 2022 before closing their online store to consumers.

- Seasonal Habits: Preferences for indica vs. sativa tend to lean toward sativa cultivars for summer and indica cultivars for winter, based on sales data.

- Outdoor Harvest: With summer comes outdoor cannabis growing, and with fall and winter comes harvest season for outdoor grows: expect cheaper bulk products around this time.

- Increasing Quality: Legal cannabis has been slowly increasing in average quality throughout legalization. Bud is getting better and better!

- Decreasing Prices: Prices have come down a long way since the legal market's inception. Once $56/3.5g products are now as low as $30/3.5g, bulk products have price per gram values as low as $3/g.

Moving Forward in Canadian Cannabis

We tread through uncharted territory as we move beyond the initial few years of cannabis legalization. Given that national cannabis legalization is still relatively new it seems complicated to predict what will come next - especially so given the pace at which this industry has been developing and changing since 2018.

However, this constant development and change points to a trend that has defined the industry thus far and will continue to define it moving forward: innovation.

THC Intimacy Oil

Through thousands of SKUs since 2018, licensed producers have been optimizing their processes and developing new and improved products and types of products.

This won't be stopping here. We're at just the beginning of improvements and new creations as an industry. With legalization 2.0, we saw the launch of edibles and cannabis beverages.

Since then, the market has featured topicals, bath products, concentrates, and even personal lubricants. I wouldn't even be shocked if we stumbled upon an entirely new consumption method! I expect tons of new types of products to be launched, along with much improvement on older technologies.

Apart from innovation, I anticipate that cannabis companies will focus on one of three outputs - biomass, bulk/value cannabis, and craft/premium cannabis.

Biomass cannabis producers will be interested in producing cannabis for its purposes as a process input for consumer goods rather than a consumer good itself. As a process input, this cannabis will have its cannabinoids extracted for use in vaporizer cartridges, beverages, edibles, and a variety of other non-flower cannabis products. In the case of biomass, some mass producers of cannabis may go this route, particularly those interested in growing quantity over quality.

Bulk and value-oriented cannabis producers make up the next group. They will primarily focus on growing large amounts of low to mid-grade cannabis. Cannabis from producers like these will likely make up a variety of pre-rolls on the market and cheaper 3.5g, 7g, 14g and 28g flower options.

Finally, we have the remaining group, my favourite group: craft flower companies.

Craft Cannabis Flower (Greybeard Afghani Drifter)

These are small to medium-sized companies with small to medium-sized grow spaces, producing the highest quality of cannabis. These companies will produce the majority of the non-value and premium cannabis out there provided they can remain competitive in the face of "the race to the bottom" with pricing in the industry. Craft producers should always have a place in the market with specialized growing practices, increased research, greater care, and unique genetics. There should always be a demand for premium quality cannabis produced at the highest standard.

The final set of trends I see developing or continuing moving forward are the trends of price, quality, and variety.

In the case of price, as it has been since legalization, cannabis prices should continue to drop until finally stabilizing for each product type. Flower 3.5g are potentially doing this already, with premium flower costing $35-$45/3.5g and average flower at $25-$35/3.5g. There may still be room to drop, however.

The quality of products will continue to increase as companies find more and more ways to improve their flower production. As industry standards continue to develop, this quality increase should be apparent, along with an increase in consistency across the board.

Lastly, the variety of products will only improve. Many brands boast seed banks of hundreds if not thousands of cultivars, and some have begun genetic breeding programs, so new cultivars will keep coming.

Attention: Stoners Across the Nation

In the years since legalization, while many trends are emerging in the cannabis industry, there is one that is most concerning: the trend of cost and convenience over the quality of cannabis and experience.

The race to the bottom in cannabis flower pricing best illustrates why this hurts the market: craft producers can't survive below a certain $/g value of cannabis.

If you're a stoner who appreciates cannabis for everything that makes cannabis remarkable: we're at war.

The fight for craft producers is well underway. Ask your budtender not just what they are smoking - ask them what they *want* to be smoking. At budtender wages, affording craft flower is difficult, but being aware of it is not. Trust in your budtenders. Trust in craft.

Brand Bios and Cultivar Reviews

Brand Score Ranking

1. Citizen Stash (94.00%)
2. Qwest (93.73%)
3. Good Buds (92.33%)
4. Whistler Cannabis Company (92.00%)
5. Joi Botanicals (92.00%)
6. Artisan Batch (91.50%)
7. Ignite (90.33%)
8. Broken Coast (90.27%)
9. Natural History (90.00%)
10. Kolab (90.00%)
11. Habitat (90.00%)
12. Highland Grow (89.50%)
13. Ogen (89.00%)
14. 18Twelve (89.00%)
15. 7Acres (88.83%)
16. Simply Bare (88.60%)
17. Reef (88.00%)
18. Fireside (87.50%)
19. Wink (86.33%)
20. Topleaf (86.30%)
21. Boaz (86.25%)
22. Skosha (85.33%)
23. Farmstead (85.00%)
24. Ness (84.50%)
25. Color (83.40%)
26. Thumbs Up Brand (82.75%)
27. San Rafael '71 (82.50%)
28. Cove (82.50%)
29. Royal City Cannabis Co. (82.40%)
30. Spinach (82.29%)
31. Strain Rec (82.14%)
32. Robinsons (82.00%)
33. Poolboy (81.50%)
34. Up (81.33%)
35. Abba Medix (81.00%)
36. Grail (81.00%)
37. Palmetto (80.67%)
38. Viridis (80.50%)
39. Redecan (80.20%)
40. Blissco (80.00%)

Brand Score Ranking

41. Marley Natural (79.75%)
42. Weed Me (78.80%)
43. Houseplant (78.33%)
44. Canna Farms (77.63%)
45. Sundial (77.44%)
46. Riff (77.38%)
47. The Green Organic Dutchman (77.25%)
48. DNA Genetics (77.20%)
49. Haven St. (76.92%)
50. Edison (76.36%)
51. Tantalus Labs (76.00%)
52. FIGR (75.67%)
53. AltaVie (75.50%)
54. Flowr (75.33%)
55. Caliber (75.33%)
56. LBS (75.25%)
57. Pure Sunfarms (75.11%)
58. Emerald Health (74.88%)
59. High Tide (74.25%)
60. Canaca (74.06%)
61. Solei (74.00%)
62. Namaste (73.75%)
63. Northern Harvest (73.50%)
64. Good Supply (73.33%)
65. Delta 9 (73.15%)
66. Kiwi (73.00%)
67. Royal High (72.50%)
68. 48North (72.40%)
69. Hexo (70.67%)
70. Vertical (70.63%)
71. Acreage Pharms (70.63%)
72. Symbl (68.43%)
73. Ankr Organics (67.00%)
74. Tokyo Smoke (66.25%)
75. Van Der Pop (65.50%)
76. Tweed (65.33%)
77. Kingsway (64.00%)
78. Aurora (63.25%)

18Twelve

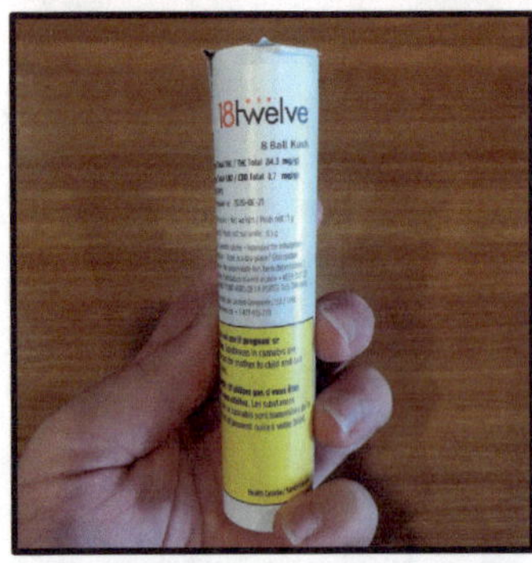

Overall Performance

Average Score: 89.00%

Brand Ranking: 14th Place

Brand Background

18Twelve is a premium cannabis brand dedicated to quality products. The 18Twelve team is proud of their BC heritage and sees themselves as "a product of the history of BC." With the core values of expertise, innovation, vision, commitment, and a growing team with over 90 years of horticultural experience, they aim to bring cannabis to the market that is premium, unique, and memorable.

18Twelve's cannabis is grown in the Cowichan Valley on Vancouver Island, using a hydroponic growth system. Plants are monitored daily to ensure successful growth and quality buds, and the finished product from 18Twelve is never irradiated.

Other Cultivars:	Canuck Cookies, King Kush, Purple Rockstar, Sour Amnesia, Wakizashi
Associated Brands:	Royal High

Cultivar Selection

8 Ball Kush	89%

8 Ball Kush

Cultivar/Product Information

Type/Effect:	Indica - Heavy
Legacy Name:	8 Ball Kush
Lineage:	Bubba Kush x King Kush
Cannabinoids:	25.7% THC / <1% CBD
Terpenes:	Caryophyllene, Limonene, Humulene

First Impression

Review #280; July 2, 2020,

After two bags of 18Twelve's 8 Ball Kush, I had already developed a substantial high, and I liked where this was going. The intensity kept on building with every lung full, the effects of the high growing more and more stupefying. The high is classic kush: very physically relaxing, cerebrally intense, but mellow; it is a typical "I'm stoned" high. My eyelids are closing on me as I struggle to write; this one is certainly sedating. A great first look at 18Twelve.

Observations

Aroma: Earthy, fresh, herbal, piney, woody

Flavour: Earthy, pungent, sour, spicy, woody

Bud Colour: Dark green

Pistil Colour: Brown/orange

Trichome Density: Medium-High

Score Details

Appearance:	4 / 5
High Quality:	5 / 5
Aroma:	12 / 15
Flavour:	12 / 15
Bud Quality:	28 / 30
High Potency:	28 / 30
Overall Score:	89%
Cultivar Ranking:	79th

48North

Overall Performance

Average Score: 72.40%

Brand Ranking: 68th Place

Brand Background

48North operates out of Ontario and produces cannabis with a focus on sustainability. The brand is "committed to delivering high-quality, accessible organic cannabis" to the recreational market. With two facilities, Delshen in Kirkland Lake and Good:House in Brantford, 48North produces their flower products with quality in mind.

Hexo Corp acquired 48North in May of 2021.

Other Cultivars:	Black Label Skull Cap, Kosher Kush, Power Plant, Where's My Bike
Associated Brands:	Hexo, Namaste, Redecan, Up

Cultivar Selection

Granddaddy Purple	75%
Green Crush	80%
Paris OG	79%
Strain Hunters' Franco's Lemon Cheese	69%
Strain Hunters' Holy Punch	59%

Granddaddy Purple

Cultivar/Product Information

Type/Effect: Indica - Light
Legacy Name: Granddaddy Purple
Lineage: Big Bud x Purple Urkle
Cannabinoids: 13.8% THC / <1% CBD
Terpenes: Pinene, Caryophyllene, Myrcene

First Impression

Review #156; December 10, 2019,

Thanks to 48North's Granddaddy Purple, I'm in for a chill and creative afternoon of computer work. Quite stimulating to the mind, I feel focused and alert, though my thoughts are slowed and come fluidly. My body is overcome with a peaceful relaxation in my chest and extremities. There is an immense pressure sensation on my face, behind my eyes. The buzz off of this flower is more significant than I had expected; I'm pretty high from 13.8% and pleasantly surprised - a good start for 48 North.

Observations

Aroma: Earthy, herbal, minty, piney, pungent, spicy

Flavour: Earthy, funky, herbal, pungent, spicy

Bud Colour: Dark green

Pistil Colour: Orange

Trichome Density: Medium High

Score Details

Appearance:	4 / 5
High Quality:	5 / 5
Aroma:	12 / 15
Flavour:	11 / 15
Bud Quality:	25 / 30
High Potency:	18 / 30

Overall Score: 75%

Cultivar Ranking: 285th

Green Crush

Cultivar/Product Information

Type/Effect: Sativa - Light
Legacy Name: Green Crack
Lineage: Afghani Indica x Skunk #1
Cannabinoids: 24% THC / <1% CBD
Terpenes: Caryophyllene, Pinene, Limonene

First Impression

Review #293; July 23, 2020,

Green Crush by 48North is a cerebral blast. I'm able to block out what I wish and zone in on what I want to while high on this flower. Although, I'm pretty up there as far as intense head highs go. My heart is racing, my mind is wired, and my mood is elevated and focused. I feel oddly sharp on this; it is a super functional experience though potent. 48North's best flower yet.

Observations

Aroma: Earthy, herbal, woody

Flavour: Earthy, grassy, herbal, woody

Bud Colour: Light green/tan

Pistil Colour: Orange/tan

Trichome Density: High

Score Details

Appearance:	4 / 5
High Quality:	5 / 5
Aroma:	11 / 15
Flavour:	10 / 15
Bud Quality:	25 / 30
High Potency:	25 / 30

Overall Score: 80%

Cultivar Ranking: 222nd

Paris OG

Cultivar/Product Information

Type/Effect: Indica - Light
Legacy Name: Paris OG
Lineage: Headband x Lemon OG Kush
Cannabinoids: 18.4% THC / <1% CBD
Terpenes: Caryophyllene, Pinene, Ocimene

First Impression

Review #231; April 5, 2020,

Man, for an indica, I'm crazy alert, focused and motivated; the creative energy is flowing, and my mind is alive on Paris OG from 48North. Not incredibly intense, but a great mood-enhancing and euphoric cultivar. I'm fantasizing about future projects, jamming out to music, and just having a grand old time.

Observations

Aroma: Chocolate, earthy, herbal, pungent, sour, spicy

Flavour: Funky, grassy, herbal, woody

Bud Colour: Green

Pistil Colour: Orange

Trichome Density: Medium

Score Details

Appearance: 4 / 5
High Quality: 5 / 5
Aroma: 13 / 15
Flavour: 11 / 15
Bud Quality: 27 / 30
High Potency: 19 / 30

Overall Score: 79%

Cultivar Ranking: 229th

Strain Hunters' Franco's Lemon Cheese

Cultivar/Product Information

Type/Effect:	Sativa Hybrid - Medium Heavy
Legacy Name:	Franco's Lemon Cheese
Lineage:	Exodus Cheese x Super Lemon Haze
Cannabinoids:	16.5% THC / <1% CBD
Terpenes:	Caryophyllene, Humulene, Myrcene

First Impression

Review #175; January 7, 2020,

48North's Strain Hunters' Franco's Lemon Cheese is a mouthful of a name and a mind-full of hazy, creative, stoned goodness. I feel useless mentally and can only focus on my stomach - an excellent tribute to Franco, with a beautiful head buzz.

Observations

Aroma: Citrusy, earthy, herbal, sour, sweet

Flavour: Citrusy, earthy, herbal, sour

Bud Colour: Dark purple/green

Pistil Colour: Brown

Trichome Density: Low-Medium

Score Details

Appearance:	2 / 5
High Quality:	5 / 5
Aroma:	13 / 15
Flavour:	12 / 15
Bud Quality:	18 / 30
High Potency:	19 / 30

Overall Score: 69%

Cultivar Ranking: 356th

Strain Hunters' Holy Punch

Cultivar/Product Information

Type/Effect: Indica Hybrid - Light
Legacy Name: Holy Punch
Lineage: Grape x The Church
Cannabinoids: 13.6% THC / <1% CBD
Terpenes: Ocimene, Myrcene, Limonene

First Impression

Review #237; April 14, 2020,

48North's Strain Hunters' Holy Punch washes over me as I listen to Behemoth's "I Loved You At Your Darkest". An ironic album choice, given the satanic lyrical content, with the name of this cultivar being "Holy Punch." Not quite the punch I was expecting came from this flower (at first, at least); the high is mellow and calm, with some cerebral stimulation and mood amplification. Not a lot physically. I'm hazy and high, not quite stoned - a good mellow buzz from a decent starter cultivar.

Observations

Aroma: Fresh, herbal, minty, piney, woody

Flavour: Herbal, spicy, woody

Bud Colour: Dark green/purple

Pistil Colour: Brown

Trichome Density: Low-Medium

Score Details

Appearance:	2 / 5
High Quality:	5 / 5
Aroma:	12 / 15
Flavour:	10 / 15
Bud Quality:	16 / 30
High Potency:	14 / 30

Overall Score: 59%

Cultivar Ranking: 412th

7Acres

Overall Performance

Average Score: 88.83%

Brand Ranking: 15th Place

Brand Background

7Acres prides itself on the knowledge and passion of those who grow their cannabis and stresses the importance of "respecting the plant." The folks at 7Acres aim to produce "high-end cannabis for enthusiasts" via their specialized growing methods.

Their bud is grown in Kincardine, Ontario, under high-pressure sodium lighting with supplemental sunlight, which they credit with giving their flower a unique look and feel.

7Acres was acquired by Canopy Growth in 2021.

Other Cultivars: Papaya, Platinum Kush Breath, Wappa 49
Associated Brands: DNA Genetics, Houseplant, LBS, Tokyo Smoke, Tweed, Van Der Pop

Cultivar Selection

Ice Cream Cake	89%
Island Pink Kush	95%
Jack Haze	89%
Jean Guy	86%
Sensi Star	88%
White Widow	86%

Ice Cream Cake

Cultivar/Product Information

Type/Effect: Indica Hybrid - Heavy
Legacy Name: Ice Cream Cake
Lineage: Gelato #33 x Wedding Cake
Cannabinoids: 23.7% THC / <1% CBD
Terpenes: Limonene, Caryophyllene, Nerolidol

First Impression

Review #340; September 29, 2020,

My body is heavy, but my spirits light after starting to consume Ice Cream Cake from 7Acres. Deeper into the bowl, my eyes became heavier, and my stomach more insatiable. I'm pretty relaxed physically, and my thoughts have slowed some, but my mood and mind are still lively. It is a good option for after work or anytime in the evening or afternoon; just beware, it is heavy and potent. Now to find some of the other kind of ice cream cake.

Observations

Aroma: Earthy, herbal, minty, piney, pungent, sweet

Flavour: Earthy, herbal, piney, pungent

Bud Colour: Dull green

Pistil Colour: Brown/orange

Trichome Density: Medium-High

Score Details

Appearance:	5 / 5
High Quality:	5 / 5
Aroma:	13 / 15
Flavour:	13 / 15
Bud Quality:	27 / 30
High Potency:	26 / 30

Overall Score: 89%

Cultivar Ranking: 78th

Island Pink Kush

Cultivar/Product Information

Type/Effect: Indica - Super Heavy
Legacy Name: Tom Ford Island Pink Kush
Lineage: OG Kush
Cannabinoids: 26.5% THC / <1% CBD
Terpenes: Limonene, Pinene, Caryophyllene

First Impression

Review #287; July 10, 2020,

My experience with 7Acres' Island Pink Kush was a heavy-eyed, red-eyed, stoned-out-of-my-mind one, that's for sure. It's lasting forever in the Volcano and inspiring one hell of a coughing fit. Thinking and writing are tricky. It is very heavy and mentally and physically sedating. Great KO weed. No doubt, one of the most potent recreational flowers I've had. Beware this bud.

Observations

Aroma: Earthy, grassy, herbal, piney, pungent, sour

Flavour: Earthy, funky, grassy, herbal, piney, pungent

Bud Colour: Dark green/purple

Pistil Colour: Brown/orange

Trichome Density: Medium-High

Score Details

Appearance:	5 / 5
High Quality:	5 / 5
Aroma:	14 / 15
Flavour:	12 / 15
Bud Quality:	29 / 30
High Potency:	30 / 30

Overall Score: 95%

Cultivar Ranking: 15th

Jack Haze

Cultivar/Product Information

Type/Effect: Sativa - Light
Legacy Name: Jack Haze
Lineage: Jack Herer x Super Silver Haze
Cannabinoids: 19.4% THC / <1% CBD
Terpenes: Terpinolene, Caryophyllene, Nerolidol

First Impression

Review #122; September 26, 2019,

Jack Haze by 7Acres is the sativa I've been waiting for from this brand. This bud punched me once in the throat with thick vapour, then again in the head, with a hefty cerebral high that delivers sharp focus, motivation, and energy. Prepare for an intense-as-can-be stoned feeling and a powerful headband effect. This cultivar is fantastic and in line with the quality I've expected from 7Acres.

Observations

Aroma: Citrusy, herbal, sour, sour candy

Flavour: Citrusy, herbal, sour, sour candy

Bud Colour: Brown/green

Pistil Colour: Brown/tan

Trichome Density: Medium

Score Details

Appearance:	4 / 5
High Quality:	5 / 5
Aroma:	15 / 15
Flavour:	12 / 15
Bud Quality:	28 / 30
High Potency:	25 / 30

Overall Score: 89%

Cultivar Ranking: 71st

Jean Guy

Cultivar/Product Information

Type/Effect: Hybrid - Neutral
Legacy Name: Jean Guy
Lineage: White Widow
Cannabinoids: 18.6% THC / <1% CBD
Terpenes: Myrcene, Limonene, Pinene

First Impression

Review #28; April 19, 2019,

7Acres has a reputation for being great in quality, and Jean Guy lived up to that reputation. This flower is a mid-high THC, sativa-dominant hybrid that hits like a truck in the most pleasant way possible. Jean Guy is blissful; I feel mellow but focused, creative and motivated, an excellent mix. As with other 7Acres products, the bud's smell, touch, appearance, and moisture quality are pretty spot-on. Impressive.

Observations

Aroma: Floral, fruity, herbal, sour, sweet

Flavour: Floral, fruity, herbal, sour, sweet

Bud Colour: Green/yellow

Pistil Colour: Brown/orange

Trichome Density: Medium-High

Score Details

Appearance:	4 / 5
High Quality:	5 / 5
Aroma:	13 / 15
Flavour:	13 / 15
Bud Quality:	28 / 30
High Potency:	23 / 30

Overall Score: 86%

Cultivar Ranking: 103rd

Sensi Star

Cultivar/Product Information

Type/Effect: Indica - Neutral
Legacy Name: Sensi Star
Lineage: "Unknown Afghani"
Cannabinoids: 24.4% THC / <1% CBD
Terpenes: Myrcene, Limonene, Caryophyllene

First Impression

Review #13; April 11, 2019,

If you're interested in a high-quality, high-potency experience, check out Sensi Star from 7Acres, you won't be disappointed. Medium-large, dense nugs are what you'll find when opening a jar of this near-perfect bud. The smell and flavour are both strong and classic, herbal and earthy. The high is potent and heavy, in the sense that I feel heavily relaxed, but not in the sense that I feel like having a rest. I certainly feel like staying up for the evening and enjoying it, and thanks to this miraculous buzz from Sensi Star, I shall.

Observations

Aroma: Earthy, herbal, minty, piney

Flavour: Earthy, herbal, piney, pungent

Bud Colour: Brown/green

Pistil Colour: Dark brown/red

Trichome Density: Medium

Score Details

Appearance:	4 / 5
High Quality:	5 / 5
Aroma:	12 / 15
Flavour:	11 / 15
Bud Quality:	28 / 30
High Potency:	28 / 30

Overall Score: 88%

Cultivar Ranking: 87th

White Widow

Cultivar/Product Information

Type/Effect: Hybrid - Light
Legacy Name: White Widow
Lineage: Brazilian Sativa x Indian Indica
Cannabinoids: 17.8% THC / <1% CBD
Terpenes: Myrcene, Limonene, Caryophyllene

First Impression

Review #35; April 23, 2019,

7Acres White Widow is a well-known cultivar, from a great brand in this case, so I'm excited. This was one of my 4/20 buds for 2019, and it was a worthy choice for the occasion. This hybrid should leave you ready to take on the day, chat with some friends, or take in some entertainment. The high is manageable, I'm not entirely mangled, and my mind is relatively clear. I feel very high, but not quite stoned, if you know what I mean - solid bud from 7 Acres, as usual.

Observations

Aroma: Citrusy, herbal, piney

Flavour: Herbal, piney, pungent

Bud Colour: Light green

Pistil Colour: Orange/red

Trichome Density: Medium

Score Details

Appearance:	4 / 5
High Quality:	5 / 5
Aroma:	13 / 15
Flavour:	13 / 15
Bud Quality:	28 / 30
High Potency:	23 / 30

Overall Score: 86%

Cultivar Ranking: 105th

Abba Medix

Overall Performance

Average Score: 81.00%

Brand Ranking: 35th Place

Brand Background

As the name may suggest, Abba Medix is a brand with origins in Canadian medical cannabis. With a focus on serving their consumer base of medical consumers, mainly veterans, Abba Medix produces premium medical cannabis - some of which has been offered on the recreational market as well.

They operate out of Pickering, Ontario, where they have a 22,000 square-foot indoor cannabis production facility. Quality being a focus for Abba Medix, their quality-assurance procedures are thorough and may even exceed Health Canada standards.

Other Cultivars: Bruce Banner, Gorilla Glue, Kosher Kush, Orange Dreamer, Sour Tangie

Cultivar Selection

Critical Orange Punch	77%
Purple Bud	75%
SAGE n' Sour	91%

Critical Orange Punch

Cultivar/Product Information

Type/Effect: Indica Hybrid - Medium Light
Legacy Name: Critical Orange Punch
Lineage: Critical x (Granddaddy Purps x Orange Bud)
Cannabinoids: 17.6% THC / <1% CBD
Terpenes: Camphene, Myrcene, Limonene

First Impression

Review #263; May 20, 2020,

In my first look at Abba Medix, I partook in their Critical Orange Punch. It was a little hazy, a bit tasty, and medium intensity. I'm relaxed mentally and physically, but not overwhelmingly so, just enough to lighten up an afternoon. My thoughts are slowed, my mind is not all over the place, so I'm pretty able to focus. The headband effect is strong here; my eyes feel heavier, slightly pressurized almost. A solid first take/toke, both for the brand and the cultivar.

Observations

Aroma: Earthy, herbal, sweet, woody

Flavour: Cheese, earthy, funky, herbal, pungent, spicy, woody

Bud Colour: Dull green

Pistil Colour: Brown/orange

Trichome Density: Medium

Score Details

Appearance:	4 / 5
High Quality:	5 / 5
Aroma:	11 / 15
Flavour:	12 / 15
Bud Quality:	24 / 30
High Potency:	21 / 30

Overall Score: 77%

Cultivar Ranking: 264th

Purple Bud

Cultivar/Product Information

Type/Effect: Indica - Medium Heavy
Legacy Name: Purple Bud
Lineage: Afghani Indica x Jamaican Sativa
Cannabinoids: 19.3% THC / <1% CBD
Terpenes: Caryophyllene, Myrcene, Pinene

First Impression

Review #271; June 10, 2020,

Quite a calm and mellow cultivar on the high, Purple Bud by Abba Medix is an enjoyable addition to any afternoon or evening. However, it may reduce productivity/ability to function. My eyes feel sleepy, and my mind is slowed, a decent pre-bed bud for winding down. Unfortunately, I have a lot to accomplish tonight, so I've set myself up poorly. Thanks to Purple Bud, though, I don't care much - not stressed about it. A good one to help you escape reality.

Observations

Aroma: Floral, fresh, herbal, sour, spicy, sweet

Flavour: Floral, fresh, herbal, sweet, woody

Bud Colour: Dark green

Pistil Colour: Brown/orange

Trichome Density: Medium

Score Details

Appearance:	3 / 5
High Quality:	5 / 5
Aroma:	12 / 15
Flavour:	12 / 15
Bud Quality:	20 / 30
High Potency:	23 / 30

Overall Score: 75%

Cultivar Ranking: 289th

SAGE n' Sour

Cultivar/Product Information

Type/Effect: Sativa - Heavy
Legacy Name: SAGE n' Sour
Lineage: SAGE x Sour Diesel
Cannabinoids: 21.2% THC / <1% CBD
Terpenes: Terpinolene, Myrcene, Limonene

First Impression

Review #295; July 25, 2020,

Hazy, heady, and intense, SAGE n' Sour by Abba Medix is their best yet. I'm struggling to decide whether I'm zoned in or out; I'm constantly switching. This stuff is a bit of a mind-melter. My mood is up, though the cultivar has profoundly affected my cognitive ability. I can write but wouldn't function well in public or on a task. I wouldn't say I'm feeling euphoric, though I am mellow, content, and stoned. Very cerebrally intense this one; my head is buzzing. My body is paralyzed and relaxed at the same time. A great time if you can handle it.

Observations

Aroma: Citrusy, herbal, pungent, sour

Flavour: Citrusy, floral, fresh, herbal, piney, pungent, sour

Bud Colour: Green

Pistil Colour: Brown/orange

Trichome Density: Medium-High

Score Details

Appearance:	5 / 5
High Quality:	5 / 5
Aroma:	14 / 15
Flavour:	14 / 15
Bud Quality:	27 / 30
High Potency:	26 / 30

Overall Score: 91%

Cultivar Ranking: 46th

Acreage Pharms

Overall Performance

Average Score: 70.63%

Brand Ranking: 71st Place

Brand Background

Acreage Pharms is located in Alberta, near the Rocky Mountains. The brand was founded to provide Canadians with access to quality cannabis consistently.

Utilizing 1500 square-foot growing areas, Acreage Pharms focuses on small-batch production with carefully-selected cultivars. This ensures that each cultivar can grow in its own environment, designed specifically for that cultivar, improving quality and consistency in the end product.

Other Cultivars: CBD Charlotte's Angel, Critical Bilbo, OG Kush

Cultivar Selection

Cultivar	Score
All Kush	61%
CBD Kush	73%
Mazar	68%
OA	70%
Rewind	69%
Scentimental	70%
Sensi Star	73%
Star Banner	81%

All Kush

Cultivar/Product Information

Type/Effect: Indica Hybrid - Medium Heavy
Legacy Name: All Kush
Lineage: Chemdog x Hindu Kush
Cannabinoids: 18.2% THC / <1% CBD
Terpenes: Caryophyllene, Pinene Limonene

First Impression

Review #36; April 23, 2019,

All Kush from Acreage Pharms is a relaxing and mellowing, medium-strength indica that should prepare you for a late-night snack, resting and recharging. A good choice for when bedtime approaches.

Observations

Aroma: Citrusy, herbal, minty, piney, sour

Flavour: Herbal, minty, sour

Bud Colour: Dark green

Pistil Colour: Brown/red

Trichome Density: Low-Medium

Score Details

Appearance:	4 / 5
High Quality:	4 / 5
Aroma:	10 / 15
Flavour:	9 / 15
Bud Quality:	18 / 30
High Potency:	16 / 30

Overall Score: 61%

Cultivar Ranking: 405th

CBD Kush

Cultivar/Product Information

Type/Effect: Indica Hybrid - Neutral
Legacy Name: CBD Kush
Lineage: Kandy Kush x Quimiotipo CBD
Cannabinoids: 6.4% THC / 9% CBD
Terpenes: Pinene, Limonene, Myrcene

First Impression

Review #63; May 21, 2019,

If you're looking for a great balanced cultivar experience, Acreage Pharms' has just that to offer in their take on CBD Kush. It produces a medium-intensity head high, coupled with a chill body high that is super relaxing. Great for any time, for any consumer. I would recommend a wake and bake with this.

Observations

Aroma: Fresh, fruity, herbal, sweet

Flavour: Fresh, herbal, sweet

Bud Colour: Dark green

Pistil Colour: Brown/orange

Trichome Density: Low-Medium

Score Details

Appearance:	4 / 5
High Quality:	5 / 5
Aroma:	12 / 15
Flavour:	10 / 15
Bud Quality:	21 / 30
High Potency:	21 / 30

Overall Score: 73%

Cultivar Ranking: 309th

Mazar

Cultivar/Product Information

Type/Effect: Indica - Heavy
Legacy Name: Mazar
Lineage: Afghani Indica x Skunk
Cannabinoids: 17.9% THC / <1% CBD
Terpenes: Terpinolene, Humulene, Limonene

First Impression

Review #98; August 31, 2019,

Mazar by Acreage Pharms offers a potent, heady, stoned feeling, with a heavy physical sensation in the head, torso, and legs. Medium-high on THC potency and high intensity, Mazar is an excellent option for evening relaxation and a midnight snack. A suitable high-impact cultivar for newcomers, or a good mid-potency bud for old pros, Acreage Pharms, has something to offer to everyone in Mazar.

Observations

Aroma: Citrusy, herbal, piney, sour

Flavour: Funky, herbal, spicy

Bud Colour: Green

Pistil Colour: Brown/red

Trichome Density: Low-Medium

Score Details

Appearance:	4 / 5
High Quality:	5 / 5
Aroma:	10 / 15
Flavour:	8 / 15
Bud Quality:	19 / 30
High Potency:	22 / 30

Overall Score: 68%

Cultivar Ranking: 370th

OA

Cultivar/Product Information

Type/Effect: Sativa Hybrid - Light
Legacy Name: Outlaw Amnesia
Lineage: Amnesia x Super Haze
Cannabinoids: 16% THC / <1% CBD
Terpenes: Myrcene, Pinene, Limonene

First Impression

Review #80; August 1, 2019,

OA from Acreage Pharms is a cerebral blast, bursting with energy and creativity. This is a very head-heavy sativa that hits harder than its 16% THC would imply. I found myself extraordinarily chatty and thoughtful on this cultivar, convenient considering it is my mom's birthday! We both felt social, energetic, and excited on this beautiful bud from Acreage Pharms.

Observations

Aroma: Fruity, herbal, sweet

Flavour: Earthy, herbal, pungent

Bud Colour: Dull green

Pistil Colour: Brown/orange

Trichome Density: Medium

Score Details

Appearance:	3 / 5
High Quality:	5 / 5
Aroma:	10 / 15
Flavour:	9 / 15
Bud Quality:	21 / 30
High Potency:	22 / 30

Overall Score: 70%

Cultivar Ranking: 350th

Rewind

Cultivar/Product Information

Type/Effect: Indica Hybrid - Medium Heavy
Legacy Name: White Widow
Lineage: Brazilian Sativa x Indian Indica
Cannabinoids: 18.7% THC / <1% CBD
Terpenes: Humulene, Myrcene, Terpinolene

First Impression

Review #83; August 9, 2019,

A heady, hazy experience is what to anticipate from Acreage Pharms' Rewind. I feel slightly stoned but not so far gone that writing is difficult. The effects are mentally stimulating, though my mind feels muted and cloudy. There is a powerful pressure sensation in my head and chest as well. Good stuff. A worthwhile cultivar to try for fans of medium-intensity, medium-high potency buds. Noteworthy: I passed out shortly after writing this review, so expect a burn-out during the high.

Observations

Aroma: Citrusy, earthy, herbal, spicy

Flavour: Earthy, herbal

Bud Colour: Green

Pistil Colour: Brown/orange

Trichome Density: Low-Medium

Score Details

Appearance:	4 / 5
High Quality:	5 / 5
Aroma:	10 / 15
Flavour:	9 / 15
Bud Quality:	19 / 30
High Potency:	22 / 30

Overall Score: 69%

Cultivar Ranking: 361st

Scentimental

Cultivar/Product Information

Type/Effect: Hybrid - Medium Heavy
Legacy Name: Ultra Skunk
Lineage: Dutch Skunk x Swiss Skunk
Cannabinoids: 19.3% THC / <1% CBD
Terpenes: Pinene, Carene

First Impression

Review #86; August 13, 2019,

I'm feeling relaxed and stoned today, thanks to Acreage Pharms' Scentimental. The taste is mild, but the smell is spicy and herbal. My mind and body are relaxed physically. I feel like having a nap, but I also think I want to jam out to some tunes or watch a movie. I'd recommend this as an afternoon or evening bud; perhaps without company - I don't feel too social on this flower. Scentimental will certainly feel strong to new consumers and should deliver a decent high.

Observations

Aroma: Earthy, herbal, pungent, spicy, sweet

Flavour: Earthy, herbal

Bud Colour: Dark green

Pistil Colour: Orange

Trichome Density: Low

Score Details

Appearance:	4 / 5
High Quality:	5 / 5
Aroma:	10 / 15
Flavour:	9 / 15
Bud Quality:	20 / 30
High Potency:	22 / 30

Overall Score: 70%

Cultivar Ranking: 351st

Sensi Star

Cultivar/Product Information

Type/Effect: Indica - Medium Heavy
Legacy Name: Sensi Star
Lineage: "Unknown Afghani"
Cannabinoids: 17.1% THC / <1% CBD
Terpenes: Limonene, Myrcene, Caryophyllene

First Impression

Review #107; September 5, 2019,

Acreage Pharms' take on the classic Sensi Star is an excellent, heavier indica bud. I'm feeling pretty foggy and stoned, relaxed, mentally and physically. The THC is medium-high, but the intensity of the high is relatively low due to how mellow it is. An excellent cultivar to introduce someone to high THC indicas that won't necessarily make them want to pass out for a nap or make them want to crawl out of their skin. One of the best available from Acreage Pharms.

Observations

Aroma: Diesel, earthy, herbal, piney, pungent, sweet

Flavour: Earthy, funky, piney, pungent, sweet

Bud Colour: Light green

Pistil Colour: Brown/orange

Trichome Density: Low-Medium

Score Details

Appearance:	4 / 5
High Quality:	5 / 5
Aroma:	11 / 15
Flavour:	9 / 15
Bud Quality:	22 / 30
High Potency:	22 / 30

Overall Score: 73%

Cultivar Ranking: 316th

Star Banner

Cultivar/Product Information

Type/Effect: Indica Hybrid - Neutral
Legacy Name: Star Banner
Lineage: Bruce Banner x Sensi Star
Cannabinoids: 21.7% THC / <1% CBD
Terpenes: Limonene, Caryophyllene, Myrcene

First Impression

Review #338; September 27, 2020,

Acreage Pharms flower has returned with Star Banner. While I've experienced both parent cultivars individually, never have I had them combined. A great introduction to the cross, as Star Banner was very potent. The high itself is pretty uplifting, euphoric, hazy, and mellow. Though I don't feel particularly motivated to do anything, my mood is elevated. A magnificent cerebral buzz and a light body buzz are comforting me as I write; it's quite pleasant. It was a great comeback from Acreage Pharms and the best flower I've had from them, without a doubt.

Observations

Aroma: Cheese, fresh, herbal, sour, spicy, woody

Flavour: Earthy, floral, fresh, herbal, woody

Bud Colour: Dull green/tan

Pistil Colour: Orange

Trichome Density: High

Score Details

Appearance:	4 / 5
High Quality:	5 / 5
Aroma:	12 / 15
Flavour:	12 / 15
Bud Quality:	25 / 30
High Potency:	23 / 30

Overall Score: 81%

Cultivar Ranking: 184th

AltaVie

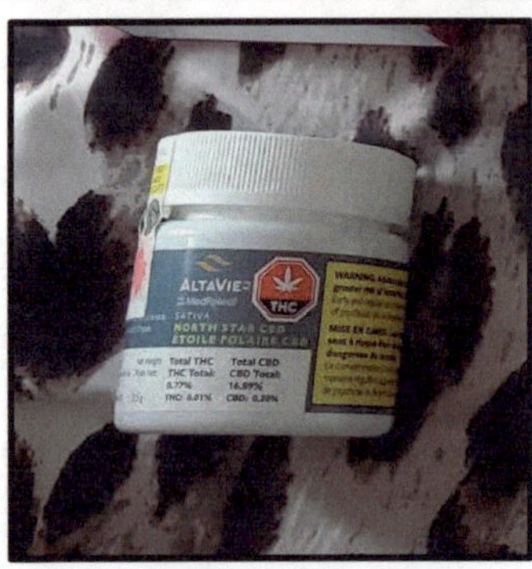

Overall Performance

Average Score: 75.50%

Brand Ranking: 53rd Place

Brand Background

A health and wellness-oriented brand, AltaVie hopes to produce products to enhance your perception and your perspective. AltaVie is focused on mindfulness and the thinking process; their cultivars aim to "enhance moments of discovery."

The AltaVie lineup of cultivars is heavily CBD-focused. Each cultivar has been selected with a specific purpose or activity in mind, often indicated by the name. Whether you want to lightly socialize with Campfire or drift away with Airplane Mode, AltaVie should have an offering for you.

AltaVie and San Rafael '71 were brands under the LP "MedReleaf" until Aurora acquired it in 2018.

Other Cultivars:	North Star CBD
Associated Brands:	Aurora, San Rafael '71, Whistler Cannabis Company

Cultivar Selection

Airplane Mode	74%
Cabaret	83%
Campfire	66%
Harmonic	79%

Airplane Mode

Cultivar/Product Information

Type/Effect: Indica - Medium Heavy
Legacy Name: Critical Kush
Lineage: Critical Mass x OG Kush
Cannabinoids: 16% THC / <1% CBD
Terpenes: Myrcene, Pinene, Caryophyllene

First Impression

Review #32; April 21, 2019,

This indica is exceptionally true to its name; Airplane Mode, by AltaVie, puts you in airplane mode. That is: stoned, checked out, and easily distracted. This bud is a great way to escape for a while and drift away.

Observations

Aroma: Chocolate, citrusy, fruity, herbal, sweet

Flavour: Cheese, citrusy, funky, herbal, sour

Bud Colour: Dark green

Pistil Colour: Brown/orange

Trichome Density: Low

Score Details

Appearance:	4 / 5
High Quality:	5 / 5
Aroma:	11 / 15
Flavour:	12 / 15
Bud Quality:	22 / 30
High Potency:	20 / 30

Overall Score: 74%

Cultivar Ranking: 300th

Cabaret

Cultivar/Product Information

Type/Effect:	Sativa - Medium Light
Legacy Name:	Island Sweet Skunk
Lineage:	Skunk #1 x Sweet Pink Grapefruit
Cannabinoids:	19.3% THC / <1% CBD
Terpenes:	Myrcene, Terpinolene, Pinene

First Impression

Review #42; April 26, 2019,

My bud of choice before I settled into a gaming session this evening, Cabaret, by AltaVie, is an excellent high that'll leave you focused yet stoned. You'll also find that this sativa settles more into a burn-out as it goes on, offering a wide range of effects for a combined experience of both an energetic and a mellow sativa. An excellent choice to pick up, Cabaret is a cultivar to look for.

Observations

Aroma: Citrusy, grapefruit, herbal, sour

Flavour: Citrusy, herbal, sour

Bud Colour: Green

Pistil Colour: Orange

Trichome Density: Medium

Score Details

Appearance:	4 / 5
High Quality:	5 / 5
Aroma:	14 / 15
Flavour:	13 / 15
Bud Quality:	24 / 30
High Potency:	23 / 30

Overall Score: 83%

Cultivar Ranking: 135th

Campfire

Cultivar/Product Information

Type/Effect: Indica Hybrid - Medium Light
Cannabinoids: 4% THC / 6.4% CBD
Terpenes: Myrcene, Pinene

First Impression

Review #8; April 9, 2019,

This has been a pleasant morning thus far, and I owe that to AltaVie's Campfire. I certainly didn't want to get out of bed, but now I'm just thrilled to be starting my day off right with this lovely balanced cultivar. I am feeling uplifted, motivated, mellow, and pleasant. While somewhat low in THC and CBD, the subtle high accented with deep relaxation that Campfire delivers might convince you otherwise. Perfect for newer consumers or those experienced who want to try a different or lighter experience.

Observations

Aroma: Earthy, fruity, herbal, pungent, sour, sweet

Flavour: Cheese, funky, herbal, sour

Bud Colour: Green

Pistil Colour: Orange

Trichome Density: Low-Medium

Score Details

Appearance:	3 / 5
High Quality:	5 / 5
Aroma:	10 / 15
Flavour:	10 / 15
Bud Quality:	22 / 30
High Potency:	16 / 30

Overall Score: 66%

Cultivar Ranking: 388th

Harmonic

Cultivar/Product Information

Type/Effect: Sativa - Medium Light
Cannabinoids: 8.9% THC / 8.7% CBD
Terpenes: Myrcene, Pinene

First Impression

Review #9; April 9, 2019,

My afternoon was going well, and now it's going great, thanks to Harmonic by AltaVie. An intense, balanced high provides a nice cerebral jolt, backed up with a potent body sensation. As the cultivar's name might suggest, I genuinely feel in harmony with myself and the moment. In no way too much or overwhelming, an enjoyable experience every time, balanced excellence has been achieved in Harmonic.

Observations

Aroma: Fresh, fruity, herbal, sweet

Flavour: Fresh, grassy, herbal

Bud Colour: Green

Pistil Colour: Brown/red

Trichome Density: Low

Score Details

Appearance:	4 / 5
High Quality:	5 / 5
Aroma:	12 / 15
Flavour:	11 / 15
Bud Quality:	23 / 30
High Potency:	24 / 30

Overall Score: 79%

Cultivar Ranking: 236th

Ankr Organics

Overall Performance

Average Score: 67.00%

Brand Ranking: 73rd Place

Ankr Organics

Brand Background

Produced in Moncton, New Brunswick, Ankr Organics is Organigram's fully organic brand offering. Launching in Alberta in 2020, the brand seeks to bring Edison-level cannabis quality and pricing from an organically grown plant.

Ankr Organics utilizes single-cultivar, indoor grow spaces for their cannabis production.

Associated Brands: Edison

Cultivar Selection

Siren	67%

Siren

Cultivar/Product Information

Type/Effect: Sativa Hybrid - Medium Heavy
Legacy Name: R2
Lineage: Afghan Haze
Cannabinoids: 16.2% THC / <1% CBD
Terpenes: Myrcene, Caryophyllene, Ocimene

First Impression

Review #310; August 15, 2020,

Ankr Organics' Siren produces a mellow and hazy high, very relaxed vs uplifting. While average in appearance, smell, and taste, this flower does deliver a high that feels relatively strong, particularly in my eyes and forehead. I lack motivation and drive; little inspiration or energy is coming to me. This is a decent one to zone out with - chill bud.

Observations

Aroma: Earthy, grassy, herbal, peas, sour, sweet

Flavour: Earthy, funky, herbal, woody

Bud Colour: Brown/green/tan

Pistil Colour: Brown

Trichome Density: Low

Score Details

Appearance:	3 / 5
High Quality:	5 / 5
Aroma:	10 / 15
Flavour:	10 / 15
Bud Quality:	21 / 30
High Potency:	18 / 30

Overall Score: 67%

Cultivar Ranking: 379th

Artisan Batch

Overall Performance

Average Score: 91.50%

Brand Ranking: 6th Place

Brand Background

Artisan Batch is not one brand but a collection of various craft cannabis brands brought to market by Indiva. Through partnerships, Artisan Batch aims to bring legacy market genetics to the recreational market.

Micro-growers and craft producers, including Coast Mountain Cannabis, Canandia, and Gnomestar Cannabis, all have near-perfect flower. Thanks to Artisan Batch, a broader consumer base can experience their expert grows.

Other Cultivars: Cereal Milk, Donny Burger, Golden Pineapple, Sour Glue, Sticky Larry, Unicorn Sherbert

Cultivar Selection

Meat Breath	93%
Original Glue	90%

Meat Breath

Cultivar/Product Information

Type/Effect: Indica Hybrid - Super Heavy
Legacy Name: Meat Breath
Lineage: Meatloaf x Mendo Breath
Cannabinoids: 21.1% THC / <1% CBD
Terpenes: Limonene, Caryophyllene, Linalool

First Impression

Review #379; December 11, 2020,

Artisan Batch & Gnomestar are making my writing process difficult with the potent power of Meat Breath. Much better smelling than one might think, Meat Breath offers a relaxing, zonk-you-out high that makes writing a challenge. I struggle to stand up, focus and think; no question, I'm stoned. I could see zoning out or passing out on this flower and not much else - well done, Gnomestar.

Observations

Aroma: Earthy, fresh, minty, piney, pungent

Flavour: Earthy, fresh, minty, piney, woody

Bud Colour: Dark green/purple

Pistil Colour: Orange/tan

Trichome Density: Medium-High

Score Details

Appearance:	5 / 5
High Quality:	5 / 5
Aroma:	14 / 15
Flavour:	13 / 15
Bud Quality:	30 / 30
High Potency:	26 / 30

Overall Score: 93%

Cultivar Ranking: 28th

Original Glue

Cultivar/Product Information

Type/Effect: Hybrid - Medium Light
Legacy Name: Original Glue
Lineage: Chem's Sister x Chocolate Diesel x Sour Dubb
Cannabinoids: 22.6% THC / <1% CBD
Terpenes: Myrcene, Pinene

First Impression

Review #326; September 4, 2020,

A pleasant, euphoric, and calm sense of wellness comes over my mind and body as I partake of Original Glue by Artisan Batch - this particular batch from Coast Mountain Cannabis. The high is intense, immense and immaculate, without ever feeling like too much. I got really into the moment on this flower, and I found my head relatively clear throughout my session, aiding in being present. I just felt great while experiencing this bud. Overall, an excellent flower and incredible high.

Observations

Aroma: Fresh, grassy, herbal, piney, spicy, sweet, woody

Flavour: Earthy, fresh, grassy, herbal, sweet

Bud Colour: Dull green

Pistil Colour: Brown/orange

Trichome Density: High

Score Details

Appearance:	5 / 5
High Quality:	5 / 5
Aroma:	13 / 15
Flavour:	12 / 15
Bud Quality:	29 / 30
High Potency:	26 / 30

Overall Score: 90%

Cultivar Ranking: 67th

Aurora

Overall Performance

Average Score: 63.25%

Brand Ranking: 78th Place

Brand Background

As Alberta's most well-known cannabis brand, Aurora is a large-scale cannabis producer focused on the mass production of cannabis. With massive facilities such as Aurora Sky, the company has produced a large portion of the cannabis the recreational market has seen, particularly in 2019.

Aurora's cannabis production takes place in large-scale greenhouses.

Associated Brands: Alta Vie, San Rafael '71, Whistler Cannabis Company

Cultivar Selection

Banana Split	55%
Blue Dream	75%
Ghost Train Haze	70%
LA Confidential	59%
MK Ultra	65%
OG Melon	68%
Summer Fling	59%
Temple	55%

Banana Split

Cultivar/Product Information

Type/Effect: Sativa Hybrid - Medium Light
Legacy Name: Banana Split
Lineage: Banana Sherbert x Tangie
Cannabinoids: 13.5% THC / <1% CBD

First Impression

Review #37; April 23, 2019,

An alright afternoon bud, Aurora's Banana Split is an enjoyable buzz. The head high from Banana Split will leave you feeling foggy and absent-minded. I played some video games while experiencing Banana Split, to limited success; considering how hazed I was, I suppose that makes sense.

Observations

Aroma: Fresh, fruity, herbal, sweet

Flavour: Fresh, herbal, sweet

Bud Colour: Dark green/purple

Pistil Colour: Orange/red

Trichome Density: Low

Score Details

Appearance:	2 / 5
High Quality:	4 / 5
Aroma:	11 / 15
Flavour:	9 / 15
Bud Quality:	15 / 30
High Potency:	14 / 30

Overall Score: 55%

Cultivar Ranking: 418th

Blue Dream

Cultivar/Product Information

Type/Effect: Sativa - Light
Legacy Name: Blue Dream
Lineage: Blueberry x Haze
Cannabinoids: 23.4% THC / <1% CBD
Terpenes: Pinene, Myrcene

First Impression

Review #45; April 27, 2019,

I found myself jamming out harder and harder to some tunes as I got higher and higher on the fantastic, blissful, motivating, and focusing Blue Dream by Aurora. It's no wonder this cultivar is so popular, its effects are delightful, and the THC comes out strong for a powerful cerebral buzz and headband effect - a pretty decent high.

Observations

Aroma: Citrusy, herbal, sour, sweet

Flavour: Citrusy, herbal, sour

Bud Colour: Light green

Pistil Colour: Brown/orange

Trichome Density: Low-Medium

Score Details

Appearance:	4 / 5
High Quality:	5 / 5
Aroma:	10 / 15
Flavour:	11 / 15
Bud Quality:	21 / 30
High Potency:	24 / 30

Overall Score: 75%

Cultivar Ranking: 292nd

Ghost Train Haze

Cultivar/Product Information

Type/Effect: Sativa - Medium Light
Legacy Name: Ghost Train Haze
Lineage: Ghost OG x Nevil's Wreck
Cannabinoids: 18.4% THC / <1% CBD
Terpenes: Terpinolene, Limonene, Ocimene

First Impression

Review #342; October 3, 2020,

Look for Aurora's Ghost Train Haze for a mind-numbing, heady high that alternates between focus and zone-out. There is a pulsing pressure sensation throughout my head from this flower's cerebral buzz. As I have more of my bowl, I find motivation fading as relaxation sets in; this is a pretty mellow sativa, though I have bouts of feeling wired. Indeed very heady in effect, my eyes look hazed over, just as my mind is - a decent ride on the Ghost Train.

Observations

Aroma: Citrusy, herbal, pungent, sour

Flavour: Citrusy, herbal, pungent, sour

Bud Colour: Green

Pistil Colour: Orange/tan

Trichome Density: Low

Score Details

Appearance:	2 / 5
High Quality:	5 / 5
Aroma:	13 / 15
Flavour:	11 / 15
Bud Quality:	16 / 30
High Potency:	23 / 30

Overall Score: 70%

Cultivar Ranking: 339th

LA Confidential

Cultivar/Product Information

Type/Effect: Indica - Medium Heavy
Legacy Name: LA Confidential
Lineage: Afghani Indica x OG LA Affie
Cannabinoids: 16.1% THC / <1% CBD
Terpenes: Pinene, Caryophyllene, Ocimene

First Impression

Review #74; June 28, 2019,

I'm talkative but relaxed, mentally alert but chill and mellow; it's odd, it's great, it's LA Confidential by Aurora, and I can't quite put my finger on where this indica is taking me, but I dig it. Mid-potency at 16% THC, feels just that too, but much more like a body-heavy hybrid than an indica on effects. Great to kick off an afternoon, evening, or get-together with.

Observations

Aroma: Earthy, fresh, sweet

Flavour: Cheese, funky, herbal, sour

Bud Colour: Dark brown/green

Pistil Colour: Brown/red

Trichome Density: Low-Medium

Score Details

Appearance:	2 / 5
High Quality:	5 / 5
Aroma:	9 / 15
Flavour:	7 / 15
Bud Quality:	18 / 30
High Potency:	18 / 30

Overall Score: 59%

Cultivar Ranking: 414th

MK Ultra

Cultivar/Product Information

Type/Effect: Indica - Heavy
Legacy Name: MK Ultra
Lineage: G13 x OG Kush
Cannabinoids: 21.4% THC / <1% CBD
Terpenes: Myrcene, Limonene, Caryophyllene

First Impression

Review #10; April 9, 2019,

Aurora's MK Ultra is a hard-hitting, potent indica that will leave you feeling stoned. Baked, wrecked, trashed, whatever your term for "extremely high", you'll be it. MK Ultra hits hard with a heavy cerebral stoned feeling and a powerful body sensation. An excellent cultivar for those who are experienced and intend to consume during the nighttime. It will either make you want to eat all the food, enjoy all the activities, or pass out on all the furniture at different points in MK's experience. Decent.

Observations

Aroma: Berry, earthy, funky, herbal, pungent, skunk, sweet

Flavour: Berry, earthy, funky, herbal, pungent, skunk

Bud Colour: Green/tan

Pistil Colour: Brown/red

Trichome Density: Medium

Score Details

Appearance:	2 / 5
High Quality:	5 / 5
Aroma:	9 / 15
Flavour:	8 / 15
Bud Quality:	18 / 30
High Potency:	23 / 30

Overall Score: 65%

Cultivar Ranking: 394th

OG Melon

Cultivar/Product Information

Type/Effect: Sativa Hybrid - Neutral
Legacy Name: OG Melon
Lineage: Captain Krypt OG x '91 Chemdog
Cannabinoids: 14.2% THC / <1% CBD
Terpenes: Caryophyllene, Limonene, Myrcene

First Impression

Review #84; August 9, 2019,

OG Melon by Aurora is a fruity cultivar, vaguely melon-like in scent. The high is medium intensity, strong in the head and chest. Focused, alert, motivated, creative, and clear-headed, that's how I'm feeling at this moment. Though only at 14.2% THC, it feels substantial in its effect; OG Melon is a great cultivar. This cultivar would be ideal for nearly any setting and any consumer, though likely not before bedtime, as it is stimulating.

Observations

Aroma: Fruity, herbal, melon, sweet

Flavour: Fruity, herbal, sweet

Bud Colour: Dark green

Pistil Colour: Brown/orange

Trichome Density: Low

Score Details

Appearance:	4 / 5
High Quality:	5 / 5
Aroma:	12 / 15
Flavour:	10 / 15
Bud Quality:	20 / 30
High Potency:	17 / 30

Overall Score: 68%

Cultivar Ranking: 366th

Summer Fling

Cultivar/Product Information

Type/Effect: Hybrid - Light
Cannabinoids: 9.7% THC / <1% CBD

First Impression

Review #82; August 8, 2019,

Relaxing and calming to the body and mind but stimulating to the senses, Summer Fling by Aurora is a lovely early morning or afternoon bud. This cultivar is ideal for new consumers and offers a very light high that shouldn't over-impair or overwhelm. I picture a day at the beach or on the porch or patio, something with company; this bud would be well enjoyed in a social setting - a good one to take the edge off on a Summer day.

Observations

Aroma: Chocolate, herbal, spicy, sweet

Flavour: Earthy, herbal, pungent, spicy

Bud Colour: Green/purple

Pistil Colour: Orange

Trichome Density: Medium

Score Details

Appearance:	3 / 5
High Quality:	5 / 5
Aroma:	11 / 15
Flavour:	10 / 15
Bud Quality:	18 / 30
High Potency:	12 / 30

Overall Score: 59%

Cultivar Ranking: 413th

Temple

Cultivar/Product Information

Type/Effect:	Hybrid - Super Light
Legacy Name:	Cannatonic
Lineage:	NYC Diesel x Reina Madre
Cannabinoids:	<1% THC / 8% CBD
Terpenes:	Myrcene, Guaiol, Pinene

First Impression

Review #91; August 18, 2019,

The experience is light, mellow, relaxed… very calm, as the name Temple by Aurora might suggest. Though not the heftiest amount of CBD in this Temple as in other CBD-only cultivars, it doesn't take away from the overall sensation, just the intensity. A great starting point for those interested in seeing what CBD in isolation, in small amounts, can do.

Observations

Aroma: Earthy, herbal, sweet

Flavour: Earthy, spicy, woody

Bud Colour: Dark brown/purple

Pistil Colour: Brown/orange

Trichome Density: Medium

Score Details

Appearance:	4 / 5
High Quality:	4 / 5
Aroma:	11 / 15
Flavour:	8 / 15
Bud Quality:	18 / 30
High Potency:	10 / 30

Overall Score: 55%

Cultivar Ranking: 416th

Blissco

Overall Performance

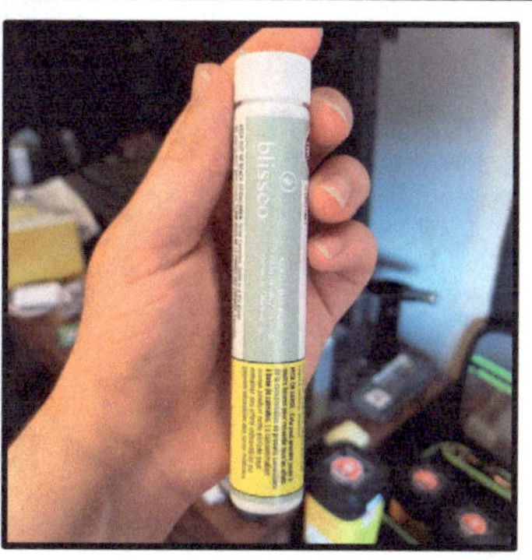

Average Score: 80.00%

Brand Ranking: 40th Place

Brand Background

Blissco is a cannabis brand focusing on wellness and sharing nature through cannabis. The brand was founded in 2013 by Damian Kettlewell, following a career of environmental activism and political ties with the BC Green Party.

The brand has released several products, but only a couple have been whole flower. While Blissco has had a limited market presence within the realm of flower, their buds have been impressive for what we have seen hit the market.

Other Cultivars: Cold Creek Kush

Cultivar Selection

Green Cush	80%

Green Cush

Cultivar/Product Information

Type/Effect: Sativa - Light
Legacy Name: Green Crack
Lineage: Afghani Indica x Skunk #1
Cannabinoids: 20% THC / <1% CBD
Terpenes: Pinene, Caryophyllene

First Impression

Review #73; June 27, 2019,

A solid sativa experience, Green Cush from Blissco, will prepare you to take on the day and its duties. I feel focused and motivated by this heady sativa and the potent cerebral high it provides. Overall, a great product from Blissco.

Observations

Aroma: Citrusy, herbal

Flavour: Cheese, fresh, funky, herbal

Bud Colour: Light green

Pistil Colour: Brown/orange

Trichome Density: Medium-High

Score Details

Appearance:	5 / 5
High Quality:	5 / 5
Aroma:	11 / 15
Flavour:	11 / 15
Bud Quality:	25 / 30
High Potency:	23 / 30

Overall Score: 80%

Cultivar Ranking: 221st

Boaz

Overall Performance

Average Score: 86.25%

Brand Ranking: 21st Place

Brand Background

Boaz is a craft producer out of Calgary, Alberta. They employ a small team of growing staff and produce higher quality bud than the average producer.

They are an eco-friendly producer working out of a 20,000 square-foot facility, utilizing grow pods with unique conditions for each cultivar. When cannabis is finished growing in its curated conditions, it is hang-dried, hand-trimmed, and cured before packaging.

Several of Boaz's reviewed cultivars were grown by other LPs, including Crescendo and Zour Apples (Atlas Growers).

Other Cultivars: Dank Rainbow, Pizza Breath, Primal Punch

Cultivar Selection

CBD Skunk Haze	73%
Crescendo	86%
Green Kraken	96%
Mandarin Cookies	87%
Platinum Gelato	89%
Wedding Cake	86%
White Russian	77%
Zour Apples	96%

CBD Skunk Haze

Cultivar/Product Information

Type/Effect: Indica Hybrid - Neutral
Legacy Name: CBD Skunk Haze
Lineage: Cannatonic x Super Haze
Cannabinoids: 5.1% THC / 6.1% CBD
Terpenes: Pinene, Guaiol, Myrcene

First Impression

Review #188; February 10, 2020,

Boaz's CBD Skunk Haze has a strong headband effect, and I feel the buzz right in the middle of my forehead. My senses are heightened, my mood calm and chill, reasonably comfortable and relaxed. A strong effect profile accompanies a slight high, and I'm ready to melt into the nearest chair; Boaz impresses again.

Observations

Aroma: Chocolate, fruity, herbal, spicy, sweet

Flavour: Chocolate, herbal, sweet, woody

Bud Colour: Green/tan

Pistil Colour: Brown/orange

Trichome Density: Medium-High

Score Details

Appearance:	4 / 5
High Quality:	5 / 5
Aroma:	13 / 15
Flavour:	11 / 15
Bud Quality:	23 / 30
High Potency:	17 / 30

Overall Score: 73%

Cultivar Ranking: 308th

Crescendo

Cultivar/Product Information

Type/Effect: Hybrid - Neutral
Legacy Name: Crescendo
Lineage: Chemdog x I-95 x Mandarin Cookies
Cannabinoids: 19.5% THC / <1% CBD

First Impression

Review #198; February 23, 2020,

Crescendo from Boaz is a great flower to enhance my afternoon off. It is a terpy, frosty delight with a unique dark purple colour that I love to see in cannabis. The high is very clear in the mind, but my face is heavy, and the headband effect is strong. I feel content and calm. The high gives a full feeling, satisfying indeed - an impressive cultivar.

Observations

Aroma: Citrusy, earthy, fruity, herbal, sweet

Flavour: Earthy, funky, herbal, pungent, sour, sweet

Bud Colour: Dark purple

Pistil Colour: Brown/orange

Trichome Density: High

Score Details

Appearance:	5 / 5
High Quality:	5 / 5
Aroma:	14 / 15
Flavour:	11 / 15
Bud Quality:	27 / 30
High Potency:	24 / 30

Overall Score: 86%

Cultivar Ranking: 97th

Green Kraken

Cultivar/Product Information

Type/Effect: Sativa Hybrid - Heavy
Legacy Name: Green Kraken
Lineage: Green Kush x Mango
Cannabinoids: 23.9% THC / <1% CBD
Terpenes: Pinene, Limonene, Myrcene

First Impression

Review #277; June 24, 2020,

Green Kraken by Boaz had me dancing around my bedroom and singing/rapping along to some Sublime. The high is full of energy, creativity, and euphoria, but it does get heavier the more you consume. A mostly cerebral cultivar, my body just feels loose and limber. I'd imagine this is an incredible social high, though my dog is my only current company. I'm stoned enough to talk to her, but the conversation isn't much between my garbled/mumbled speech and her being a dog. Superb quality, with a potent aroma to match the high, Green Kraken has it all. Boaz's best.

Observations

Aroma: Citrusy, diesel, earthy, fresh, herbal, pungent, sour

Flavour: Earthy, fresh, grassy, herbal, woody

Bud Colour: Light green

Pistil Colour: Orange

Trichome Density: High

Score Details

Appearance:	5 / 5
High Quality:	5 / 5
Aroma:	15 / 15
Flavour:	12 / 15
Bud Quality:	30 / 30
High Potency:	29 / 30

Overall Score: 96%

Cultivar Ranking: 8th

Mandarin Cookies

Cultivar/Product Information

Type/Effect: Sativa Hybrid - Neutral
Legacy Name: Mandarin Cookies
Lineage: Forum Cut GSC x Mandarin Sunset
Cannabinoids: 21.2% THC / <1% CBD
Terpenes: Caryophyllene, Limonene, Cedrene

First Impression

Review #366; November 9, 2020,

Mandarin Cookies by Boaz is a heavy head high with a mellow body sensation. I dwelled on some serious thoughts on this one and got very much in my head - a wild and weird time. Once that passed, I was very calm and relaxed throughout the experience and could think when I needed to. I also had bouts of zoning out throughout the high - kind of all over the place, but a great time nonetheless.

Observations

Aroma: Fresh, herbal, pungent, sour, spicy, sweet

Flavour: Floral, fresh, grassy, herbal, woody

Bud Colour: Dull green

Pistil Colour: Brown/red

Trichome Density: Medium-High

Score Details

Appearance:	4 / 5
High Quality:	5 / 5
Aroma:	13 / 15
Flavour:	11 / 15
Bud Quality:	28 / 30
High Potency:	26 / 30

Overall Score: 87%

Cultivar Ranking: 94th

Platinum Gelato

Cultivar/Product Information

Type/Effect: Hybrid - Light
Legacy Name: Gelato
Lineage: Sunset Sherbet x Thin Mint GSC
Cannabinoids: 17.4% THC / <1% CBD
Terpenes: Limonene, Caryophyllene, Myrcene

First Impression

Review #282; July 1, 2020,

Boaz's Platinum Gelato is an immaculate high, potent and enjoyable; it pairs well with sour candy and early-career Gojira songs. I had the munchies, a euphoric head high, an electrifying body buzz, and a spark of creativity while high on this beautiful flower. The highest quality is nothing I don't expect from Boaz at this point.

Observations

Aroma: Earthy, fresh, fruity, herbal, pungent, sweet

Flavour: Earthy, fresh, grassy, herbal, pungent, sweet

Bud Colour: Green/purple

Pistil Colour: Orange

Trichome Density: High

Score Details

Appearance:	4 / 5
High Quality:	5 / 5
Aroma:	14 / 15
Flavour:	13 / 15
Bud Quality:	29 / 30
High Potency:	24 / 30

Overall Score: 89%

Cultivar Ranking: 74th

Wedding Cake

Cultivar/Product Information

Type/Effect: Indica - Medium Heavy
Legacy Name: Wedding Cake
Lineage: Cherry Pie x Girl Scout Cookies
Cannabinoids: 18.9% THC / <1% CBD
Terpenes: Caryophyllene, Myrcene, Limonene

First Impression

Review #380; December 12, 2020,

Wedding Cake by Boaz got my mind wandering with many creative, engaging, inspiring thoughts, and also nonsense. I'm relaxed physically, and the high is slightly heavy, but my mind is cerebrally active. My creative ideas and the effects from this high are lovely, but as I got deeper into the bowl, I found creativity fading and spacey-ness creeping in - a great experience on one of my favourite cultivars.

Observations

Aroma: Earthy, fruity, herbal, pungent, sweet

Flavour: Earthy, funky, herbal, pungent

Bud Colour: Dull green/purple

Pistil Colour: Brown

Trichome Density: Medium

Score Details

Appearance:	4 / 5
High Quality:	5 / 5
Aroma:	13 / 15
Flavour:	12 / 15
Bud Quality:	28 / 30
High Potency:	24 / 30

Overall Score: 86%

Cultivar Ranking: 101st

White Russian

Cultivar/Product Information

Type/Effect: Sativa Hybrid - Medium Light
Legacy Name: White Russian
Lineage: AK-47 x White Widow
Cannabinoids: 13.1% THC / <1% CBD
Terpenes: Myrcene, Guaiol, Limonene

First Impression

Review #173; January 5, 2020,

If to be used as a morning cultivar, I'd say it's a good thing this Boaz White Russian has just 13% THC, as it is pretty potent for its percentage. It lasted longer in the Volcano than expected, indicating a higher than usual terpene content. My body and mood are relaxed, but my mind has a sharp focus to it; this is a solid functional high: a great time and an excellent first look at Boaz.

Observations

Aroma: Floral, fresh, grassy, herbal, sour, sweet

Flavour: Floral, fresh, grassy, herbal, sweet

Bud Colour: Light green

Pistil Colour: Orange

Trichome Density: Medium

Score Details

Appearance:	5 / 5
High Quality:	5 / 5
Aroma:	13 / 15
Flavour:	12 / 15
Bud Quality:	25 / 30
High Potency:	17 / 30

Overall Score: 77%

Cultivar Ranking: 257th

Zour Apples

Cultivar/Product Information

Type/Effect: Sativa Hybrid - Medium Light
Legacy Name: Zour Apples
Lineage: Ethos Glue x Plantman Jack Herer
Cannabinoids: 21.3% THC / <1% CBD
Terpenes: Myrcene, Caryophyllene, Terpinolene

First Impression

Review #233; April 8, 2020,

Zour Apples by Boaz is a masterpiece, a genuinely stunning craft grow. My thoughts are relaxed, but everything else is bursting with life and energy, the euphoria of this flower is precisely what I wanted this afternoon. The bulk of the physical sensation is in the head, especially on the face/forehead. I feel amazing. Aroma, flavour, and quality were superb; the moisture content/bud texture was incredible, super squishy and sticky. Long-lasting in the Volcano and intense as a consequence, Zour Apples is one best left to the experienced with cannabis - a gift to stoners everywhere.

Observations

Aroma: Citrusy, diesel, fruity, herbal, pungent, sour

Flavour: Diesel, earthy, funky, herbal, pungent, woody

Bud Colour: Light green

Pistil Colour: Orange/tan

Trichome Density: High

Score Details

Appearance:	5 / 5
High Quality:	5 / 5
Aroma:	15 / 15
Flavour:	13 / 15
Bud Quality:	30 / 30
High Potency:	28 / 30

Overall Score: 96%

Cultivar Ranking: 9th

Broken Coast

Overall Performance

Average Score: 90.27%

Brand Ranking: 8th Place

Brand Background

Broken Coast is producing some of the best small-batch flower on the market from the shores of Vancouver Island.

At Broken Coast, buds are grown indoors under cultivar-specific conditions, and they are hand-trimmed as well. They also slow-cure the cultivars, giving them full time to develop character after drying.

Other Cultivars:	Amnesia Haze, Kush Mints, Pipe Dream, Platinum Garlic, Sunset Sherbert
Associated Brands:	Canaca, Good Supply, Grail, Marley Natural, Riff, Solei

Cultivar Selection

Denman	92%
Gabriola	93%
Galiano	88%
Keats	89%
Moresby	80%
Quadra	93%
Ruxton	92%
Saturna	91%
Savary	91%
Sonora	94%
Stryker	90%

Denman

Cultivar/Product Information

Type/Effect: Sativa - Neutral
Legacy Name: Up in the Sky
Cannabinoids: 19.3% THC / <1% CBD
Terpenes: Myrcene, Caryophyllene, Limonene

First Impression

Review #199; February 24, 2020,

A warm, glowing, euphoric buzz envelopes my mind and soul as I struggle to stand up properly while consuming Broken Coast's Denman. My mind is clear but rendered pretty useless by the intensity of the cerebral high. My forehead feels like it will burst with pressure, the headband effect enough to make me squint at times. I'm coughing up a storm from the thick and terpy vapour, so much so that I began drooling a little. A hazy, heady experience, Denman stands among the best.

Observations

Aroma: Citrusy, fresh, fruity, herbal, orange, sweet

Flavour: Diesel, earthy, herbal, pungent, sweet

Bud Colour: Dark green/purple

Pistil Colour: Brown/orange

Trichome Density: High

Score Details

Appearance: 5 / 5
High Quality: 5 / 5
Aroma: 14 / 15
Flavour: 13 / 15
Bud Quality: 30 / 30
High Potency: 25 / 30

Overall Score: 92%

Cultivar Ranking: 37th

Gabriola

Cultivar/Product Information

Type/Effect: Indica - Neutral
Legacy Name: Frost Monster
Cannabinoids: 20.8% THC / <1% CBD
Terpenes: Caryophyllene, Limonene, Linalool

First Impression

Review #242; April 19, 2020,

Gabriola, from Broken Coast, is easily one of the best cultivars on the market, based on quality, potency and several other criteria; one of which is the abundance of trichomes on the nugs of Gabriola, that earned it the nickname "Frost Monster" from the folks who grew it. I feel like doing things and maybe getting some work done, though, with the heavy body sensation, perhaps not. This is excellent flower from Broken Coast, my favourite of their super impressive, high-quality bud.

Observations

Aroma: Fresh, herbal, minty, piney

Flavour: Fresh, herbal, minty, piney

Bud Colour: Green/tan

Pistil Colour: Orange/red

Trichome Density: High

Score Details

Appearance:	5 / 5
High Quality:	5 / 5
Aroma:	14 / 15
Flavour:	13 / 15
Bud Quality:	30 / 30
High Potency:	26 / 30

Overall Score: 93%

Cultivar Ranking: 27th

Galiano

Cultivar/Product Information

Type/Effect: Sativa - Light
Legacy Name: Northern Lights Haze
Lineage: Haze x Northern Lights
Cannabinoids: 17.3% THC / <1% CBD
Terpenes: Myrcene, Limonene, Caryophyllene

First Impression

Review #2; April 3, 2019,

Expect a hefty cerebral jolt from Broken Coast's Galiano. This sativa is uplifting, energizing, and elevating. This is an excellent cultivar for taking on a day and getting things done, or taking on an afternoon or evening and doing something exciting and fun. The head buzz is clear, focused, and blissful. Based on my elevated mood and creativity, this cultivar pairs well with some tunes and friends, making for a great occasion.

Observations

Aroma: Earthy, herbal, pungent, woody

Flavour: Herbal, woody

Bud Colour: Green/tan

Pistil Colour: Brown/orange

Trichome Density: Medium

Score Details

Appearance:	5 / 5
High Quality:	5 / 5
Aroma:	13 / 15
Flavour:	12 / 15
Bud Quality:	30 / 30
High Potency:	23 / 30

Overall Score: 88%

Cultivar Ranking: 85th

Keats

Cultivar/Product Information

Type/Effect: Indica Hybrid - Medium Heavy
Legacy Name: White-Walker Kush
Lineage: Skywalker x White Widow
Cannabinoids: 17.8% THC / <1% CBD
Terpenes: Caryophyllene, Myrcene, Ocimene

First Impression

Review #1; April 2, 2019,

Not a bad buzz for 3pm on a Tuesday; Keats from Broken Coast was good procrastination material for me. Nothing particularly stands out about the effects of the high, but it certainly delivers a kick that feels more substantial than 17.8% THC. I enjoy its simplicity; the high is average effect-wise but done to perfection. Enjoy this gem any time of day, and expect a strong cerebral kick and a light body sensation. Very impressive.

Observations

Aroma: Fresh, fruity, pungent, sweet, woody

Flavour: Cheese, earthy, fruity, funky, pungent, sweet

Bud Colour: Dark green

Pistil Colour: Brown/orange

Trichome Density: Medium-High

Score Details

Appearance:	5 / 5
High Quality:	5 / 5
Aroma:	13 / 15
Flavour:	12 / 15
Bud Quality:	30 / 30
High Potency:	24 / 30

Overall Score: 89%

Cultivar Ranking: 75th

Moresby

Cultivar/Product Information

Type/Effect: Sativa - Light
Legacy Name: Healing Fields
Lineage: Sannie's Jack x The One
Cannabinoids: 12.4% THC / <1% CBD
Terpenes: Caryophyllene, Ocimene, Pinene

First Impression

Review #200; February 27, 2020,

The light high provided by Broken Coast's Moresby elevated my mood and overall alertness during my morning review session. While a lower than usual potency for a Broken Coast cultivar, it is still of exceptional quality; this flower should yield the ideal experience for a functional but still fun morning or afternoon. At this THC percentage, this cultivar is an excellent way for lower-tolerance consumers to enjoy the quality of Broken Coast without the usual high-intensity experience.

Observations

Aroma: Chocolate, earthy, herbal, spicy, sweet

Flavour: Chocolate, citrusy, earthy, funky, herbal, sour

Bud Colour: Dark brown/green

Pistil Colour: Brown

Trichome Density: Medium

Score Details

Appearance:	5 / 5
High Quality:	5 / 5
Aroma:	13 / 15
Flavour:	12 / 15
Bud Quality:	29 / 30
High Potency:	16 / 30

Overall Score: 80%

Cultivar Ranking: 196th

Quadra

Cultivar/Product Information

Type/Effect: Indica - Heavy
Legacy Name: Headstash
Lineage: Biker Kush x (Cherry Pie x Girl Scout Cookies x KarmaRado OG)
Cannabinoids: 17.9% THC / <1% CBD
Terpenes: Myrcene, Limonene, Caryophyllene

First Impression

Review #15; April 12, 2019,

Quadra, from Broken Coast, is a near-perfect indica that hits hard and feels heavy. I'm watching game shows and zoning out hard while enjoying this bud before bed; I'm stoned and unable to keep up with what is happening on screen. I'm certainly ready to end my night, but I feel great enough that I want it to continue. Quadra looks, smells, and tastes as great as the high it produces. Minty and herbal, and a gorgeous appearance - a deep purple and green bud. Excellent stuff, as usual, from the expert cultivators at Broken Coast.

Observations

Aroma: Earthy, herbal, minty, piney, pungent

Flavour: Earthy, herbal, minty, piney, pungent

Bud Colour: Dark green/purple

Pistil Colour: Brown/red

Trichome Density: High

Score Details

Appearance:	5 / 5
High Quality:	5 / 5
Aroma:	14 / 15
Flavour:	14 / 15
Bud Quality:	30 / 30
High Potency:	25 / 30

Overall Score: 93%

Cultivar Ranking: 26th

Ruxton

Cultivar/Product Information

Type/Effect: Sativa Hybrid - Medium Heavy
Legacy Name: Sour OG
Lineage: OG Kush x Sour Diesel
Cannabinoids: 19.2% THC / <1% CBD
Terpenes: Myrcene, Caryophyllene, Limonene

First Impression

Review #43; April 26, 2019,

Ruxton, from Broken Coast, is an excellent bud that provides a strong head high and a light body sensation, mainly in the chest. The headband effect is here in full force too. Despite how stoned I am, I feel focused and alert while motivated to take on my day. This is a rather intense cultivar - so much so that it famously made my personal trainer friend afraid of the dark. As usual with Broken Coast bud, my eighth was almost one whole nug and was exceptional in quality. A solid addition to the lineup.

Observations

Aroma: Diesel, earthy, herbal, piney, sour

Flavour: Diesel, earthy, herbal, piney, sour

Bud Colour: Green/purple/tan

Pistil Colour: Orange

Trichome Density: High

Score Details

Appearance:	5 / 5
High Quality:	5 / 5
Aroma:	14 / 15
Flavour:	13 / 15
Bud Quality:	30 / 30
High Potency:	25 / 30

Overall Score: 92%

Cultivar Ranking: 36th

Saturna

Cultivar/Product Information

Type/Effect: Indica Hybrid - Heavy
Legacy Name: Muskmelon OG
Cannabinoids: 18.9% THC / <1% CBD
Terpenes: Myrcene, Limonene, Caryophyllene

First Impression

Review #239; April 15, 2020,

Heavy-eyed for a hybrid, Broken Coast's Saturna offers a hazy, intense headband effect and cerebral stimulation while overall being quite chill and relaxing. Most of this cultivar's physical effects are a pulsing sensation in the head; though my body feels loose, I feel like I'm floating on a cloud. My mood, demeanour, and energy are all dampened by the high. I feel like a sloth. A heavy-hitter for sure, stoners should be satisfied and connoisseurs impressed with the unique flavour and potent high.

Observations

Aroma: Earthy, fruity, piney, pungent, sour, sweet

Flavour: Earthy, fruity, melon, sweet

Bud Colour: Green

Pistil Colour: Orange

Trichome Density: High

Score Details

Appearance:	5 / 5
High Quality:	5 / 5
Aroma:	13 / 15
Flavour:	13 / 15
Bud Quality:	30 / 30
High Potency:	25 / 30

Overall Score: 91%

Cultivar Ranking: 50th

Savary

Cultivar/Product Information

Type/Effect: Indica - Heavy
Legacy Name: Pink Kush
Lineage: OG Kush
Cannabinoids: 16.4% THC / <1% CBD
Terpenes: Myrcene, Caryophyllene, Limonene

First Impression

Review #150; December 2, 2019,

Oh boy, was I ever excited when I found out that Broken Coast's Savary was hitting the recreational market, and damn, was it worth the anticipation. I'm stoned out of my mind; the terpene content of this bud must be significant, as the modest 16.4% THC feels like a solid 20+% with the effect potency factored in. My mind is racing, and my head is throbbing (in a good way); my body is relaxed and overcome with a sense of comfort. I could easily see myself A: melting into the couch, B: munching on snacks, or C: falling asleep during both. Amazing.

Observations

Aroma: Diesel, earthy, piney, pungent

Flavour: Diesel, earthy, pungent

Bud Colour: Dark green/purple

Pistil Colour: Brown/red

Trichome Density: High

Score Details

Appearance:	5 / 5
High Quality:	5 / 5
Aroma:	14 / 15
Flavour:	14 / 15
Bud Quality:	30 / 30
High Potency:	23 / 30

Overall Score: 91%

Cultivar Ranking: 47th

Sonora

Cultivar/Product Information

Type/Effect: Indica - Super Heavy
Legacy Name: Stargazer
Lineage: "Unknown Indica" x Starkiller
Cannabinoids: 24.9% THC / <1% CBD
Terpenes: Caryophyllene, Limonene, Myrcene

First Impression

Review #203; February 29, 2020,

My head is throbbing, mind racing, heart pounding, and I'm stoned off my rocker on Sonora by Broken Coast. The most potent Broken Coast flower I've had at nearly 25% THC, I feel it has melted my mind and body, leaving my soul to wander about, lost in the cerebral fog. I feel nearly overwhelmed, a sensation I haven't felt in a while, but I'll have to ride it out (PS., I made it!). Excellent on all fronts; I'd recommend this flower to anyone looking to get paralyzed by their high.

Observations

Aroma: Earthy, fresh, piney, pungent

Flavour: Berry, diesel, earthy, piney, pungent, sweet

Bud Colour: Dull green/purple

Pistil Colour: Brown/red

Trichome Density: High

Score Details

Appearance:	4 / 5
High Quality:	5 / 5
Aroma:	13 / 15
Flavour:	13 / 15
Bud Quality:	30 / 30
High Potency:	29 / 30

Overall Score: 94%

Cultivar Ranking: 20th

Stryker

Cultivar/Product Information

Type/Effect: Indica - Heavy
Legacy Name: Starkiller
Lineage: Rare Dankness #2 x Skywalker OG
Cannabinoids: 16.1% THC / <1% CBD
Terpenes: Myrcene, Caryophyllene, Limonene

First Impression

Review #163; December 18, 2019,

"I feel like a, like a slice of butter… melting on top of a big-ol' pile of flapjacks" doesn't even begin to describe the physical sensation of Stryker by Broken Coast (credit to the film Pineapple Express for the quote). A chill and relaxing to the body but stimulating to the mind indica, Stryker is powerful; the 16% THC is deceiving. It should impress the heaviest of consumers by smell alone and blow away casual consumers with the potency of its effects; Stryker is superb.

Observations

Aroma: Berry, blueberry, earthy, fresh, fruity, piney, sweet

Flavour: Berry, citrusy, earthy, funky, herbal, pungent

Bud Colour: Light green

Pistil Colour: Brown/red

Trichome Density: Medium-High

Score Details

Appearance:	5 / 5
High Quality:	5 / 5
Aroma:	15 / 15
Flavour:	13 / 15
Bud Quality:	30 / 30
High Potency:	22 / 30

Overall Score: 90%

Cultivar Ranking: 54th

Caliber

Overall Performance

Average Score: 75.33%

Brand Ranking: 55th Place

Brand Background

Caliber, a small-batch producer, believes it is all in the details regarding cannabis production. Processes are never rushed but are dictated by when the plant is ready - part of Caliber's promise to "maximize the potential of every cultivar."

Caliber grows cannabis indoors in cultivar-specific grow rooms, allowing them a great deal of environmental control over their plants. Buds are hand-trimmed before entering a slow-cure process and then trimmed once more after curing and before packaging.

Cultivar Selection

Berry White	73%
Koffee	80%
Lemon Z	73%

Berry White

Cultivar/Product Information

Type/Effect: Indica Hybrid - Light
Legacy Name: White Berry
Lineage: Blueberry x White Widow
Cannabinoids: 12.2% THC / <1% CBD
Terpenes: Myrcene, Limonene, Guaiol

First Impression

Review #169; December 31, 2019,

I was singing and dancing around to Devin Townsend songs all morning in my room; the great Berry White (no relation) from Caliber brought up the upbeat, creative, and inspired mood. Though medium on potency and mild on intensity, this bud creates a good chest and head rush coupled with a very functional high that is mood-elevating and relaxing - a great start to this New Year's Eve Day.

Observations

Aroma: Berry, herbal, sour, sweet

Flavour: Herbal, sour, spicy, sweet

Bud Colour: Dark green/purple

Pistil Colour: Orange

Trichome Density: High

Score Details

Appearance:	5 / 5
High Quality:	5 / 5
Aroma:	12 / 15
Flavour:	12 / 15
Bud Quality:	24 / 30
High Potency:	15 / 30

Overall Score: 73%

Cultivar Ranking: 311th

Koffee

Cultivar/Product Information

Type/Effect: Hybrid - Medium Heavy
Legacy Name: Kaya's Koffee
Lineage: Alien Kush x Alien OG
Cannabinoids: 20.6% THC / <1% CBD
Terpenes: Myrcene, Limonene, Caryophyllene

First Impression

Review #419; February 14, 2021,

Koffee by Caliber was a euphoric, hazy, and primarily lazy experience (and a great pick for my Valentine's Day review, thanks for the suggestion Kelsie, my love). My mind is experiencing less distraction than I anticipated, surprising, given the immense headband effect and physical relaxation. I do find myself nodding along to my Dead Kennedys playlist rather than singing, indicating that I'm feeling rather chill. A great addition to your day, or evening, that will make you feel mellow and baked.

Observations

Aroma: Coffee, diesel, earthy, fresh, pungent, woody

Flavour: Diesel, earthy, pungent, woody

Bud Colour: Green/tan

Pistil Colour: Brown/orange

Trichome Density: Medium-High

Score Details

Appearance:	3 / 5
High Quality:	5 / 5
Aroma:	12 / 15
Flavour:	12 / 15
Bud Quality:	25 / 30
High Potency:	23 / 30

Overall Score: 80%

Cultivar Ranking: 208th

Lemon Z

Cultivar/Product Information

Type/Effect: Sativa Hybrid - Light
Legacy Name: Lemon Z
Lineage: Lemon Skunk x Zkittlez
Cannabinoids: 12.1% THC / <1% CBD
Terpenes: Pinene, Terpineol, Guaiol

First Impression

Review #189; February 10, 2020,

I got a light, heady buzz that is clear and focused from Lemon Z by Caliber. The kind of high to brighten your day, heighten your creativity, and elevate your mood to make the most of any morning. The quality of the flower was great, and the appearance was gorgeous - a worthwhile experience, no doubt.

Observations

Aroma: Citrusy, herbal, sour, sweet, woody

Flavour: Herbal, sour, woody

Bud Colour: Dark green/purple

Pistil Colour: Brown/orange

Trichome Density: Medium-High

Score Details

Appearance:	4 / 5
High Quality:	5 / 5
Aroma:	13 / 15
Flavour:	12 / 15
Bud Quality:	24 / 30
High Potency:	15 / 30

Overall Score: 73%

Cultivar Ranking: 307th

Canaca

Overall Performance

Average Score: 74.06%

Brand Ranking: 60th Place

Brand Background

Canaca is a cannabis brand with facilities in BC and Ontario focusing on large-scale production. The brand is meant to be a tribute to Canadian culture and cannabis.

At Canaca, a "Love of the Leaf" is essential. Genetics-wise, Canaca aims to seek out the most fragrant varieties of the cultivars they bring to market.

Other Cultivars: Purps
Associated Brands: Broken Coast, Good Supply, Grail, Marley Natural, Riff, Solei

Cultivar Selection

Cultivar	Score	Cultivar	Score
Alien Dawg	61%	Jean Guy	81%
Citrus Tangerine	71%	Mango	65%
Ghost Train Haze	63%	OG Kush	61%
Glue	75%	Oregon Golden Goat	84%
Glueberry	76%	Sensi Star	78%
Great North CBD	79%	Shishkaberry	70%
Green Cush	80%	White Widow	75%
GSC	80%	White Widow Haze	86%
Hash Plant	74%		

Alien Dawg

Cultivar/Product Information

Type/Effect: Indica - Medium Heavy
Legacy Name: Alien Dawg
Lineage: Alien Technology x Chemdog
Cannabinoids: 17.4% THC / <1% CBD
Terpenes: Humulene, Limonene, Caryophyllene

First Impression

Review #46; April 28, 2019,

Canaca's Alien Dawg is a good, mid-high THC indica suitable for late-day or evening use. The effects weren't exceptionally energizing or draining, but I felt relaxed, pleasant and, well, high! To the senses, herbal and grassy, but there was also something different about the taste, something "Alien," if you will. Decent enough flower from Canaca; I would recommend this bud to those looking for a mid-strength indica.

Observations

Aroma: Cheese, diesel, earthy, funky, herbal, pungent, sour

Flavour: Funky, grassy, herbal

Bud Colour: Dark green

Pistil Colour: Brown/red

Trichome Density: Medium-High

Score Details

Appearance:	2 / 5
High Quality:	5 / 5
Aroma:	9 / 15
Flavour:	7 / 15
Bud Quality:	18 / 30
High Potency:	20 / 30

Overall Score: 61%

Cultivar Ranking: 408th

Citrus Tangerine

Cultivar/Product Information

Type/Effect: Sativa - Light
Legacy Name: Tangerine Dream
Lineage: Afghani Indica x G13 x Nevil's A5 Haze
Cannabinoids: 16.7% THC / <1% CBD

First Impression

Review #264; May 20, 2020,

Effect-wise, Canaca's Citrus Tangerine is both calming and focusing. My ability to think is unimpeded, and my motor skills seem typical; relatively speaking, I'm unimpaired. But, a subtle buzz is growing in my mind as I delve deeper into my bowl. Hardly as vibrant or flavorful as some other takes on the same genetics but still hits the same notes. Decent quality here from Canaca - the flower is bright, fruity and uplifting, a good way to start the day.

Observations

Aroma: Citrusy, floral, fruity, herbal, orange, woody

Flavour: Citrusy, floral, fruity, grassy, herbal, sweet

Bud Colour: Dark green

Pistil Colour: Brown/orange

Trichome Density: Medium

Score Details

Appearance:	3 / 5
High Quality:	5 / 5
Aroma:	12 / 15
Flavour:	13 / 15
Bud Quality:	22 / 30
High Potency:	16 / 30

Overall Score: 71%

Cultivar Ranking: 331st

Ghost Train Haze

Cultivar/Product Information

Type/Effect: Sativa - Medium Light
Legacy Name: Ghost Train Haze
Lineage: Ghost OG x Nevil's Wreck
Cannabinoids: 17.3% THC / <1% CBD

First Impression

Review #97; August 29, 2019,

Canaca's Ghost Train Haze is an energetic sativa high, motivating and focusing while mood-elevating. My mind is clear, and I'm eager to get stuff done, but my thoughts and mind are relaxed, calmed by the effects of this flower. I'm stoned but alert - a good sativa option for any tolerance.

Observations

Aroma: Citrusy, earthy, herbal, sour

Flavour: Earthy, pungent, spicy, woody

Bud Colour: Dull green

Pistil Colour: Brown/orange

Trichome Density: Low-Medium

Score Details

Appearance:	2 / 5
High Quality:	5 / 5
Aroma:	12 / 15
Flavour:	9 / 15
Bud Quality:	14 / 30
High Potency:	21 / 30

Overall Score: 63%

Cultivar Ranking: 396th

Glue

Cultivar/Product Information

Type/Effect: Hybrid - Medium Light
Legacy Name: Original Glue
Lineage: Chem's Sister x Chocolate Diesel x Sour Dubb
Cannabinoids: 17% THC / <1% CBD
Terpenes: Bisabolol, Limonene, Caryophyllene

First Impression

Review #258; May 13, 2020,

Canaca's Glue is a mellow head buzz with a full-body relaxing sensation. I found it certainly stronger than anticipated. The flower left me with a clear head and a heightened mood, but I drifted out into space repeatedly: constantly daydreaming while juggling writing and a phone call. Glue was a great time.

Observations

Aroma: Cheese, fresh, grassy, herbal, sour, sweet

Flavour: Fresh, grassy, herbal, sour

Bud Colour: Dark green

Pistil Colour: Brown/red

Trichome Density: Low-Medium

Score Details

Appearance:	3 / 5
High Quality:	5 / 5
Aroma:	12 / 15
Flavour:	11 / 15
Bud Quality:	23 / 30
High Potency:	21 / 30

Overall Score: 75%

Cultivar Ranking: 290th

Glueberry

Cultivar/Product Information

Type/Effect:	Hybrid - Medium Heavy
Legacy Name:	Glueberry
Lineage:	Blueberry x Original Glue
Cannabinoids:	17.6% THC / <1% CBD

First Impression

Review #216; March 15, 2020,

My mind is alive, but my mood is mellow on Glueberry by Canaca. I can think clearly and quickly, but my body, mood, and spirit are all relaxed; this is the perfect couch flower. I don't feel chatty, but I wish I had company; this would be an appropriate flower for "bedtime" too. Chill bud, for anytime you want to enjoy yourself just a little more.

Observations

Aroma: Berry, earthy, fruity, grass, herbal, sour, sweet

Flavour: Berry, earthy, funky, pungent, sweet

Bud Colour: Green

Pistil Colour: Orange

Trichome Density: Medium

Score Details

Appearance:	4 / 5
High Quality:	5 / 5
Aroma:	12 / 15
Flavour:	11 / 15
Bud Quality:	24 / 30
High Potency:	20 / 30

Overall Score: 76%

Cultivar Ranking: 277th

Great North CBD

Cultivar/Product Information

Type/Effect: Hybrid - Super Light
Cannabinoids: <1% THC / 16.5% CBD

First Impression

Review #123; September 26, 2019,

Great North CBD by Canaca is the affordable, high-CBD flower I've been waiting to see. I feel at peace; my mind is like a cool winter's day, but no wind, no extreme chill, just crisp and calm. My thoughts are clear and come quickly; no racing, no difficulty thinking. The headband pressure effect is light, but the effects of the CBD on my mood, body and mind are all strong, given the 16.5% CBD potency. A great way to start a day, or anything really, because you'll be unimpaired and unwound. Lovely flower indeed.

Observations

Aroma: Cheesy, funky, herbal, sour, sweet

Flavour: Earthy, herbal, spicy, woody

Bud Colour: Dark green

Pistil Colour: Brown/orange

Trichome Density: Medium

Score Details

Appearance:	4 / 5
High Quality:	5 / 5
Aroma:	12 / 15
Flavour:	11 / 15
Bud Quality:	25 / 30
High Potency:	22 / 30

Overall Score: 79%

Cultivar Ranking: 237th

Green Cush

Cultivar/Product Information

Type/Effect: Sativa - Light
Legacy Name: Green Crack
Lineage: Afghani Indica x Skunk #1
Cannabinoids: 18.4% THC / <1% CBD
Terpenes: Pinene, Myrcene, Caryophyllene

First Impression

Review #75; June 29, 2019,

I feel awake, alive and motivated, "pumped up" in energy, spirit, creativity, the whole lot, all due to this Green Cush from Canaca. The high is bright and cerebral, very heady. This bud is challenging to grind in the best way possible; super sticky stuff. Great stuff to consume before the doing gets done for the day.

Observations

Aroma: Earthy, fresh, herbal, piney, sour

Flavour: Fresh, herbal, sour

Bud Colour: Dull green

Pistil Colour: Brown-red

Trichome Density: Low

Score Details

Appearance:	4 / 5
High Quality:	5 / 5
Aroma:	12 / 15
Flavour:	11 / 15
Bud Quality:	25 / 30
High Potency:	23 / 30

Overall Score: 80%

Cultivar Ranking: 211th

GSC

Cultivar/Product Information

Type/Effect: Hybrid - Neutral
Legacy Name: Girl Scout Cookies
Lineage: Durban Poison x OG Kush
Cannabinoids: 23.4% THC / <1% CBD
Terpenes: Humulene, Myrcene, Caryophyllene

First Impression

Review #339; September 28, 2020,

Canaca's GSC had me all over the place… I was moving frantically, trying to do a few things simultaneously, accomplishing nothing while stoned off my ass. I got super distracted for twenty minutes by my phone and singing along to Opeth. This was a pretty heady and active-minded GSC variety. My body was relaxed, but I felt rejuvenated, full of energy, and easily distracted. GSC is a great way to spend the post-work hours on whatever you enjoy most, assuming you can focus on it.

Observations

Aroma: Grassy, herbal, sour, spicy, sweet, woody

Flavour: Earthy, fresh, grassy, herbal, sour

Bud Colour: Brown/green

Pistil Colour: Orange/tan

Trichome Density: Low-Medium

Score Details

Appearance:	4 / 5
High Quality:	5 / 5
Aroma:	11 / 15
Flavour:	11 / 15
Bud Quality:	25 / 30
High Potency:	24 / 30

Overall Score: 80%

Cultivar Ranking: 223rd

Hash Plant

Cultivar/Product Information

Type/Effect: Indica - Medium Heavy
Legacy Name: Hash Plant
Lineage: Afghani Indica x Northern Lights
Cannabinoids: 16.4% THC / <1% CBD

First Impression

Review #130; October 12, 2019,

Canaca Hash Plant provides a strong cerebral "stoned" high, coupled with a powerful pulsing sensation in the head and throughout the body. I don't feel tired notably, but I'm relaxed and would be couch-locked if not for the fact that I should be writing. I got mega-distracted by cartoons mid-review on this one; I blame this high, but I'm not bothered either.

Observations

Aroma: Herbal, sour

Flavour: Herbal, sour

Bud Colour: Green

Pistil Colour: Brown/orange

Trichome Density: Low-Medium

Score Details

Appearance:	4 / 5
High Quality:	5 / 5
Aroma:	12 / 15
Flavour:	11 / 15
Bud Quality:	21 / 30
High Potency:	21 / 30

Overall Score: 74%

Cultivar Ranking: 299th

Jean Guy

Cultivar/Product Information

Type/Effect:	Sativa Hybrid - Neutral
Legacy Name:	Jean Guy
Lineage:	White Widow
Cannabinoids:	18.1% THC / <1% CBD
Terpenes:	Terpinolene, Caryophyllene, Guaiol

First Impression

Review #77; June 30, 2019,

I'm stoned, having a grand old time jamming to some metal tunes; it's very early in the morning for me, but with Jean Guy, it's bearable and better yet, enjoyable. The high is heavy and heady; expect a pressure sensation in the head for physical effects. A cultivar to ease you into the day, not one to make you dive in head first, but gradually, slowly, in a soft sativa haze.

Observations

Aroma: Citrusy, herbal, piney, sour

Flavour: Citrusy, herbal, piney

Bud Colour: Green

Pistil Colour: Brown/orange

Trichome Density: Low-Medium

Score Details

Appearance:	4 / 5
High Quality:	5 / 5
Aroma:	13 / 15
Flavour:	12 / 15
Bud Quality:	25 / 30
High Potency:	22 / 30

Overall Score: 81%

Cultivar Ranking: 179th

Mango

Cultivar/Product Information

Type/Effect: Indica Hybrid - Medium Heavy
Legacy Name: Mango
Lineage: Afghani Indica x KC33
Cannabinoids: 18.5% THC / <1% CBD
Terpenes: Myrcene, Limonene, Humulene

First Impression

Review #48; May 4, 2019,

For a moderate head high and strong body high, look for Canaca's Mango. I don't feel overly tired despite fatigue from work and hunger. Still, I don't feel like doing much, maybe some TV; classic symptoms from consuming a medium-strength indica - an overall fine experience.

Observations

Aroma: Fruity, herbal, mango, sweet

Flavour: Earthy, funky, herbal, woody

Bud Colour: Dark green

Pistil Colour: Orange/red

Trichome Density: Low

Score Details

Appearance:	3 / 5
High Quality:	4 / 5
Aroma:	10 / 15
Flavour:	9 / 15
Bud Quality:	19 / 30
High Potency:	20 / 30

Overall Score: 65%

Cultivar Ranking: 393rd

OG Kush

Cultivar/Product Information

Type/Effect: Hybrid - Medium Heavy
Legacy Name: OG Kush
Lineage: "Northern Californian" x Hindu Kush
Cannabinoids: 12.4% THC / <1% CBD

First Impression

Review #104; September 3, 2019,

OG Kush by Canaca delivers a solid high, present in the head and chest as a powerful physical sensation and the mind as a cerebral stoned feeling. It was more intense than anticipated, given its medium-low THC %. Not too shabby.

Observations

Aroma: Fruity, herbal, spicy, sweet

Flavour: Earthy, funky, herbal, spicy, woody

Bud Colour: Dark green

Pistil Colour: Brown

Trichome Density: Low

Score Details

Appearance:	3 / 5
High Quality:	4 / 5
Aroma:	11 / 15
Flavour:	8 / 15
Bud Quality:	18 / 30
High Potency:	17 / 30

Overall Score: 61%

Cultivar Ranking: 403rd

Oregon Golden Goat

Cultivar/Product Information

Type/Effect: Sativa Hybrid - Light
Legacy Name: Oregon Golden Goat
Lineage: Florida OG x Lemon Haze x Zelly's Gift
Cannabinoids: 21.8% THC / <1% CBD
Terpenes: Humulene, Caryophyllene, Terpinolene

First Impression

Review #334; September 23, 2020,

A clean and clear cerebral high with light and social effects and a robust physical head buzz, Oregon Golden Goat by Canaca is a great time. I wish I had company, as I feel uniquely uplifted, euphoric, talkative, and enthused. I keep getting distracted by texting on my phone and petting my dog (she’s so damn cute!). My mind is focused, just not on things it should be. A great AM or afternoon high that should please most consumers.

Observations

Aroma: Citrusy, herbal, lemon, sour, spicy, woody

Flavour: Citrusy, herbal, lemon, sour, spicy, woody

Bud Colour: Dull green

Pistil Colour: Orange

Trichome Density: Low-Medium

Score Details

Appearance:	4 / 5
High Quality:	5 / 5
Aroma:	13 / 15
Flavour:	12 / 15
Bud Quality:	25 / 30
High Potency:	25 / 30

Overall Score: 84%

Cultivar Ranking: 123rd

Sensi Star

Cultivar/Product Information

Type/Effect: Indica - Medium Light
Legacy Name: Sensi Star
Lineage: "Unknown Afghani"
Cannabinoids: 14.2% THC / <1% CBD

First Impression

Review #34; April 22, 2019,

On Canaca's Sensi Star, I partook of many chicken wings and experimental metal; everything involved was fantastic. The high was less heavy than anticipated. I was somewhat energetic, feeling uniquely creative and focused but hungry. The buzz was medium-light for me but plenty enjoyable.

Observations

Aroma: Fruity, herbal, sweet

Flavour: Herbal, piney, spicy, sweet

Bud Colour: Green/yellow

Pistil Colour: Brown/red

Trichome Density: Low-Medium

Score Details

Appearance:	4 / 5
High Quality:	5 / 5
Aroma:	12 / 15
Flavour:	12 / 15
Bud Quality:	25 / 30
High Potency:	20 / 30

Overall Score: 78%

Cultivar Ranking: 252nd

Shishkaberry

Cultivar/Product Information

Type/Effect: Indica Hybrid - Neutral
Legacy Name: Shishkaberry
Lineage: "Unknown Afghani" x DJ Short Blueberry
Cannabinoids: 15% THC / <1% CBD

First Impression

Review #29; April 19, 2019,

Canaca's Shishkaberry is a surprisingly heady experience for an indica. It has a significant headband effect and distracting cerebral buzz. My thoughts aren't focused at all, but I'm not complaining. An enjoyable high from Canaca was found in Shishkaberry.

Observations

Aroma: Floral, fruity, herbal, sour, sweet

Flavour: Herbal, spicy

Bud Colour: Brown/green

Pistil Colour: Brown/red

Trichome Density: Low

Score Details

Appearance:	3 / 5
High Quality:	4 / 5
Aroma:	12 / 15
Flavour:	10 / 15
Bud Quality:	22 / 30
High Potency:	19 / 30

Overall Score: 70%

Cultivar Ranking: 347th

White Widow

Cultivar/Product Information

Type/Effect: Hybrid - Medium Light
Legacy Name: White Widow
Lineage: Brazilian Sativa x Indian Indica
Cannabinoids: 15.7% THC / <1% CBD
Terpenes: Limonene, Caryophyllene, Myrcene

First Impression

Review #71; June 10, 2019,

Canaca's White Widow is an enjoyable medium-light potency option. The effects of this flower are mild, calming, and focusing, leaving the mind clear and the body relaxed. I could see myself using this cultivar before getting some serious work done, but I am a chronic consumer - a good take on a classic from Canaca.

Observations

Aroma: Fruity, herbal, sour, sweet

Flavour: Herbal, sour, sweet

Bud Colour: Green/tan

Pistil Colour: Orange

Trichome Density: Low-Medium

Score Details

Appearance:	4 / 5
High Quality:	5 / 5
Aroma:	12 / 15
Flavour:	11 / 15
Bud Quality:	24 / 30
High Potency:	19 / 30

Overall Score: 75%

Cultivar Ranking: 287th

White Widow Haze

Cultivar/Product Information

Type/Effect: Sativa Hybrid - Medium Light
Legacy Name: White Widow Haze
Lineage: Super Silver Haze x White Widow
Cannabinoids: 20.9% THC / <1% CBD

First Impression

Review #93; August 19, 2019,

I'm wired on the most wonderful sativa I've had this month, White Widow Haze by Canaca. I'm mentally alert and focused, motivated and energetic. The creative juices are flowing, and my mood is elevated AND… I'm stoned out of my mind: exceptionally high intensity for a 21% THC flower. Not a great choice for beginners or those sensitive to high THC sativas, but for the seasoned consumer or connoisseur, this should deliver an impressive experience.

Observations

Aroma: Citrusy, herbal, sour

Flavour: Citrusy, herbal, sour, woody

Bud Colour: Green

Pistil Colour: Brown

Trichome Density: Medium

Score Details

Appearance:	4 / 5
High Quality:	5 / 5
Aroma:	14 / 15
Flavour:	12 / 15
Bud Quality:	26 / 30
High Potency:	25 / 30

Overall Score: 86%

Cultivar Ranking: 99th

Canna Farms

Overall Performance

Average Score: 77.63%

Brand Ranking: 44th Place

Brand Background

The first BC cannabis producer to receive licensing, Canna Farms, has roots in the Canadian medical cannabis market and has brought a handful of products to the recreational market. Canna Farms is "dedicated to delivering world-class experiences" through their cannabis. Located in Hope, BC, Canna Farms operates a 15,000 square-foot facility for cannabis production, featuring 31 grow rooms.

Canna Farms grows cannabis in small batches, focusing on craft production practices. They take great pride in their cannabis at Canna Farms and look to do so for the foreseeable future.

Associated Brands: Fireside

Cultivar Selection

Blue Dream	84%
Bubba Kush	81%
CBD Critical Mass	70%
Critical Super Silver Haze	75%
GSC	78%
Hash Plant	69%
Pink Kush	83%
Tangerine Dream	81%

Blue Dream

Cultivar/Product Information

Type/Effect:	Sativa - Neutral
Legacy Name:	DJ's Azure Haze
Lineage:	DJ Short Blueberry x Super Silver Haze
Cannabinoids:	20% THC / <1% CBD
Terpenes:	Myrcene, Pinene, Limonene

First Impression

Review #133; October 21, 2019,

Canna Farms' Blue Dream is potent, relaxing and mood-elevating; a sativa that is great for watching TV or enjoying anything with some friends. I feel giggly and social; Futurama and this flower keep me entertained. This is a cut above some other Blue Dream varieties on the market.

Observations

Aroma: Citrusy, fruity, herbal, sour, sweet

Flavour: Grassy, herbal, sweet

Bud Colour: Dull green

Pistil Colour: Orange

Trichome Density: Medium-High

Score Details

Appearance:	4 / 5
High Quality:	5 / 5
Aroma:	13 / 15
Flavour:	12 / 15
Bud Quality:	27 / 30
High Potency:	23 / 30

Overall Score: 84%

Cultivar Ranking: 125th

Bubba Kush

Cultivar/Product Information

Type/Effect: Indica - Medium Heavy
Legacy Name: Bubba Kush
Lineage: Northern Lights x Triangle Kush
Cannabinoids: 20.3% THC / <1% CBD
Terpenes: Myrcene, Caryophyllene, Limonene

First Impression

Review #143; November 24, 2019,

Bubba Kush by Canna Farms has me feeling relaxed, chill, stoned, and bubbly. I want to stay up all night, given how euphoric this bud is. However, sleep will come quickly with the heavy body sensation this flower provides. Canna Farms always delivers an impressive high, and Bubba Kush is no different.

Observations

Aroma: Earthy, fresh, pungent, sweet

Flavour: Earthy, funky, herbal, pungent

Bud Colour: Light green

Pistil Colour: Brown/orange

Trichome Density: Medium-High

Score Details

Appearance:	4 / 5
High Quality:	5 / 5
Aroma:	13 / 15
Flavour:	10 / 15
Bud Quality:	24 / 30
High Potency:	25 / 30

Overall Score: 81%

Cultivar Ranking: 174th

CBD Critical Mass

Cultivar/Product Information

Type/Effect: Indica - Medium Heavy
Legacy Name: CBD Critical Mass
Lineage: Cannatonic x Critical Mass
Cannabinoids: 5.7% THC / 10.1% CBD

First Impression

Review #171; January 3, 2020,

Canna Farms' CBD Critical Mass was a solid indica balanced experience. The THC high was mild, not too potent, but enough to take the edge off, and the CBD increased the relaxation and calm. I'm chill and content: Canna Farms always pleases me.

Observations

Aroma: Cheese, earthy, herbal, sweet

Flavour: Cheese, funky, herbal, sweet

Bud Colour: Brown/green

Pistil Colour: Brown

Trichome Density: Low

Score Details

Appearance:	4 / 5
High Quality:	5 / 5
Aroma:	12 / 15
Flavour:	12 / 15
Bud Quality:	19 / 30
High Potency:	18 / 30

Overall Score: 70%

Cultivar Ranking: 346th

Critical Super Silver Haze

Cultivar/Product Information

Type/Effect: Sativa - Light
Legacy Name: Critical Super Silver Haze
Lineage: Critical Mass x Super Silver Haze
Cannabinoids: 20.2% THC / <1% CBD
Terpenes: Caryophyllene, Myrcene, Limonene

First Impression

Review #78; July 6, 2019,

Critical Super Silver Haze by Canna Farms is an aromatic blast with a focused, calm, and ready-for-the-day feeling high. This is a sativa experience a tad milder than the THC% would suggest on overall intensity, so an excellent high-potency option for newer and experienced consumers alike. A perfect bud for morning consumption or before tasks/the gym/work/etc. The effects aren't overly impairing, and it shouldn't leave you too stoned - a good first batch for me from Canna Farms.

Observations

Aroma: Citrusy, fruity, herbal, sweet

Flavour: Fruity, herbal

Bud Colour: Green/purple

Pistil Colour: Brown/orange

Trichome Density: Medium

Score Details

Appearance:	4 / 5
High Quality:	4 / 5
Aroma:	13 / 15
Flavour:	11 / 15
Bud Quality:	23 / 30
High Potency:	20 / 30

Overall Score: 75%

Cultivar Ranking: 281st

GSC

Cultivar/Product Information

Type/Effect: Indica Hybrid - Medium Heavy
Legacy Name: Girl Scout Cookies
Lineage: Durban Poison x OG Kush
Cannabinoids: 21.1% THC / <1% CBD
Terpenes: Limonene, Linalool, Caryophyllene

First Impression

Review #85; August 9, 2019,

GSC by Canna Farms is a relaxing and calming high-potency indica hybrid that offers a powerful high and body sensation. I'm also stoned and have the munchies. I spontaneously ordered pizza on this bud at 11pm. A favourite cultivar of mine, GSC is one to look out for.

Observations

Aroma: Cheese, earthy, funky, herbal, piney, sour

Flavour: Cheese, earthy, funky, herbal, piney

Bud Colour: Dark green

Pistil Colour: Brown

Trichome Density: Low-Medium

Score Details

Appearance:	4 / 5
High Quality:	5 / 5
Aroma:	12 / 15
Flavour:	9 / 15
Bud Quality:	23 / 30
High Potency:	25 / 30

Overall Score: 78%

Cultivar Ranking: 251st

Hash Plant

Cultivar/Product Information

Type/Effect: Indica - Heavy
Legacy Name: Hash Plant
Lineage: Hash Plant x Northern Lights #1
Cannabinoids: 15.4% THC / <1% CBD

First Impression

Review #112; September 12, 2019,

The high from Canna Farms' Hash Plant is intense and cerebral; a very in-your-face stoned feeling should overwhelm your consciousness. There is less body high than anticipated, but the head high exceeded expectations. This showcases something typical of Canna Farms products I've tried: a strong terpene profile. Hash Plant is an excellent high for those looking for a head rush.

Observations

Aroma: Earthy, herbal, piney, sour, sweet

Flavour: Earthy, funky, herbal, sour

Bud Colour: Green/tan

Pistil Colour: Orange

Trichome Density: Medium

Score Details

Appearance:	4 / 5
High Quality:	5 / 5
Aroma:	11 / 15
Flavour:	9 / 15
Bud Quality:	20 / 30
High Potency:	20 / 30

Overall Score: 69%

Cultivar Ranking: 359th

Pink Kush

Cultivar/Product Information

Type/Effect: Indica - Heavy
Legacy Name: Pink Kush
Lineage: OG Kush
Cannabinoids: 18.8% THC / <1% CBD
Terpenes: Caryophyllene, Limonene, Myrcene

First Impression

Review #147; November 28, 2019,

Canna Farms' Pink Kush makes for a tremendous end-of-the-night session. A heavy and cerebrally potent indica, Pink Kush packs an intense head high and pounding sensation, with complete body relaxation. This bud is not for the faint of heart, nor is it for those who desire to stay awake and productive - a great rendition of this popular cultivar.

Observations

Aroma: Earthy, minty, piney, pungent, sweet

Flavour: Earthy, pungent, sweet

Bud Colour: Dark green/purple

Pistil Colour: Brown

Trichome Density: Medium-High

Score Details

Appearance:	4 / 5
High Quality:	5 / 5
Aroma:	13 / 15
Flavour:	12 / 15
Bud Quality:	25 / 30
High Potency:	24 / 30

Overall Score: 83%

Cultivar Ranking: 145th

Tangerine Dream

Cultivar/Product Information

Type/Effect: Sativa Hybrid - Neutral
Legacy Name: Tangerine Dream
Lineage: Afghani Indica x G13 x Nevil's A5 Haze
Cannabinoids: 21.1% THC / <1% CBD
Terpenes: Myrcene, Limonene, Linalool

First Impression

Review #161; December 17, 2019,

Canna Farms' Tangerine Dream is a productive, functional, strong sativa buzz with a mellow and relaxed body feel. Not necessarily a get-up-and-go, more like a get-up-and-flow sativa, great for getting things done. It is pretty potent, with a decent terpene profile, which comes through in the aroma and flavour. A much more high-intensity take on this year's sativa of the year.

Observations

Aroma: Cheese, citrusy, fruity, orange, sweet

Flavour: Cheese, fruity, herbal, orange, sweet

Bud Colour: Light green

Pistil Colour: Brown/red

Trichome Density: Medium

Score Details

Appearance:	4 / 5
High Quality:	5 / 5
Aroma:	13 / 15
Flavour:	12 / 15
Bud Quality:	24 / 30
High Potency:	23 / 30

Overall Score: 81%

Cultivar Ranking: 175th

Citizen Stash

Overall Performance

Average Score: 94.00%

Brand Ranking: 1st Place

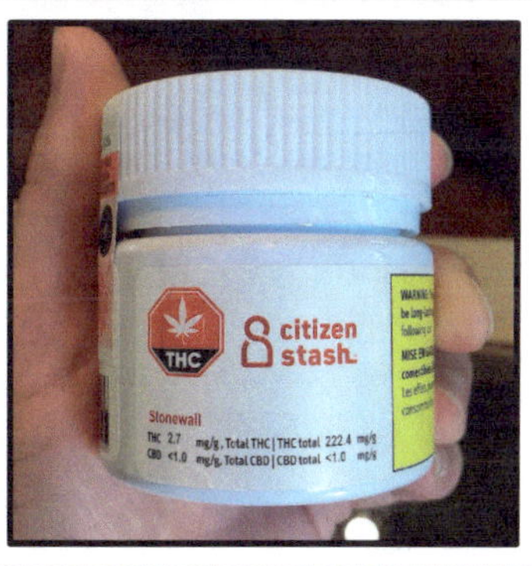

Brand Background

Out of Mission, BC, Citizen Stash is a small batch cannabis producer with the goal to become a world leader in craft production. The brand sees cannabis as a unifying force between people and urges consumers to "stand for something" and be active in their communities.

The craft approach to cannabis production of Citizen Stash involves small batch grows in indoor grow rooms. The brand also focuses on genetics that are unique in cultivar selection. To ensure quality, every part of their production process is performed by hand.

The Valens Company acquired Citizen Stash in November 2021.

Other Cultivars: Chocolate Sour Diesel, Cookie Puss, FPOG, Jungle Breath, Sundae Driver

Cultivar Selection

MAC1	97%
SAGE n' Sour	96%
Stonewall	93%
Sunset Sherbet	90%

MAC1

Cultivar/Product Information

Type/Effect: Hybrid - Super Heavy
Legacy Name: Miracle Alien Cookies 1
Lineage: Alien Cookies x (Columbian x Starfighter)
Cannabinoids: 25.6% THC / <1% CBD
Terpenes: Limonene, Caryophyllene, Linalool

First Impression

Review #177; January 11, 2020,

MAC1… oh boy, did the debut in AB from Citizen Stash hit hard. I was pretty cooked within the first three bags, then it just got real spacy and chilled out after that, with the intensity amping up each pull. Extremely frosty and immensely strong in aroma and effect, this flower rivals the best on the market. The quality is immaculate; in structure and appearance, this is perfect. It was stunning in every way, a strong start from Citizen Stash.

Observations

Aroma: Diesel, earthy, minty, piney, pungent, woody

Flavour: Diesel, earthy, funky, grassy, herbal, piney, pungent

Bud Colour: Dark green/purple

Pistil Colour: Brown/orange

Trichome Density: High

Score Details

Appearance:	5 / 5
High Quality:	5 / 5
Aroma:	15 / 15
Flavour:	12 / 15
Bud Quality:	30 / 30
High Potency:	30 / 30

Overall Score: 97%

Cultivar Ranking: 4th

SAGE n' Sour

Cultivar/Product Information

Type/Effect: Sativa - Medium Heavy
Legacy Name: SAGE 'n Sour
Lineage: SAGE x Sour Diesel
Cannabinoids: 26.4% THC / <1% CBD
Terpenes: Terpinolene, Limonene, Caryophyllene

First Impression

Review #274; June 16, 2020,

Citizen Stash's SAGE n' Sour amplifies my creativity and dulls my cognitive ability. As Jello Biafra belts out political ramblings in the background, I switch between creatively writing and blankly staring at the page before me. My concerns have faded away; the high washes over my soul in a most cleansing fashion. If you can't tell from the weird "soul-cleansing" stuff, I'm pretty stoned. I'm slow when I want to be, fast when I need to be: this is a "Goldilocks sativa"… SAGE n' Sour is just right. An outstanding cultivar, grow, and overall product, it meets the standard that Citizen Stash has set for itself.

Observations

Aroma: Citrusy, herbal, piney, sour, sweet, woody

Flavour: Citrusy, floral, herbal, sour, spicy, woody

Bud Colour: Light green

Pistil Colour: Brown/orange

Trichome Density: Medium-High

Score Details

Appearance:	5 / 5
High Quality:	5 / 5
Aroma:	14 / 15
Flavour:	12 / 15
Bud Quality:	30 / 30
High Potency:	30 / 30

Overall Score: 96%

Cultivar Ranking: 10th

Stonewall

Cultivar/Product Information

Type/Effect: Sativa Hybrid - Light
Legacy Name: Mimosa
Lineage: Clementine x Purple Punch
Cannabinoids: 22.7% THC / <1% CBD
Terpenes: Myrcene, Caryophyllene, Pinene

First Impression

Review #250; April 26, 2020,

On Stonewall by Citizen Stash, I've hardly hit a wall mentally speaking; my mind is alive, and it feels like it could fill the whole room. The high is cerebrally light and bright, and physically calming and chill. I could do anything, but I know I shouldn't, as I'm quite high. I better waste my ambition and apply my energy and creativity to some serious gaming (Minecraft, so not so 'serious,' I suppose). A tremendous high to spend active, no matter how you enjoy your activities or socializing (in non-quarantine times). A great achievement.

Observations

Aroma: Citrusy, earthy, floral, fruity, herbal, orange, sweet

Flavour: Citrusy, earthy, floral, fruity, orange, sweet

Bud Colour: Dark green/purple

Pistil Colour: Brown

Trichome Density: Medium-High

Score Details

Appearance:	5 / 5
High Quality:	5 / 5
Aroma:	15 / 15
Flavour:	15 / 15
Bud Quality:	28 / 30
High Potency:	25 / 30

Overall Score: 93%

Cultivar Ranking: 24th

Sunset Sherbet

Cultivar/Product Information

Type/Effect:	Indica Hybrid - Heavy
Legacy Name:	Sunset Sherbet
Lineage:	Girl Scout Cookies x Pink Panties
Cannabinoids:	23.6% THC / <1% CBD
Terpenes:	Limonene, Caryophyllene, Linalool

First Impression

Review #253; May 2, 2020,

Citizen Stash always seems to impress with their flower, and the case is no different with Sunset Sherbet. The effects are heavy and hazy, my eyes reflecting this. My whole body is loose and experiencing waves of sensations from the flower; it feels like I'm on a cloud. Euphoric and relaxing, my mind is also melting from the intensity of the high. I'm ready to become one with the couch.

Observations

Aroma: Cheese, earthy, floral, fresh, grassy, woody

Flavour: Earthy, floral, fresh, funky, sweet

Bud Colour: Green/purple

Pistil Colour: Orange

Trichome Density: Medium-High

Score Details

Appearance:	5 / 5
High Quality:	5 / 5
Aroma:	13 / 15
Flavour:	12 / 15
Bud Quality:	28 / 30
High Potency:	27 / 30

Overall Score: 90%

Cultivar Ranking: 68th

Color

Overall Performance

Average Score: 83.40%

Brand Ranking: 25th Place

Brand Background

Color is a cannabis brand that sees cannabis as "a unique and subjective experience for everyone", allowing individuals to "see the world differently." Cannabis is a means of connecting on a greater level with the world and those around us, and Color hopes for people to achieve this via their cultivars.

Color cannabis is grown both indoors and outdoors in Strathroy, Ontario. They have a few cultivars on their lineup, all with unique terpene profiles and effects. Most unique possibly is Pedro's Sweet Sativa, the cultivar best known across the market from Color.

Other Cultivars: Black Sugar Rose

Cultivar Selection

Cultivar	Score
Blueberry Seagal	80%
Ghost Train Haze	83%
Mango Haze	82%
Pedro's Sweet Sativa	87%
White Shark	85%

Blueberry Seagal

Cultivar/Product Information

Type/Effect: Indica Hybrid - Medium Light
Cannabinoids: 15.3% THC / <1% CBD
Terpenes: Caryophyllene, Nerolidol

First Impression

Review #128; October 11, 2019,

For a creative, medium-intensity, mood-elevating high, look for Blueberry Seagal by Color. I'm not stoned or out of my mind; pleasantly high, it is a manageable and functional indica flower. It won't couch-lock you either, but may induce a soothing body sensation. I'm alone at the moment, but I feel it would be a social flower. Super chill, typical great bud from Color.

Observations

Aroma: Berry, blueberry, earthy, piney, sweet

Flavour: Earthy, funky, sweet

Bud Colour: Green

Pistil Colour: Brown/orange

Trichome Density: Medium

Score Details

Appearance:	4 / 5
High Quality:	5 / 5
Aroma:	15 / 15
Flavour:	11 / 15
Bud Quality:	25 / 30
High Potency:	20 / 30

Overall Score: 80%

Cultivar Ranking: 192nd

Ghost Train Haze

Cultivar/Product Information

Type/Effect:	Sativa - Medium Light
Legacy Name:	Ghost Train Haze
Lineage:	Ghost OG x Nevil's Wreck
Cannabinoids:	20.4% THC / <1% CBD
Terpenes:	Caryophyllene, Terpinolene, Pinene

First Impression

Review #76; June 29, 2019,

This is one of my faves from before legalization; a true gem of a sativa, Ghost Train Haze offers a heady cerebral lift that boosts creativity, heightens the senses, livens the spirit, and makes you feel pleasant and alive. This could be useful before doing some chores or even a gym visit - I haven't exercised in a while, but I feel like tackling a marathon while riding the Ghost Train. A great first look at Color.

Observations

Aroma: Citrusy, earthy, herbal, sour

Flavour: Citrusy, fruity, earthy, herbal

Bud Colour: Green

Pistil Colour: Brown

Trichome Density: Medium-High

Score Details

Appearance:	4 / 5
High Quality:	5 / 5
Aroma:	14 / 15
Flavour:	12 / 15
Bud Quality:	26 / 30
High Potency:	22 / 30

Overall Score: 83%

Cultivar Ranking: 136th

Mango Haze

Cultivar/Product Information

Type/Effect: Sativa Hybrid - Light
Legacy Name: CBD Mango Haze
Lineage: "High CBD Cultivar" x Mango Haze
Cannabinoids: 5.6% THC / 8.8% CBD
Terpenes: Caryophyllene, Cymene, Pinene

First Impression

Review #79; July 31, 2019,

For a hefty and cerebral CBD experience, look no further than Color's Mango Haze. The buzz is intense and epically strong for a balanced cultivar. Though a bit hazy and not as clear-headed as expected, I feel creative and energized. The flavour, aroma, and quality of the bud are all exceptional. I'm super impressed and hope to see more balanced cultivars from Color in the future.

Observations

Aroma: Floral, fresh, fruity, herbal

Flavour: Floral, fresh, herbal

Bud Colour: Dull green

Pistil Colour: Brown/orange

Trichome Density: Low-Medium

Score Details

Appearance:	4 / 5
High Quality:	5 / 5
Aroma:	14 / 15
Flavour:	11 / 15
Bud Quality:	26 / 30
High Potency:	22 / 30

Overall Score: 82%

Cultivar Ranking: 147th

Pedro's Sweet Sativa

Cultivar/Product Information

Type/Effect: Sativa - Medium Light
Lineage: "Unknown Indica" x Dominican Sativa x White Russian
Cannabinoids: 23.5% THC / <1% CBD
Terpenes: Caryophyllene, Pinene

First Impression

Review #17; April 14, 2019,

Pedro's Sweet Sativa from Color packs a heavy cerebral punch - I'm stoned after enjoying a bowl of this potent sativa over episodes of an animated podcast. The high is relatively clear, doesn't fog the mind much, and is motivating and focused. This lasted forever in the Volcano, producing many more bags than anticipated. Those accustomed to hefty head highs will likely find a friend in Pedro and his Sweet Sativa. I'd vote for Pedro.

Observations

Aroma: Fresh, grassy, herbal, sweet

Flavour: Fresh, grassy, herbal, sweet

Bud Colour: Light green

Pistil Colour: Brown/orange

Trichome Density: Medium-High

Score Details

Appearance:	4 / 5
High Quality:	5 / 5
Aroma:	13 / 15
Flavour:	14 / 15
Bud Quality:	26 / 30
High Potency:	25 / 30

Overall Score: 87%

Cultivar Ranking: 93rd

White Shark

Cultivar/Product Information

Type/Effect: Sativa - Heavy
Legacy Name: White Shark
Lineage: Brazilian Sativa x South Indian Sativa x Super Skunk
Cannabinoids: 17.2% THC / <1% CBD
Terpenes: Caryophyllene, Pinene

First Impression

Review #134; October 28, 2019,

I got super high, distracted by Futurama while enjoying Color's White Shark in the Volcano. I feel stoned and stupid, not ready to do much except chill and watch TV with this great day off bud. Strong stuff for a 17.2% THC flower, with the higher terpene content I expect from Color. Super enjoyable.

Observations

Aroma: Berry, earthy, fruity, funky, sweet

Flavour: Earthy, funky, herbal, spicy, sweet

Bud Colour: Green/purple

Pistil Colour: Brown/red

Trichome Density: High

Score Details

Appearance:	5 / 5
High Quality:	5 / 5
Aroma:	14 / 15
Flavour:	11 / 15
Bud Quality:	27 / 30
High Potency:	23 / 30

Overall Score: 85%

Cultivar Ranking: 110th

Cove

Overall Performance

Average Score: 82.50%

Brand Ranking: 28th Place

Brand Background

Cove produces cultivars with specific purposes in mind, hence their naming scheme for their products. Cove believes that "the right moment doesn't just happen, it's crafted," and they carry this philosophy on to their growing, producing cannabis to highlight those moments.

Cove grows cannabis in specialized grow rooms for each cultivar, ensuring the proper conditions for optimal growth. Only top cola flowers are used for their dried flower products, adding another layer of quality to their flower. Cove is grown in the Okanagan Valley in BC.

Associated Brands: Spinach

Cultivar Selection

Reflect	82%
Rest	83%
Revive	83%
Rise	82%

Reflect

Cultivar/Product Information

Type/Effect: Hybrid - Medium Light
Lineage: Chemdog x Tangerine OG
Cannabinoids: 19.8% THC / <1% CBD

First Impression

Review #145; November 25, 2019,

Cove's Reflect has me reflecting on the superb quality of Cove's flower. This flower is super long-lasting in the Volcano; it produced more bags than usual, indicating a high combined terpene and cannabinoid content. I feel a clear-headed cerebral buzz and a racing chest sensation. I feel motivated and ready to attack my day, and my mood is also elevated. I'm stoked to be stoned on Reflect.

Observations

Aroma: Earthy, herbal, piney, sweet

Flavour: Earthy, piney, sweet

Bud Colour: Dark green/purple

Pistil Colour: Brown

Trichome Density: Medium-High

Score Details

Appearance:	4 / 5
High Quality:	5 / 5
Aroma:	12 / 15
Flavour:	11 / 15
Bud Quality:	26 / 30
High Potency:	24 / 30

Overall Score: 82%

Cultivar Ranking: 160th

Rest

Cultivar/Product Information

Type/Effect: Indica - Heavy
Legacy Name: Pink Bubba
Lineage: Bubba Kush x Pink Kush
Cannabinoids: 16.9% THC / <1% CBD

First Impression

Review #151; December 3, 2019,

Cove's Rest is super chill and relaxing to the body and mind and a relatively high-quality flower. In the experience, I'm periodically nodding off, losing focus, and fading out. Not recommended for any time but the evening if you intend to accomplish much. My eyes are heavy, my legs weak, and my body is throbbing with a mellow pulsing sensation. I think I ought to get some more Rest - and some real rest, this bud compels me.

Observations

Aroma: Berry, earthy, fruity, piney, sweet

Flavour: Berry, earthy, funky, grass, sweet

Bud Colour: Green/tan

Pistil Colour: Brown/orange

Trichome Density: Medium

Score Details

Appearance:	5 / 5
High Quality:	5 / 5
Aroma:	14 / 15
Flavour:	10 / 15
Bud Quality:	27 / 30
High Potency:	22 / 30

Overall Score: 83%

Cultivar Ranking: 138th

Revive

Cultivar/Product Information

Type/Effect: Sativa Hybrid - Neutral
Lineage: Lucinda Williams x Thin Mint GSC
Cannabinoids: 20.4% THC / <1% CBD

First Impression

Review #154; December 5, 2019,

The potency of Cove products is always a cut above your average bud, and their Revive is no different. The high cannabinoid and terpene content had me coughing a lot from the Volcano, and the vapour was super thick. The high is mellow, uplifting for the mood and spirit, and very cerebral. My head is throbbing, and I can feel this flower in my face, right behind the eyes. It's intense, not recommended for beginners, but should impress regular stoners.

Observations

Aroma: Herbal, piney, sour, sweet

Flavour: Earthy, herbal, sweet, woody

Bud Colour: Dull green

Pistil Colour: Brown

Trichome Density: Medium

Score Details

Appearance:	4 / 5
High Quality:	5 / 5
Aroma:	13 / 15
Flavour:	12 / 15
Bud Quality:	25 / 30
High Potency:	24 / 30

Overall Score: 83%

Cultivar Ranking: 143rd

Rise

Cultivar/Product Information

Type/Effect: Sativa - Light
Lineage: Green Crack x Sonoma Coma
Cannabinoids: 22.1% THC / <1% CBD

First Impression

Review #204; February 29, 2020,

A cerebral rush is what to expect from Rise by Cove. I feel this one in the back of my head, and the sensation is creeping its way to my forehead, the headband effect making me squint. My mind is surprisingly calm and focused; I can write easily despite the high THC %. The high from this flower is serene, very euphoric, and uplifting. An excellent AM or pre-task cultivar, as I feel like being productive and active on this bud. A worthy addition to the Cove lineup.

Observations

Aroma: Citrusy, fresh, herbal, pungent, sour, woody

Flavour: Citrusy, fresh, herbal, sour, woody

Bud Colour: Dark green

Pistil Colour: Brown/orange

Trichome Density: Medium

Score Details

Appearance:	4 / 5
High Quality:	5 / 5
Aroma:	13 / 15
Flavour:	11 / 15
Bud Quality:	25 / 30
High Potency:	24 / 30

Overall Score: 82%

Cultivar Ranking: 156th

Delta 9

Overall Performance

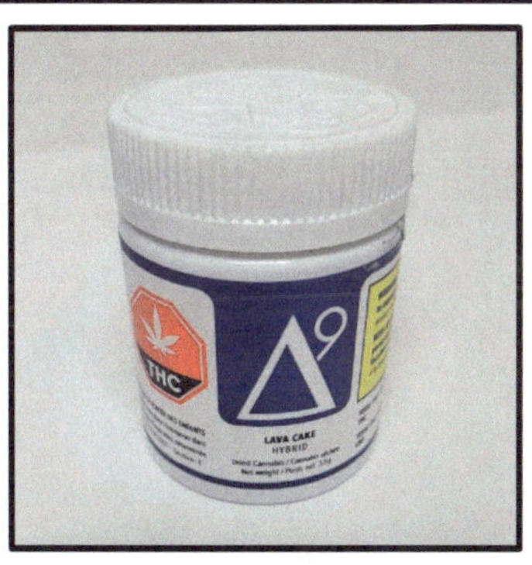

Average Score: 73.15%

Brand Ranking: 65th Place

Brand Background

Founded in 2012 by Bill and John Arbuthnot, Delta 9 was Canada's 4th licensed producer. Delta 9 operates an 80,000 square-foot facility in Winnipeg, Manitoba, where they grow in their proprietary grow pod system.

Delta 9 grows hydroponically, focusing on small-batch production. With over 20 cultivars brought to the recreational market since 2018, Delta 9 has one of the widest catalogues of cultivars I have experienced.

Cultivar Selection

Cultivar	Score	Cultivar	Score
Afghan Kush	67%	Lemon Meringue	76%
Apple Fritter	78%	Lemon Skunk	71%
Blue Venom	67%	OG Kush	68%
CBD Skunk Haze	62%	Sinaloa Gold	80%
Electric Punch	77%	Space Cake	80%
GGIV	71%	Stargazer	67%
Headbanger	77%	Super Lemon Haze	68%
Jack Herer	75%	White Out	80%
Kali Mist	72%	White Russian	67%
Lava Cake	80%	White Widow	80%

Afghan Kush

Cultivar/Product Information

Type/Effect: Indica Hybrid - Medium Heavy
Legacy Name: Afghan Kush
Lineage: Afghani Indica
Cannabinoids: 15.1% THC / <1% CBD
Terpenes: Caryophyllene, Myrcene, Ocimene

First Impression

Review #285; July 7, 2020,

Afghan Kush by Delta 9 is an indica that is relatively medium in heaviness and potency. It is relaxing and mellow without being too sedating or inebriating - a great couch or afternoon indica. My mood is calm and collected, my thoughts come quickly, and I'm not too zoned-out. A very manageable high, this would be an ideal starter cultivar.

Observations

Aroma: Fruity, grassy, herbal, sweet

Flavour: Grassy, herbal, sweet

Bud Colour: Green

Pistil Colour: Orange

Trichome Density: Low-Medium

Score Details

Appearance:	3 / 5
High Quality:	5 / 5
Aroma:	12 / 15
Flavour:	10 / 15
Bud Quality:	21 / 30
High Potency:	16 / 30

Overall Score: 67%

Cultivar Ranking: 376th

Apple Fritter

Cultivar/Product Information

Type/Effect: Hybrid - Neutral
Legacy Name: Apple Fritter
Cannabinoids: 16.3% THC / <1% CBD
Terpenes: Caryophyllene, Limonene, Nerolidol

First Impression

Review #309; August 13, 2020,

With an aroma of weedy granny smith apples and a high that surprised me with its intensity and rapid intoxication, Apple Fritter by Delta 9 is a grand old time and a tasty treat. I'm indeed experiencing an array of physical sensations in my head and chest and a mental melting. I'm zoning out mid-sentence, staring intently at nothing. My stance is wobbly, and I'm pretty baked. An excellent cultivar, ideal for times where mental focus is not necessary and euphoric relaxation is desired.

Observations

Aroma: Apple, fruity, herbal, sour, sweet

Flavour: Earthy, fresh, grassy, herbal, pungent, sour

Bud Colour: Dark green/purple

Pistil Colour: Brown/orange

Trichome Density: Medium

Score Details

Appearance:	4 / 5
High Quality:	5 / 5
Aroma:	13 / 15
Flavour:	12 / 15
Bud Quality:	22 / 30
High Potency:	22 / 30

Overall Score: 78%

Cultivar Ranking: 242nd

Blue Venom

Cultivar/Product Information

Type/Effect:	Indica Hybrid - Medium Heavy
Legacy Name:	White Berry
Lineage:	Blueberry x White Widow
Cannabinoids:	11.1% THC / <1% CBD
Terpenes:	Humulene, Caryophyllene, Ocimene

First Impression

Review #301; August 2, 2020,

A mild-medium strength experience with mellow moments and physical relaxation is in store for those who consume Delta 9's Blue Venom. A great way to chill out after work, chill out with some food and friends, or just chill out. Get the idea here? It's a chill flower. Not too potent, just chill. A decent introductory cultivar that isn't overly sedating, leaving the consumer with plenty of options for activities that pair with the high rather than just a pillow. Good flower from Delta 9.

Observations

Aroma: Berry, earthy, fruity, herbal, sour, sweet

Flavour: Berry, earthy, herbal, sweet, woody

Bud Colour: Dull green

Pistil Colour: Brown/orange

Trichome Density: Low

Score Details

Appearance:	3 / 5
High Quality:	5 / 5
Aroma:	13 / 15
Flavour:	11 / 15
Bud Quality:	23 / 30
High Potency:	12 / 30

Overall Score: 67%

Cultivar Ranking: 372nd

CBD Skunk Haze

Cultivar/Product Information

Type/Effect: Sativa Hybrid - Super Light
Legacy Name: CBD Skunk Haze
Lineage: Cannatonic x Super Haze
Cannabinoids: 3.6% THC / 6.3% CBD
Terpenes: Pinene, Caryophyllene, Myrcene

First Impression

Review #288; July 11, 2020,

Delta 9's CBD Skunk Haze is a mild cerebral buzz paired with a mellow body sensation and a sense of focus and clarity. I feel calm and serene, ready to start my day, whatever it may bring. Not crazy impressive to look at, but this CBD Skunk Haze has pleasant effects that should leave you wanting another bowl. Given the potency, you may also like another bowl. Not too shabby.

Observations

Aroma: Fresh, herbal, sour, sweet

Flavour: Fresh, herbal, sour

Bud Colour: Dull green

Pistil Colour: Brown/red

Trichome Density: Low

Score Details

Appearance:	3 / 5
High Quality:	4 / 5
Aroma:	11 / 15
Flavour:	9 / 15
Bud Quality:	21 / 30
High Potency:	14 / 30

Overall Score: 62%

Cultivar Ranking: 402nd

Electric Punch

Cultivar/Product Information

Type/Effect: Hybrid - Neutral
Cannabinoids: 19.2% THC / <1% CBD
Terpenes: Limonene, Caryophyllene, Linalool

First Impression

Review #383; December 17, 2020,

Delta 9's Electric Punch was just that: a cerebral jolt and, in other words, an electric punch to the head. My body is quite chill-feeling, not heavy, but comfy. Mentally, I'm thinking pretty normally, but there's a mellow haze blanketing my consciousness. Everything is a bit slower, but I possess the urge to go a-mile-a-minute: the cultivar is uplifting and motivating mood-wise. Electric Punch is a fantastic addition to any day and any time; it is one of Delta 9's best additions to their lineup.

Observations

Aroma: Fresh, herbal, spicy, sweet

Flavour: Fresh, grassy, herbal, sweet

Bud Colour: Dark green/purple

Pistil Colour: Brown/orange

Trichome Density: Medium

Score Details

Appearance:	4 / 5
High Quality:	5 / 5
Aroma:	12 / 15
Flavour:	11 / 15
Bud Quality:	24 / 30
High Potency:	21 / 30

Overall Score: 77%

Cultivar Ranking: 260th

GGIV

Cultivar/Product Information

Type/Effect:	Hybrid - Neutral
Legacy Name:	Original Glue
Lineage:	Chem's Sister x Chocolate Diesel x Sour Dubb
Cannabinoids:	14.4% THC / <1% CBD
Terpenes:	Pinene, Myrcene, Caryophyllene

First Impression

Review #311; August 15, 2020,

The effects of Delta 9's GGIV are potent, mellow, and euphoric. My mood is improved, and much more relaxed than before consumption. A powerful feeling for a <15% cultivar, GGIV never disappoints me. I'm not zoning out, and I can remain focused on review writing. The high is not too impairing to my ability, but I'm experiencing a strong headband effect and certainly feel stoned. I'd recommend this anytime you want to slow down and appreciate the moment.

Observations

Aroma: Earthy, fresh, herbal, minty, piney, sour, spicy, sweet

Flavour: Earthy, funky, grassy, herbal, pungent

Bud Colour: Brown/green

Pistil Colour: Brown/orange

Trichome Density: Low

Score Details

Appearance:	4 / 5
High Quality:	5 / 5
Aroma:	11 / 15
Flavour:	10 / 15
Bud Quality:	23 / 30
High Potency:	18 / 30

Overall Score: 71%

Cultivar Ranking: 334th

Headbanger

Cultivar/Product Information

Type/Effect: Sativa Hybrid - Neutral
Cannabinoids: 18.8% THC / <1% CBD
Terpenes: Limonene, Nerolidol, Pinene

First Impression

Review #374; December 2, 2020,

I'd be headbanging on Headbanger by Delta 9, but I'm currently in a room with no music. I'm pretty lively mood-wise and energy-wise, but the haze is a little heavy cerebrally. A kind of sensation that feels like you've been headbanging at a concert for a while. My eyes don't feel heavy - everything else about the high is uplifting. Headbanger is a great time solo or with company, given the social high.

Observations

Aroma: Earthy, fresh, fruity, herbal, sour, sweet

Flavour: Earthy, fresh, pungent, woody

Bud Colour: Dark green

Pistil Colour: Brown/orange

Trichome Density: Medium

Score Details

Appearance:	4 / 5
High Quality:	5 / 5
Aroma:	13 / 15
Flavour:	10 / 15
Bud Quality:	24 / 30
High Potency:	21 / 30

Overall Score: 77%

Cultivar Ranking: 255th

Jack Herer

Cultivar/Product Information

Type/Effect:	Hybrid - Light
Legacy Name:	Jack Herer
Lineage:	Haze x (Northern Lights #5 x Shiva Skunk)
Cannabinoids:	14.9% THC / <1% CBD
Terpenes:	Pinene, Caryophyllene, Nerolidol

First Impression

Review #344; October 8, 2020,

Delta 9's Jack Herer is a social and functional delight. The high is relatively clear-headed and mood-enhancing, a good morning or daytime option to brighten your day. Though I find myself texting more than writing my review, not entirely focused on what I should be, my mind is awake and alive. Inspiring and uplifting, and a great coffee replacement, Jack Herer is worth a try.

Observations

Aroma: Floral, fresh, fruity, herbal, sour, sweet

Flavour: Floral, fresh, funky, grassy, herbal

Bud Colour: Dark green/purple

Pistil Colour: Brown/orange

Trichome Density: Medium

Score Details

Appearance:	4 / 5
High Quality:	5 / 5
Aroma:	14 / 15
Flavour:	11 / 15
Bud Quality:	24 / 30
High Potency:	17 / 30

Overall Score: 75%

Cultivar Ranking: 280th

Kali Mist

Cultivar/Product Information

Type/Effect: Sativa Hybrid - Medium Light
Legacy Name: Kali Mist
Cannabinoids: 18.1% THC / <1% CBD

First Impression

Review #261; May 15, 2020,

The effects of Delta 9's Kali Mist are mood-elevating, hazy, and mellow. My mind is relatively clear, and thoughts come easily and quickly still. But everything is a little fuzzy, a little slow, and I like it - a great option to start a day off right.

Observations

Aroma: Citrusy, fresh, fruity, herbal, lemon, sour

Flavour: Herbal, sweet, woody

Bud Colour: Dark green

Pistil Colour: Brown/orange

Trichome Density: Low-Medium

Score Details

Appearance:	4 / 5
High Quality:	4 / 5
Aroma:	14 / 15
Flavour:	10 / 15
Bud Quality:	23 / 30
High Potency:	17 / 30

Overall Score: 72%

Cultivar Ranking: 317th

Lava Cake

Cultivar/Product Information

Type/Effect: Hybrid - Neutral
Legacy Name: Lava Cake
Cannabinoids: 17.8% THC / <1% CBD
Terpenes: Caryophyllene, Humulene, Limonene

First Impression

Review #281; July 4, 2020,

Delta 9's Lava Cake has one of the loveliest purple colors in cannabis and is a tremendous high considering the price point and percentage. The high itself is euphoric and mellow, with a very pleasant headband and physical effect. The aroma and flavour are above average and thoroughly enjoyable all around. I would liken Lava Cake to a nice dessert, a treat for yourself, but an affordable one worthy of being an everyday smoke.

Observations

Aroma: Earthy, fresh, grassy, piney, pungent, sweet, woody

Flavour: Earthy, fresh, grassy, piney, pungent, sweet, woody

Bud Colour: Dark green/purple

Pistil Colour: Orange/tan

Trichome Density: Medium-High

Score Details

Appearance:	4 / 5
High Quality:	5 / 5
Aroma:	13 / 15
Flavour:	12 / 15
Bud Quality:	24 / 30
High Potency:	22 / 30

Overall Score: 80%

Cultivar Ranking: 198th

Lemon Meringue

Cultivar/Product Information

Type/Effect: Sativa Hybrid - Light
Legacy Name: Lemon Meringue
Cannabinoids: 13.8% THC / <1% CBD
Terpenes: Myrcene, Caryophyllene, Terpinolene

First Impression

Review #240; April 15, 2020,

Lemon Meringue by Delta 9 is one of the few cultivars I've encountered to taste even better than it smells. The sweet and sour lemon and cream flavour is excellent, and the high is satisfying. Mellow cerebral stimulation to get the creative juices flowing and improve my mood, and a calm, gentle headband effect to haze up my afternoon. A stand-out Lemon Skunk cross, well done Delta 9.

Observations

Aroma: Citrusy, floral, fresh, fruity, lemon, sour, sweet

Flavour: Citrusy, fresh, fruity, herbal, lemon, sour, sweet

Bud Colour: Dull green

Pistil Colour: Brown/orange

Trichome Density: Low-Medium

Score Details

Appearance:	4 / 5
High Quality:	5 / 5
Aroma:	14 / 15
Flavour:	14 / 15
Bud Quality:	23 / 30
High Potency:	16 / 30

Overall Score: 76%

Cultivar Ranking: 267th

Lemon Skunk

Cultivar/Product Information

Type/Effect: Sativa Hybrid - Light
Legacy Name: Lemon Skunk
Lineage: Skunk
Cannabinoids: 13.7% THC / <1% CBD
Terpenes: Myrcene, Pinene

First Impression

Review #267; May 28, 2020,

Lemon Skunk from Delta 9 offers a bright cerebral buzz, and mellow body feels. I would recommend this to anyone looking to feel "a'ight." I'm not motivated to accomplish much, but my creative juices flow, and my mind is alive with ideas. I'm rocking back and forth with the physical sensation I'm experiencing - a great way to spend an afternoon under the spell of this significant Lemon Skunk high.

Observations

Aroma: Citrusy, earthy, floral, grassy, herbal, lemon, sour

Flavour: Citrusy, earthy, floral, grassy, herbal, sweet

Bud Colour: Dull green

Pistil Colour: Brown/orange

Trichome Density: Low-Medium

Score Details

Appearance:	3 / 5
High Quality:	5 / 5
Aroma:	13 / 15
Flavour:	11 / 15
Bud Quality:	23 / 30
High Potency:	16 / 30

Overall Score: 71%

Cultivar Ranking: 326th

OG Kush

Cultivar/Product Information

Type/Effect: Indica Hybrid - Neutral
Legacy Name: OG Kush
Lineage: "Northern Californian" x Hindu Kush
Cannabinoids: 18.8% THC / <1% CBD
Terpenes: Nerolidol, Limonene, Caryophyllene

First Impression

Review #372; November 26, 2020.

OG Kush by Delta 9 is a mellow high, perfect for chilling with some friends or chilling on your own - it'll keep you entertained, with company or otherwise. I've been all over the place during this high, texting and sending emails. The cerebral activity and motivated mood are a stark contrast to the physical relaxation. Usually, these kinds of effects are not paired, but OG Kush variants are often both relaxing and cerebrally active, I've found (as opposed to sedating). Deeper into the bowl, I do find motivation fading. Now I want to do nothing and enjoy it.

Observations

Aroma: Grassy, herbal, pungent, sour

Flavour: Earthy, herbal, woody

Bud Colour: Dark green

Pistil Colour: Brown/orange

Trichome Density: Medium

Score Details

Appearance:	3 / 5
High Quality:	5 / 5
Aroma:	11 / 15
Flavour:	9 / 15
Bud Quality:	18 / 30
High Potency:	22 / 30

Overall Score: 68%

Cultivar Ranking: 369th

Sinaloa Gold

Cultivar/Product Information

Type/Effect: Hybrid - Medium Light
Cannabinoids: 22.8% THC / <1% CBD
Terpenes: Caryophyllene, Nerolidol, Limonene

First Impression

Review #347; October 12, 2020,

The high from Delta 9's Sinaloa Gold has awakened my mind and stomach. I feel uplifted and clear-headed, though I lose focus from time to time. The buzz is primarily heady, and I don't feel much of a body effect. My eyes feel wide open. I'm alert, very aware of everything; I'm high, but not quite stoned - a strong high, it hits a bit harder than you may expect.

Observations

Aroma: Earthy, floral, fresh, herbal

Flavour: Fresh, grassy, herbal

Bud Colour: Dark green/purple

Pistil Colour: Brown/red

Trichome Density: Medium-High

Score Details

Appearance:	4 / 5
High Quality:	5 / 5
Aroma:	12 / 15
Flavour:	11 / 15
Bud Quality:	24 / 30
High Potency:	24 / 30

Overall Score: 80%

Cultivar Ranking: 217th

Space Cake

Cultivar/Product Information

Type/Effect: Hybrid - Medium Light
Legacy Name: Space Cake
Cannabinoids: 17.5% THC / <1% CBD
Terpenes: Caryophyllene, Limonene, Nerolidol

First Impression

Review #307; August 12, 2020,

Space Cake by Delta 9 has me less "far-out man" and more zoned-in, in-the-moment, and present. I feel fantastic and relieved of my mental and physical stresses. A partial escape from reality in that I've found momentary reprieve from my stress, but I'm still here, and my thoughts aren't wandering too much. I'm not entirely cooked (more than half-baked, though). A perfect hybrid with a mix of uplifting and relaxing effects, suitable for anytime you want to feel great and feel more. Beautiful to look at as well, given its gorgeous colour.

Observations

Aroma: Earthy, fresh, herbal, pungent, sweet

Flavour: Earthy, fresh, piney, pungent, woody

Bud Colour: Dark green/purple

Pistil Colour: Orange

Trichome Density: High

Score Details

Appearance:	4 / 5
High Quality:	5 / 5
Aroma:	13 / 15
Flavour:	12 / 15
Bud Quality:	24 / 30
High Potency:	22 / 30

Overall Score: 80%

Cultivar Ranking: 197th

Stargazer

Cultivar/Product Information

Type/Effect: Sativa Hybrid - Medium Heavy
Legacy Name: Stargazer
Cannabinoids: 14.1% THC / <1% CBD
Terpenes: Pinene, Caryophyllene, Limonene

First Impression

Review #298; July 29, 2020,

A lazy-eyed, mellow feel with an uplifting effect on mood and perspective, Stargazer by Delta 9 is a solid option for day or night. Whether you're gazing at the stars, grazing the munchies, or just hazing up the room, Stargazer should ground you, center you, and zone you out of your concerns. Slowed thoughts and lethargic movement are symptoms of this bud; it brings you back down to earth rather than shooting you into space - a worthwhile high.

Observations

Aroma: Earthy, floral, fresh, herbal, mint, piney, pungent

Flavour: Earthy, floral, fresh, grassy, herbal, mint, woody

Bud Colour: Dark green

Pistil Colour: Brown/red

Trichome Density: Low

Score Details

Appearance:	3 / 5
High Quality:	4 / 5
Aroma:	12 / 15
Flavour:	9 / 15
Bud Quality:	22 / 30
High Potency:	17 / 30

Overall Score: 67%

Cultivar Ranking: 377th

Super Lemon Haze

Cultivar/Product Information

Type/Effect: Sativa Hybrid - Light
Legacy Name: Super Lemon Haze
Lineage: Lemon Skunk x Super Silver Haze
Cannabinoids: 19.9% THC / <1% CBD
Terpenes: Caryophyllene, Myrcene, Pinene

First Impression

Review #214; March 14, 2020,

A clear, focused, cerebrally-active high is what I got out of Super Lemon Haze by Delta 9. Though it's not a very intense feeling, I'm certainly relatively high; I can sense it in my mood and alertness. This is another incredible high for getting stuff done or lazing around for an afternoon with your thoughts, myself opting for the latter.

Observations

Aroma: Citrusy, herbal, pungent, sour, woody

Flavour: Citrusy, herbal, piney, sour, woody

Bud Colour: Light green

Pistil Colour: Orange/tan

Trichome Density: Low-Medium

Score Details

Appearance:	3 / 5
High Quality:	4 / 5
Aroma:	14 / 15
Flavour:	13 / 15
Bud Quality:	15 / 30
High Potency:	19 / 30

Overall Score: 68%

Cultivar Ranking: 364th

White Out

Cultivar/Product Information

Type/Effect: Hybrid - Heavy
Legacy Name: White Out
Cannabinoids: 21.3% THC / <1% CBD
Terpenes: Humulene, Caryophyllene, Ocimene

First Impression

Review #187; February 7, 2020,

On Delta 9's White Out, my first taste of Delta 9, I found it challenging to think and breathe simultaneously. My room, dead silent as I wrote, was foggy even with the door open from the copious amount of vapour this flower produced. I was stoned, ripped, smashed, wasted, and super high that fateful afternoon. A decent product, I'm excited now to try more Delta 9.

Observations

Aroma: Earthy, grassy, piney, pungent, sour, woody

Flavour: Earthy, funky, grassy, piney, pungent

Bud Colour: Dark green/purple

Pistil Colour: Orange

Trichome Density: Medium-High

Score Details

Appearance:	4 / 5
High Quality:	5 / 5
Aroma:	13 / 15
Flavour:	12 / 15
Bud Quality:	23 / 30
High Potency:	23 / 30

Overall Score: 80%

Cultivar Ranking: 200th

White Russian

Cultivar/Product Information

Type/Effect: Indica Hybrid - Light
Legacy Name: White Russian
Lineage: AK-47 x White Widow
Cannabinoids: 14.9% THC / <1% CBD

First Impression

Review #205; February 29, 2020,

Mildly stoned on White Russian from Delta 9, I attempted to recall Newton's Laws of Motion, to little success - strange how the mind wanders. On the topic of physics, I had a customer say to me yesterday, "remember Einstein, Emc^2= hash," and in no way is that relevant, but it's hilarious, and this flower has me in the mood for stories. The buzz is mellow, clear and cerebral. A solid option, not tiring like some other indicas, so appropriate for a wake and bake session.

Observations

Aroma: Fresh, fruity, herbal, sour, sweet

Flavour: Fresh, herbal, sour, woody

Bud Colour: Dull green

Pistil Colour: Brown/tan

Trichome Density: Low

Score Details

Appearance:	4 / 5
High Quality:	5 / 5
Aroma:	13 / 15
Flavour:	10 / 15
Bud Quality:	20 / 30
High Potency:	15 / 30

Overall Score: 67%

Cultivar Ranking: 373rd

White Widow

Cultivar/Product Information

Type/Effect: Hybrid - Medium Heavy
Legacy Name: White Widow
Lineage: Brazilian Sativa x Indian Indica
Cannabinoids: 18% THC / <1% CBD

First Impression

Review #241; April 15, 2020,

I have a hazy afternoon ahead of me after consuming Delta 9's White Widow. Excellent quality considering the year-old packaging date. My mind is clouded over, and my mood is elevated and happy. I don't feel like accomplishing too much after this flower and might not be capable enough at the moment to be productive anyway - a potent and worthwhile White Widow.

Observations

Aroma: Fruity, herbal, pungent, sour

Flavour: Floral, funky, herbal, sour, woody

Bud Colour: Green

Pistil Colour: Brown

Trichome Density: Medium

Score Details

Appearance:	4 / 5
High Quality:	5 / 5
Aroma:	13 / 15
Flavour:	11 / 15
Bud Quality:	24 / 30
High Potency:	23 / 30

Overall Score: 80%

Cultivar Ranking: 204th

DNA Genetics

Overall Performance

Average Score: 77.20%

Brand Ranking: 48th Place

Brand Background

DNA Genetics, the Canadian cannabis brand associated with the seed company of the same name, is a premium cannabis producer. They operate a 60,000 square-foot facility where they grow cultivars from the DNA Genetics catalogue. Since 2004, Don and Aaron of DNA Genetics have accumulated a High Times Cannabis Cup win in every category, so consumers can be confident knowing the genetics they're consuming have been bred by some of the best.

DNA Genetics cannabis is grown indoors by Canopy Growth Corporation in Bowmanville, Ontario.

Other Cultivars:	Golden Lemons
Associated Brands:	7Acres, Houseplant, LBS, Tokyo Smoke, Tweed, Van Der Pop

Cultivar Selection

Chocolate Fondue	81%
Kosher Kush	74%
Lemon Skunk	79%
Sour Kush	79%
Sour Tangie	73%

Chocolate Fondue

Cultivar/Product Information

Type/Effect: Sativa - Medium Heavy
Legacy Name: Chocolate Fondue
Lineage: Chocolope x Exodus UK Cheese
Cannabinoids: 23% THC / <1% CBD
Terpenes: Caryophyllene, Limonene, Santalene

First Impression

Review #23; April 17, 2019,

Before starting work in the cannabis industry, this was my favourite recreational cultivar, and still, Chocolate Fondue remains one of my favourites. Chocolate Fondue by DNA Genetics is a heavy, heady sativa with potent effects. It provides a powerful head high that motivates and inspires while still being hazy and quite powerful cerebrally. A great experience all around, especially if you dig some cheesy, funky goodness.

Observations

Aroma: Cheese, earthy, funky, herbal, sour, spicy, sweet

Flavour: Cheese, earthy, funky, herbal, sour, spicy

Bud Colour: Dull green

Pistil Colour: Brown/red

Trichome Density: Medium

Score Details

Appearance:	4 / 5
High Quality:	5 / 5
Aroma:	14 / 15
Flavour:	12 / 15
Bud Quality:	21 / 30
High Potency:	25 / 30

Overall Score: 81%

Cultivar Ranking: 168th

Kosher Kush

Cultivar/Product Information

Type/Effect: Indica - Medium Heavy
Legacy Name: Kosher Kush
Lineage: OG Kush
Cannabinoids: 16% THC / <1% CBD
Terpenes: Limonene, Caryophyllene, Myrcene

First Impression

Review #24; April 17, 2019,

Rumour has it that DNA Genetics' Kosher Kush is the first rec market cultivar to be blessed by a Rabbi; thus, it is actually, factually kosher. Apart from that, it's also the type of indica that makes your dream scenario a couch, some snacks, and a TV for the evening. It creates a delightful head high coupled with an equally excellent body sensation. My head remains clear, but I find myself slower in many ways - an ideal state for evening relaxation.

Observations

Aroma: Earthy, fresh, grassy, herbal, sour

Flavour: Earthy, herbal

Bud Colour: Dark green

Pistil Colour: Brown/orange

Trichome Density: Medium

Score Details

Appearance:	4 / 5
High Quality:	5 / 5
Aroma:	12 / 15
Flavour:	10 / 15
Bud Quality:	21 / 30
High Potency:	22 / 30

Overall Score: 74%

Cultivar Ranking: 295th

Lemon Skunk

Cultivar/Product Information

Type/Effect: Sativa Hybrid - Light
Legacy Name: Lemon Skunk
Lineage: Skunk
Cannabinoids: 14.3% THC / <1% CBD
Terpenes: Terpinolene, Caryophyllene, Pinene

First Impression

Review #52; May 7, 2019,

Head high to the max: euphoric and creative, DNA's Lemon Skunk is an enjoyable experience. Also, the high is quite productive and motivational, and I could probably accomplish a lot on this bud if not distracted by the noises outside. Are those kids that sound like birds, or birds that sound like kids? I don't know, but I digress: I'm stoned, and this is some good stuff.

Observations

Aroma: Citrusy, herbal, lemon, pungent, sour, woody

Flavour: Citrusy, herbal, woody

Bud Colour: Light green

Pistil Colour: Orange

Trichome Density: Low-Medium

Score Details

Appearance:	5 / 5
High Quality:	5 / 5
Aroma:	14 / 15
Flavour:	14 / 15
Bud Quality:	22 / 30
High Potency:	19 / 30

Overall Score: 79%

Cultivar Ranking: 224th

Sour Kush

Cultivar/Product Information

Type/Effect: Indica - Neutral
Legacy Name: Sour Kush
Lineage: OG Kush x Sour Diesel
Cannabinoids: 19% THC / <1% CBD

First Impression

Review #66; June 1, 2019,

My heart races, mind pulses, head throbs, and I'm super stoned thanks to DNA's take on the well-known Sour Kush. A tremendous high has me alert and focused enough to write this review but relaxed enough that it can ease me into the evening, early or late. I could see enjoying a night out, or in, with Sour Kush as the highlight; great bud for any setting, particularly those involving company, laughs, and conversation.

Observations

Aroma: Earthy, herbal, minty, piney, sweet

Flavour: Cheese, earthy, funky, herbal, minty, piney

Bud Colour: Dark green

Pistil Colour: Brown/red

Trichome Density: Low-Medium

Score Details

Appearance:	4 / 5
High Quality:	5 / 5
Aroma:	13 / 15
Flavour:	12 / 15
Bud Quality:	21 / 30
High Potency:	24 / 30

Overall Score: 79%

Cultivar Ranking: 231st

Sour Tangie

Cultivar/Product Information

Type/Effect: Sativa - Super Light
Legacy Name: Sour Tangie
Lineage: East Coast Sour Diesel x Tangie
Cannabinoids: 15% THC / <1% CBD

First Impression

Review #30; April 19, 2019,

Sour Tangie by DNA Genetics is a flavorful, pleasant-smelling bud that offers a focused cerebral jolt and a powerful headband effect. The terpene profile is typically unique from DNA Genetics, and Sour Tangie is no different. 15% THC doesn't do enough to describe the true potency of this flower, and the entourage effect comes through in full force here. Sour Tangie is a fantastic cultivar at any THC potency, worth it just for the subtle tangerine flavour.

Observations

Aroma: Fruity, herbal, orange, spicy, sweet

Flavour: Fruity, herbal, mint, orange, sweet

Bud Colour: Light green

Pistil Colour: Brown/red

Trichome Density: Low

Score Details

Appearance:	4 / 5
High Quality:	5 / 5
Aroma:	14 / 15
Flavour:	14 / 15
Bud Quality:	18 / 30
High Potency:	18 / 30

Overall Score: 73%

Cultivar Ranking: 305th

Edison

Overall Performance

Average Score: 76.36%

Brand Ranking: 50th Place

Brand Background

From Moncton, New Brunswick, comes Edison, a recreational cannabis brand that's been around since legalization. The folks at Edison believe in the "infinite potential" of both their team and their cannabis.

Edison cannabis is grown in cultivar-specific, indoor environments, suited to the needs of each cultivar. Utilizing data-driven growing practices, Edison is constantly improving their cannabis production, and the result is consistent cannabis that is consistently getting better.

Other Cultivars: Frozen Lemons, GMO Cookies, Kush Cake, MAC-1, Sour OG Cheese
Associated Brands: Ankr Organics

Cultivar Selection

Cultivar	Score	Cultivar	Score
Black Cherry Punch	84%	La Strada	70%
Blue Velvet	85%	Limelight	86%
Casa Blanca	67%	Lola Montes	70%
Chemdog	74%	Rio Bravo	71%
City Lights	61%	Samurai Spy	82%
El Dorado	78%	Slurricane	78%
Ice Cream Cake	82%	The General	81%

Black Cherry Punch

Cultivar/Product Information

Type/Effect: Indica - Neutral
Legacy Name: Black Cherry Punch
Lineage: Black Cherry Pie x Purple Punch
Cannabinoids: 20% THC / <1% CBD
Terpenes: Limonene, Beta Caryophyllene, Linalool

First Impression

Review #406; January 17, 2021,

Black Cherry Punch by Edison delivers a mellow punch to the body and mind without being too relaxing, sedating, or inebriating. I can still think quickly and move around in a coordinated fashion. My mood is calm and chill, and I'm perfectly content just doing nothing but listening to music and existing. It is a very manageable 20% THC high but also super enjoyable. The aroma is next level for Edison, as is the flavour; I'm impressed.

Observations

Aroma: Berry, cherry, fruity, herbal, sour, spicy, sweet

Flavour: Berry, cherry, floral, fruity, herbal, sweet

Bud Colour: Green/purple

Pistil Colour: Orange

Trichome Density: Medium-High

Score Details

Appearance:	4 / 5
High Quality:	5 / 5
Aroma:	15 / 15
Flavour:	13 / 15
Bud Quality:	25 / 30
High Potency:	22 / 30

Overall Score: 84%

Cultivar Ranking: 121st

Blue Velvet

Cultivar/Product Information

Type/Effect: Indica - Neutral
Legacy Name: Blueberry Kush
Lineage: Blueberry x OG Kush
Cannabinoids: 23.3% THC / <1% CBD
Terpenes: Myrcene, Caryophyllene, Pinene

First Impression

Review #72; June 24, 2019,

Before this review, I was restless, but not anymore: after a bowl of Edison's Blue Velvet, I feel mellow, chill, and relaxed. I'm more brought-up than put-down; the high is heady and intense. My head is pulsing, and my body feels comfortable as a sensation throbs from my chest to my feet. The best Edison bud I've had yet, especially on quality.

Observations

Aroma: Berry, earthy, herbal, sweet

Flavour: Berry, earthy, herbal, sweet

Bud Colour: Green/purple

Pistil Colour: Orange

Trichome Density: Medium

Score Details

Appearance:	4 / 5
High Quality:	5 / 5
Aroma:	14 / 15
Flavour:	12 / 15
Bud Quality:	26 / 30
High Potency:	24 / 30

Overall Score: 85%

Cultivar Ranking: 114th

Casa Blanca

Cultivar/Product Information

Type/Effect: Indica - Medium Heavy
Legacy Name: Mongolian
Cannabinoids: 14.1% THC / <1% CBD
Terpenes: Myrcene, Caryophyllene, Pinene

First Impression

Review #19; April 15, 2019,

I zoned out several times before writing this review - Casa Blanca by Edison will do that to you. I felt a slight body sensation, but most of this one went straight to the dome. This heavy, impairing, and distracting high will leave you asking everyone to repeat themselves in conversation and rewinding the TV show repeatedly. In short, Casa Blanca will leave you stoned and stupid.

Observations

Aroma: Cheese, earthy, funky, herbal, sour

Flavour: Herbal, sour

Bud Colour: Dull green

Pistil Colour: Orange/tan

Trichome Density: Medium

Score Details

Appearance:	4 / 5
High Quality:	5 / 5
Aroma:	10 / 15
Flavour:	9 / 15
Bud Quality:	21 / 30
High Potency:	18 / 30

Overall Score: 67%

Cultivar Ranking: 300th

Chemdog

Cultivar/Product Information

Type/Effect: Hybrid - Medium Heavy
Legacy Name: Chemdog
Lineage: Dogbud
Cannabinoids: 18.9% THC / <1% CBD
Terpenes: Limonene, Caryophyllene, Linalool

First Impression

Review #341; September 30, 2020,

Chemdog by Edison is heady and hazy, an outstanding cerebral cultivar. The flavour and aroma are light, but the high is a mid-heavy one for sure; not too get-up and go, more get-down and go-with-the-flow. I feel like I look baked, definitely squinting at the moment. A decent cultivar to enhance a day or night with, but don't expect to get much done. I lack the will to do anything on this flower that doesn't involve sprawling out on the couch - a good lazy high from Edison.

Observations

Aroma: Herbal, sour, spicy, woody

Flavour: Grassy, herbal, woody

Bud Colour: Dull green

Pistil Colour: Orange/tan

Trichome Density: Medium-High

Score Details

Appearance:	4 / 5
High Quality:	5 / 5
Aroma:	10 / 15
Flavour:	9 / 15
Bud Quality:	23 / 30
High Potency:	23 / 30

Overall Score: 74%

Cultivar Ranking: 304th

City Lights

Cultivar/Product Information

Type/Effect: Hybrid - Neutral
Legacy Name: Critical Kush
Lineage: Critical Mass x OG Kush
Cannabinoids: 15% THC / <1% CBD
Terpenes: Myrcene, Caryophyllene, Limonene

First Impression

Review #20; April 15, 2019,

On Edison's City Lights, my mind and body are satisfied by the stoned feeling created. Nothing stands out as incredibly unique about this cultivar, but it does the average and predictable thing quite well. At 15%, this is a great medium-strength option, and it can be consumed any time of day without the risk of overstimulation or couch-lock. City Lights is a solid flower option for those new to cannabis or experienced consumers looking for a lighter buzz.

Observations

Aroma: Earthy, herbal, sour

Flavour: Earthy, herbal

Bud Colour: Light green

Pistil Colour: Brown/orange

Trichome Density: Low

Score Details

Appearance:	3 / 5
High Quality:	5 / 5
Aroma:	10 / 15
Flavour:	8 / 15
Bud Quality:	18 / 30
High Potency:	17 / 30

Overall Score: 61%

Cultivar Ranking: 404th

El Dorado

Cultivar/Product Information

Type/Effect: Hybrid - Neutral
Legacy Name: Kanata
Cannabinoids: 16.9% THC / <1% CBD
Terpenes: Pinene, Caryophyllene

First Impression

Review #69; June 6, 2019,

I feel a boost in my creativity and overall interest in everything. El Dorado has me feeling great. The high is a heady cerebral buzz coupled with a pleasant, peaceful body sensation that I feel most in my legs and chest. Also, this bud is beautiful: dense and moist. A good experience from great bud, El Dorado is brilliance from the geniuses at Edison.

Observations

Aroma: Chocolate, earthy, sour, spicy

Flavour: Herbal, sour, woody

Bud Colour: Dark brown/green

Pistil Colour: Brown/orange

Trichome Density: Medium

Score Details

Appearance:	4 / 5
High Quality:	5 / 5
Aroma:	13 / 15
Flavour:	12 / 15
Bud Quality:	25 / 30
High Potency:	19 / 30

Overall Score: 78%

Cultivar Ranking: 243rd

Ice Cream Cake

Cultivar/Product Information

Type/Effect: Indica - Heavy
Legacy Name: Ice Cream Cake
Lineage: Gelato #33 x Wedding Cake
Cannabinoids: 21.6% THC / <1% CBD
Terpenes: Limonene, Caryophyllene, Linalool

First Impression

Review #414; February 8, 2021,

The potent power of Edison's Ice Cream Cake packs a hit that should leave you feeling relaxed and on the edge of passing out. Even though I'm consuming this mid-day, I'm feeling heavy-eyed, squinty, and sedated. My thought process, like my writing process, is slowed way down. I may need to take a nap.

Observations

Aroma: Earthy, herbal, minty, piney, pungent

Flavour: Earthy, piney, pungent

Bud Colour: Dark green/purple

Pistil Colour: Brown/orange

Trichome Density: Medium

Score Details

Appearance:	4 / 5
High Quality:	5 / 5
Aroma:	13 / 15
Flavour:	13 / 15
Bud Quality:	22 / 30
High Potency:	25 / 30

Overall Score: 82%

Cultivar Ranking: 153rd

La Strada

Cultivar/Product Information

Type/Effect: Sativa - Medium Light
Legacy Name: Blue Dream
Lineage: Blueberry x Haze
Cannabinoids: 16% THC / <1% CBD
Terpenes: Caryophyllene, Myrcene, Humulene

First Impression

Review #108; September 7, 2019,

Edison's La Strada paired well with waking up to my Thursday errands. A high strong enough to keep me from thinking and worrying about my duties, but not so strong that I forget about them. While it was a tad milder at first, I found La Strada crept up on me as I wrote the review. A mid-strength sativa, this cultivar was uplifting but more relaxing than energizing - decent enough stuff.

Observations

Aroma: Citrusy, fresh, grassy, herbal, sour, sweet

Flavour: Earthy, funky, herbal, sour

Bud Colour: Dull green

Pistil Colour: Orange

Trichome Density: Low-Medium

Score Details

Appearance:	4 / 5
High Quality:	5 / 5
Aroma:	11 / 15
Flavour:	9 / 15
Bud Quality:	22 / 30
High Potency:	19 / 30

Overall Score: 70%

Cultivar Ranking: 348th

Limelight

Cultivar/Product Information

Type/Effect: Sativa - Neutral
Legacy Name: Ultra Sour
Lineage: East Coast Sour Diesel x MK Ultra
Cannabinoids: 25.8% THC / <1% CBD
Terpenes: Terpinolene, Caryophyllene, Humulene

First Impression

Review #182; January 31, 2020,

Oh, the power of Ultra Sour, or Limelight by Edison. A robust and clear-headed high, but distractions come easily. My body is relaxed to the point where my dresser/review desk has become comfortable to rest against. I feel the high throughout my body, especially in the eyes and forehead. At this %, new consumers should stay away, as the cerebral intensity of this flower is hardcore - a beast of a high.

Observations

Aroma: Cheese, citrusy, herbal, piney, sour, woody

Flavour: Citrusy, herbal, sour, woody

Bud Colour: Green

Pistil Colour: Orange

Trichome Density: Low-Medium

Score Details

Appearance:	4 / 5
High Quality:	5 / 5
Aroma:	13 / 15
Flavour:	13 / 15
Bud Quality:	25 / 30
High Potency:	26 / 30

Overall Score: 86%

Cultivar Ranking: 106th

Lola Montes

Cultivar/Product Information

Type/Effect: Indica - Medium Heavy
Legacy Name: Hash Plant
Lineage: Hash Plant x Northern Lights #1
Cannabinoids: 14.9% THC / <1% CBD
Terpenes: Myrcene, Caryophyllene, Guaiol

First Impression

Review #99; August 31, 2019,

I'm stoned on Edison's Lola Montes but not sleepy at all. I'm pretty zoned out, and I'm struggling to write. The head buzz is a hazy one, and it comes with a potent and heavy body sensation. Decent.

Observations

Aroma: Fruity, funky, herbal, sour, sweet

Flavour: Earthy, funky, herbal, sweet

Bud Colour: Green/tan

Pistil Colour: Orange

Trichome Density: Medium

Score Details

Appearance:	4 / 5
High Quality:	5 / 5
Aroma:	10 / 15
Flavour:	9 / 15
Bud Quality:	22 / 30
High Potency:	20 / 30

Overall Score: 70%

Cultivar Ranking: 352nd

Rio Bravo

Cultivar/Product Information

Type/Effect: Sativa - Light
Legacy Name: Jack Herer
Lineage: Haze x (Northern Lights #5 x Shiva Skunk)
Cannabinoids: 16.8% THC / <1% CBD
Terpenes: Terpinolene, Caryophyllene, Myrcene

First Impression

Review #38; April 24, 2019,

Edison's Rio Bravo is an impressive, medium-potency sativa that delivers a boost to focus and creativity, as well as a powerful head buzz and body sensation for a complete experience. This bud is excellent to kick off a morning with, and I certainly feel ready to take on my day.

Observations

Aroma: Citrusy, herbal, sour, sweet

Flavour: Citrusy, herbal

Bud Colour: Green

Pistil Colour: Brown/tan

Trichome Density: Low-Medium

Score Details

Appearance:	4 / 5
High Quality:	5 / 5
Aroma:	11 / 15
Flavour:	12 / 15
Bud Quality:	19 / 30
High Potency:	20 / 30

Overall Score: 71%

Cultivar Ranking: 333rd

Samurai Spy

Cultivar/Product Information

Type/Effect: Hybrid - Neutral
Legacy Name: Ninja Fruit
Lineage: Grape Ape x Grapefruit Haze
Cannabinoids: 21.9% THC / <1% CBD
Terpenes: Caryophyllene, Myrcene, Limonene

First Impression

Review #318; August 26, 2020,

I find myself lost in the cerebral haze brought on by Edison's Samurai Spy. A bright and uplifting effect on mood, but you'll have heavy eyes and a calm and chill demeanour. It seems like a wonderful flower for an afternoon off or an occasion with friends; I feel like chatting, though I'm pretty relaxed. A peaceful and calm high, one of Edison's best yet.

Observations

Aroma: Fruity, herbal, orange, sweet, woody

Flavour: Cherry, fruity, herbal, orange, sweet, woody

Bud Colour: Dull green

Pistil Colour: Orange

Trichome Density: Medium

Score Details

Appearance:	4 / 5
High Quality:	5 / 5
Aroma:	15 / 15
Flavour:	13 / 15
Bud Quality:	22 / 30
High Potency:	23 / 30

Overall Score: 82%

Cultivar Ranking: 148th

Slurricane

Cultivar/Product Information

Type/Effect: Indica - Medium Light
Legacy Name: Slurricane
Lineage: Do-Si-Dos x Purple Punch
Cannabinoids: 18.9% THC / <1% CBD
Terpenes: Caryophyllene, Myrcene, Humulene

First Impression

Review #404; January 14, 2021,

I forgot I was writing a review while I indulged in Edison's Slurricane. I was in a great mood and easily distracted from my task. My mind is pretty alive with thoughts, but it feels all over the place. I'm pretty decently high. Not too heavy, not too light, just right. This was great as my first of the day, not too impairing or relaxing for an indica, which is nice. After this, I'm excited to see what's next from Edison.

Observations

Aroma: Berry, earthy, fruity, herbal, sour, spicy, sweet

Flavour: Grassy, herbal, sweet, woody

Bud Colour: Dull green/purple

Pistil Colour: Brown/orange

Trichome Density: Medium-High

Score Details

Appearance:	4 / 5
High Quality:	5 / 5
Aroma:	13 / 15
Flavour:	10 / 15
Bud Quality:	25 / 30
High Potency:	21 / 30

Overall Score: 78%

Cultivar Ranking: 244th

The General

Cultivar/Product Information

Type/Effect: Sativa - Light
Legacy Name: Grapefruit GG
Lineage: Grapefruit x Original Glue
Cannabinoids: 21.1% THC / <1% CBD
Terpenes: Terpinolene, Limonene, Myrcene

First Impression

Review #316; August 23, 2020,

Uplifting and hazy, The General by Edison is perfect for a morning or afternoon that you want to spend wired. My mood is elevated; I feel much less tired than before consumption. I got lost on my phone texting people mid-review. I'm easily distracted, and feel social and euphoric. My brain is throbbing, and a strong head high is the culprit. Things are getting spacey and weird, so I'm finished writing now. Great stuff, one of Edison's best to date.

Observations

Aroma: Citrusy, earthy, fresh, fruity, grapefruit, herbal, sour

Flavour: Citrusy, grassy, herbal, woody

Bud Colour: Dull green

Pistil Colour: Orange

Trichome Density: Medium

Score Details

Appearance:	4 / 5
High Quality:	5 / 5
Aroma:	13 / 15
Flavour:	11 / 15
Bud Quality:	24 / 30
High Potency:	24 / 30

Overall Score: 81%

Cultivar Ranking: 173rd

Emerald Health

Overall Performance

Average Score: 74.88%

Brand Ranking: 58th Place

Brand Background

A group of scientists interested in the therapeutic benefits of cannabis formed Emerald Health in 2014. Producing for both the recreational and medical markets, Emerald focuses on midrange cannabis production. Beyond flower, the team at Emerald Health also works tirelessly to innovate and develop new products for their consumers.

The Emerald Health team grows cannabis in Richmond, BC, out of a two-greenhouse, 156,000 square-foot facility.

Other Cultivars: Grapefruit GG1

Cultivar Selection

Afghan Kush	74%
Black Widow	80%
Chemdog	82%
Durga Mata	77%
Hash Plant	71%
Jack the Ripper	79%
Timewarp A3	59%
White Rhino	77%

Afghan Kush

Cultivar/Product Information

Type/Effect: Indica - Neutral
Legacy Name: Afghan Kush
Lineage: Afghani Indica
Cannabinoids: 17% THC / <1% CBD
Terpenes: Myrcene, Caryophyllene, Linalool

First Impression

Review #121; September 25, 2019,

Afghan Kush from Emerald Health packs a stupefying and distracting punch. Although I seem to have a particular animation about my mood, my demeanour is anything but that. I feel relaxed and chill; my body is heavy, but my mind is racing, alert, and alive. Engaging, entertaining, fun, creative, just great.

Observations

Aroma: Earthy, fresh, grassy, herbal, sour, woody

Flavour: Earthy, funky, herbal, spicy, woody

Bud Colour: Light green/tan

Pistil Colour: Dark brown

Trichome Density: Medium

Score Details

Appearance:	4 / 5
High Quality:	5 / 5
Aroma:	11 / 15
Flavour:	10 / 15
Bud Quality:	23 / 30
High Potency:	21 / 30

Overall Score: 74%

Cultivar Ranking: 303rd

Black Widow

Cultivar/Product Information

Type/Effect: Hybrid - Light
Legacy Name: Black Widow
Lineage: Brazilian Sativa x South Indian Indica
Cannabinoids: 19.3% THC / <1% CBD
Terpenes: Myrcene, Limonene, Caryophyllene

First Impression

Review #279; June 27, 2020,

Emerald Health Therapeutics offers a potent, heady high in its take on Black Widow. The buzz is cerebral and physically present in the face and chest. Quite hazy and foggy mentally, but I'm not distracted or dumbfounded, and I can form thoughts. More relaxing than stimulating, the high is great for days off. An excellent quality, Emerald Health Therapeutics has improved much since last year.

Observations

Aroma: Bubblegum, floral, fresh, herbal, sour, sweet, woody

Flavour: Floral, fresh, herbal, woody

Bud Colour: Green/tan

Pistil Colour: Orange/tan

Trichome Density: Medium

Score Details

Appearance:	4 / 5
High Quality:	5 / 5
Aroma:	13 / 15
Flavour:	12 / 15
Bud Quality:	24 / 30
High Potency:	22 / 30

Overall Score: 80%

Cultivar Ranking: 205th

Chemdog

Cultivar/Product Information

Type/Effect: Sativa Hybrid - Medium Heavy
Legacy Name: Chemdog
Lineage: Dogbud
Cannabinoids: 22.3% THC / <1% CBD
Terpenes: Limonene, Linalool, Myrcene

First Impression

Review #272; June 10, 2020,

Emerald Health Therapeutics' Chemdog is a rather heavy sativa, my eyes are relaxed, and my mind is moving slowly. Mentally, my cognition is stumbling around in the dark - I fade out, then hit something, and jump back into a focused state, only to have myself fade out again. A distracting and distracted high that makes your mental focus dart around. I don't feel too bright on this stuff either. Chemdog is relaxing for a sativa, and it will make you forget about everything and cause you to recall very little - a great cerebral ride.

Observations

Aroma: Earthy, fresh, herbal, sour

Flavour: Earthy, herbal, woody

Bud Colour: Dark green

Pistil Colour: Brown/orange

Trichome Density: Medium

Score Details

Appearance:	4 / 5
High Quality:	5 / 5
Aroma:	12 / 15
Flavour:	11 / 15
Bud Quality:	25 / 30
High Potency:	25 / 30

Overall Score: 82%

Cultivar Ranking: 164th

Durga Mata

Cultivar/Product Information

Type/Effect: Indica - Heavy
Legacy Name: Durga Mata
Lineage: South Asian Indica
Cannabinoids: 19.1% THC / <1% CBD
Terpenes: Terpinolene, Limonene, Myrcene

First Impression

Review #276; June 23, 2020,

My experience with Emerald Health Therapeutics' Durga Mata was rudely interrupted by a work call but then livened up with some "Pirate Metal." The effects were mentally and physically relaxing, slightly sedating, and supremely heavy on the eyes. I'm pretty distracted from this review by the prospect of sleep, so off to dreamland, I go.

Observations

Aroma: Herbal, piney, pungent, sour, woody

Flavour: Herbal, pungent, sour, spicy, woody

Bud Colour: Green

Pistil Colour: Brown/orange

Trichome Density: Medium

Score Details

Appearance:	3 / 5
High Quality:	5 / 5
Aroma:	13 / 15
Flavour:	12 / 15
Bud Quality:	23 / 30
High Potency:	21 / 30

Overall Score: 77%

Cultivar Ranking: 258th

Hash Plant

Cultivar/Product Information

Type/Effect:	Indica - Medium Heavy
Legacy Name:	Hash Plant
Lineage:	Hash Plant x Northern Lights #1
Cannabinoids:	15.5% THC / <1% CBD
Terpenes:	Myrcene, Guaiol, Caryophyllene

First Impression

Review #120; September 19, 2019,

I'm thoroughly stoned and thoroughly distracted from my review by the TV while on Hash Plant by Emerald Health Therapeutics. Surprisingly heady for an indica, but not lacking physical sensation - my shoulders and legs are relaxed too. Great bud, but don't expect any sort of focus.

Observations

Aroma: Earthy, floral, fresh, herbal, piney, sour, sweet

Flavour: Earthy, funky, herbal, spicy, woody

Bud Colour: Green/tan

Pistil Colour: Orange

Trichome Density: Medium

Score Details

Appearance:	4 / 5
High Quality:	5 / 5
Aroma:	12 / 15
Flavour:	10 / 15
Bud Quality:	20 / 30
High Potency:	20 / 30

Overall Score: 71%

Cultivar Ranking: 329th

Jack the Ripper

Cultivar/Product Information

Type/Effect: Sativa - Medium Light
Legacy Name: Jack the Ripper
Lineage: Jack's Cleaner x Space Queen
Cannabinoids: 14.1% THC / <1% CBD
Terpenes: Terpinolene, Pinene, Limonene

First Impression

Review #305; August 6, 2020,

A bright, functional, daytime-oriented high is expected from Emerald Health Therapeutics' Jack the Ripper. The buzz is light and energetic, though a bit hazy at times, so I occasionally zone out. I still feel quite able to do stuff, maybe even hold a conversation and socialize! It smells and tastes lovely, and comes in large, fluffy buds. A moderate-potency bud I'd suggest to anyone looking to liven up a day.

Observations

Aroma: Citrusy, fresh, herbal, sour, spicy, sweet, woody

Flavour: Citrusy, grassy, herbal, lemon, sour, woody

Bud Colour: Light green

Pistil Colour: Orange

Trichome Density: Medium

Score Details

Appearance:	5 / 5
High Quality:	5 / 5
Aroma:	13 / 15
Flavour:	12 / 15
Bud Quality:	27 / 30
High Potency:	17 / 30

Overall Score: 79%

Cultivar Ranking: 228th

Timewarp A3

Cultivar/Product Information

Type/Effect: Hybrid - Super Light
Legacy Name: Timewarp
Cannabinoids: 9.7% THC / <1% CBD
Terpenes: Myrcene, Caryophyllene, Pinene

First Impression

Review #158; December 11, 2019,

The experience is a light and simple one, Timewarp A3 by Emerald Health Therapeutics is a decent low-THC option that delivers a mild head buzz and chest sensation. I wouldn't recommend this flower to anyone looking for a "seriously stoned" experience, but a day out on the town, a day at the gym, or a morning at home all sound great when accented by this bud's effects. My mood is elevated, and I'm mellow and worry-free, thanks to Timewarp A3.

Observations

Aroma: Berry, earthy, fruity, herbal, sweet

Flavour: Earthy, funky, herbal, sweet

Bud Colour: Dull green

Pistil Colour: Brown/tan

Trichome Density: Low

Score Details

Appearance:	4 / 5
High Quality:	5 / 5
Aroma:	12 / 15
Flavour:	9 / 15
Bud Quality:	15 / 30
High Potency:	14 / 30

Overall Score: 59%

Cultivar Ranking: 411th

White Rhino

Cultivar/Product Information

Type/Effect: Indica - Medium Heavy
Legacy Name: White Rhino
Lineage: "Unknown Indica" x White Widow
Cannabinoids: 18.7% THC / <1% CBD
Terpenes: Myrcene, Caryophyllene, Pinene

First Impression

Review #152; December 3, 2019,

Emerald Health Therapeutics did well with their grow of White Rhino; I feel relaxed, calm, serene, and pretty high as well. Not overly intense due to the nature of the effects, but the body sensation is certainly immense and potent. I find my thoughts coming quickly; I wouldn't say I'm "stoned," but "high" more accurately describes my state. I feel neither tired nor social, so I imagine this would be great flower for an evening alone. I envision a night on the couch with video games, maybe some snacks. White Rhino is a mellow dream.

Observations

Aroma: Grassy, herbal, sweet

Flavour: Funky, grassy, herbal, sweet

Bud Colour: Dull green

Pistil Colour: Brown/red

Trichome Density: Medium

Score Details

Appearance:	4 / 5
High Quality:	5 / 5
Aroma:	11 / 15
Flavour:	11 / 15
Bud Quality:	24 / 30
High Potency:	22 / 30

Overall Score: 77%

Cultivar Ranking: 266th

Farmstead

Overall Performance

Average Score: 85.00%

Brand Ranking: 23rd Place

Brand Background

Farmstead is a brand rooted in the Canadian heartland from the LP AgroGreens, a family-run cannabis company. With their extensive history of agricultural expertise, the cultivators at Farmstead pride themselves on experience and high standards. Utilizing "pharmaceutical processing and packaging technology," Farmstead consistently produces products that are both clean and of high quality.

The cannabis in Farmstead products is produced in the AgroGreens production facility in Macklin, Saskatchewan.

Other Cultivars: Cafe Racer, Canuck Cookies

Cultivar Selection

Colada	85%

Colada

Cultivar/Product Information

Type/Effect: Sativa Hybrid - Neutral
Legacy Name: Colada
Lineage: Banana OG x Do-Si-Dos x Papaya
Cannabinoids: 18.8% THC / <1% CBD
Terpenes: Myrcene, Farnesene, Limonene

First Impression

Review #329; September 10, 2020,

Colada, by Farmstead, is thought-provoking and mind-numbing at the same time; I keep switching between bouts of creativity and moments of zoning out. A mellow, soothing to the body/mind/soul hybrid that feels much larger than 19%. I feel like I could be high on this flower anywhere and anytime. However, I don't feel too active, chatty, or motivated, so I'll prefer to stay home. Colada is an experience of long-lasting impairment and a pretty decent introduction to Farmstead.

Observations

Aroma: Earthy, fresh, herbal, sweet, woody

Flavour: Earthy, fresh, grassy, herbal, woody

Bud Colour: Dull green/tan

Pistil Colour: Orange/tan

Trichome Density: Medium

Score Details

Appearance:	5 / 5
High Quality:	5 / 5
Aroma:	12 / 15
Flavour:	11 / 15
Bud Quality:	29 / 30
High Potency:	23 / 30

Overall Score: 85%

Cultivar Ranking: 119th

FIGR

Overall Performance

Average Score: 75.67%

Brand Ranking: 52nd Place

Brand Background

FIGR, a cannabis brand out of P.E.I., has a combined 150 years of growing experience, providing an excellent foundation to support its cannabis products. At FIGR, a 10-step growing process is followed to ensure consistency with their cannabis.

Buds of FIGR's are hand-trimmed, then machine-trimmed, and then cured. Jars of FIGR cannabis are also hand-packed.

Other Cultivars: Black Cherry Punch, CBD Shark, Kali Mist, Mandarin Cookies, Mmmosa, Powdered Doughnuts

Cultivar Selection

No. 7	72%
No. 8	76%
No. 14	79%

No. 7

Cultivar/Product Information

Type/Effect: Indica - Medium Light
Legacy Name: Afghan Kush
Lineage: Afghani Indica
Cannabinoids: 18.1% THC / <1% CBD
Terpenes: Pinene, Linalool, Caryophyllene

First Impression

Review #234; August 24, 2020,

A calm, if not relaxed experience, is in store for those who partake in FIGR's No. 7. My mind is pretty focused still, not drifting too much, and my thoughts are calm and coming at an average pace. I still find myself wandering around my room, headbanging to some "Ensiferum," as usual. This flower isn't overly inebriating, but I'd say I'm high. My body is very relaxed, as is my overall mood. However, I'm nowhere near tired, given that it is a more active-feeling Afghan Kush than anticipated.

Observations

Aroma: Earthy, grassy, herbal, sour, sweet

Flavour: Earthy, herbal, woody

Bud Colour: Dull green

Pistil Colour: Brown/red

Trichome Density: Medium

Score Details

Appearance:	3 / 5
High Quality:	5 / 5
Aroma:	11 / 15
Flavour:	11 / 15
Bud Quality:	22 / 30
High Potency:	20 / 30

Overall Score: 72%

Cultivar Ranking: 238th

No. 8

Cultivar/Product Information

Type/Effect: Sativa - Medium Light
Legacy Name: Green Crack
Lineage: Afghani Indica x Skunk #1
Cannabinoids: 18.8% THC / <1% CBD
Terpenes: Nerolidol, Pinene, Caryophyllene

First Impression

Review #317; August 16, 2020,

It's a pretty active, stoned experience from FIGR's No. 8. My head is buzzing, my body is loose and limber, and I'm amped-up, no longer yawning! My head high is strong and heavy - a pounding in my forehead highlights this. Not heavy in the sense that it is relaxing, just quite distracting. My concerns and useful thoughts fade away as I delve deeper into the bowl. Uplifting, energetic, and functional, No.8 is a solid choice for daytime consumption.

Observations

Aroma: Fresh, herbal, sour, spicy, sweet

Flavour: Earthy, fresh, grassy, herbal

Bud Colour: Dark brown/green

Pistil Colour: Brown

Trichome Density: Low-Medium

Score Details

Appearance:	4 / 5
High Quality:	5 / 5
Aroma:	12 / 15
Flavour:	10 / 15
Bud Quality:	22 / 30
High Potency:	23 / 30

Overall Score: 76%

Cultivar Ranking: 323rd

No. 14

Cultivar/Product Information

Type/Effect: Indica - Neutral
Legacy Name: Sour Lemon Kush
Cannabinoids: 20.7% THC / <1% CBD
Terpenes: Myrcene, Limonene, Linalool

First Impression

Review #312; April 9, 2020,

I'm zoned in on the TV on FIGR's No. 14, the music videos a distraction from everything, along with the potent, cerebrally active high. I'm pretty relaxed in both my body and mood. As the high intensifies, things become foggier, and I'm just staring at the page for minutes between sentences sometimes. This is terrific flower for daydreaming (or regular dreaming). I'm digging the music I've got playing, but not dancing along today, as I am way too chilled out.

Observations

Aroma: Cheese, earthy, floral, fruity, funky, herbal, piney, sour

Flavour: Cheese, floral, funky, herbal, sour

Bud Colour: Light green/tan

Pistil Colour: Orange

Trichome Density: Medium-High

Score Details

Appearance:	4 / 5
High Quality:	5 / 5
Aroma:	12 / 15
Flavour:	11 / 15
Bud Quality:	24 / 30
High Potency:	23 / 30

Overall Score: 79%

Cultivar Ranking: 276th

Fireside

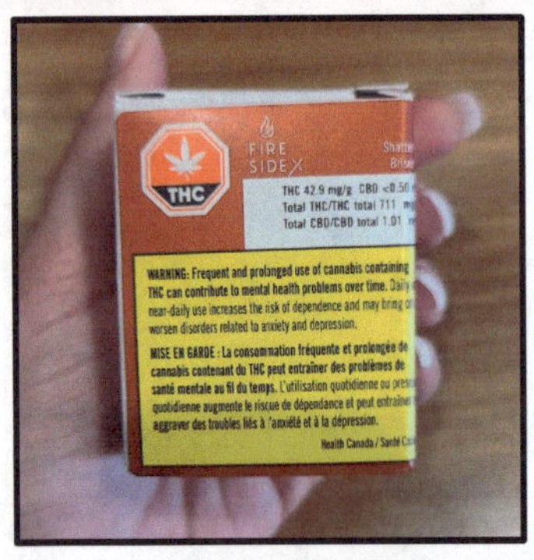

Overall Performance

Average Score: 87.50%

Brand Ranking: 18th Place

Brand Background

Fireside is a brand built upon quality, as well as connections. Through their cannabis, they hope to inspire consumers to connect in every sense of the word - with nature, others, and themselves.

Cannabis from Fireside is produced in small batches to help ensure a quality product.

Other Cultivars: Sour Kush, The Purps
Associated Brands: Canna Farms

Cultivar Selection

Sensi Star	85%
Wappa	90%

Sensi Star

Cultivar/Product Information

Type/Effect: Indica - Medium Heavy
Legacy Name: Sensi Star
Lineage: "Unknown Afghani"
Cannabinoids: 18.9% THC / <1% CBD
Terpenes: Myrcene, Caryophyllene, Limonene

First Impression

Review #185; February 5, 2020,

I was chilling in my room, reflecting on my reviews, introspectiveness inspired in me by the great Sensi Star from Fireside. Musing about things - my mind was open wide. Relaxing and thought-provoking, this is a great afternoon or evening-in cultivar for those also looking for a hefty head high. The flower quality from Fireside is always superb, and Sensi Star is no different.

Observations

Aroma: Citrusy, earthy, fruity, herbal, sour, sweet

Flavour: Citrusy, earthy, herbal, sour, woody

Bud Colour: Green

Pistil Colour: Brown/orange

Trichome Density: Medium

Score Details

Appearance:	4 / 5
High Quality:	5 / 5
Aroma:	14 / 15
Flavour:	12 / 15
Bud Quality:	27 / 30
High Potency:	23 / 30

Overall Score: 85%

Cultivar Ranking: 113th

Wappa

Cultivar/Product Information

Type/Effect: Indica - Medium Heavy
Legacy Name: Wappa
Lineage: "Unknown Cultivar" x Sweet Skunk
Cannabinoids: 18.7% THC / <1% CBD
Terpenes: Myrcene, Caryophyllene, Pinene

First Impression

Review #57; May 9, 2019,

One morning, while watching Austin Powers: International Man of Mystery, Dylan, our hero, decided to consume the legendary "Wappa" from Fireside. The power of the Wappa was too strong for the morning-time; he was overcome with creativity, and a powerful restful force, which took hold of his consciousness as he wrote his reviews. Dylan was compelled against his will by this powerful force to write his review as though it were a story. He knew this to be temporary but that the high would last far beyond the creative spark, for this was the great Fireside Wappa that he had consumed.

Observations

Aroma: Fruity, herbal, sweet

Flavour: Cheese, fresh, fruity, funky, sweet

Bud Colour: Green/purple

Pistil Colour: Orange

Trichome Density: Medium-High

Score Details

Appearance:	5 / 5
High Quality:	5 / 5
Aroma:	14 / 15
Flavour:	14 / 15
Bud Quality:	28 / 30
High Potency:	24 / 30

Overall Score: 90%

Cultivar Ranking: 63rd

Flowr

Overall Performance

Average Score: 75.33%

Brand Ranking: 54th Place

Brand Background

Established sometime before 2000, Flowr prides itself on cultivating cannabis that is "Grown True" and believe that that standard "defines their purpose." With a focus on well-grown, craft cannabis, Flowr produces out of the Okanagan Valley in BC.

From researching genetics to curated growing environments to a careful and thoughtful trim, Flowr goes an extra step further to "Grow True."

Other Cultivars: Black Cherry Punch, LB33, Sour Sis, Strawnana

Cultivar Selection

Cultivar	Score
Atomical Haze	70%
Delahaze	70%
Diesel	70%
Durga Mata	66%
Durga Mata 2 CBD	79%
Intergalactic Princess	74%
Pink Kush	88%
Sensi Star	79%
Tahoe OG	82%

Atomical Haze

Cultivar/Product Information

Type/Effect: Sativa - Light
Cannabinoids: 7.9% THC / <1% CBD

First Impression

Review #222; March 28, 2020,

The high from Flowr's Atomical Haze is almost all in the head, except for this full-body calm I'm feeling. My mind and mood are alive and motivated, but my eyes reveal through their squinting and redness that I'm hazy, under the spell of this impressive low-THC flower. Given the aroma's strength and the intensity of the high, I'd assume a ridiculous terpene content here is responsible for the bulk of what I'm feeling, which I love, of course - one of Flowr's best low-THC cultivars.

Observations

Aroma: Citrusy, diesel, earthy, herbal, sour, spicy

Flavour: Citrusy, earthy, sour, spicy, woody

Bud Colour: Light green

Pistil Colour: Brown/orange

Trichome Density: Low-Medium

Score Details

Appearance:	4 / 5
High Quality:	5 / 5
Aroma:	13 / 15
Flavour:	11 / 15
Bud Quality:	24 / 30
High Potency:	13 / 30

Overall Score: 70%

Cultivar Ranking: 337th

Delahaze

Cultivar/Product Information

Type/Effect: Sativa - Super Light
Legacy Name: Delahaze
Lineage: Lemon Skunk x Mango Haze
Cannabinoids: 8.5% THC / <1% CBD

First Impression

Review #211; March 13, 2020,

Flowr's Delahaze is certainly not the most potent variety of this cultivar I've had, but one of the more terpy ones. It's incredibly distinct, sour, and tangy in the aroma and flavour. The high is very light, like a cerebrally stimulating balanced flower. I feel relatively focused and motivated, ready for the day now that I've had my session with Delahaze. Not bad for <10% THC flower, decent in fact.

Observations

Aroma: Citrusy, herbal, pungent, sour, woody

Flavour: Citrusy, herbal, pungent, sour, woody

Bud Colour: Dull green

Pistil Colour: Brown/orange

Trichome Density: Low-Medium

Score Details

Appearance:	4 / 5
High Quality:	5 / 5
Aroma:	14 / 15
Flavour:	12 / 15
Bud Quality:	24 / 30
High Potency:	11 / 30

Overall Score: 70%

Cultivar Ranking: 335th

Diesel

Cultivar/Product Information

Type/Effect: Sativa Hybrid - Medium Light
Cannabinoids: 7.9% THC / <1% CBD

First Impression

Review #141; November 19, 2019,

Diesel by Flowr is a light and mellow buzz, ideal for a morning or afternoon, tending to responsibilities or taking time to yourself. Just a solid, middle-of-the-road high on this one, offering mood elevation, focus and calm. Great quality option for light to moderate consumers.

Observations

Aroma: Fruity, herbal, sour, sweet

Flavour: Funky, herbal, sour

Bud Colour: Light green

Pistil Colour: Orange

Trichome Density: Low

Score Details

Appearance:	5 / 5
High Quality:	5 / 5
Aroma:	13 / 15
Flavour:	10 / 15
Bud Quality:	24 / 30
High Potency:	13 / 30

Overall Score: 70%

Cultivar Ranking: 338th

Durga Mata

Cultivar/Product Information

Type/Effect: Indica - Medium Light
Legacy Name: Durga Mata
Lineage: South Asian Indica
Cannabinoids: 6.2% THC / <1% CBD

First Impression

Review #159; December 11, 2019,

Flowr offers a light and chill indica experience in their version of Durga Mata. My body feels loose, and my thoughts are fluid. My mood is uplifted and relaxed, and this is a great couch-lock-free evening option that shouldn't overstimulate before bedtime. Good flower from Flowr. Though much too mild for the regular stoner, should satisfy less frequent consumers.

Observations

Aroma: Fruity, herbal, piney, sour, sweet

Flavour: Herbal, pungent, sour, spicy

Bud Colour: Dark green

Pistil Colour: Brown/red

Trichome Density: Low-Medium

Score Details

Appearance:	4 / 5
High Quality:	5 / 5
Aroma:	12 / 15
Flavour:	10 / 15
Bud Quality:	23 / 30
High Potency:	12 / 30

Overall Score: 66%

Cultivar Ranking: 385th

Durga Mata 2 CBD

Cultivar/Product Information

Type/Effect: Indica Hybrid - Neutral
Legacy Name: Durga Mata 2
Lineage: "High CBD Cultivar" x Durga Mata
Cannabinoids: 5.8% THC / 11.5% CBD

First Impression

Review #168; December 29, 2019,

Flowr has the best rendition of Durga Mata 2 CBD I've had on the recreational market. Everything I want in an indica balanced flower: calm, focus, serenity, peace, and mellow relaxation. Great for anytime you want to unwind and feel well but can't afford to be intensely high. Another decent flower from Flowr.

Observations

Aroma: Citrusy, herbal, sour

Flavour: Citrusy, herbal, sour, woody

Bud Colour: Dark green

Pistil Colour: Orange

Trichome Density: Medium

Score Details

Appearance:	4 / 5
High Quality:	5 / 5
Aroma:	13 / 15
Flavour:	12 / 15
Bud Quality:	24 / 30
High Potency:	21 / 30

Overall Score: 79%

Cultivar Ranking: 234th

Intergalactic Princess

Cultivar/Product Information

Type/Effect: Hybrid - Super Light
Cannabinoids: <1% THC / 6.2% CBD

First Impression

Review #238; April 14, 2020,

Flowr's Intergalactic Princess is a serene, grounded experience that provides a sense of calm and wellbeing. Mentally, I'm active and functional. Physically I'm relaxed, limber, loose. A higher-quality way to get your CBD, and though I could do with a higher CBD %, the experience is not lacking.

Observations

Aroma: Floral, fruity, herbal, spicy, sweet

Flavour: Floral, fruity, herbal, sweet

Bud Colour: Dull green/tan

Pistil Colour: Orange

Trichome Density: Low

Score Details

Appearance:	5 / 5
High Quality:	5 / 5
Aroma:	13 / 15
Flavour:	12 / 15
Bud Quality:	25 / 30
High Potency:	14 / 30

Overall Score: 74%

Cultivar Ranking: 293rd

Pink Kush

Cultivar/Product Information

Type/Effect: Indica - Super Heavy
Legacy Name: Pink Kush
Lineage: OG Kush
Cannabinoids: 23.2% THC / <1% CBD
Terpenes: Caryophyllene, Nerolidol, Limonene

First Impression

Review #192; February 12, 2020,

I got into a massive coughing fit midway through a potent, powerful, pungent Pink Kush by Flowr. The smell and taste of this bud is classic Pink Kush but amped right up, and terpene content must be massive like the THC content. I'm stoned out of my mind, useless. I forgot how to breathe for a second. I'm super in my head, but nothing is going on; I'm comatose. Waves of sensation overwhelm my body as I write this review; a full, massive, intense high is what this Pink Kush will provide; brace yourself.

Observations

Aroma: Diesel, earthy, fresh, herbal, minty, piney, pungent

Flavour: Diesel, earthy, funky, piney, pungent

Bud Colour: Dark green/purple

Pistil Colour: Brown/orange

Trichome Density: Medium-High

Score Details

Appearance:	4 / 5
High Quality:	5 / 5
Aroma:	13 / 15
Flavour:	13 / 15
Bud Quality:	25 / 30
High Potency:	28 / 30

Overall Score: 88%

Cultivar Ranking: 83rd

Sensi Star

Cultivar/Product Information

Type/Effect: Indica - Medium Heavy
Legacy Name: Sensi Star
Lineage: "Unknown Afghani"
Cannabinoids: 14.2% THC / <1% CBD

First Impression

Review #236; April 13, 2020,

Sensi Star by Flowr is undoubtedly one of the most potent 14% THC flowers I've had and also one that induced the most coughing. Much more substantial of a high than anticipated. Heavy on the mind and body, but not too slowing on the mind - my thoughts are coming quickly. I wish to collapse into the nearest couch/chair/bed and just zone out on this cultivar. This is one of my favourite Sensi Star varieties. Great job, Flowr.

Observations

Aroma: Diesel, earthy, herbal, pungent, spicy, sweet

Flavour: Earthy, floral, herbal, spicy, woody

Bud Colour: Dull brown/green

Pistil Colour: Brown/orange

Trichome Density: Low

Score Details

Appearance:	4 / 5
High Quality:	5 / 5
Aroma:	12 / 15
Flavour:	11 / 15
Bud Quality:	26 / 30
High Potency:	21 / 30

Overall Score: 79%

Cultivar Ranking: 235th

Tahoe OG

Cultivar/Product Information

Type/Effect: Sativa Hybrid - Medium Heavy
Legacy Name: Tahoe OG
Lineage: OG Kush
Cannabinoids: 19.5% THC / <1% CBD
Terpenes: Pinene, Myrcene, Nerolidol

First Impression

Review #296; July 25, 2020,

My mood is calm, and my spirits uplifted on Flowr's Tahoe OG. I'm a little spaced out, and my mind is wandering from time to time. Not a particularly motivational sativa in energy or mood; I feel like chilling out rather than accomplishing something. Hazy and foggy for sure, my thoughts come slowly, and my eyes are heavy. Some great ideas managed to make it through the cerebral mist obscuring my cognition - this cultivar is also inspiring and creative. Tahoe OG was a super well-rounded and superb experience, from an unassuming and average-seeming flower by Flowr.

Observations

Aroma: Floral, herbal, sour, spicy, sweet

Flavour: Earthy, floral, herbal, sour, spicy, woody

Bud Colour: Dark green

Pistil Colour: Orange/tan

Trichome Density: Medium

Score Details

Appearance:	4 / 5
High Quality:	5 / 5
Aroma:	12 / 15
Flavour:	12 / 15
Bud Quality:	26 / 30
High Potency:	23 / 30

Overall Score: 82%

Cultivar Ranking: 163rd

Good Buds

Overall Performance

Average Score: 92.33%

Brand Ranking: 3rd Place

Brand Background

Good Buds are a small-batch, FVOPA certified organic premium cannabis producer from Salt Spring Island, BC. The company was founded by brothers Tyler and Alex Rumi, and their mission is simple: "to deliver you the stickiest nugs available."

Good Buds cannabis is grown organically, without any pesticides, in living organic soil. All plants are hang-dried and slow-cured and then finished with either a hand-trim or hand-roll for their pre-rolled products.

Other Cultivars: Dosi Melon, Glueranguta n

Cultivar Selection

Mango Taffie	90%
Salty God	93%
Sapphire OG	94%

Mango Taffie

Cultivar/Product Information

Type/Effect: Sativa - Medium Light
Legacy Name: Mango Taffie
Lineage: Hawaiian x OG LA Affie
Cannabinoids: 17.6% THC / <1% CBD
Terpenes: Caryophyllene, Myrcene, Terpinolene

First Impression

Review #178; January 11, 2020,

Mango Taffie by Good Buds is a treat. It heightened my mood so far that I was entirely immersed in what I was watching on TV… almost some "Pleasantville" stuff going on here, crazy. Or, at least it felt like it with the intense high I experienced. This is a hazy buzz ideal for social scenarios or creative endeavours. Great bud, flavour, aroma, and quality-wise. Definitely a great start for a more than just "Good" brand.

Observations

Aroma: Citrusy, fruity, lemon, mango, sour, sweet

Flavour: Citrusy, herbal, lemon, sour, woody

Bud Colour: Light green

Pistil Colour: Orange

Trichome Density: Medium-High

Score Details

Appearance:	4 / 5
High Quality:	5 / 5
Aroma:	15 / 15
Flavour:	15 / 15
Bud Quality:	29 / 30
High Potency:	22 / 30

Overall Score: 90%

Cultivar Ranking: 57th

Salty God

Cultivar/Product Information

Type/Effect:	Indica - Medium Light
Legacy Name:	Salty God
Lineage:	God
Cannabinoids:	20.5% THC / <1% CBD
Terpenes:	Ocimene, Linalool, Limonene

First Impression

Review #246; April 23, 2020,

Good Buds' Salty God - an epic, long-lasting and potent indica flower - paired well with an equally epic and long-lasting song by Rush, "Natural Science." Fantastic work here and an excellent cultivar indeed. I am a massive fan of both the cultivar and the music, making my mood joyful, carefree, and creative. I'm calm and serene, relaxed and rejuvenated. Given its supreme excellence, this flower is worthy of a title like "God."

Observations

Aroma: Citrusy, earthy, fruity, pungent, sweet

Flavour: Diesel, earthy, funky, pungent, spicy, sweet, woody

Bud Colour: Green

Pistil Colour: Brown/orange

Trichome Density: Medium-High

Score Details

Appearance:	4 / 5
High Quality:	5 / 5
Aroma:	15 / 15
Flavour:	14 / 15
Bud Quality:	30 / 30
High Potency:	25 / 30

Overall Score: 93%

Cultivar Ranking: 21st

Sapphire OG

Cultivar/Product Information

Type/Effect: Indica - Heavy
Legacy Name: Sapphire OG
Lineage: Afghan Kush x OG Kush x OG Kush
Cannabinoids: 21.2% THC / <1% CBD
Terpenes: Caryophyllene, Limonene, Linalool

First Impression

Review #247; April 24, 2020,

The character of Good Buds Sapphire OG has me at a loss for words, and it is truly unique. The cheesiest, funkiest, stinkiest cultivar I've had in a bit. It induces a potent, relaxing, "stoned out in space" feeling that is to die for. I'm ready to sink into some munchies and my bed; I'm impaired to sedation. My eyes are heavy, and my vision is fading as my eyes lose focus on the page. Standing is difficult; I'm not the most coordinated under the spell of Sapphire OG… good job, Good Buds.

Observations

Aroma: Cheese, earthy, fruity, funky, pungent, sour

Flavour: Cheese, earthy, funky, herbal, pungent, spicy, woody

Bud Colour: Green/purple

Pistil Colour: Brown/red

Trichome Density: Medium-High

Score Details

Appearance:	5 / 5
High Quality:	5 / 5
Aroma:	15 / 15
Flavour:	14 / 15
Bud Quality:	29 / 30
High Potency:	26 / 30

Overall Score: 94%

Cultivar Ranking: 17th

Good Supply

Overall Performance

Average Score: 73.33%

Brand Ranking: 64th Place

Brand Background

Good Supply is a value-oriented cannabis brand from Aphria, one of Canada's largest LPs (before being acquired by Tilray). The brand focused initially on cheaper 3.5g flower products but has since moved up to mainly supplying 28g units.

Good Supply cannabis is mass-produced via a greenhouse grow in Leamington, Ontario.

Other Cultivars:	Golden Goat, Grand Daddy Purps, Monkey Butter, Pineapple Express, Sour Kush, Starwalker Kush, Sweet Berry Kush, Tangie Green
Associated Brands:	Broken Coast, Canaca, Grail, Marley Natural, Riff, Solei

Cultivar Selection

Jean Guy	72%
Monkey Glue	76%
Royal Highness	72%

Jean Guy

Cultivar/Product Information

Type/Effect: Sativa - Neutral
Legacy Name: Jean Guy
Lineage: White Widow
Cannabinoids: 19.7% THC / <1% CBD
Terpenes: Caryophyllene, Guaiol, Limonene

First Impression

Review #41; April 25, 2019,

Mental alertness is high, but response time is low; Good Supply's Jean Guy is impairing. A potent cerebral experience that'll leave you baked but still alert and aware. I'm also feeling creative, hungry, and easily distracted. Jean Guy is worth trying when done well, and Good Supply has done well with their version of this French-Canadian classic.

Observations

Aroma: Chocolate, earthy, herbal, sour, spicy, sweet

Flavour: Herbal, pungent, sour, spicy

Bud Colour: Green

Pistil Colour: Brown/orange

Trichome Density: Low

Score Details

Appearance:	3 / 5
High Quality:	5 / 5
Aroma:	12 / 15
Flavour:	9 / 15
Bud Quality:	20 / 30
High Potency:	23 / 30

Overall Score: 72%

Cultivar Ranking: 319th

Monkey Glue

Cultivar/Product Information

Type/Effect: Hybrid - Neutral
Cannabinoids: 16.6% THC / <1% CBD
Terpenes: Caryophyllene, Nerolidol, Humulene

First Impression

Review #266; May 26, 2020,

It's mellow but far from relaxed; the high from Good Supply's Monkey Glue feels very lively to me, uplifting and euphoric. There is a slight mental fog, but it is not too impairing to my thought process. Not necessarily a cultivar that motivates me to accomplish anything meaningful, but one inspiring me to indulge in whatever I feel is best for the moment. Right now, that's a long walk with my doggo, Kally, and a bunch of pizza. Solid stuff from Good Supply, something I'm used to at this point.

Observations

Aroma: Earthy, floral, herbal, pungent, sweet

Flavour: Earthy, floral, grassy, herbal, sweet

Bud Colour: Green

Pistil Colour: Orange/tan

Trichome Density: Medium

Score Details

Appearance:	4 / 5
High Quality:	5 / 5
Aroma:	12 / 15
Flavour:	12 / 15
Bud Quality:	23 / 30
High Potency:	20 / 30

Overall Score: 76%

Cultivar Ranking: 272nd

Royal Highness

Cultivar/Product Information

Type/Effect: Hybrid - Neutral
Cannabinoids: 23.1% THC / <1% CBD
Terpenes: Myrcene, Limonene, Caryophyllene

First Impression

Review #254; May 3, 2020,

Royal Highness by Good Supply is a medium potency, high THC, clear-headed, but slow high. I feel sluggish, but my thoughts are clear, and my ability to think is unimpeded. I feel neither up nor down on this flower, just high. A good supply from Good Supply, indeed.

Observations

Aroma: Diesel, earthy, grassy, herbal, pungent, sour, sweet

Flavour: Earthy, grassy, herbal, pungent, sour

Bud Colour: Green

Pistil Colour: Brown

Trichome Density: Medium

Score Details

Appearance:	4 / 5
High Quality:	5 / 5
Aroma:	10 / 15
Flavour:	9 / 15
Bud Quality:	22 / 30
High Potency:	22 / 30

Overall Score: 72%

Cultivar Ranking: 324th

Grail

Overall Performance

Average Score: 81.00%

Brand Ranking: 36th Place

Brand Background

Grail operates out of Vancouver Island, BC, producing a premium flower. Grail cannabis was founded in the spirit of "celebrating the journey" and the "quest for the unknown."

Operating indoors in pristine environments, Grail utilizes BC cultivar genetics carefully selected to provide the best quality in cannabis and experience.

Other Cultivars:	Purps
Associated Brands:	Broken Coast, Canaca, Good Supply, Marley Natural, Riff, Solei

Cultivar Selection

Headband	81%
Pink Kush	82%
Rockstar	80%

Headband

Cultivar/Product Information

Type/Effect:	Sativa Hybrid - Heavy
Legacy Name:	Headband
Lineage:	OG Kush x Sour Diesel
Cannabinoids:	23.6% THC / <1% CBD
Terpenes:	Caryophyllene, Nerolidol, Limonene

First Impression

Review #114; September 13, 2019,

A strong, heady, heavy, stoned feeling high to rival the best is what you'll get from Grail's Headband. I'm crazy stoned from this potent flower and about to go to a family dinner; I hope I'm not too far gone - a genuine concern given the intense and powerful high. Excellent bud, but not for those new to THC.

Observations

Aroma: Cheese, earthy, funky, herbal, pungent, sour

Flavour: Earthy, funky, herbal, sour, woody

Bud Colour: Dark green

Pistil Colour: Brown/red

Trichome Density: Low-Medium

Score Details

Appearance:	3 / 5
High Quality:	5 / 5
Aroma:	12 / 15
Flavour:	9 / 15
Bud Quality:	25 / 30
High Potency:	27 / 30

Overall Score: 81%

Cultivar Ranking: 188th

Pink Kush

Cultivar/Product Information

Type/Effect: Indica Hybrid - Heavy
Legacy Name: Pink Kush
Lineage: OG Kush
Cannabinoids: 23.4% THC / <1% CBD
Terpenes: Limonene, Caryophyllene, Linalool

First Impression

Review #286; July 9, 2020,

Grail's Pink Kush is a relaxing and heady high that will leave you stoned, heavy-eyed, and low-energy. I want to collapse into my couch after a bowl of this potent bud. The high is cerebral mainly, with a pulsing sensation throughout my head and body. My mind is racing, unfocused, and zoned out; I'm distracted thinking about nothing. Typical stoner stuff, inspired by Pink Kush - time to go chill.

Observations

Aroma: Earthy, fresh, grassy, herbal, piney, pungent, sour

Flavour: Earthy, funky, grassy, herbal, piney, pungent, woody

Bud Colour: Dark green

Pistil Colour: Brown/orange

Trichome Density: Medium

Score Details

Appearance:	4 / 5
High Quality:	5 / 5
Aroma:	12 / 15
Flavour:	12 / 15
Bud Quality:	25 / 30
High Potency:	24 / 30

Overall Score: 82%

Cultivar Ranking: 162nd

Rockstar

Cultivar/Product Information

Type/Effect: Indica - Heavy
Legacy Name: Rockstar
Lineage: Rock Bud x Sensi Star
Cannabinoids: 20.3% THC / <1% CBD
Terpenes: Caryophyllene, Terpinolene, Limonene

First Impression

Review #7; April 8, 2019,

I was exhausted before writing this review, and now, I can't tell if I'm ready for bed, some munchies, or both. Grail's Rockstar is heavy and appetite-inducing. This potent indica will knock you on your ass if you're not careful. It's a powerful one; I blanked for several minutes on what to write - this is great cannabis.

Observations

Aroma: Cheese, fresh, funky, grassy, herbal, piney, pungent

Flavour: Herbal, piney

Bud Colour: Dark green

Pistil Colour: Brown/red

Trichome Density: Medium

Score Details

Appearance:	4 / 5
High Quality:	5 / 5
Aroma:	12 / 15
Flavour:	10 / 15
Bud Quality:	25 / 30
High Potency:	24 / 30

Overall Score: 80%

Cultivar Ranking: 214th

Habitat

Overall Performance

Average Score: 90.00%

Brand Ranking: 11th Place

Brand Background

Habitat cultivates in Chase, BC, producing more than just cannabis from their 1,000 square-foot micro-cultivation facility. Rudi Schiebel and Laine Keyes, the founders of Habitat, saw an opportunity in 2018's legalization of cannabis to combine their passions for sustainability, cannabis, and agriculture. As an aquaponics-utilizing organic producer, Habitat grows cannabis and raises coho salmon simultaneously in the same process.

Habitat focuses on small-batch craft practices to ensure the highest quality in their products and has no interest in deviating from that model in the future.

Cultivar Selection

Cake	90%

Cake

Cultivar/Product Information

Type/Effect:	Hybrid - Heavy
Legacy Name:	Cake
Lineage:	Do-Si-Dos x Mandarin Sunset
Cannabinoids:	21.6% THC / <1% CBD
Terpenes:	Limonene, Myrcene, Caryophyllene

First Impression

Review #327; September 5, 2020,

Habitat's first addition to the recreational market, Cake, is an excellent premium flower in both quality and effect. I'm mentally zoned-out and foggy, as this is a great way to shut down the mind. My brain is experiencing a relaxing pounding sensation from the high, as are my torso and limbs. It's a heavy cultivar overall, and I definitely could see chilling with some tunes and munchies for a while, stoned on Cake. Thoroughly enjoyable.

Observations

Aroma: Diesel, earthy, fresh, grassy, herbal, pungent, sweet

Flavour: Earthy, fresh, grassy, herbal, piney, sweet, woody

Bud Colour: Dull green

Pistil Colour: Orange/tan

Trichome Density: High

Score Details

Appearance:	5 / 5
High Quality:	5 / 5
Aroma:	13 / 15
Flavour:	13 / 15
Bud Quality:	30 / 30
High Potency:	24 / 30

Overall Score: 90%

Cultivar Ranking: 66th

Haven St.

Overall Performance

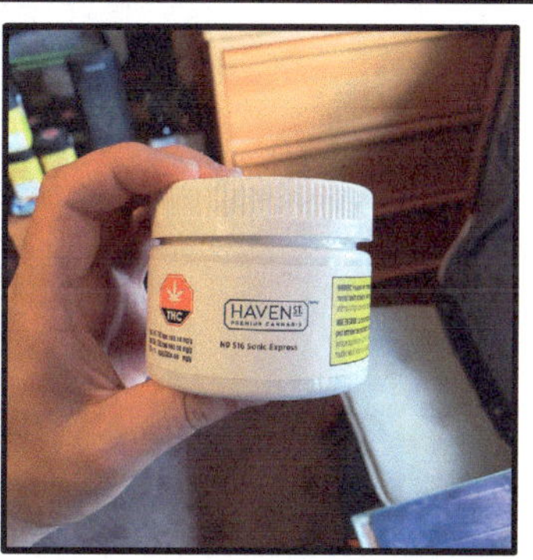

Average Score: 76.92%

Brand Ranking: 49th Place

Brand Background

Haven St. is a midrange cannabis brand operating out of Ontario. They have offered various products, including flower, since early legalization. Their flower catalogue spans a variety of different cannabis experiences, outlined by the brand's "5-block address system" for categorizing their products.

Cannabis from Haven St. is grown in large indoor greenhouse facilities.

Other Cultivars: Banana Punch, Retrograde, Secret Address, Lemon Pound Cake

Cultivar Selection

Cultivar	Score	Cultivar	Score
Beach Hammock	73%	Indigo Daze	86%
Big Dipper	80%	Midnight Jam	78%
Blue Comet	80%	Napali CBD	63%
Blueberry Kush	54%	Noisy Neighbour	93%
Cosmic Thunder	80%	Sonic Express	80%
Couch Surf	72%	Twilight	84%

Beach Hammock

Cultivar/Product Information

Type/Effect: Hybrid - Medium Light
Cannabinoids: 5.3% THC / 11.2% CBD

First Impression

Review #119; September 18, 2019,

Beach Hammock by Haven St. is a weird name at first, but I feel like I just woke up from a nice rest in a hammock. I'm calm, peaceful, rested, and pretty motivated and hazy - an interesting mood. A pretty low-intensity high, but enough to elevate the mood and senses. A solid, balanced flower.

Observations

Aroma: Earthy, floral, herbal, spicy, sweet

Flavour: Earthy, floral, fresh, herbal, spicy

Bud Colour: Dark brown/green

Pistil Colour: Orange/tan

Trichome Density: Low-Medium

Score Details

Appearance:	4 / 5
High Quality:	5 / 5
Aroma:	12 / 15
Flavour:	11 / 15
Bud Quality:	19 / 30
High Potency:	22 / 30

Overall Score: 73%

Cultivar Ranking: 312th

Big Dipper

Cultivar/Product Information

Type/Effect: Indica Hybrid - Heavy
Legacy Name: Pink Kush
Lineage: OG Kush
Cannabinoids: 19.3% THC / <1% CBD
Terpenes: Caryophyllene, Linalool, Limonene

First Impression

Review #180; January 16, 2020,

I'm heavily stoned on Haven St.'s Big Dipper. Waves of sensation are overwhelming my head and chest, a physical assault that should confine you to any furniture and melt you away. I find it hard to focus between sentences - this stuff is not for before meaningful work is done. A relaxing and potent high, Big Dipper gets the job done well.

Observations

Aroma: Chocolate, earthy, herbal, piney, sour, spicy

Flavour: Earthy, herbal, piney, pungent, spicy

Bud Colour: Dark green

Pistil Colour: Brown/orange

Trichome Density: Low-Medium

Score Details

Appearance:	4 / 5
High Quality:	5 / 5
Aroma:	13 / 15
Flavour:	9 / 15
Bud Quality:	25 / 30
High Potency:	24 / 30

Overall Score: 80%

Cultivar Ranking: 206th

Blue Comet

Cultivar/Product Information

Type/Effect: Sativa Hybrid - Neutral
Legacy Name: Lemon Z
Lineage: Lemon Skunk x Zkittlez
Cannabinoids: 17.1% THC / <1% CBD
Terpenes: Myrcene, Pinene, Caryophyllene

First Impression

Review #124; September 26, 2019,

I'm pretty spaced out on Blue Comet by Haven St. - they did it right with this flower. I had two nugs in my eighth. One was a 3.0g, a colossal bud with excellent quality and sensory features. The high is not too relaxing, not too stimulating, but mood-elevating, mellowing, and hazy. Worth a try for sure.

Observations

Aroma: Earthy, fresh, fruity, grass, herbal, sweet

Flavour: Earthy, fresh, funky, grass, herbal, spicy

Bud Colour: Dull green/tan

Pistil Colour: Orange

Trichome Density: Medium

Score Details

Appearance:	5 / 5
High Quality:	5 / 5
Aroma:	13 / 15
Flavour:	10 / 15
Bud Quality:	26 / 30
High Potency:	21 / 30

Overall Score: 80%

Cultivar Ranking: 199th

Blueberry Kush

Cultivar/Product Information

Type/Effect: Indica - Medium Light
Legacy Name: Shishkaberry
Lineage: "Unknown Afghani" x DJ Short Blueberry
Cannabinoids: 11% THC / <1% CBD
Terpenes: Pinene, Caryophyllene, Limonene

First Impression

Review #53; May 7, 2019,

For a lighter, mellow experience, Haven St. offers its take on Shishkaberry. The flavour isn't great, but the mild-medium high is decent. I feel at peace, very chill, and I feel a powerful urge to pet my animals and give people hugs, and I'm pretty uplifted and cheery. For new consumers or fans of lighter cannabis, Shishkaberry should provide a worthwhile experience.

Observations

Aroma: Berry, floral, fruity, sweet

Flavour: Berry, earthy, herbal, woody

Bud Colour: Light green

Pistil Colour: Orange/tan

Trichome Density: Low-Medium

Score Details

Appearance:	3 / 5
High Quality:	4 / 5
Aroma:	10 / 15
Flavour:	7 / 15
Bud Quality:	20 / 30
High Potency:	10 / 30

Overall Score: 54%

Cultivar Ranking: 419th

Cosmic Thunder

Cultivar/Product Information

Type/Effect: Indica Hybrid - Heavy
Legacy Name: Cold Creek Kush
Lineage: Chemdog x MK Ultra
Cannabinoids: 24.3% THC / <1% CBD
Terpenes: Myrcene, Ocimene, Caryophyllene

First Impression

Review #174; January 6, 2020,

Oh, Haven St., the name Cosmic Thunder makes no sense (in space, no one can hear you cough). While stoned on this flower, I struggle to hold my head and body upright, and thinking is a chore. My eyes and body are heavy, exceptionally so. My mind is alive but pretty much rendered useless by the epic potency of this flower. Zoning out is likely on this flower.

Observations

Aroma: Citrusy, floral, fresh, grass, herbal, sour

Flavour: Earthy, funky, herbal, spicy, woody

Bud Colour: Light green

Pistil Colour: Orange

Trichome Density: Medium

Score Details

Appearance:	4 / 5
High Quality:	5 / 5
Aroma:	13 / 15
Flavour:	11 / 15
Bud Quality:	20 / 30
High Potency:	27 / 30

Overall Score: 80%

Cultivar Ranking: 201st

Couch Surf

Cultivar/Product Information

Type/Effect: Indica - Neutral
Legacy Name: Afghan Kush
Lineage: Afghani Indica
Cannabinoids: 17.1% THC / <1% CBD
Terpenes: Limonene, Pinene, Myrcene

First Impression

Review #190; February 10, 2020,

Haven St.'s Couch Surf makes me want to sprawl out on the couch and take in a movie with some company. It's an ideal evening-in option if socialization is in mind, as it wasn't so strong that I would have trouble speaking or communicating effectively. An active cerebral high is present, but my body is relaxed and loose from this great mid-range THC option.

Observations

Aroma: Cheese, funky, herbal, sour

Flavour: Cheese, grass, herbal, sour, sweet

Bud Colour: Light green

Pistil Colour: Brown/red

Trichome Density: Low-Medium

Score Details

Appearance:	3 / 5
High Quality:	5 / 5
Aroma:	12 / 15
Flavour:	12 / 15
Bud Quality:	20 / 30
High Potency:	20 / 30

Overall Score: 72%

Cultivar Ranking: 320th

Indigo Haze

Cultivar/Product Information

Type/Effect: Indica - Heavy
Legacy Name: Sensi Star
Lineage: "Unknown Afghani"
Cannabinoids: 25.8% THC / <1% CBD
Terpenes: Myrcene, Limonene, Caryophyllene

First Impression

Review #394; December 30, 2020.

Haven St.'s Indigo Daze was some of the densest, rock-hard flower I've seen yet, and the 3.5g looked like 2g. Super potent, this flower is not for beginners. It is a cerebral meltdown of a head high paired with heavy eyes and a heavier body, but is not tiring, just absurdly relaxing. An excellent option for those seeking a strong couch-lock sensation. Some of the most powerful flower from Haven St. I've had.

Observations

Aroma: Earthy, herbal, piney, pungent, sweet

Flavour: Earthy, herbal, woody

Bud Colour: Dark green

Pistil Colour: Brown

Trichome Density: Medium

Score Details

Appearance:	4 / 5
High Quality:	5 / 5
Aroma:	13 / 15
Flavour:	10 / 15
Bud Quality:	28 / 30
High Potency:	26 / 30

Overall Score: 86%

Cultivar Ranking: 107th

Midnight Jam

Cultivar/Product Information

Type/Effect: Indica - Heavy
Legacy Name: 8 Ball Kush
Lineage: Bubba Kush x King Kush
Cannabinoids: 21.2% THC / <1% CBD
Terpenes: Caryophyllene, Myrcene, Humulene

First Impression

Review #376; December 5, 2020,

I had Haven St.'s Midnight Jam a tad early to live up to the name, but this would be my jam at midnight. Heavy on the body and mind, my thoughts slowly come to me, and the motivation to accomplish anything with my evening is gone. I just want to feast and then lie down. Not a great option for waking and baking, but perfect for counting some sheep, though you'll likely lose count.

Observations

Aroma: Fresh, herbal, sour, spicy, sweet, woody

Flavour: Earthy, fresh, funky, grassy, herbal, woody

Bud Colour: Dark green

Pistil Colour: Brown/orange

Trichome Density: Low-Medium

Score Details

Appearance:	4 / 5
High Quality:	5 / 5
Aroma:	13 / 15
Flavour:	11 / 15
Bud Quality:	22 / 30
High Potency:	23 / 30

Overall Score: 78%

Cultivar Ranking: 246th

Napali CBD

Cultivar/Product Information

Type/Effect: Indica Hybrid - Neutral
Legacy Name: CBD God Bud
Lineage: "High CBD Cultivar" x God Bud
Cannabinoids: 5.5% THC / 9.4% CBD
Terpenes: Ocimene, Limonene, Pinene

First Impression

Review #101; September 1, 2019,

Napali CBD, from Haven St., offers a light head buzz, an elevated mood, and a sense of calm. I feel like I've just enjoyed a soothing cup of tea or a candle-lit bath or something; it is very chill. Pretty tame for THC fans, but a good choice for those looking to feel "just right."

Observations

Aroma: Chocolate, earthy, fresh, grass, herbal, sweet

Flavour: Citrusy, fresh, funky, herbal, sour, woody

Bud Colour: Dark brown/green

Pistil Colour: Brown/orange

Trichome Density: Low-Medium

Score Details

Appearance:	3 / 5
High Quality:	4 / 5
Aroma:	11 / 15
Flavour:	10 / 15
Bud Quality:	17 / 30
High Potency:	18 / 30

Overall Score: 63%

Cultivar Ranking: 401st

Noisy Neighbour

Cultivar/Product Information

Type/Effect: Sativa Hybrid - Medium Light
Legacy Name: Ultra Sour
Lineage: East Coast Sour Diesel x MK Ultra
Cannabinoids: 22.4% THC / <1% CBD
Terpenes: Terpinolene, Limonene, Caryophyllene

First Impression

Review #283; July 5, 2020,

I never thought I'd find an Ultra Sour that pleased me more than Namaste's, but Noisy Neighbour from Haven St. did just that. My head and body are buzzing, but this is no mere "buzz": this monster of a high is a full-on mental assault. I'm able to write and focus while my thoughts remain mellow. I'm motivated, excited, euphoric, and full of energy. A very active and functional high, but I am stoned and zoned-in to what I'm doing. One of my favourite cultivars, the best I've ever had. Well done, Haven St.

Observations

Aroma: Citrusy, herbal, lemon, sour

Flavour: Citrusy, herbal, lemon, sour, sour candy

Bud Colour: Light green

Pistil Colour: Orange

Trichome Density: Medium

Score Details

Appearance:	5 / 5
High Quality:	5 / 5
Aroma:	15 / 15
Flavour:	15 / 15
Bud Quality:	27 / 30
High Potency:	26 / 30

Overall Score: 93%

Cultivar Ranking: 25th

Sonic Express

Cultivar/Product Information

Type/Effect: Sativa Hybrid - Medium Light
Legacy Name: Sage 'n Sour
Lineage: SAGE x Sour Diesel
Cannabinoids: 24.3% THC / <1% CBD
Terpenes: Terpinolene, Caryophyllene, Limonene

First Impression

Review #390; December 26, 2020,

Sonic Express by Haven St. has me glued to the TV and lost within my head. The high is super elevating; my energy levels are to the max, and I'm in an upbeat and motivated mood. However, I do find myself occasionally lost in thought. I could see this as a great early-afternoon pick me up, with or without company (I feel I'd be chatty/social on this flower). A super heady ride on Sonic Express should satisfy any daytime stoner's needs.

Observations

Aroma: Citrusy, herbal, lemon, pungent, sour, sour candy

Flavour: Citrusy, fresh, grassy, herbal, sour, woody

Bud Colour: Green

Pistil Colour: Brown/orange

Trichome Density: Medium-High

Score Details

Appearance: 4 / 5
High Quality: 4 / 5
Aroma: 14 / 15
Flavour: 12 / 15
Bud Quality: 23 / 30
High Potency: 23 / 30

Overall Score: 80%

Cultivar Ranking: 194th

Twilight

Cultivar/Product Information

Type/Effect: Indica Hybrid - Medium Heavy
Legacy Name: Northern Berry
Lineage: Blueberry x Northern Lights #5
Cannabinoids: 21.5% THC / <1% CBD
Terpenes: Pinene, Caryophyllene, Humulene

First Impression

Review #289; July 11, 2020,

Twilight from Haven St. offers mellow relaxation and cerebral bliss, ideal for any evening occasion. More hazy than heavy, this cultivar is calm and euphoric instead of sleepy and sedating. The high from this flower provides a momentary escape from reality and its concerns and transports you into a spacey daydream. A decent couch-bound option, or for those just looking to chill and not be overwhelmed by cerebral intensity.

Observations

Aroma: Berry, cheesy, fruity, funky, herbal, sour, sweet

Flavour: Berry, earthy, fruity, funky, herbal, sour, sweet

Bud Colour: Dull green

Pistil Colour: Orange

Trichome Density: Medium

Score Details

Appearance:	4 / 5
High Quality:	5 / 5
Aroma:	13 / 15
Flavour:	12 / 15
Bud Quality:	27 / 30
High Potency:	23 / 30

Overall Score: 84%

Cultivar Ranking: 129th

Hexo

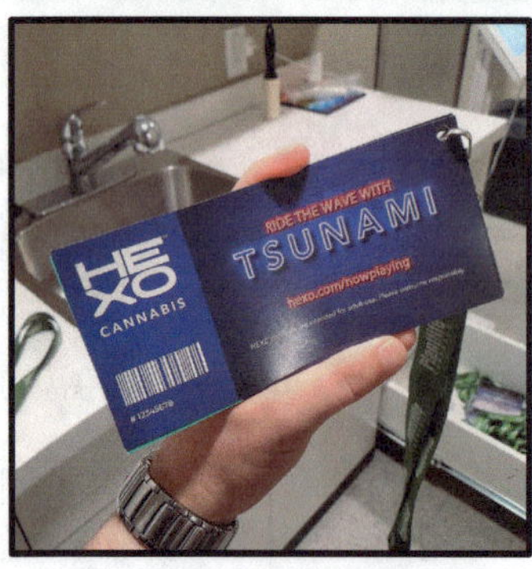

Overall Performance

Average Score: 70.67%

Brand Ranking: 69th Place

Brand Background

Hexo, based in Gatineau, Quebec, is a recreational cannabis brand focusing on large-scale production. Hexo sees the potential for the industry to end the stigma around cannabis, as well as the potential for cannabis to bring people together, and grows with those goals in mind.

Hexo flower is greenhouse-grown in Masson-Angers, Quebec, in highly controlled environments.

Associated Brands: 48North, Namaste, Redecan

Cultivar Selection

Atlantis	70%
Bayou	63%
Helios	67%
Horizon	73%
Lagoon	74%
Nebula	63%
Sierra	77%
Terra	70%
Tsunami	80%

Atlantis

Cultivar/Product Information

Type/Effect: Sativa Hybrid - Light
Legacy Name: AK-47
Lineage: Afghani Indica x Mexican Sativa x South American Sativa x Thai Sativa
Cannabinoids: 13.9% THC / <1% CBD
Terpenes: Caryophyllene, Myrcene, Humulene

First Impression

Review #129; October 11, 2019,

I got freakin' pumped for my day jamming out to Mastodon's "Leviathan" album (it's a heavy metal "Moby Dick," check it out) while getting high on this Hexo Atlantis. A heady high that is uplifting and focusing. It is pretty functional, and I feel ready to take on my day. It's also distracting me from my empty stomach, neat!

Observations

Aroma: Cheese, diesel, earthy, funky, herbal, sour, sweet

Flavour: Earthy, funky, herbal

Bud Colour: Dull green

Pistil Colour: Orange

Trichome Density: Medium

Score Details

Appearance:	4 / 5
High Quality:	5 / 5
Aroma:	12 / 15
Flavour:	10 / 15
Bud Quality:	20 / 30
High Potency:	19 / 30

Overall Score: 70%

Cultivar Ranking: 344th

Bayou

Cultivar/Product Information

Type/Effect: Indica - Medium Heavy
Legacy Name: Dark Desire
Lineage: Double Deth x Gooey 84% x Zinn
Cannabinoids: 8.1% THC / <1% CBD
Terpenes: Myrcene, Caryophyllene, Guaiol

First Impression

Review #95; August 27, 2019,

Mind-numbing and physically sedating, Bayou from Hexo is an ideal bud for helping you unwind and count the sheep at night. The flower is a gorgeous and uniquely dark purple, and the high is chill and soothing; it calms everything, mind, body, and soul. Certainly on the lighter side for THC content, but the buzz is entirely one-of-a-kind, heavy despite its lightness in THC. A great bud for anyone looking to rest and recharge.

Observations

Aroma: Chocolate, earthy, herbal, spicy, sweet

Flavour: Earthy, spicy, woody

Bud Colour: Dark purple

Pistil Colour: Brown/orange

Trichome Density: Low

Score Details

Appearance:	4 / 5
High Quality:	5 / 5
Aroma:	11 / 15
Flavour:	11 / 15
Bud Quality:	20 / 30
High Potency:	12 / 30

Overall Score: 63%

Cultivar Ranking: 400th

Helios

Cultivar/Product Information

Type/Effect:	Sativa - Medium Light
Legacy Name:	Snow Leopard
Lineage:	Snow Lotus x Tiger Melon
Cannabinoids:	14.1% THC / <1% CBD
Terpenes:	Myrcene, Caryophyllene, Pinene

First Impression

Review #81; August 1, 2019,

Hexo's Helios is relaxing to the body but stimulating to the mind. My senses are heightened, but I feel calm and mellow, and I'm ready to sit and relax for the day. Ideal for a morning or afternoon off, as you might not feel like doing much after consuming this bud. A good time-killer for getting some daydreaming done.

Observations

Aroma: Earthy, funky, herbal, sweet

Flavour: Cheese, earthy, funky, herbal

Bud Colour: Dull green

Pistil Colour: Orange/tan

Trichome Density: Low-Medium

Score Details

Appearance:	4 / 5
High Quality:	5 / 5
Aroma:	11 / 15
Flavour:	10 / 15
Bud Quality:	20 / 30
High Potency:	18 / 30

Overall Score: 68%

Cultivar Ranking: 368th

Horizon

Cultivar/Product Information

Type/Effect: Sativa Hybrid - Medium Light
Legacy Name: Serious Happiness
Lineage: AK-47 x Warlock
Cannabinoids: 15.8% THC / <1% CBD
Terpenes: Myrcene, Caryophyllene, Pinene

First Impression

Review #137; November 8, 2019,

A relaxing body experience and an extremely mood elevating high, Hexo's Horizon is a super satisfying flower. I'm not too high, but enough that I wouldn't want to be in public. I'm focused, relaxed, uplifted, and I feel at peace. Decent stuff.

Observations

Aroma: Cheese, funky, herbal, sour

Flavour: Cheese, funky, grassy, herbal, sour

Bud Colour: Light green

Pistil Colour: Orange

Trichome Density: Medium

Score Details

Appearance:	4 / 5
High Quality:	5 / 5
Aroma:	13 / 15
Flavour:	10 / 15
Bud Quality:	21 / 30
High Potency:	20 / 30

Overall Score: 73%

Cultivar Ranking: 306th

Lagoon

Cultivar/Product Information

Type/Effect: Indica - Heavy
Legacy Name: Northern Berry
Lineage: Blueberry x Northern Lights #5
Cannabinoids: 16.9% THC / <1% CBD
Terpenes: Myrcene, Caryophyllene, Humulene

First Impression

Review #115; September 13, 2019,

I'm feeling chill, relaxed, and mellow on Lagoon by Hexo. My mind is foggy and calm, and a powerful sensation is developing in my torso and legs. Not ideal for the morning - I now feel like crawling back into bed. Great stuff for an evening-in.

Observations

Aroma: Berry, earthy, fruity, herbal, sweet

Flavour: Berry, earthy, fresh, funky, grassy, herbal, sweet

Bud Colour: Dull green

Pistil Colour: Brown/orange

Trichome Density: Low-Medium

Score Details

Appearance:	4 / 5
High Quality:	5 / 5
Aroma:	11 / 15
Flavour:	10 / 15
Bud Quality:	23 / 30
High Potency:	21 / 30

Overall Score: 74%

Cultivar Ranking: 302nd

Nebula

Cultivar/Product Information

Type/Effect: Indica - Medium Light
Legacy Name: White Widow
Lineage: Brazilian Sativa x Indian Indica
Cannabinoids: 11.8% THC / <1% CBD
Terpenes: Myrcene, Caryophyllene, Limonene

First Impression

Review #113; September 12, 2019,

This bud is a lighter experience due to the medium-low THC potency of Hexo's Nebula, but the high is very focusing, pleasant, and euphoric. Before writing this review, I was distracted by the music I was listening to and cuddling with my dog. The flower made that detour from my review process all the more enjoyable. An excellent cultivar to suggest to newer consumers at this THC level. A good, clean, fun high.

Observations

Aroma: Fresh, herbal, sour, sweet

Flavour: Funky, herbal, sour

Bud Colour: Dark green

Pistil Colour: Brown/orange

Trichome Density: Medium

Score Details

Appearance:	4 / 5
High Quality:	5 / 5
Aroma:	11 / 15
Flavour:	7 / 15
Bud Quality:	21 / 30
High Potency:	15 / 30

Overall Score: 63%

Cultivar Ranking: 399th

Sierra

Cultivar/Product Information

Type/Effect: Indica - Medium Light
Legacy Name: CBD Shark Shock
Lineage: Cannatonic x Shark Shock
Cannabinoids: 5.9% THC / 10% CBD
Terpenes: Myrcene, Bisabolol, Caryophyllene

First Impression

Review #87; August 14, 2019,

My mind is numb yet focused, my body and spirit are calm and relaxed, and "zen," if you will, is how I'm feeling - thanks to Hexo's Sierra. I want to give hugs and pet animals. I want to melt into the couch and enjoy something. I want to experience this balanced excellence again and again.

Observations

Aroma: Citrusy, herbal, sour, sweet

Flavour: Earthy, herbal, sour, spicy

Bud Colour: Dark brown/green

Pistil Colour: Brown

Trichome Density: Medium

Score Details

Appearance:	3 / 5
High Quality:	5 / 5
Aroma:	12 / 15
Flavour:	11 / 15
Bud Quality:	22 / 30
High Potency:	22 / 30

Overall Score: 75%

Cultivar Ranking: 284th

Terra

Cultivar/Product Information

Type/Effect:	Indica Hybrid - Super Light
Legacy Name:	CBD Remedy
Lineage:	Afghan Skunk x Cannatonic
Cannabinoids:	<1% THC / 11% CBD
Terpenes:	Myrcene, Pinene, Caryophyllene

First Impression

Review #157; December 10, 2019,

Terra, by Hexo, provides a super light headband effect and head sensation, as well as focus, calm, and a sense of overall wellness. While the sensation is absent of THC, it's still gratifying, great when getting stoned won't be beneficial. A solid CBD-only cultivar option.

Observations

Aroma: Fresh, fruity, herbal, sour, spicy, sweet

Flavour: Fresh, funky, herbal, spicy

Bud Colour: Dark green

Pistil Colour: Brown/orange

Trichome Density: Low

Score Details

Appearance:	4 / 5
High Quality:	5 / 5
Aroma:	13 / 15
Flavour:	9 / 15
Bud Quality:	23 / 30
High Potency:	16 / 30

Overall Score: 70%

Cultivar Ranking: 341st

Tsunami

Cultivar/Product Information

Type/Effect:	Indica - Heavy
Legacy Name:	Northern Berry
Lineage:	Blueberry x Northern Lights #5
Cannabinoids:	18.7% THC / <1% CBD
Terpenes:	Myrcene, Caryophyllene, Humulene

First Impression

Review #125; September 26, 2019,

Hexo's Tsunami has me feeling waves of sensation throughout my head, torso and legs, and a potent head buzz that is very relaxed despite its relatively high intensity and potency. This flower is quite heavy for <20% THC. The quality, smell, and flavour were all pretty decent here as well. Hexo can make some decent flower, and Tsunami is a prime example of that.

Observations

Aroma: Berry, earthy, fruity, sweet

Flavour: Berry, earthy, fruity, sweet

Bud Colour: Dark green

Pistil Colour: Brown/red

Trichome Density: Medium

Score Details

Appearance:	4 / 5
High Quality:	5 / 5
Aroma:	12 / 15
Flavour:	12 / 15
Bud Quality:	24 / 30
High Potency:	23 / 30

Overall Score: 80%

Cultivar Ranking: 213th

High Tide

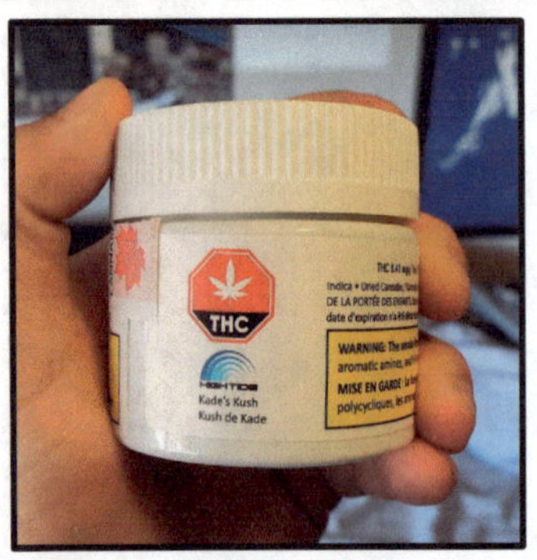

Overall Performance

Average Score: 74.25%

Brand Ranking: 59th Place

Brand Background

High Tide, the cannabis brand, not to be confused with the cannabis retailer of the same name, produce midrange cannabis products out of Ontario. High Tide seeks to bring medical-grade cannabis to recreational consumers.

High Tide cannabis is grown in a large indoor facility under strict quality assurance practices.

Other Cultivars: Dark Star
Associated Brands: Kiwi, Northern Harvest

Cultivar Selection

Amnesia Haze	73%
Ghost Train Haze	77%
Headband	72%
Kade's Kush	75%

Amnesia Haze

Cultivar/Product Information

Type/Effect: Sativa - Medium Light
Legacy Name: Amnesia Haze
Lineage: Afghani Hawaiian x Jamaican Sativa x Laotian Sativa
Cannabinoids: 14.2% THC / <1% CBD
Terpenes: Caryophyllene, Pinene, Nerolidol

First Impression

Review #186; February 5, 2020,

Amnesia Haze from High Tide provides a mental fog but leaves you with your high beams working at least. A weird analogy, I know, but it works. My mind and head are buzzing, my shoulders are relaxed, and everything is hazy - a focused midday buzz for doing stuff around the house.

Observations

Aroma: Chocolate, earthy, herbal, sour, sweet

Flavour: Earthy, herbal, sour, sweet

Bud Colour: Dull green

Pistil Colour: Brown/orange

Trichome Density: Medium

Score Details

Appearance:	4 / 5
High Quality:	5 / 5
Aroma:	11 / 15
Flavour:	11 / 15
Bud Quality:	24 / 30
High Potency:	18 / 30

Overall Score: 73%

Cultivar Ranking: 315th

Ghost Train Haze

Cultivar/Product Information

Type/Effect:	Sativa - Light
Legacy Name:	Ghost Train Haze
Lineage:	Ghost OG x Nevil's Wreck
Cannabinoids:	20.2% THC / <1% CBD
Terpenes:	Terpinolene, Caryophyllene, Myrcene

First Impression

Review #382; December 15, 2020,

I was in a terrible mood, but High Tide hit me with Ghost Train Haze, and everything got better. The haze primarily affects the head, my mind is moving rather quickly, and my thoughts are still relatively clear. Uplifting and energetic, definitely a get-up-and-go cultivar. Euphoric and inspiring, this cultivar eased my worries, lifted my spirits, and elevated my mood - a good take on one of my go-to sativas.

Observations

Aroma: Citrusy, floral, fresh, herbal, pungent, sour

Flavour: Citrusy, floral, fresh, herbal, lemon, pungent, sour

Bud Colour: Green

Pistil Colour: Brown/tan

Trichome Density: Low-Medium

Score Details

Appearance:	4 / 5
High Quality:	5 / 5
Aroma:	12 / 15
Flavour:	12 / 15
Bud Quality:	21 / 30
High Potency:	23 / 30

Overall Score: 77%

Cultivar Ranking: 261st

Headband

Cultivar/Product Information

Type/Effect: Hybrid - Neutral
Legacy Name: Headband
Lineage: OG Kush x Sour Diesel
Cannabinoids: 18.3% THC / <1% CBD
Terpenes: Limonene, Nerolidol, Caryophyllene

First Impression

Review #118; September 15, 2019,

Look for Headband by High Tide for a chill but still heady cultivar. I feel my body is relaxed, despite the lack of an apparent physical sensation. My thoughts are calm and peaceful: instead of racing or lacking focus, a strong and clear high is present. This strikes me as a high-potency flower that is approachable and mellow, not too intense either, which isn't my usual Headband experience.

Observations

Aroma: Diesel, earthy, fresh, grassy, herbal, piney, pungent

Flavour: Earthy, funky, herbal, pungent, sour

Bud Colour: Light green

Pistil Colour: Orange/red

Trichome Density: Medium

Score Details

Appearance:	3 / 5
High Quality:	5 / 5
Aroma:	12 / 15
Flavour:	9 / 15
Bud Quality:	22 / 30
High Potency:	21 / 30

Overall Score: 72%

Cultivar Ranking: 321st

Kade's Kush

Cultivar/Product Information

Type/Effect: Indica - Neutral
Legacy Name: Kade's Kush
Lineage: "Northern Californian" x Afghani Indica
Cannabinoids: 18.4% THC / <1% CBD
Terpenes: Nerolidol, Caryophyllene, Pinene

First Impression

Review #413; February 7, 2021,

My eyes are heavy and lazy-looking, and my body and mind are relieved and relaxed while high on Kade's Kush by High Tide. I'm not zoning out too much, definitely more present-feeling than reality-escaping. Everything feels more calm and bright under the influence of Kade's Kush. Excellent for winding down and chilling out.

Observations

Aroma: Earthy, herbal, spicy, sour, woody

Flavour: Earthy, funky, grassy, herbal

Bud Colour: Dark green

Pistil Colour: Brown/orange

Trichome Density: Medium

Score Details

Appearance:	4 / 5
High Quality:	5 / 5
Aroma:	12 / 15
Flavour:	11 / 15
Bud Quality:	21 / 30
High Potency:	22 / 30

Overall Score: 75%

Cultivar Ranking: 288th

Highland Grow

Overall Performance

Average Score: 89.50%

Brand Ranking: 12th Place

Brand Background

Highland Grow is a cannabis brand out of Nova Scotia focused on cultivating premium cannabis. Between careful cultivar selection and dedication to the plant, all backed by the expertise of the Highland Grow team, the flower they produce certainly is top-shelf.

Cannabis produced by Highland Grow is grown on the coast near Antigonish, Nova Scotia.

Other Cultivars: Animal Crasher, Cold Creek Kush, Diamond Breath, Eastern Dank, Gaelic Fire, Gas Tank, Mendo Sunset, Sensi Wizard

Cultivar Selection

Cherry Burst	87%
White Lightning	92%

Cherry Burst

Cultivar/Product Information

Type/Effect: Hybrid - Neutral
Legacy Name: Cherry Burst
Lineage: Forum Cut GSC x OG Kush
Cannabinoids: 25.5% THC / <1% CBD
Terpenes: Caryophyllene, Myrcene, Bisabolol

First Impression

Review #361; November 2, 2020,

Cherry Burst from Highland Grow offered a burst of energy, a clear and wired head high, and plenty of coughing. I danced around my room, singing along to Dead Kennedys, The Clash, and Misfits, for a fantastic and lively time. I could think pretty clearly, but the cerebral sensations grew more distracting the further into the bowl I got. Functional, but in small doses. A potent experience for my first from Highland Grow.

Observations

Aroma: Earthy, fresh, fruity, herbal, piney, spicy, sweet

Flavour: Earthy, herbal, sweet, woody

Bud Colour: Green/tan

Pistil Colour: Orange/red

Trichome Density: Medium-High

Score Details

Appearance:	5 / 5
High Quality:	5 / 5
Aroma:	12 / 15
Flavour:	11 / 15
Bud Quality:	29 / 30
High Potency:	25 / 30

Overall Score: 87%

Cultivar Ranking: 95th

White Lightning

Cultivar/Product Information

Type/Effect: Indica - Super Heavy
Legacy Name: White Lightning
Lineage: Hindu Kush x Northern Lights
Cannabinoids: 24% THC / <1% CBD
Terpenes: Caryophyllene, Myrcene, Limonene

First Impression

Review #367; November 13, 2020,

Highland Grow nailed it with White Lightning, a cultivar that offers a strong, "stoned" effect on both the body and mind. I soon struggled to keep my eyes open after several bags of this potent indica. Relaxing doesn't quite cut it - the effects make my legs weak and my mind vacant. I'm ready to pass out on my bed. Not one for beginners or for wake-n-bake sessions as it is too strong and too sedating for that. Well done, Highland Grow.

Observations

Aroma: Earthy, herbal, piney, pungent, spicy, sweet, woody

Flavour: Earthy, floral, grassy, herbal, pungent

Bud Colour: Dark green/purple

Pistil Colour: Brown/red

Trichome Density: High

Score Details

Appearance:	5 / 5
High Quality:	5 / 5
Aroma:	13 / 15
Flavour:	13 / 15
Bud Quality:	29 / 30
High Potency:	27 / 30

Overall Score: 92%

Cultivar Ranking: 42nd

Houseplant

Overall Performance

Average Score: 78.33%

Brand Ranking: 43rd Place

Brand Background

Houseplant, Seth Rogen and Evan Goldberg's cannabis brand brought to Canada by Canopy Growth, was founded on "giving weed the treatment it deserves." Both founders were closely involved with cultivar selection for the brand's lineup of products. They had the requirement that the cultivars selected be appropriate for use in their own daily lives and the consumers'.

At Houseplant, a strong passion for educating the public about cannabis and support for organizations that aim to erase cannabis stigma is also core to their mission.

Associated Brands: 7Acres, DNA Genetics, LBS, Tokyo Smoke, Tweed, Van Der Pop

Cultivar Selection

Hybrid	67%
Indica	88%
Sativa	80%

Hybrid

Cultivar/Product Information

Type/Effect: Hybrid - Light
Legacy Name: Blue Cheese
Lineage: Blueberry x UK Cheese
Cannabinoids: 14% THC / <1% CBD
Terpenes: Myrcene, Caryophyllene, Limonene

First Impression

Review #224; March 31, 2020,

Houseplant's Hybrid is a mellow, lighter option suited for any time use. I don't feel lethargic or heavy but pleasantly high with a mild headband effect. My thoughts and mind are clear, and my focus is typical. Some slight mood elevation reveals the extent of this high. This is a good option for those with lower tolerances or anyone with an afternoon to improve.

Observations

Aroma: Earthy, floral, fresh, grassy, herbal, sweet

Flavour: Fresh, grassy, herbal, sour, sweet

Bud Colour: Green

Pistil Colour: Brown/orange

Trichome Density: Medium

Score Details

Appearance:	4 / 5
High Quality:	5 / 5
Aroma:	13 / 15
Flavour:	10 / 15
Bud Quality:	20 / 30
High Potency:	15 / 30

Overall Score: 67%

Cultivar Ranking: 374th

Indica

Cultivar/Product Information

Type/Effect: Indica - Neutral
Legacy Name: 91 Krypt
Lineage: Captain Krypt OG x '91 Chemdog
Cannabinoids: 24.6% THC / <1% CBD
Terpenes: Linalool, Caryophyllene, Myrcene

First Impression

Review #208; March 9, 2020,

I'm pretty high on Houseplant's Indica. My mood and mind are clear, focused and calm. In the background, the creative juices are flowing, an immense body buzz is pulsing, and a high is elevating me to great heights. A high-potency, full experience is to be had when consuming this. A very active indica despite its body-calming sensation. Wonderful, a delight. Wonderful, a delight. The flower so nice, I said it twice (that's for you, Dale Denton). Hats off to Canopy and Seth Rogen for this bud.

Observations

Aroma: Cheese, floral, fresh, grassy, sour, sweet

Flavour: Floral, fresh, funky, grassy, herbal, melon, sweet

Bud Colour: Dark green/purple

Pistil Colour: Brown/orange

Trichome Density: High

Score Details

Appearance:	5 / 5
High Quality:	5 / 5
Aroma:	14 / 15
Flavour:	13 / 15
Bud Quality:	26 / 30
High Potency:	25 / 30

Overall Score: 88%

Cultivar Ranking: 82nd

Sativa

Cultivar/Product Information

Type/Effect: Sativa - Neutral
Legacy Name: Chemdog
Lineage: Dogbud
Cannabinoids: 20% THC / <1% CBD
Terpenes: Myrcene, Pinene

First Impression

Review #207; March 5, 2020,

Houseplant's Sativa is a high THC cultivar, offering a potent, high-intensity experience that hits heavily in the eyes, face, head, and chest. I can feel so much of my face and yet none of my face simultaneously. My heart is racing, the physical and cerebral effects overwhelming my mind and body; this cultivar is a full-on mental and physical assault. This flower is great for an afternoon you can afford to write off completely. I'm baked beyond belief: this is not the snicklefritz.

Observations

Aroma: Earthy, fresh, grassy, herbal, sour, sweet

Flavour: Herbal, sour, woody

Bud Colour: Green

Pistil Colour: Brown/orange

Trichome Density: Medium

Score Details

Appearance:	4 / 5
High Quality:	5 / 5
Aroma:	12 / 15
Flavour:	10 / 15
Bud Quality:	25 / 30
High Potency:	24 / 30

Overall Score: 80%

Cultivar Ranking: 209th

Ignite

Overall Performance

Average Score: 90.33%

Brand Ranking: 7th Place

Brand Background

Ignite, a cannabis brand brought to you by Dan Bilzerian, brought a few decent flower products to the recreational market. Little information is available on Ignite, given their poor performance in Canada and lack of product availability.

Ignite's cannabis was purchased from other licensed producers, though I'm not sure which ones specifically. I did enjoy their cannabis. I know that much.

Cultivar Selection

Crescendo	89%
GG4	93%
Tropicana Cookies	89%

Crescendo

Cultivar/Product Information

Type/Effect: Sativa Hybrid - Medium Heavy
Legacy Name: Crescendo
Lineage: Chemdog x I-95 x Mandarin Cookies
Cannabinoids: 21.9% THC / <1% CBD

First Impression

Review #322; August 29, 2020,

Ignite's Crescendo messes my head a bunch; my mind is alive, and my focus is darting around. I'm pretty stoned. My brain feels like it's growing out of my skull, or trying to at least. My eyes feel heavy, but they're still wide open. Overall, I'm mellow, mood-wise and physically speaking, but upstairs is a different story: I feel focused on everything, all at once. It's almost unsettling, but I like it anyway. The cerebral intensity is overwhelming in the best kind of way.

Observations

Aroma: Earthy, fruity, herbal, spicy, sweet

Flavour: Earthy, fruity, herbal, sweet, woody

Bud Colour: Dark green/purple

Pistil Colour: Orange

Trichome Density: Medium-High

Score Details

Appearance:	5 / 5
High Quality:	5 / 5
Aroma:	13 / 15
Flavour:	12 / 15
Bud Quality:	29 / 30
High Potency:	25 / 30

Overall Score: 89%

Cultivar Ranking: 76th

GG4

Cultivar/Product Information

Type/Effect: Hybrid - Medium Heavy
Legacy Name: Original Glue
Lineage: Chem's Sister x Chocolate Diesel x Sour Dubb
Cannabinoids: 22.1% THC / <1% CBD

First Impression

Review #321; August 27, 2020,

Paired with pizza and Futurama, Ignite's GG4 offered me a wondrous high, with which I thoroughly enjoyed the dinner and show. That is to say, I overate and couldn't comprehend the show, as I was super stoned. The effects of GG4 are euphoric, distracting, chill, and inebriating. The vapour in the Volcano bags I inhaled was milky white for longer than typical, indicating a potent flower rich in cannabinoids and terpenes - a great Glue.

Observations

Aroma: Earthy, fresh, pungent, spicy, sweet, woody

Flavour: Earthy, fresh, herbal, piney, pungent, woody

Bud Colour: Light green

Pistil Colour: Brown/red

Trichome Density: High

Score Details

Appearance:	5 / 5
High Quality:	5 / 5
Aroma:	14 / 15
Flavour:	14 / 15
Bud Quality:	29 / 30
High Potency:	26 / 30

Overall Score: 93%

Cultivar Ranking: 29th

Tropicana Cookies

Cultivar/Product Information

Type/Effect: Sativa Hybrid - Medium Light
Legacy Name: Tropicana Cookies
Lineage: Girl Scout Cookies x Tangie
Cannabinoids: 15.5% THC / <1% CBD

First Impression

Review #319; August 26, 2020,

Ignite's Tropicana Cookies was an absolute treat to vaporize. It produces a tasty, fruity flavour and an aroma to match, coupled with a mellow mood and hazy high. A cross of two favourite cultivars of mine, Girl Scout Cookies and Tangie, Tropicana Cookies is great for anytime you want to feel high and bask in the moment's joy. A pleasure to experience all around and with a potency that should satisfy most low-medium tolerance consumers.

Observations

Aroma: Citrusy, earthy, fruity, herbal, orange, sweet

Flavour: Citrusy, fruity, herbal, orange, sweet

Bud Colour: Green/purple

Pistil Colour: Brown/orange

Trichome Density: Medium-High

Score Details

Appearance:	5 / 5
High Quality:	5 / 5
Aroma:	15 / 15
Flavour:	14 / 15
Bud Quality:	29 / 30
High Potency:	21 / 30

Overall Score: 89%

Cultivar Ranking: 72nd

Joi Botanicals

Overall Performance

Average Score: 92.00%

Brand Ranking: 5th Place

Brand Background

The folks at Joi Botanicals love cannabis, which shines through in their growing practices and their end products. Their approach is to grow in an automated environment operated by a team of highly experienced cannabis cultivators. Cannabis is produced in small batches at Joi, with cultivar-specific conditions for each plant.

Joi Botanicals cannabis is grown at their facility in Alberta. Extra care is taken to ensure quality products, including growing by the plant's schedule rather than by the calendar (harvesting when ready, not when due for harvest) and some expert after-care in the drying, curing, and trimming.

Other Cultivars: Electric Ave, Jet Fuel Funk, OG Kush, Purple Punch Mints, Rainmaker, Super Lemon Haze CBD

Cultivar Selection

Cake Crasher #1	92%

Cake Crasher #1

Cultivar/Product Information

Type/Effect: Hybrid - Neutral
Legacy Name: Cake Crasher #1
Lineage: Wedding Cake x Wedding Crasher
Cannabinoids: 24.1% THC / <1% CBD
Terpenes: Limonene, Nerolidol, Myrcene

First Impression

Review #375; December 4, 2020,

Cake Crasher #1 by Joi Botanicals is a joy indeed, in every sense of the word. This is the best fruity-smelling cannabis I've had since Strawberry Cream. I want this as a candle. The effects are strong and quite mellow physically and active cerebrally. I texted up a storm while high on this flower and thought about the future. It's very uplifting, social, and inspiring; it's still relatively calm as well - I feel like I just woke up from a nap. This is a fantastic cultivar and a great time.

Observations

Aroma: Berry, cheese, earthy, fruity, funky, sweet, sweet candy

Flavour: Berry, cherry, earthy, fruity, sweet

Bud Colour: Dark green/purple

Pistil Colour: Brown/tan

Trichome Density: High

Score Details

Appearance:	5 / 5
High Quality:	5 / 5
Aroma:	15 / 15
Flavour:	14 / 15
Bud Quality:	27 / 30
High Potency:	26 / 30

Overall Score: 92%

Cultivar Ranking: 33rd

Kingsway

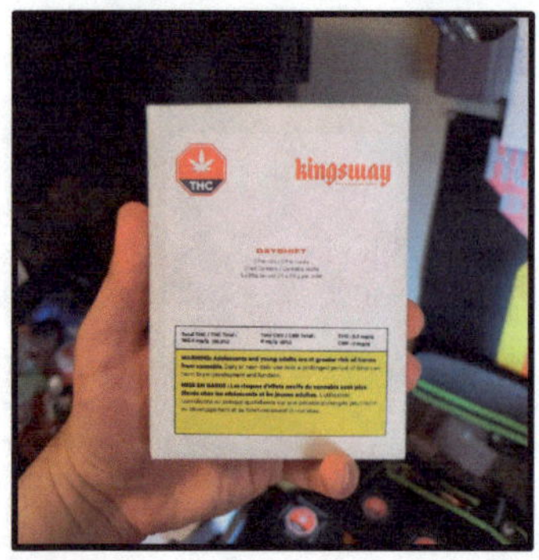

Overall Performance

Average Score: 64.00%

Brand Ranking: 77th Place

Brand Background

Kingsway is a cannabis brand that seeks to provide experienced consumers with a value-oriented product to suit their needs. I was able to find little information on them apart from a large rotating letter "K" on their website.

Kingsway cannabis is purchased from other licensed producers and packaged into Kingsway products. Both products reviewed were grown by Aurora.

Associated Brands: Strain Rec

Cultivar Selection

Dayshift	67%
Nightshift	61%

Dayshift

Cultivar/Product Information

Type/Effect: Sativa - Neutral
Legacy Name: OG Melon
Lineage: Captain Krypt OG x '91 Chemdog
Cannabinoids: 15% THC / <1% CBD

First Impression

Review #363; November 4, 2020,

Kingsway's Dayshift is a mellow but heady experience. My eyes are slightly heavy, my mind is pretty hazy, and I'm experiencing a calm euphoria. An average afternoon turned into a semi-zoned-out, enjoyable ride with Dayshift.

Observations

Aroma: Cheese, earthy, fruity, herbal, pungent, spicy, sweet

Flavour: Earthy, fruity, funky, grassy, herbal, sweet

Bud Colour: Dark green

Pistil Colour: Brown

Trichome Density: Low

Score Details

Appearance:	3 / 5
High Quality:	5 / 5
Aroma:	13 / 15
Flavour:	12 / 15
Bud Quality:	15 / 30
High Potency:	19 / 30

Overall Score: 67%

Cultivar Ranking: 375th

Nightshift

Cultivar/Product Information

Type/Effect: Indica - Medium Heavy
Legacy Name: LA Confidential
Lineage: Afghani Indica x OG L.A. Affie
Cannabinoids: 15.2% THC / <1% CBD

First Impression

Review #362; November 3, 2020,

Nightshift by Kingsway, my first introduction to the brand, is a mellow and relaxed high on both the body and mind. It would be a great bedtime bud. Not too intense cerebrally, so it won't keep you up, and very chill overall in effect. Not too bad.

Observations

Aroma: Earthy, funky, grassy, herbal, woody

Flavour: Earthy, funky, grassy, herbal, woody

Bud Colour: Dark green

Pistil Colour: Brown/red

Trichome Density: Low

Score Details

Appearance:	4 / 5
High Quality:	5 / 5
Aroma:	9 / 15
Flavour:	8 / 15
Bud Quality:	18 / 30
High Potency:	17 / 30

Overall Score: 61%

Cultivar Ranking: 407th

Kiwi

Overall Performance

Average Score: 73.00%

Brand Ranking: 66th Place

Kiwi

Brand Background

Accessibility is core to the goal Kiwi has in mind with their cannabis. They seek to provide clear and concise information on their products and products that speak for themselves. The Kiwi portfolio of cultivars is balanced-focused.

Kiwi cannabis is grown in Ontario in a large indoor facility.

Associated Brands: High Tide, Northern Harvest

Cultivar Selection

Cali-O	76%
Mango Haze	76%
San Fernando Valley	67%

Cali-O

Cultivar/Product Information

Type/Effect: Hybrid - Light
Legacy Name: California Orange
Cannabinoids: 7.5% THC / 9.3% CBD
Terpenes: Limonene, Pinene, Linalool

First Impression

Review #67; June 1, 2019,

Cali-O by Kiwi feels like the perfect bud for an afternoon on the beach, or in general, just any nice summer day. I enjoyed this one in the morning - the THC provided a nice cerebral jolt of a high, and the CBD relaxed me to help me ease into the day. This is an uplifting balanced cultivar with a great aroma and flavour - a favourite.

Observations

Aroma: Citrusy, fruity, herbal, orange, sweet

Flavour: Herbal, sweet

Bud Colour: Dark green

Pistil Colour: Orange

Trichome Density: Low-Medium

Score Details

Appearance:	4 / 5
High Quality:	5 / 5
Aroma:	14 / 15
Flavour:	12 / 15
Bud Quality:	20 / 30
High Potency:	21 / 30

Overall Score: 76%

Cultivar Ranking: 268th

Mango Haze

Cultivar/Product Information

Type/Effect: Sativa - Light
Legacy Name: CBD Mango Haze
Lineage: "High CBD Cultivar" x Mango Haze
Cannabinoids: 7.4% THC / 11.2% CBD
Terpenes: Pinene, Caryophyllene, Cymene

First Impression

Review #110; September 10, 2019,

The balance of Mango Haze by Kiwi is stimulating to the mind, relaxing to the body, and calming to the soul. The haze comes through strong, as does the THC and CBD, producing a mentally focused experience with an excellent body buzz. A wake and bake with this flower would make for a wonderful morning.

Observations

Aroma: Citrusy, fruity, herbal, mango, orange, sweet

Flavour: Funky, herbal

Bud Colour: Dark green

Pistil Colour: Orange

Trichome Density: Low-Medium

Score Details

Appearance:	4 / 5
High Quality:	5 / 5
Aroma:	13 / 15
Flavour:	8 / 15
Bud Quality:	23 / 30
High Potency:	23 / 30

Overall Score: 76%

Cultivar Ranking: 269th

San Fernando Valley

Cultivar/Product Information

Type/Effect: Hybrid - Light
Cannabinoids: 5.8% THC / 8.1% CBD

First Impression

Review #217; March 19, 2020,

Kiwi's San Fernando Valley is a light head buzz and physical sensation, one that left me checked out in conversation and tuned in to my daydreams. A calm, soft, mild high, suited for times best spent in a mellow haze.

Observations

Aroma: Chocolate, earthy, herbal, spicy, sweet

Flavour: Funky, herbal, sour, spicy, woody

Bud Colour: Light green

Pistil Colour: Orange

Trichome Density: Medium

Score Details

Appearance:	3 / 5
High Quality:	5 / 5
Aroma:	13 / 15
Flavour:	10 / 15
Bud Quality:	17 / 30
High Potency:	19 / 30

Overall Score: 67%

Cultivar Ranking: 371st

Kolab

Overall Performance

Average Score: 90.00%

Brand Ranking: 10th Place

Brand Background

Kolab, another brand that sources some of its flower from other cultivators, brings quality, craft cannabis to market. Their lineup has consisted mostly of heavy indicas.

Kolab flower is grown by various small producers, often using automated systems to control environmental conditions. All flower is also dried, hand-trimmed and slow-cured.

Other Cultivars: Slurricane

Cultivar Selection

Ice Cream Cake	90%
Kalifornia	90%

Ice Cream Cake

Cultivar/Product Information

Type/Effect:	Indica - Heavy
Legacy Name:	Ice Cream Cake
Lineage:	Gelato #33 x Wedding Cake
Cannabinoids:	23.5% THC / <1% CBD
Terpenes:	Limonene, Caryophyllene, Linalool

First Impression

Review #397; January 2, 2021,

Ice Cream Cake is always a super potent experience, and this batch by Kolab and Safari Flower Co. is no different: I'm stoned out of my mind. My mind is an empty void; I'm struggling with vocabulary choices in my writing as I nearly collapse from standing stoned - my legs are pretty relaxed. The high has conquered my body and cognition and rendered both relatively useless. Overall, I'm chillaxed, if not thoroughly sedated; Kolab has delivered a great version of a kickass cultivar.

Observations

Aroma: Earthy, minty, piney, pungent, sweet

Flavour: Earthy, herbal, minty, piney, pungent

Bud Colour: Dark green/purple

Pistil Colour: Orange

Trichome Density: Medium

Score Details

Appearance:	4 / 5
High Quality:	5 / 5
Aroma:	14 / 15
Flavour:	13 / 15
Bud Quality:	26 / 30
High Potency:	28 / 30

Overall Score: 90%

Cultivar Ranking: 62nd

Kalifornia

Cultivar/Product Information

Type/Effect: Indica - Heavy
Legacy Name: Kalifornia
Lineage: Nepali OG x '88 G13 Hashplant
Cannabinoids: 22.3% THC / <1% CBD
Terpenes: Myrcene, Limonene, Caryophyllene

First Impression

Review #328; September 6, 2020,

A heavy high, Kalifornia by Kolab and Lotus Cannabis Co. is an experience best enjoyed before bedtime to avoid an accidental nap. My brain is pretty vacant (shout out to Sex Pistols) and heavily sedated. The relaxing nature of this flower soothes my body, and a sense of calm comes over me despite the potency of effect. Never overwhelming, but a good paralyzer, I feel comfortable and comatose on my couch.

Observations

Aroma: Diesel, earthy, fruity, herbal, pungent, sour, sweet

Flavour: Earthy, fresh, funky, herbal, piney, pungent, sweet

Bud Colour: Dull green

Pistil Colour: Brown/red

Trichome Density: Medium

Score Details

Appearance:	4 / 5
High Quality:	5 / 5
Aroma:	14 / 15
Flavour:	13 / 15
Bud Quality:	29 / 30
High Potency:	25 / 30

Overall Score: 90%

Cultivar Ranking: 64th

LBS

Overall Performance

Average Score: 75.25%

Brand Ranking: 56th Place

Brand Background

LBS, otherwise known as Leafs by Snoop, is a cannabis brand from Canopy Growth. Now, when I say Snoop, yes, I mean that Snoop, the one who enjoys his gin with juice. Cannabis featured by LBS on their brand lineup consists of cultivars that serve as an ode to California that covers a whole day's worth of cannabis experiences: from early day sessions with Ocean View and Palm Tree CBD to evenings with Moonbeam and Sunset.

Canopy Growth grows mid-grade, mass-produced cannabis in Ontario for the LBS brand.

Associated Brands: 7Acres, DNA Genetics, Houseplant, Tokyo Smoke, Tweed, Van Der Pop

Cultivar Selection

Moonbeam	77%
Ocean View	70%
Palm Tree CBD	79%
Sunset	75%

Moonbeam

Cultivar/Product Information

Type/Effect: Indica - Light
Legacy Name: Strawberry Banana
Lineage: Banana Kush x Bubblegum
Cannabinoids: 22% THC / <1% CBD
Terpenes: Limonene, Caryophyllene

First Impression

Review #26; April 18, 2019,

A start to an evening at home, but certainly not the end, Moonbeam by LBS is a relatively light indica on effects, but the high itself is pretty strong. The smell and flavour in a vaporizer are unreal. This batch reminds me a bit of strawberry licorice. A social indica, very little couch-lock, but exceptional for chilling out, relaxing, and unwinding midday to evening. All around a lovely, pleasant, enjoyable experience.

Observations

Aroma: Berry, floral, fruity, herbal, sweet

Flavour: Berry, floral, fruity, sweet

Bud Colour: Dull green

Pistil Colour: Brown/tan

Trichome Density: Low

Score Details

Appearance:	3 / 5
High Quality:	5 / 5
Aroma:	14 / 15
Flavour:	14 / 15
Bud Quality:	18 / 30
High Potency:	23 / 30

Overall Score: 77%

Cultivar Ranking: 254th

Ocean View

Cultivar/Product Information

Type/Effect:	Sativa - Light
Legacy Name:	Strawberry Cough
Lineage:	Haze x Strawberry Fields
Cannabinoids:	11.6% THC / <1% CBD
Terpenes:	Myrcene, Caryophyllene, Ocimene

First Impression

Review #49; May 4, 2019,

Ocean View by LBS would be a perfect beach bud, and the name is fitting. The flavour in a vaporizer is noteworthy on this one, with excellent taste from this great low-strength offering from LBS. Being a mellow and relaxing but uplifting sativa with a mild high, Ocean View would be great for new and experienced consumers alike.

Observations

Aroma: Berry, fresh, fruity, herbal, strawberry, sweet

Flavour: Berry, fresh, fruity, strawberry, sweet

Bud Colour: Dark green

Pistil Colour: Orange/red

Trichome Density: Low-Medium

Score Details

Appearance:	5 / 5
High Quality:	5 / 5
Aroma:	14 / 15
Flavour:	14 / 15
Bud Quality:	17 / 30
High Potency:	15 / 30

Overall Score: 70%

Cultivar Ranking: 336th

Palm Tree CBD

Cultivar/Product Information

Type/Effect: Indica - Medium Light
Legacy Name: Super Nordle
Lineage: CBD Nordle
Cannabinoids: 6.2% THC / 7.3% CBD
Terpenes: Myrcene, Pinene, Guaiol

First Impression

Review #58; May 11, 2019,

Palm Tree CBD by LBS is an excellent balanced option that leaves you feeling like you've enjoyed a day off in the sun. Gorgeous smell and flavour, excellent thick vapour and a great mild high. A mellow, "I just wanna chill for ages" kinda high that feels just right.

Observations

Aroma: Floral, fresh, herbal

Flavour: Floral, fresh, fruity, sweet

Bud Colour: Dark green

Pistil Colour: Orange

Trichome Density: Medium

Score Details

Appearance:	4 / 5
High Quality:	5 / 5
Aroma:	14 / 15
Flavour:	13 / 15
Bud Quality:	24 / 30
High Potency:	19 / 30

Overall Score: 79%

Cultivar Ranking: 225th

Sunset

Cultivar/Product Information

Type/Effect: Indica - Medium Heavy
Legacy Name: Sour Kush
Lineage: OG Kush x Sour Diesel
Cannabinoids: 23% THC / <1% CBD
Terpenes: Caryophyllene, Humulene, Linalool

First Impression

Review #39; April 24, 2019,

Sunset by LBS is a great way to kick off an evening. The high is chill and quite potent - I can't think of things to write because I'm that kind of stoned. It would be a great bud before sitting down and watching some TV or playing games. A potent indica option from LBS with a relaxing and stupefying effect, Sunset is a worthwhile try.

Observations

Aroma: Fresh, grassy, herbal, minty, piney

Flavour: Fresh, herbal, piney

Bud Colour: Dark brown/green

Pistil Colour: Brown

Trichome Density: Medium

Score Details

Appearance:	3 / 5
High Quality:	5 / 5
Aroma:	13 / 15
Flavour:	11 / 15
Bud Quality:	18 / 30
High Potency:	25 / 30

Overall Score: 75%

Cultivar Ranking: 282nd

Marley Natural

Overall Performance

Average Score: 79.75%

Brand Ranking: 41st Place

Brand Background

Marley Natural, a brand that bears the name of the late cannabis great Bob Marley, is a midrange quality cannabis producer. Their lineup of cultivars features a colour system that has each colour corresponding to a different experience for the consumer (and also the Rastafarian flag's colour scheme).

In Canada, Marley Natural was brought to the market by the licensed producer High Park Company, which operates mainly out of Ontario.

Other Cultivars: Master Kush
Associated Brands: Broken Coast, Canaca, Good Supply, Grail, Riff, Solei

Cultivar Selection

Berry Lights	84%
Blue Dream	78%
Cannatonic	77%
Island Sweet Skunk	80%

Berry Lights

Cultivar/Product Information

Type/Effect: Indica - Heavy
Legacy Name: Northern Berry
Lineage: Blueberry x Northern Lights #5
Cannabinoids: 24.5% THC / <1% CBD
Terpenes: Caryophyllene, Myrcene, Humulene

First Impression

Review #415; February 9, 2021,

Berry Lights (Marley Black) by Marley Natural has me feeling blissful, relaxed, and stoned. It strikes me as an evening-oriented cultivar, and I certainly wouldn't want to wake and bake with this; it is far too potent and heavy. My head, chest, and limbs are soothed and relieved by the gentle body buzz provided by the high. I could get real cozy, real easily right about now, but first: DINNER (he thought, resisting the urge to drool) - an excellent bud for a night to enjoy and perhaps forget.

Observations

Aroma: Berry, cheese, earthy, funky, herbal, pungent

Flavour: Earthy, funky, herbal

Bud Colour: Dull green

Pistil Colour: Brown/tan

Trichome Density: Medium-High

Score Details

Appearance:	5 / 5
High Quality:	5 / 5
Aroma:	12 / 15
Flavour:	10 / 15
Bud Quality:	27 / 30
High Potency:	25 / 30

Overall Score: 84%

Cultivar Ranking: 132nd

Blue Dream

Cultivar/Product Information

Type/Effect: Sativa Hybrid - Medium Light
Legacy Name: Blue Dream
Lineage: Blueberry x Haze
Cannabinoids: 21.2% THC / <1% CBD
Terpenes: Pinene, Myrcene, Caryophyllene

First Impression

Review #228; April 2, 2020,

Blue Dream (Marley Green) by Marley Natural is a mellow sativa hybrid that livens the mind, calms the thoughts, relaxes the body, and awakens the soul. I should be listening to reggae right now, the cultivar making me feel just as the music typically does. It is not overwhelming for a high-THC variety, and my mellow mood is evidence of this - super peaceful flower, fitting and enjoyable.

Observations

Aroma: Earthy, fresh, herbal, sweet, woody

Flavour: Funky, grassy, herbal, sweet

Bud Colour: Dark green

Pistil Colour: Brown/purple

Trichome Density: Medium

Score Details

Appearance:	4 / 5
High Quality:	5 / 5
Aroma:	12 / 15
Flavour:	10 / 15
Bud Quality:	25 / 30
High Potency:	22 / 30

Overall Score: 78%

Cultivar Ranking: 248th

Cannatonic

Cultivar/Product Information

Type/Effect: Hybrid - Light
Legacy Name: Cannatonic
Lineage: NYC Diesel x Reina Madre
Cannabinoids: 9.9% THC / 6.7% CBD
Terpenes: Myrcene, Caryophyllene, Pinene

First Impression

Review #420; February 28, 2021,

A powerful balanced cultivar, Cannatonic by Marley Natural (Marley Red) is not a CBD-only variety but one boasting nearly 10% THC in addition to some CBD. Effect-wise, I feel a strong headband though I'm not too impaired, just more aware and alive and functional. A great way to calm yourself and straighten out. Before bedtime, I wouldn't necessarily recommend this, but it would be fantastic for waking and baking.

Observations

Aroma: Floral, fresh, herbal, spicy, sweet

Flavour: Floral, fresh, herbal

Bud Colour: Dark brown/green

Pistil Colour: Brown/red

Trichome Density: Low

Score Details

Appearance:	4 / 5
High Quality:	5 / 5
Aroma:	12 / 15
Flavour:	11 / 15
Bud Quality:	23 / 30
High Potency:	22 / 30

Overall Score: 77%

Cultivar Ranking: 263rd

Island Sweet Skunk

Cultivar/Product Information

Type/Effect:	Sativa - Medium Light
Legacy Name:	Island Sweet Skunk
Lineage:	Skunk #1 x Sweet Pink Grapefruit
Cannabinoids:	26.1% THC / <1% CBD
Terpenes:	Terpinolene, Myrcene, Caryophyllene

First Impression

Review #313; August 16, 2020,

A cerebral melting is what's in store for consumers of Island Sweet Skunk (Marley Gold) by Marley Natural. The most potent version of this cultivar I've ever had doesn't disappoint in intensity. I'm not too lacking in writing ability, thinking process, or physical coordination, but this flower produces a razor-sharp, powerful mental buzz. My focus is all over the place the deeper into the Volcano session I go; this is a cultivar and THC % that might make some folks antsy. But, if you are looking for a potent high and elevated mood and alertness, look no further than Island Sweet Skunk.

Observations

Aroma: Citrusy, fruity, grapefruit, herbal, sour, sweet

Flavour: Citrusy, grassy, herbal, sour, sweet, woody

Bud Colour: Light green

Pistil Colour: Brown/red

Trichome Density: Medium

Score Details

Appearance:	4 / 5
High Quality:	5 / 5
Aroma:	12 / 15
Flavour:	11 / 15
Bud Quality:	22 / 30
High Potency:	26 / 30

Overall Score: 80%

Cultivar Ranking: 210th

Namaste

Overall Performance

Average Score: 73.75%

Brand Ranking: 62nd Place

Brand Background

Namaste "elevates every day" for its consumers by providing THC and CBD experiences. With a team featuring doctors, scientists, researchers, cultivators and educators, Namaste creates cannabis products designed for consumers, both new and experienced.

Initially launched as a brand by Zenabis, a large-scale licensed producer of cannabis, Namaste was acquired by Hexo Corp. in 2021.

Other Cultivars: Cream Caramel, Green Banner, GSC
Associated Brands: 48North, Hexo, Redecan, Up

Cultivar Selection

Citrique	81%
D. Bubba	79%
Durga Mata 2	69%
MK Ultra	69%
Sensi Star	74%
Shishkaberry	66%
Ultra Sour	85%
Wappa	67%

Citrique

Cultivar/Product Information

Type/Effect: Sativa Hybrid - Light
Legacy Name: Citrique
Lineage: Lime Skunk x Orange Valley OG
Cannabinoids: 18% THC / <1% CBD
Terpenes: Terpinolene, Myrcene, Caryophyllene

First Impression

Review #314; August 17, 2020,

I'm wired, excited, and I almost knocked over a bong (oh no!) while experiencing the citrusy wonder that is Namaste's Citrique. After a long 11-hour day at work, I was exhausted, but now I'm perked up as though some caffeine hit me - a very energetic, motivating, and functional high. I spent most of it headbanging along to Between the Buried and Me's "Alaska" and dancing around my room. I also just got really into my phone for a good 20 minutes. It is a focused high, a great daytime option, and a great pick-me-up.

Observations

Aroma: Citrusy, herbal, lemon, lime, pungent, sour

Flavour: Citrusy, grassy, herbal, pungent, sour

Bud Colour: Green/tan

Pistil Colour: Orange/tan

Trichome Density: Low-Medium

Score Details

Appearance:	4 / 5
High Quality:	5 / 5
Aroma:	15 / 15
Flavour:	13 / 15
Bud Quality:	23 / 30
High Potency:	21 / 30

Overall Score: 81%

Cultivar Ranking: 165th

D. Bubba

Cultivar/Product Information

Type/Effect: Indica Hybrid - Heavy
Legacy Name: Death Bubba
Lineage: Bubba Kush x Death Star
Cannabinoids: 19% THC / <1% CBD
Terpenes: Caryophyllene, Myrcene, Humulene

First Impression

Review #323; August 30, 2020,

Namaste's D. Bubba started slowing my brain down after bag 4 or 5, but by bag 10, it had come to a grinding halt. My thoughts are few and far between, my empty head throbbing just as my chest and torso, with physical sensation - soothing, relieving, calming. I feel detached from concern and worry (and reality); it is relaxing, and my body feels great. If it weren't 6pm, I'd be looking for a bed, but instead, I'm left with my eyes half shut, stumbling on the search for snacks. A heavy indica, D. Bubba got me pretty baked.

Observations

Aroma: Diesel, earthy, fresh, funky, piney, pungent, sour

Flavour: Earthy, fresh, funky, grassy, herbal, spicy, woody

Bud Colour: Dark green

Pistil Colour: Brown/orange

Trichome Density: Low-Medium

Score Details

Appearance: 4 / 5
High Quality: 5 / 5
Aroma: 13 / 15
Flavour: 11 / 15
Bud Quality: 23 / 30
High Potency: 23 / 30

Overall Score: 79%

Cultivar Ranking: 233rd

Durga Mata 2

Cultivar/Product Information

Type/Effect: Indica - Medium Light
Legacy Name: Durga Mata 2
Lineage: "High CBD Cultivar" x Durga Mata
Cannabinoids: 6% THC / 11% CBD
Terpenes: Terpinolene, Myrcene, Limonene

First Impression

Review #102; September 1, 2019,

Durga Mata 2 delivers a mentally calming and soothing high that is also physically relaxing. An excellent way to chill out after a hard day or kick off a slow day in the right mood. An affordable, hard-hitting, 2:1 CBD:THC balanced cultivar. It is fitting that a Namaste product has me feeling so "zen."

Observations

Aroma: Citrusy, earthy, fruity, herbal, sour, woody

Flavour: Herbal, sour, spicy, woody

Bud Colour: Dark brown/green

Pistil Colour: Brown/orange

Trichome Density: Low-Medium

Score Details

Appearance:	3 / 5
High Quality:	5 / 5
Aroma:	10 / 15
Flavour:	9 / 15
Bud Quality:	20 / 30
High Potency:	22 / 30

Overall Score: 69%

Cultivar Ranking: 362nd

MK Ultra

Cultivar/Product Information

Type/Effect: Indica - Medium Light
Legacy Name: MK Ultra
Lineage: G13 x OG Kush
Cannabinoids: 15.4% THC / <1% CBD
Terpenes: Terpinolene, Myrcene, Limonene

First Impression

Review #92; August 18, 2019,

Namaste's MK Ultra is a less-heavy-than-anticipated indica that delivers a head-high and body sensation that makes you feel slightly stoned. That is to say, high and relaxed, but not overly so - a decent indica option.

Observations

Aroma: Earthy, herbal, minty, piney, sour

Flavour: Earthy, spicy, woody

Bud Colour: Green/tan

Pistil Colour: Orange

Trichome Density: Low-Medium

Score Details

Appearance:	4 / 5
High Quality:	5 / 5
Aroma:	10 / 15
Flavour:	10 / 15
Bud Quality:	22 / 30
High Potency:	18 / 30

Overall Score: 69%

Cultivar Ranking: 360th

Sensi Star

Cultivar/Product Information

Type/Effect: Indica - Neutral
Legacy Name: Sensi Star
Lineage: "Unknown Afghani"
Cannabinoids: 16.5% THC / <1% CBD
Terpenes: Limonene, Caryophyllene, Myrcene

First Impression

Review #96; August 28, 2019,

A relaxing, cerebral, and distinctly not-sleepy indica, Namaste's Sensi Star is chill but exciting at the same time. There is a robust body sensation and headband effect, and my heart is racing. But I'm calm and sedated by the stoned feeling enveloping my consciousness. The progressive metal I'm listening to has me feeling particularly creative when combined with this cultivar as well.

Observations

Aroma: Earthy, herbal, piney, sour

Flavour: Earthy, piney, woody

Bud Colour: Dull green

Pistil Colour: Brown/orange

Trichome Density: Medium

Score Details

Appearance:	4 / 5
High Quality:	5 / 5
Aroma:	12 / 15
Flavour:	10 / 15
Bud Quality:	22 / 30
High Potency:	21 / 30

Overall Score: 74%

Cultivar Ranking: 297th

Shishkaberry

Cultivar/Product Information

Type/Effect:	Indica - Medium Light
Legacy Name:	Shishkaberry
Lineage:	"Unknown Afghani" x DJ Short Blueberry
Cannabinoids:	18.5% THC / <1% CBD
Terpenes:	Myrcene, Caryophyllene, Limonene

First Impression

Review #59; May 13, 2019,

This medium-high potency indica will hit you in the head and chest with a physical sensation and in the mind with an intense cerebral high. Shishkaberry by Namaste hits slightly more energetic than anticipated, I kinda feel less like lounging around and more like accomplishing something. A good option if you want to get stoned in the early to mid evening and still want to do some stuff at home. A good indica option for those not looking for a heavy experience.

Observations

Aroma: Berry, citrusy, earthy, herbal, sour, sweet

Flavour: Earthy, herbal, pungent, spicy, woody

Bud Colour: Dark green/purple

Pistil Colour: Brown/orange

Trichome Density: Medium

Score Details

Appearance:	3 / 5
High Quality:	5 / 5
Aroma:	10 / 15
Flavour:	8 / 15
Bud Quality:	20 / 30
High Potency:	20 / 30

Overall Score: 66%

Cultivar Ranking: 386th

Ultra Sour

Cultivar/Product Information

Type/Effect: Sativa Hybrid - Medium Light
Legacy Name: Ultra Sour
Lineage: East Coast Sour Diesel x MK Ultra
Cannabinoids: 19.6% THC / <1% CBD
Terpenes: Terpinolene, Caryophyllene, Limonene

First Impression

Review #11; April 10, 2019,

This review of Ultra Sour by Namaste was a Plantlife team experience. Ultra Sour is an excellent sativa for a little extra-curricular team-building exercise. Jessie has requested that I inform you all of my "raccoon skin" hat that she is now wearing. MK wishes for those reading to know that she craves Mary Brown's "taters." Travis has been going full Kenny McCormick in a stylish pink hoodie and has nothing to add. We're all conversing in my bedroom over a bowl of this wonderful Ultra Sour. An excellent cultivar for socializing and giggling and enjoying the company of some stoner friends. A heady, cerebral, and fun experience.

Observations

Aroma: Citrusy, fruity, herbal, sour, sour candy

Flavour: Citrusy, herbal, sour, sour candy

Bud Colour: Dull green

Pistil Colour: Orange

Trichome Density: Medium

Score Details

Appearance:	4 / 5
High Quality:	5 / 5
Aroma:	15 / 15
Flavour:	15 / 15
Bud Quality:	23 / 30
High Potency:	23 / 30

Overall Score: 85%

Cultivar Ranking: 109th

Wappa

Cultivar/Product Information

Type/Effect: Indica Hybrid - Medium Light
Legacy Name: Wappa
Lineage: "Unknown Cultivar" x Sweet Skunk
Cannabinoids: 13.6% THC / <1% CBD
Terpenes: Myrcene, Caryophyllene, Pinene

First Impression

Review #27; April 18, 2019,

Namaste's version of the cultivar Wappa certainly feels pleasant and relaxed, as an indica hybrid ideally should. As the THC level is below 15%, the high is relatively light but enjoyable. I consumed this nug for a wake and bake session, so I think it's pretty good for anytime consumption at this potency.

Observations

Aroma: Chocolate, fruity, herbal, spicy, sweet

Flavour: Fresh, herbal, spicy

Bud Colour: Light green

Pistil Colour: Brown/orange

Trichome Density: Medium

Score Details

Appearance:	4 / 5
High Quality:	5 / 5
Aroma:	10 / 15
Flavour:	10 / 15
Bud Quality:	22 / 30
High Potency:	16 / 30

Overall Score: 67%

Cultivar Ranking: 381st

Natural History

Overall Performance

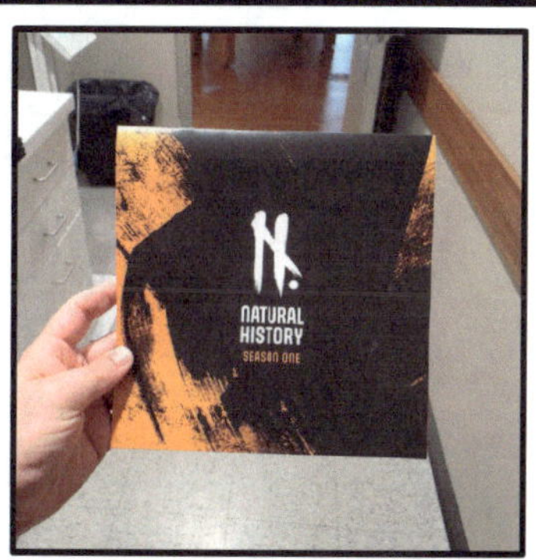

Average Score: 90.00%

Brand Ranking: 9th Place

Brand Background

At Natural History, cannabis legalization is seen as a new chapter in the story of cannabis and, in a greater sense, humanity. As a cannabis producer, their goals are centred around preserving the rich history of cannabis genetics and promoting that history through their line of quality cannabis products.

Natural History's facility is located just outside Edmonton, Alberta, where they produce premium flower in a strictly controlled environment.

Other Cultivars: Garlicane, Meat Breath, Supreme Grapes, Tally Man

Cultivar Selection

ACDC Cookies	84%
Crescendo	90%
Fruit Cake	91%
LA Kush Cake	95%
Mandarin Cookies	92%
Melon Cookies	86%
Zour Apples	92%

ACDC Cookies

Cultivar/Product Information

Type/Effect: Hybrid - Medium Light
Legacy Name: ACDC Cookies F2
Lineage: ACDC Cookies x ACDC Cookies
Cannabinoids: 3.9% THC / 9.8% CBD
Terpenes: Myrcene, Farnesene, Bisabolol

First Impression

Review #350; October 17, 2020,

ACDC Cookies by Natural History is a unique flower; the colour is exceptionally dark, and the flavour seems to develop into something new in each bag. Way more of a headband effect than I anticipated from a 4% THC cultivar. The effect profile is calm and relaxing to the body and mind. I would prefer to pair this balanced cultivar with a day-off rather than a day-on; while I'm not inebriated, I'm also not motivated. I just want to chill, jam to some "Ne Obliviscaris," and contemplate the limits of my creativity. ACDC Cookies slowed me down so I could enjoy my day.

Observations

Aroma: Cheesy, funky, herbal, pungent, sour, spicy, woody

Flavour: Floral, fruity, funky, herbal, sour, spicy, sweet, woody

Bud Colour: Dark green/purple

Pistil Colour: Brown/red

Trichome Density: Low-Medium

Score Details

Appearance:	5 / 5
High Quality:	5 / 5
Aroma:	13 / 15
Flavour:	13 / 15
Bud Quality:	27 / 30
High Potency:	21 / 30

Overall Score: 84%

Cultivar Ranking: 126th

Crescendo

Cultivar/Product Information

Type/Effect: Hybrid - Medium Heavy
Legacy Name: Crescendo
Lineage: ((Chemdog x I-95) x Mandarin Cookies) x (Headband x I-95)
Cannabinoids: 21.8% THC / <1% CBD
Terpenes: Myrcene, Caryophyllene, Limonene

First Impression

Review #355; October 25, 2020,

Natural History always impresses, and Crescendo is no different. The high is very full-feeling; it's hitting me in the head and throughout my body. My eyes are beet-red and barely open, my brain has melted, and my body vibrates with physical sensation. I'm stoned. A super intense and powerful high that'll leave your mind empty. Zoning out on this flower is something I would highly recommend - well done, Natural History.

Observations

Aroma: Chocolate, earthy, fresh, herbal, pungent, sweet

Flavour: Earthy, fresh, funky, grassy, herbal, pungent

Bud Colour: Dark purple

Pistil Colour: Orange

Trichome Density: High

Score Details

Appearance:	4 / 5
High Quality:	5 / 5
Aroma:	14 / 15
Flavour:	12 / 15
Bud Quality:	29 / 30
High Potency:	26 / 30

Overall Score: 90%

Cultivar Ranking: 60th

Fruit Cake

Cultivar/Product Information

Type/Effect: Hybrid - Heavy
Legacy Name: Fruit Cake
Lineage: Cookies & Cream x Plum Wine
Cannabinoids: 23.1% THC / <1% CBD
Terpenes: Caryophyllene, Limonene, Myrcene

First Impression

Review #378; December 8, 2020,

Fruit Cake by Natural History isn't anything like Grandma used to make (unless you had a pretty kickass Grandma), but it is delicious. Delicious in the "I'm super baked and can't see straight" kind of sense, not too notable on taste this one. But the high is potent and a decent mind-f***, so I'm not focused on the flavour. I'm not focused on anything, and I feel pretty spacey, more chill than uplifted, and out of it more than anything. Great munchie/movie material in a unique and powerful cultivar.

Observations

Aroma: Diesel, earthy, fruity, herbal, pungent, sweet

Flavour: Diesel, earthy, funky, herbal, pungent, woody

Bud Colour: Dark green/purple

Pistil Colour: Orange/tan

Trichome Density: High

Score Details

Appearance:	4 / 5
High Quality:	5 / 5
Aroma:	14 / 15
Flavour:	12 / 15
Bud Quality:	29 / 30
High Potency:	27 / 30

Overall Score: 91%

Cultivar Ranking: 44th

LA Kush Cake

Cultivar/Product Information

Type/Effect: Indica - Super Heavy
Legacy Name: LA Kush Cake
Lineage: Kush Mints x Wedding Cake
Cannabinoids: 23.9% THC / <1% CBD
Terpenes: Farnesene, Caryophyllene, Limonene

First Impression

Review #333; September 22, 2020,

Three bags in, and Natural History already has me hooked and high on LA Kush Cake. Six bags in, I'm stoned and stumbling around; this is some powerfully potent herb. The effects are overwhelming my body and mind with relaxation and a sense of bliss. I won't accomplish much more than indulging in some food and cartoons with this kind of high, and I'll be perfectly content with that, baked as I am on this flower. Fifteen bags in, my eyes are heavy, I'm dazed, confused, and thoroughly stoned on LA Kush Cake. A wonderful experience from Natural History, one I'd recommend to most experienced stoners.

Observations

Aroma: Earthy, fresh, grassy, herbal, piney, pungent

Flavour: Earthy, grassy, herbal, piney, pungent, woody

Bud Colour: Dark green/purple

Pistil Colour: Brown/orange

Trichome Density: High

Score Details

Appearance:	5 / 5
High Quality:	5 / 5
Aroma:	14 / 15
Flavour:	12 / 15
Bud Quality:	30 / 30
High Potency:	29 / 30

Overall Score: 95%

Cultivar Ranking: 12th

Mandarin Cookies

Cultivar/Product Information

Type/Effect: Sativa Hybrid - Medium Heavy
Legacy Name: Mandarin Cookies
Lineage: Ethos Cookies #12 x Mandarin Sunset
Cannabinoids: 24.5% THC / <1% CBD
Terpenes: Myrcene, Caryophyllene, Farnesene

First Impression

Review #377; December 6, 2020,

While stoned out of my mind on Natural History's Mandarin Cookies, I tried doing math, but it didn't go well. I'm having a fantastic time while fully cooked, and my mind is gone, miles away. Uplifted in mood, but energy and thinking capacity certainly are not. Other than that, I feel more mellow/chill than anything else. I feel heavy in mind but light in body, ready to take in dinner and some TV. Natural History did a great job with this cultivar, as per usual.

Observations

Aroma: Earthy, herbal, sweet, woody

Flavour: Funky, grassy, herbal, woody

Bud Colour: Dark green/purple

Pistil Colour: Brown/orange

Trichome Density: High

Score Details

Appearance:	5 / 5
High Quality:	5 / 5
Aroma:	13 / 15
Flavour:	11 / 15
Bud Quality:	30 / 30
High Potency:	28 / 30

Overall Score: 92%

Cultivar Ranking: 41st

Melon Cookies

Cultivar/Product Information

Type/Effect: Hybrid - Neutral
Legacy Name: Melon Cookies
Lineage: Forum Cut GSC x Watermelon OG
Cannabinoids: 18.8% THC / <1% CBD
Terpenes: Caryophyllene, Limonene, Myrcene

First Impression

Review #336; September 24, 2020,

An outstanding member of the GSC family, Melon Cookies by Natural History did not disappoint. The heaviness of my eyes and body is bogging me down. A pressure sensation is growing in my skull, as though someone hooked my head up to a bicycle pump. The high itself is on the relaxing side, more mellow than uplifting on the body. Melon Cookies is a unique cultivar you won't want to miss.

Observations

Aroma: Diesel, earthy, herbal, piney, pungent, sour, woody

Flavour: Diesel, earthy, fresh, herbal, pungent

Bud Colour: Dark green/purple

Pistil Colour: Orange

Trichome Density: High

Score Details

Appearance:	4 / 5
High Quality:	5 / 5
Aroma:	13 / 15
Flavour:	13 / 15
Bud Quality:	28 / 30
High Potency:	23 / 30

Overall Score: 86%

Cultivar Ranking: 102nd

Zour Apples

Cultivar/Product Information

Type/Effect:	Sativa Hybrid - Medium Light
Legacy Name:	Zour Apples
Lineage:	Ethos Glue x Plantman Jack Herer
Cannabinoids:	19.5% THC / <1% CBD
Terpenes:	Terpinolene, Caryophyllene, Myrcene

First Impression

Review #354; October 23, 2020,

Ah, Zour Apples - Natural History is spoiling me with one of my favourite cultivars. Uplifting effects and a euphoric blast accompany a light haze and a potent cerebral rush. Don't mistake the sub 20% THC for being weak… it is a very focused, clear, intense high. I think it would fit nicely as a pre-workout, pre-household-chores, or post-work cultivar. Zour Apples is electrifying, euphoric excellence.

Observations

Aroma: Citrusy, herbal, pungent, sour, woody

Flavour: Citrusy, floral, herbal, sour, woody

Bud Colour: Dull green

Pistil Colour: Orange/tan

Trichome Density: Medium-High

Score Details

Appearance:	5 / 5
High Quality:	5 / 5
Aroma:	15 / 15
Flavour:	13 / 15
Bud Quality:	29 / 30
High Potency:	25 / 30

Overall Score: 92%

Cultivar Ranking: 35th

Ness

Overall Performance

Average Score: 84.50%

Brand Ranking: 24th Place

Brand Background

Ness, a midrange cannabis brand from BZAM, seeks to inspire consumers to find their "-ness" Whether it be high-ness, baked-ness, or stoned-ness that you desire, their selection of flavour-forward products should get you there.

Grown indoors at any of BZAM's three cultivation facilities, Ness' cannabis comes from an environment of ideal conditions. Their nugs are also hand-selected by their team before packaging.

Other Cultivars: Black Cherry Punch, Citrus Rush, Gelato Mint, Guava Kush, Nice Cream Peachy Mack, Rainmaker, Secret Garden, Strawberry Tahoe

Cultivar Selection

Lemon Berry	86%
Mint Sour	83%

Lemon Berry

Cultivar/Product Information

Type/Effect: Sativa Hybrid - Neutral
Legacy Name: Lemon Berry
Lineage: Dabney Blue x Lemon Thai
Cannabinoids: 26.2% THC / <1% CBD
Terpenes: Caryophyllene, Limonene, Camphene

First Impression

Review #385; December 19, 2020,

An attractive aroma, a delicious taste, and an incredible, mellow, uplifting high are all bundled together into one cultivar - Lemon Berry by Ness. I want candy that tastes like this and incense that smells like this. Effect-wise, the experience is lighter than it is heavy. My body feels pretty normal, a little more comfortable than before. My mind feels calm and collected; despite the euphoric haze that accents my perception, I lack energy and motivation. However, I feel at peace, as though I've been meditating or chilling in a bath for a while. Lemon Berry is a blissful experience that will brighten any day.

Observations

Aroma: Berry, citrusy, fruity, lemon, sweet, sweet candy

Flavour: Berry, citrusy, fruity, herbal, orange, sweet, sweet candy

Bud Colour: Green

Pistil Colour: Brown

Trichome Density: Medium

Score Details

Appearance:	4 / 5
High Quality:	4 / 5
Aroma:	15 / 15
Flavour:	14 / 15
Bud Quality:	25 / 30
High Potency:	24 / 30

Overall Score: 86%

Cultivar Ranking: 96th

Mint Sour

Cultivar/Product Information

Type/Effect: Sativa Hybrid - Neutral
Legacy Name: Sage 'n Sour
Lineage: SAGE x Sour Diesel
Cannabinoids: 22.4% THC / <1% CBD
Terpenes: Terpinolene, Caryophyllene, Limonene

First Impression

Review #369; November 18, 2020,

Barely four bags into Ness' Mint Sour, I got lost in the depths of the internet while playing around on my phone. A tremendous uplifting and social high, but my mind wanders from time to time; focused, but the focus is drifting off of my task consistently. The aroma on this cultivar was unique: classic Sour Diesel with a hint of mint - as though some Tic-Tacs were thrown in the bag with my nugs. An excellent and euphoric time, a great way to reset after work and catch a new burst of energy. My first introduction to Ness was a pleasant and impressive one.

Observations

Aroma: Citrusy, herbal, lemon, minty, sour

Flavour: Citrusy, grassy, herbal, minty, sour, woody

Bud Colour: Green

Pistil Colour: Orange/tan

Trichome Density: Medium

Score Details

Appearance:	4 / 5
High Quality:	5 / 5
Aroma:	13 / 15
Flavour:	13 / 15
Bud Quality:	25 / 30
High Potency:	23 / 30

Overall Score: 83%

Cultivar Ranking: 140th

Northern Harvest

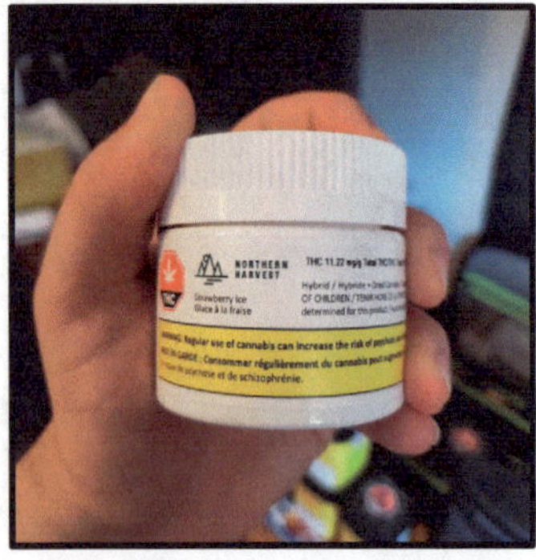

Overall Performance

Average Score: 73.50%

Brand Ranking: 63rd Place

Brand Background

A recreational cannabis brand from Maricann, Northern Harvest brought to market several different sativa cultivars. The brand was active mainly during the first year of legalization, with a limited market presence (at least in Alberta) since then.

Cannabis for the Northern Harvest brand is grown in Ontario.

Other Cultivars: Jack Herer
Associated Brands: High Tide, Kiwi

Cultivar Selection

Blue Haze	67%
Strawberry Ice	80%

Blue Haze

Cultivar/Product Information

Type/Effect: Sativa - Light
Cannabinoids: 13.6% THC / <1% CBD

First Impression

Review #105; September 3, 2019,

Northern Harvest's Blue Haze doesn't have me feeling too hazy; pretty uplifted, clear-headed, and focused. I feel like I'd be really into it if some music were playing. This is somewhat euphoric as well, and my mood is super elevated. Blue Haze should be good for most consumers at this THC potency; it provides a very relaxed but heady high and experience that should please most.

Observations

Aroma: Earthy, fruity, sour, sweet

Flavour: Funky, herbal, sweet

Bud Colour: Light green

Pistil Colour: Brown/orange

Trichome Density: Medium

Score Details

Appearance:	4 / 5
High Quality:	5 / 5
Aroma:	12 / 15
Flavour:	8 / 15
Bud Quality:	21 / 30
High Potency:	17 / 30

Overall Score: 67%

Cultivar Ranking: 378th

Strawberry Ice

Cultivar/Product Information

Type/Effect: Sativa Hybrid - Light
Cannabinoids: 21.5% THC / <1% CBD
Terpenes: Nerolidol, Terpinolene, Caryophyllene

First Impression

Review #50; May 5, 2019,

Strawberry Ice from Northern Harvest is a potent head buzz with substantial effects that are focusing, motivating, and uplifting for me. I feel amazing after a bowl of this lovely bud - a true testament to how great this stuff is when you consider that I hardly slept last night. Strawberry Ice provides an enjoyable energized experience.

Observations

Aroma: Citrusy, herbal, sour

Flavour: Citrusy, herbal, sour, woody

Bud Colour: Green

Pistil Colour: Orange/tan

Trichome Density: Medium

Score Details

Appearance:	4 / 5
High Quality:	5 / 5
Aroma:	13 / 15
Flavour:	12 / 15
Bud Quality:	22 / 30
High Potency:	24 / 30

Overall Score: 80%

Cultivar Ranking: 195th

Ogen

Overall Performance

Average Score: 89.00%

Brand Ranking: 13th Place

Brand Background

A high-quality, mid-priced brand, Ogen cultivates craft cannabis via a modern approach to old-school practices. Beginning their genetic selection process with a pheno-hunt, Ogen seeks out the best of their best to be grown for consumers. The selected genetics are developed using small-batch hydroponics under strict environmental control.

Ogen cannabis is grown near Calgary, Alberta, in small, indoor grow rooms. Whole plants are harvested, hang-dried intact, then hand-trimmed and slow-cured to achieve the highest quality possible in their end product.

Other Cultivars: Bacio Punch, Dosi-GMO-si, Space Flight Superstar

Cultivar Selection

Early Glue RBx1 #15	87%
Gas Berries #112	90%
Lemon Z #42	90%

Early Glue RBx1 #15

Cultivar/Product Information

Type/Effect:	Indica - Medium Heavy
Legacy Name:	Early Glue RBx1
Lineage:	Original Glue x (Original Glue x Blackfire F-1)
Cannabinoids:	19.6% THC / <1% CBD
Terpenes:	Caryophyllene, Limonene, Humulene

First Impression

Review #359; November 1, 2020,

Ogen's Early Glue RBx1 #15 offers a mellow head buzz and physical comfort and relaxation. A calm euphoria comes over my mind as I consume this flower, improving my mood and lifting my spirits. Overall, a medium-heavy cultivar for me, one that's likely to sit me down on the couch with some snacks. It was not sedating, though, something I appreciated, given the great time I had.

Observations

Aroma: Earthy, floral, fresh, herbal, minty, pungent

Flavour: Earthy, fresh, herbal, minty, piney, pungent, woody

Bud Colour: Dull green

Pistil Colour: Orange/tan

Trichome Density: High

Score Details

Appearance:	4 / 5
High Quality:	5 / 5
Aroma:	14 / 15
Flavour:	13 / 15
Bud Quality:	27 / 30
High Potency:	24 / 30

Overall Score: 87%

Cultivar Ranking: 91st

Gas Berries #112

Cultivar/Product Information

Type/Effect: Indica Hybrid - Medium Heavy
Legacy Name: Gas Berries
Lineage: Blueberry x OG Kush x Sour Diesel
Cannabinoids: 18.2% THC / <1% CBD
Terpenes: Pinene, Myrcene, Caryophyllene

First Impression

Review #331; September 14, 2020,

Ogen's Gas Berries #112 lasts longer than anticipated in the Volcano, a good sign for terpene and cannabinoid content. The high is hitting me everywhere. Body sensations overwhelm me while the cerebral meltdown zones me out nearly completely. Yet, I can still hone in on writing when I need to. It would seem this high gets you spaced out, but you're the captain of the spaceship still. Relaxing and blissful, a great combination of effects from a great combination of cultivars in Gas Berries.

Observations

Aroma: Berry, diesel, earthy, fruity, pungent, sweet

Flavour: Berry, diesel, earthy, grassy, herbal, pungent, sour

Bud Colour: Dull green

Pistil Colour: Brown/tan

Trichome Density: High

Score Details

Appearance:	5 / 5
High Quality:	5 / 5
Aroma:	15 / 15
Flavour:	13 / 15
Bud Quality:	29 / 30
High Potency:	23 / 30

Overall Score: 90%

Cultivar Ranking: 56th

Lemon Z #42

Cultivar/Product Information

Type/Effect: Sativa Hybrid - Medium Light
Legacy Name: Lemon Z
Lineage: Lemon Skunk x Zkittlez
Cannabinoids: 20.2% THC / <1% CBD
Terpenes: Caryophyllene, Linalool, Limonene

First Impression

Review #294; July 24, 2020,

My first Ogen product, Lemon Z #42, was a grand introduction. The high is euphoric and mellow, and quite clear-headed. I could see this as a tremendous functional high for AM or before any tasks you wish to be pleasantly stoned during. Better looking than I could've hoped, and the same goes for aroma and feel. Lemon Z #42 is a stand-out flower.

Observations

Aroma: Citrusy, diesel, earthy, herbal, pungent, sour, woody

Flavour: Citrusy, herbal, sour, woody

Bud Colour: Light green

Pistil Colour: Orange/tan

Trichome Density: High

Score Details

Appearance:	5 / 5
High Quality:	5 / 5
Aroma:	15 / 15
Flavour:	12 / 15
Bud Quality:	29 / 30
High Potency:	24 / 30

Overall Score: 90%

Cultivar Ranking: 55th

Palmetto

Overall Performance

Average Score: 80.67%

Brand Ranking: 37th Place

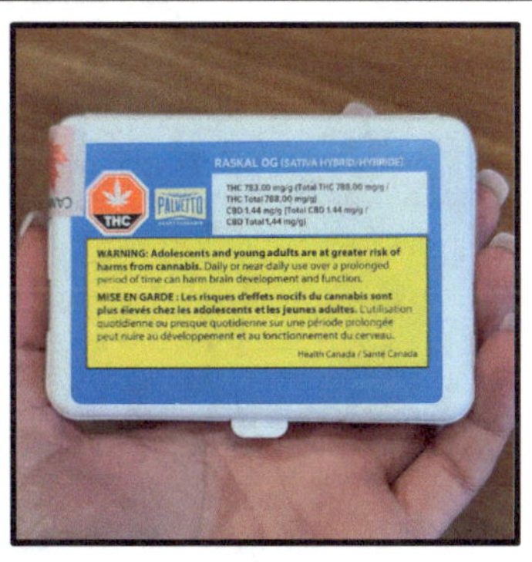

Brand Background

Palmetto cannabis is a recreational brand from Sundial Growers, an Albertan licensed producer. Featuring creative and colourful advertising and packaging, Palmetto is a brand inspired by the fun side of cannabis.

Grown indoors in a facility near Olds, Alberta, Palmetto cannabis is monitored carefully and grown, dried, and cured under strict controls.

Other Cultivars: Lemon Royale, OG Kush, Pink Kush, Platinum Cookies, Romulan

Associated Brands: Sundial, Topleaf

Cultivar Selection

Chemdog	81%
Headband	78%
Nuken	83%

Chemdog

Cultivar/Product Information

Type/Effect: Sativa Hybrid - Medium Heavy
Legacy Name: Chemdog
Lineage: Dogbud
Cannabinoids: 17.8% THC / <1% CBD

First Impression

Review #315; August 21, 2020,

A less foggy high than I anticipated, Palmetto's Chemdog is super heady and intense for a mid-teen THC % flower. I find myself getting lost in deep thought, staring blankly at whatever is in front of me all the while. I feel I want to socialize, but I'm high enough that I fear I might not speak very well. This one is a pretty good mind-melter, ideal for days meant to be wasted.

Observations

Aroma: Earthy, fruity, herbal, spicy, sweet, woody

Flavour: Earthy, fresh, fruity, herbal, sweet, woody

Bud Colour: Dull green

Pistil Colour: Brown/orange

Trichome Density: Medium

Score Details

Appearance:	4 / 5
High Quality:	5 / 5
Aroma:	13 / 15
Flavour:	12 / 15
Bud Quality:	24 / 30
High Potency:	23 / 30

Overall Score: 81%

Cultivar Ranking: 180th

Headband

Cultivar/Product Information

Type/Effect: Sativa Hybrid - Medium Heavy
Legacy Name: Headband
Lineage: OG Kush x Sour Diesel
Cannabinoids: 19.2% THC / <1% CBD

First Impression

Review #345; October 9, 2020,

Headband by Palmetto has produced a full-feeling, cerebral high in me. A high that certainly lives up to the name, the headband effect is extreme, my eyes are watery and half-shut, I can't think too clearly, and I'm cooked. Not half-baked either; I'm well-done for sure. I was expecting the cerebral intensity, but I certainly didn't expect this much of a kick. Now it's creeping down to my shoulders and chest - a potent and worthwhile cultivar to zone out on.

Observations

Aroma: Diesel, earthy, fresh, grassy, herbal, sour

Flavour: Earthy, grassy, herbal, sour

Bud Colour: Green

Pistil Colour: Brown/red

Trichome Density: Low-Medium

Score Details

Appearance:	4 / 5
High Quality:	5 / 5
Aroma:	12 / 15
Flavour:	10 / 15
Bud Quality:	24 / 30
High Potency:	23 / 30

Overall Score: 78%

Cultivar Ranking: 247th

Nuken

Cultivar/Product Information

Type/Effect: Indica Hybrid - Medium Heavy
Legacy Name: Nuken
Lineage: God Bud x Kish
Cannabinoids: 20.3% THC / <1% CBD

First Impression

Review #290; July 11, 2020,

My first look at Palmetto is my review of their take on Nuken. The aroma is sweet and fruity, very inviting. My mind is pretty relaxed, as is my mood. Physically, I feel heavy and lethargic. I feel like this may be a good social or creative indica. Palmetto has made a decent first impression with a great taste, smell, and quality all around.

Observations

Aroma: Fruity, herbal, sour, sweet

Flavour: Fruity, herbal, sweet

Bud Colour: Dark green

Pistil Colour: Orange/tan

Trichome Density: Medium

Score Details

Appearance:	4 / 5
High Quality:	5 / 5
Aroma:	14 / 15
Flavour:	12 / 15
Bud Quality:	25 / 30
High Potency:	23 / 30

Overall Score: 83%

Cultivar Ranking: 137th

Poolboy

Overall Performance

Average Score: 81.50%

Brand Ranking: 33rd Place

Brand Background

Brought to market by licensed producer 314 Pure, Poolboy is a recreational cannabis brand featuring tongue-in-cheek marketing, colourful packaging, and flavourful product profiles.

The facility where Poolboy cannabis is grown occupies a 16-acre plot in southern Alberta. Features of the facility are a no-waste approach to cultivation and building specifications up to EU standards.

Other Cultivars: Strawberry Banana, Super Lemon Haze

Cultivar Selection

Bruce	83%
Chemdog	82%
King T	80%
Raspberry Cough	81%

Bruce

Cultivar/Product Information

Type/Effect:	Sativa Hybrid - Medium Heavy
Legacy Name:	Bruce Banner
Lineage:	OG Kush x Strawberry Diesel
Cannabinoids:	19.4% THC / <1% CBD
Terpenes:	Myrcene, Caryophyllene, Linalool

First Impression

Review #395; December 30, 2020,

Bruce has finally made his way onto the recreational market, and Poolboy has done an excellent job with this cultivar. These sticky, dense buds are full of aroma and flavour and offer a high that could chill out the consciousness of even the Hulk himself. The headband from this one is hazy and full of zoned-out, stoned-out effects. Everything seems brighter, more vivid, but my mind is dull; it is a euphoric but stupefying high that offers little motivation and functionality. In other words: I'm messed up. Bruce is a great guy to waste away a day with.

Observations

Aroma: Diesel, earthy, fresh, herbal, pungent, sweet

Flavour: Earthy, funky, herbal, pungent, spicy, woody

Bud Colour: Dark green

Pistil Colour: Brown/orange

Trichome Density: Medium

Score Details

Appearance:	4 / 5
High Quality:	5 / 5
Aroma:	13 / 15
Flavour:	11 / 15
Bud Quality:	27 / 30
High Potency:	23 / 30

Overall Score: 83%

Cultivar Ranking: 142nd

Chemdog

Cultivar/Product Information

Type/Effect: Indica Hybrid - Medium Heavy
Legacy Name: Chemdog
Lineage: Dogbud
Cannabinoids: 17.1% THC / <1% CBD
Terpenes: Myrcene, Caryophyllene, Pinene

First Impression

Review #365; November 8, 2020,

Poolboy's Chemdog is a great time and a heady haze. Mellow, but it still has that "I feel f***ed up" factor. I chowed down on some delicious three-cheese pepperoni pizza while stoned on this strong-smelling flower - a solid appetite-inspiring option for any time.

Observations

Aroma: Fruity, grassy, herbal, sweet

Flavour: Funky, grassy, herbal, sweet

Bud Colour: Dark green

Pistil Colour: Brown

Trichome Density: Low-Medium

Score Details

Appearance:	4 / 5
High Quality:	5 / 5
Aroma:	13 / 15
Flavour:	12 / 15
Bud Quality:	26 / 30
High Potency:	22 / 30

Overall Score: 82%

Cultivar Ranking: 158th

King T

Cultivar/Product Information

Type/Effect: Sativa - Light
Legacy Name: King Tut
Lineage: AK-47
Cannabinoids: 19.5% THC / <1% CBD
Terpenes: Myrcene, Caryophyllene, Pinene

First Impression

Review #364; November 4, 2020.

King T by Poolboy offers a mostly cerebral, energetic high. It perked me right up after a few bags and brightened my mood. I don't feel that intoxicated, and it's super clear-headed and functional. This bud would pair well with household chores or a get-together with some friends. Hell, I would consider this pre-gym flower too. It's that bright and active feeling. I can't wait to try a wake 'n bake with my liege, King T.

Observations

Aroma: Fresh, herbal, woody

Flavour: Funky, grassy, herbal, woody

Bud Colour: Dark green/purple

Pistil Colour: Orange

Trichome Density: Medium

Score Details

Appearance:	4 / 5
High Quality:	5 / 5
Aroma:	12 / 15
Flavour:	11 / 15
Bud Quality:	26 / 30
High Potency:	22 / 30

Overall Score: 80%

Cultivar Ranking: 216th

Raspberry Cough

Cultivar/Product Information

Type/Effect: Sativa Hybrid - Medium Light
Legacy Name: Raspberry Cough
Lineage: Cambodian Sativa x ICE
Cannabinoids: 17.3% THC / <1% CBD
Terpenes: Bisabolol, Caryophyllene, Limonene

First Impression

Review #393; December 29, 2020,

Raspberry Cough (aptly named, I'm coughing a ton) by Poolboy offers a focused but hazy daytime buzz, ideal for mornings or afternoons to give the day some spice. I feel mellow but uplifted and euphoric as well. I'm feeling quite functional… one for tackling housework or video games (I want to grind) - a great, active-minded buzz.

Observations

Aroma: Berry, fruity, herbal, sweet

Flavour: Floral, fresh, grassy, herbal, sweet

Bud Colour: Dark green/purple

Pistil Colour: Brown/orange

Trichome Density: Medium

Score Details

Appearance:	4 / 5
High Quality:	5 / 5
Aroma:	13 / 15
Flavour:	12 / 15
Bud Quality:	26 / 30
High Potency:	21 / 30

Overall Score: 81%

Cultivar Ranking: 176th

Pure Sunfarms

Overall Performance

Average Score: 75.11%

Brand Ranking: 57th Place

Brand Background

Found in the Fraser Valley in BC, Pure Sunfarms operates as an ode to BC bud. They seek to honour the traditions and practices of past cultivators and see it as a privilege to be able to grow in a place so renowned for excellent cannabis.

Pure Sunfarms' facility for cannabis production is located in Delta, BC. Utilizing a greenhouse setup (with the entire space making up 16 grow rooms) and legacy growing techniques, Pure Sunfarms produces large quantities of BC bud for the recreational market.

Other Cultivars: Black Cherry Punch, Blueberry Kush, Jet Fuel Gelato, Pennywise

Cultivar Selection

Afghan Kush	70%
Critical Kali Mist	69%
D. Bubba	81%
Headband	80%
Island Honey	65%
Pink Kush	77%
Pure Sun CBD	85%
Purple Sun God	70%
White Rhino	79%

Afghan Kush

Cultivar/Product Information

Type/Effect: Indica - Neutral
Legacy Name: Afghan Kush
Lineage: Hindu Kush
Cannabinoids: 19.1% THC / <1% CBD
Terpenes: Myrcene, Caryophyllene, Linalool

First Impression

Review #244; April 21, 2020,

Pure Sunfarms' take on Afghan Kush was calm and mellow but not overwhelming or sedating, and it didn't feel as strong as anticipated. Despite this, the medium potency high was fuel for a great walk with my dog, a good gaming session, and a feast of munchies. It is a solid higher THC option for folks newer to cannabis or those looking for a mellow buzz.

Observations

Aroma: Cheese, earthy, herbal, sour, woody

Flavour: Earthy, herbal, sour, woody

Bud Colour: Green

Pistil Colour: Brown/red

Trichome Density: Medium

Score Details

Appearance:	4 / 5
High Quality:	4 / 5
Aroma:	12 / 15
Flavour:	10 / 15
Bud Quality:	22 / 30
High Potency:	18 / 30

Overall Score: 70%

Cultivar Ranking: 345th

Critical Kali Mist

Cultivar/Product Information

Type/Effect: Sativa - Light
Legacy Name: Critical Kali Mist
Cannabinoids: 15.7% THC / <1% CBD
Terpenes: Pinene, Myrcene, Caryophyllene

First Impression

Review #259; May 14, 2020,

Critical Kali Mist by Pure Sunfarms is a great, light afternoon smoke that offers a clear and mellow head buzz. A very comfortable feeling high, particularly for a sativa. I don't feel too different after consuming this flower, except I'm high and drifting off in thought more often.

Observations

Aroma: Citrusy, fresh, grassy, herbal, sour, sweet

Flavour: Grassy, herbal, sour, woody

Bud Colour: Dark green

Pistil Colour: Brown/orange

Trichome Density: Medium

Score Details

Appearance:	4 / 5
High Quality:	5 / 5
Aroma:	11 / 15
Flavour:	10 / 15
Bud Quality:	23 / 30
High Potency:	16 / 30

Overall Score: 69%

Cultivar Ranking: 358th

D. Bubba

Cultivar/Product Information

Type/Effect: Indica - Medium Heavy
Legacy Name: Death Bubba
Lineage: Bubba Kush x Death Star
Cannabinoids: 17.7% THC / <1% CBD
Terpenes: Caryophyllene, Limonene, Humulene

First Impression

Review #302; August 2, 2020,

One of the best yet from Pure Sunfarms is their take on D. Bubba. It is potent and feels more substantial than the average 17.7% flower. The high is heavy on the mind and body. My eyes feel drowsy, and my mood is thoroughly sedated. I'm zoning out and jiving to some stoner metal jams, a great pairing with the slow, lethargic high. It is a grungy high bogging me down; I feel like a sloth. I'm pretty happy with this selection from Pure Sunfarms.

Observations

Aroma: Earthy, herbal, pungent, sour

Flavour: Diesel, earthy, grassy, herbal, pungent

Bud Colour: Dark green

Pistil Colour: Brown/orange

Trichome Density: Medium

Score Details

Appearance:	4 / 5
High Quality:	5 / 5
Aroma:	12 / 15
Flavour:	13 / 15
Bud Quality:	24 / 30
High Potency:	23 / 30

Overall Score: 81%

Cultivar Ranking: 189th

Headband

Cultivar/Product Information

Type/Effect: Hybrid - Medium Heavy
Legacy Name: Headband
Lineage: OG Kush x Sour Diesel
Cannabinoids: 18.7% THC / <1% CBD
Terpenes: Caryophyllene, Linalool, Humulene

First Impression

Review #351; October 18, 2020,

I feel Pure Sunfarms' Headband in my skull; there is an extreme physical sensation of pressure in my head. The high is cerebral and potent. A bit of a mind-f***, you'll be zoned in on something one second and then BAM, nothing in your mind at all, completely vacant. An excellent cultivar for inspiring munchie consumption and creativity with euphoric and spacey effects. With an immense head-high for its THC percentage, Headband lives up to its name and the expectations I have of Pure Sunfarms products.

Observations

Aroma: Cheese, funky, earthy, herbal, pungent, sour, woody

Flavour: Earthy, funky, grassy, herbal

Bud Colour: Dull green

Pistil Colour: Brown/orange

Trichome Density: Low-Medium

Score Details

Appearance:	4 / 5
High Quality:	5 / 5
Aroma:	12 / 15
Flavour:	11 / 15
Bud Quality:	24 / 30
High Potency:	24 / 30

Overall Score: 80%

Cultivar Ranking: 215th

Island Honey

Cultivar/Product Information

Type/Effect:	Sativa - Super Light
Legacy Name:	Island Honey
Lineage:	Early Pearl x Jack Herer
Cannabinoids:	15.3% THC / <1% CBD
Terpenes:	Myrcene, Bisabolol, Linalool

First Impression

Review #210; March 12, 2020,

For a lighter sativa flower, Island Honey from Pure Sunfarms is one that still packs a decent headband effect. I'm relatively unimpaired on this flower; peering through the mental fog is pretty effortless. My mood and spirit are uplifted, and my body is relieved. The slight buzz I've got going is doing just the trick without being apparent in the foreground of my mind - a functional and manageable high.

Observations

Aroma: Herbal, sour, sweet, woody

Flavour: Funky, herbal, sweet, woody

Bud Colour: Light green

Pistil Colour: Brown/red

Trichome Density: Low-Medium

Score Details

Appearance:	4 / 5
High Quality:	4 / 5
Aroma:	11 / 15
Flavour:	9 / 15
Bud Quality:	23 / 30
High Potency:	14 / 30

Overall Score: 65%

Cultivar Ranking: 390th

Pink Kush

Cultivar/Product Information

Type/Effect: Indica - Heavy
Legacy Name: Pink Kush
Lineage: OG Kush
Cannabinoids: 22.5% THC / <1% CBD
Terpenes: Myrcene, Bisabolol, Humulene

First Impression

Review #306; August 7, 2020,

My mind feels heavy and slow, my mood is quite chill, and I'm pretty baked on Pure Sunfarms' Pink Kush. It's much more a lay-you-out-on-the-couch flower than anything else. I feel lazy after vaporizing a bowl of this bud, not too motivated, and I'm craving food - a decent pick for an evening in and pretty intense.

Observations

Aroma: Earthy, funky, grassy, herbal, sour

Flavour: Earthy, grassy, herbal, piney, pungent

Bud Colour: Dark green

Pistil Colour: Brown/red

Trichome Density: Medium

Score Details

Appearance:	4 / 5
High Quality:	5 / 5
Aroma:	11 / 15
Flavour:	10 / 15
Bud Quality:	24 / 30
High Potency:	23 / 30

Overall Score: 77%

Cultivar Ranking: 265th

Pure Sun CBD

Cultivar/Product Information

Type/Effect: Hybrid - Super Light
Legacy Name: Cannatonic
Lineage: NYC Diesel x Reina Madre
Cannabinoids: <1% THC / 18.2% CBD
Terpenes: Myrcene, Bisabolol, Linalool

First Impression

Review #303; August 5, 2020,

Pure Sun CBD, by Pure Sunfarms, is pure satisfaction and pleasantness in a bag. Peaceful and serene, calm and zen, flavourful, and CBD-rich, this bud is lovely in both effect and quality. I feel a slight tightness in the eyes and forehead but not much else physical; I've been relieved of such sensations by this flower, and I'm pretty loose and limber. My mind is slowed slightly and a bit hazy, though the focus inspired by the high-CBD cuts through the mental fog. I'm not high, but I am sky-high, on a cloud, in a blissful state of calm.

Observations

Aroma: Floral, fresh, fruity, melon, sour, sweet

Flavour: Floral, fresh, fruity, herbal, sweet

Bud Colour: Green/tan

Pistil Colour: Brown

Trichome Density: Low

Score Details

Appearance:	4 / 5
High Quality:	5 / 5
Aroma:	13 / 15
Flavour:	13 / 15
Bud Quality:	26 / 30
High Potency:	24 / 30

Overall Score: 85%

Cultivar Ranking: 118th

Purple Sun God

Cultivar/Product Information

Type/Effect: Indica - Light
Legacy Name: Purple Sun God
Lineage: Purple God Bud x UBC Chemo
Cannabinoids: 11.4% THC / <1% CBD
Terpenes: Caryophyllene, Limonene, Ocimene

First Impression

Review #255; May 7, 2020,

There's a certain tightness and heaviness to my eyes while under the spell of Purple Sun God by Pure Sunfarms. Sleep's "Marijuanaut's Theme" plays in the background as my forehead pulses with physical sensation. Most of the high is in the eyes and forehead area, with little body effect. As a result, it's not too heavy overall and made for some calm and mellow wake and bake material. At this potency, an excellent starter cultivar, or one for those interested in lower intensity, high effect highs. Everything seems brighter and more pleasant with Purple Sun God lighting the way. Praise the Sun!

Observations

Aroma: Fresh, herbal, sour, sweet, woody

Flavour: Fresh, grassy, herbal, sour

Bud Colour: Dull green

Pistil Colour: Brown/orange

Trichome Density: Low

Score Details

Appearance:	4 / 5
High Quality:	5 / 5
Aroma:	10 / 15
Flavour:	11 / 15
Bud Quality:	25 / 30
High Potency:	15 / 30

Overall Score: 70%

Cultivar Ranking: 349th

White Rhino

Cultivar/Product Information

Type/Effect: Indica - Neutral
Legacy Name: White Rhino
Lineage: "Unknown Indica" x White Widow
Cannabinoids: 19% THC / <1% CBD
Terpenes: Myrcene, Ocimene, Humulene

First Impression

Review #230; April 4, 2020,

White Rhino by Pure Sunfarms is a calm, full-body sensation coupled with a mellow buzz right in the center of your brain. It's a weird description, but it feels like something is emanating from the center of my skull - in a good way! I'm pretty together still, entirely functional, but certainly high and having an excellent time chilling.

Observations

Aroma: Chocolate, fresh, fruity, herbal, sweet

Flavour: Fruity, grassy, herbal, sweet

Bud Colour: Dark green

Pistil Colour: Brown

Trichome Density: Medium

Score Details

Appearance:	4 / 5
High Quality:	5 / 5
Aroma:	13 / 15
Flavour:	12 / 15
Bud Quality:	23 / 30
High Potency:	22 / 30

Overall Score: 79%

Cultivar Ranking: 232nd

Qwest

Overall Performance

Average Score: 93.73%

Brand Ranking: 2nd Place

Brand Background

Given the quality of their cannabis, it is no surprise that Qwest is of the top-rated brands in the market.

Qwest produces cannabis in either of two facilities, one in Battleford, Saskatchewan, and one in the Creston Valley of BC. Utilizing small-batch production and hang-drying and hand-trimming, Qwest produces cannabis to the highest standard.

Other Cultivars: Grape Pie, Papaya Cake, Redneck Wedding, Stuffed French Toast, Sunset MAC

Cultivar Selection

Cultivar	Score
Black Lime Reserve	89%
Death Bubba	92%
Ex-Wife	91%
Forbidden Fruit	96%
Gelato #33	93%
Gelato #41	92%
Goji OG	94%
Ice Cream Cake	96%
JB Cookies	93%
Kalifornia	92%
Kush Mints	98%
MAC1	97%
OG Kush 25	91%
Oregon Lemons	92%
Original Glue	94%
Phenome OG Spike	95%
Pineapple Upside Down Cake	93%
Point Break	98%
Strawberry Cough	93%
Super Silver Skunk	97%
Wedding Breath	89%
Wedding Cake	97%

Black Lime Reserve

Cultivar/Product Information

Type/Effect: Indica Hybrid - Neutral
Legacy Name: Black Lime Reserve
Lineage: Chemdog Reserve x Northern Lights x Purple Kush
Cannabinoids: 14.7% THC / <1% CBD
Terpenes: Caryophyllene, Myrcene, Pinene

First Impression

Review #162; December 17, 2019,

I never thought I'd smell bud that reminded me of lime zest and fresh herbs, but this Black Lime Reserve by Qwest is that bud: it smells like something I want to put in a delicious salsa recipe. The quality: immaculate. The aroma: unique. The high: cerebral, clear-minded and in the back of the skull. Physically, there's a medium potency chest and head sensation. Thoroughly enjoyable. It's excellent in every way and not so potent that it'll give less serious stoners a rough time. Great flavour and flower from Qwest, as usual.

Observations

Aroma: Citrusy, fresh, herbal, lime, piney

Flavour: Citrusy, fresh, herbal, lime, piney

Bud Colour: Light green

Pistil Colour: Orange/tan

Trichome Density: Medium-High

Score Details

Appearance:	4 / 5
High Quality:	5 / 5
Aroma:	15 / 15
Flavour:	14 / 15
Bud Quality:	30 / 30
High Potency:	21 / 30

Overall Score: 89%

Cultivar Ranking: 73rd

Death Bubba

Cultivar/Product Information

Type/Effect: Indica Hybrid - Super Heavy
Legacy Name: Death Bubba
Lineage: Bubba Kush x Death Star
Cannabinoids: 22.2% THC / <1% CBD
Terpenes: Caryophyllene, Limonene, Myrcene

First Impression

Review #201; February 27, 2020,

I'm only halfway through my bags of Death Bubba by Qwest, and I'm wondering whether I should tap out or not - it's deadly potent. This is one you'll feel in the face, head, throat, lungs, torso, limbs, extremities, etc. It's a full-bodied, "chillax and let your mind roam the universe, so spaced out and stoned you'll lose track of space and time," kinda high (to quote my exact inner monologue). My brain, now thoroughly melted, struggles to formulate new sentences to write. I must go, for my snacks and my bed are calling me.

Observations

Aroma: Earthy, herbal, pungent, sweet

Flavour: Earthy, funky, pungent, sweet

Bud Colour: Dark green/purple

Pistil Colour: Brown/orange

Trichome Density: High

Score Details

Appearance:	5 / 5
High Quality:	5 / 5
Aroma:	13 / 15
Flavour:	10 / 15
Bud Quality:	30 / 30
High Potency:	29 / 30

Overall Score: 92%

Cultivar Ranking: 43rd

Ex-Wife

Cultivar/Product Information

Type/Effect: Indica Hybrid - Heavy
Legacy Name: Ex-Wife
Lineage: Ghost OG x Trophy Wife
Cannabinoids: 25.5% THC / <1% CBD
Terpenes: Caryophyllene, Bisabolol, Linalool

First Impression

Review #343; October 3, 2020,

So far, Qwest's Ex-Wife is potent, relaxing, and sedating. Given the effect profile, this flower should be consumed in the PM, or at least when you've set time aside to be useless and sleepy. My eyes are heavy, and my brain is melting; my body is loose and relieved of its usual stresses. Lasting forever in the Volcano, so many bags have been produced that I've lost count. My will to continue writing fades as my inebriation intensifies. Not a light cultivar at all. Heavy indeed, and powerful highs are to be expected.

Observations

Aroma: Earthy, fresh, grassy, herbal, piney

Flavour: Earthy, fresh, grassy, herbal, piney, woody

Bud Colour: Dull green

Pistil Colour: Brown/tan

Trichome Density: High

Score Details

Appearance:	4 / 5
High Quality:	5 / 5
Aroma:	12 / 15
Flavour:	12 / 15
Bud Quality:	30 / 30
High Potency:	28 / 30

Overall Score: 91%

Cultivar Ranking: 53rd

Forbidden Fruit

Cultivar/Product Information

Type/Effect: Indica Hybrid - Medium Heavy
Legacy Name: Forbidden Fruit
Lineage: Cherry Pie x Tangie
Cannabinoids: 19.1% THC / <1% CBD
Terpenes: Caryophyllene, Guaiol, Linalool

First Impression

Review #269; June 8, 2020,

Qwest's Forbidden Fruit tempts me as though it were an apple of Eden, luring me in with its extraordinary sensory qualities. As I, uh, Adam in this case, I guess, partake of the Forbidden Fruit, I am impressed, as it tastes just as wonderful and fruity as it smells. I'd also like to make note that my inner monologue at the moment is voiced by Futurama's Zapp Brannigan; the Adam and Eve reference made me think of the episode "In a Gadda Da Leela." But, I digress; the high itself is exceptionally mellow, and there is also a sharp throbbing in my head (not a bad kind). Perfect for any time you want to be chilling. One of my favourites.

Observations

Aroma: Floral, fruity, herbal, orange, sweet

Flavour: Fruity, herbal, orange, sweet, woody

Bud Colour: Green/purple

Pistil Colour: Orange/red

Trichome Density: High

Score Details

Appearance:	5 / 5
High Quality:	5 / 5
Aroma:	15 / 15
Flavour:	15 / 15
Bud Quality:	30 / 30
High Potency:	26 / 30

Overall Score: 96%

Cultivar Ranking: 7th

Gelato #33

Cultivar/Product Information

Type/Effect: Hybrid - Medium Heavy
Legacy Name: Gelato
Lineage: Sunset Sherbet x Thin Mint GSC
Cannabinoids: 19.7% THC / <1% CBD
Terpenes: Caryophyllene, Myrcene, Limonene

First Impression

Review #160; December 11, 2019,

Qwest did incredible things with one of my favourite cultivars, Gelato #33. This potent cross of two different GSC cultivars is cerebrally intense and paralyzingly powerful on both the body and mind. I'm mentally alert but super stoned; focused but high as a kite. My body is overcome with waves of sensation from head to toe, and I could easily lock myself into any couch. This fantastic high should impress most stoners, but new or infrequent consumers should be wary: this bud is potent.

Observations

Aroma: Earthy, minty, piney, pungent, sweet

Flavour: Earthy, funky, grassy, herbal, piney, pungent

Bud Colour: Dark purple

Pistil Colour: Orange

Trichome Density: High

Score Details

Appearance:	5 / 5
High Quality:	5 / 5
Aroma:	15 / 15
Flavour:	12 / 15
Bud Quality:	30 / 30
High Potency:	26 / 30

Overall Score: 93%

Cultivar Ranking: 22nd

Gelato #41

Cultivar/Product Information

Type/Effect: Hybrid - Neutral
Legacy Name: Gelato
Lineage: Sunset Sherbet x Thin Mint GSC
Cannabinoids: 20% THC / <1% CBD
Terpenes: Limonene, Myrcene, Caryophyllene

First Impression

Review #249; April 25, 2020,

Oh, Qwest's Gelato 41, you're everything I need in a post-morning-shift flower: potent, physically rejuvenating and relaxing, mentally inspiring, uplifting, and euphoric. A damn near perfect hybrid for any occasion that you just want to feel happy, enthused, or excited for. The high is present mainly in the head, forehead, and face and partially in the chest and limbs. A wonderful grow from the masters at Qwest.

Observations

Aroma: Earthy, floral, fresh, grassy, piney, sweet, woody

Flavour: Earthy, floral, fresh, grassy, sweet, woody

Bud Colour: Dark green/purple

Pistil Colour: Brown/tan

Trichome Density: High

Score Details

Appearance:	4 / 5
High Quality:	5 / 5
Aroma:	14 / 15
Flavour:	13 / 15
Bud Quality:	30 / 30
High Potency:	26 / 30

Overall Score: 92%

Cultivar Ranking: 38th

Goji OG

Cultivar/Product Information

Type/Effect: Sativa - Heavy
Legacy Name: Goji OG
Lineage: Nepali OG x Snow Lotus
Cannabinoids: 19.8% THC / <1% CBD
Terpenes: Limonene, Myrcene, Pinene

First Impression

Review #268; June 4, 2020,

Three bags in, and Goji OG already has me squinting, a tightness behind the eyes provided by this masterful grow from Qwest. Now ten bags in, my mind is gone, melting, fading away. I pause every sentence as I write, too stoned to stay focused. I seriously don't know what else to say. It's crazy potent, at a much higher perceived intensity than the actual THC potency... it feels way more potent than 20%. Super uplifting, I'm no longer tired but nearly overwhelmed by this fantastic flower.

Observations

Aroma: Earthy, floral, herbal, piney, sour, sweet

Flavour: Floral, grassy, herbal, woody

Bud Colour: Light green

Pistil Colour: Brown/tan

Trichome Density: High

Score Details

Appearance:	5 / 5
High Quality:	5 / 5
Aroma:	14 / 15
Flavour:	13 / 15
Bud Quality:	30 / 30
High Potency:	27 / 30

Overall Score: 94%

Cultivar Ranking: 19th

Ice Cream Cake

Cultivar/Product Information

Type/Effect: Indica Hybrid - Super Heavy
Legacy Name: Ice Cream Cake
Lineage: Gelato #33 x Wedding Cake
Cannabinoids: 23.1% THC / <1% CBD
Terpenes: Limonene, Caryophyllene, Myrcene

First Impression

Review #117; September 14, 2019,

Ice Cream Cake by Qwest, at 23.1% THC, might be the most potent feeling flower I've had on the recreational market (so far). A heavy, cerebral stoned feeling is coupled with a powerful sensation throughout the body. I suspect I would be ultra couch-locked if not standing at the moment. I am craving munchies and some TV… this bud is not conducive to focus. The quality is perfect, the smell and flavour amazing, and the high is immaculate, rivalling the best of the best.

Observations

Aroma: Diesel, earthy, fresh, piney, pungent, sweet

Flavour: Diesel, earthy, piney, pungent

Bud Colour: Dull green

Pistil Colour: Orange

Trichome Density: High

Score Details

Appearance:	5 / 5
High Quality:	5 / 5
Aroma:	14 / 15
Flavour:	13 / 15
Bud Quality:	30 / 30
High Potency:	29 / 30

Overall Score: 96%

Cultivar Ranking: 11th

JB Cookies

Cultivar/Product Information

Type/Effect: Hybrid - Super Heavy
Legacy Name: JB Cookies
Lineage: Girl Scout Cookies x Romulan
Cannabinoids: 27.5% THC / <1% CBD
Terpenes: Caryophyllene, Limonene, Linalool

First Impression

Review #402; January 12, 2021,

The immense headband effect of Qwest's JB Cookies is hitting me hard, just a few Volcano bags in. The high is washing over my body and mind like a tsunami, an endless torrent of stoned-ness. My overall demeanour is chill, but my brain has become mush inside, and I'm aware of it but can't do anything; it's like stoner sleep paralysis, except I'm awake. Not a tiring cultivar, the cerebral stone is so potent you'll look very relaxed as you stand there still, frozen, and dumbfounded by this powerful herb.

Observations

Aroma: Earthy, pungent, spicy, woody

Flavour: Earthy, grassy, herbal, spicy, woody

Bud Colour: Dark green/purple

Pistil Colour: Brown/red

Trichome Density: High

Score Details

Appearance:	5 / 5
High Quality:	5 / 5
Aroma:	12 / 15
Flavour:	12 / 15
Bud Quality:	30 / 30
High Potency:	29 / 30

Overall Score: 93%

Cultivar Ranking: 32nd

Kalifornia

Cultivar/Product Information

Type/Effect: Indica - Heavy
Legacy Name: Kalifornia
Lineage: Nepali OG x '88 G13 Hashplant
Cannabinoids: 22.9% THC / <1% CBD
Terpenes: Myrcene, Limonene, Camphene

First Impression

Review #256; May 7, 2020,

The effects of Qwest's Kalifornia are potent, in-your-face, and euphoric, though quite relaxed - if I were tired, I'd pass out. My whole body is melting into my chair as I write. A powerful pounding sensation in my chest and head is assaulting me; the euphoric rush from the high embraces me. The further I get into my Volcano session with Kalifornia, the more soothing the effects are and the heavier my eyes feel. A wonderful creation to annihilate an afternoon with or kick off an evening.

Observations

Aroma: Earthy, grassy, herbal, pungent, sour, spicy, sweet

Flavour: Earthy, floral, herbal, spicy, sweet, woody

Bud Colour: Light green

Pistil Colour: Orange/red

Trichome Density: High

Score Details

Appearance:	5 / 5
High Quality:	5 / 5
Aroma:	14 / 15
Flavour:	12 / 15
Bud Quality:	30 / 30
High Potency:	26 / 30

Overall Score: 92%

Cultivar Ranking: 40th

Kush Mints

Cultivar/Product Information

Type/Effect: Indica Hybrid - Super Heavy
Legacy Name: Kush Mints
Lineage: Animal Mints x Bubba Kush
Cannabinoids: 33.3% THC / <1% CBD
Terpenes: Caryophyllene, Limonene, Linalool

First Impression

Review #348; October 14, 2020,

Three bags in, and I feel baked on Kush Mints from Qwest. I was coughing my brains out due to the extra thick vapour produced by this incredibly potent bud. The most potent cultivar that Alberta has seen yet, Kush Mints is a marvel. I'm struggling to figure out what to write. I'm cooked. It's more so on the relaxing side physically and mentally, but a mind-f*** of a paralyzing high above all. Set aside some time, I'd recommend an entire evening for this one, or a day you're okay with forgetting about, and let Kush Mints melt your mind and body. This is ultra-premium and uber-potent, another one of the best.

Observations

Aroma: Diesel, earthy, fresh, herbal, pungent

Flavour: Earthy, fresh, herbal, pungent

Bud Colour: Dark green/purple

Pistil Colour: Brown/tan

Trichome Density: High

Score Details

Appearance:	5 / 5
High Quality:	5 / 5
Aroma:	14 / 15
Flavour:	14 / 15
Bud Quality:	30 / 30
High Potency:	30 / 30

Overall Score: 98%

Cultivar Ranking: 2nd

MAC1

Cultivar/Product Information

Type/Effect: Hybrid - Super Heavy
Legacy Name: Miracle Alien Cookies 1
Lineage: Alien Cookies x (Columbian x Starfighter)
Cannabinoids: 28.2% THC / <1% CBD
Terpenes: Limonene, Linalool, Pinene

First Impression

Review #275; June 20, 2020,

MAC1 has never failed me, and Qwest may be top dog brand-wise, so I knew that I was in for a treat with this one. Then my brain was plucked from my skull by the claws of the high I was experiencing, and I was left lobotomized. Or at least, that's what it felt like at first. The high kept growing, but eventually, I got my brain back, and it was empty. I keep staring ahead at my wall, forgetting about the task of writing. Crazily potent, as expected, given previous MAC1 and Qwest experiences. Excellent as an all-purpose, zone-out, bliss-out hybrid, though very intense.

Observations

Aroma: Earthy, fresh, herbal, minty, piney, pungent, sour

Flavour: Earthy, funky, herbal, piney, pungent

Bud Colour: Dark green/purple

Pistil Colour: Brown/orange

Trichome Density: High

Score Details

Appearance:	5 / 5
High Quality:	5 / 5
Aroma:	15 / 15
Flavour:	12 / 15
Bud Quality:	30 / 30
High Potency:	30 / 30

Overall Score: 97%

Cultivar Ranking: 3rd

OG Kush 25

Cultivar/Product Information

Type/Effect: Indica Hybrid - Heavy
Legacy Name: OG Kush
Lineage: "Northern Californian" x Hindu Kush
Cannabinoids: 19.6% THC / <1% CBD
Terpenes: Myrcene, Limonene, Caryophyllene

First Impression

Review #262; May 15, 2020,

Qwest's take on the classic Kush, OG Kush 25, is a punch straight in the head, maybe a KO if you have too much. Certainly potent, much stronger than I had initially suspected. A powerful throbbing overwhelms my body and mind. The physical sensation reverberating within me from this high is intense and immaculate. Not crazy relaxing, just in-your-face, inebriating, and all-encompassing. Stupidly stoned.

Observations

Aroma: Diesel, earthy, piney, pungent, sour

Flavour: Earthy, funky, grass, herbal, sour

Bud Colour: Dark green/tan

Pistil Colour: Brown/tan

Trichome Density: High

Score Details

Appearance:	4 / 5
High Quality:	5 / 5
Aroma:	13 / 15
Flavour:	13 / 15
Bud Quality:	30 / 30
High Potency:	26 / 30

Overall Score: 91%

Cultivar Ranking: 51st

Oregon Lemons

Cultivar/Product Information

Type/Effect: Hybrid - Medium Heavy
Legacy Name: Oregon Lemons
Lineage: Faceoff OG x Lemon Diesel
Cannabinoids: 23.7% THC / <1% CBD
Terpenes: Limonene, Myrcene, Caryophyllene

First Impression

Review #195; February 14, 2020,

Oregon Lemons by Qwest is a citrus-fuel masterpiece and a testament to what the quality of cannabis can be and should be. The high is hazy and heady, but my eyes feel heavy without wanting to close; my mind is alive, my face and body not so much. There is a lot of forehead sensation on this flower, and the headband effect comes through in full force - a truly remarkable product.

Observations

Aroma: Citrusy, diesel, earthy, herbal, pungent, sour

Flavour: Citrusy, diesel, earthy, funky, herbal, pungent, sour

Bud Colour: Dull green

Pistil Colour: Orange

Trichome Density: High

Score Details

Appearance:	4 / 5
High Quality:	5 / 5
Aroma:	14 / 15
Flavour:	12 / 15
Bud Quality:	30 / 30
High Potency:	27 / 30

Overall Score: 92%

Cultivar Ranking: 39th

Original Glue

Cultivar/Product Information

Type/Effect: Indica Hybrid - Neutral
Legacy Name: Original Glue
Lineage: Chem's Sister x Chocolate Diesel x Sour Dubb
Cannabinoids: 21.2% THC / <1% CBD
Terpenes: Caryophyllene, Limonene, Myrcene

First Impression

Review #197; February 20, 2020.

I spent most of my time enjoying Original Glue by Qwest cerebrally stoned and elevated in mood, emotion, creativity, and perception. I zoned out for long periods in a blissful fantasy about a potential road trip with my best friends and jammed out to some great tunes. This is one of my favourites done to perfection.

Observations

Aroma: Chocolate, earthy, fresh, herbal, pungent, sweet

Flavour: Fresh, herbal, sweet

Bud Colour: Dark green

Pistil Colour: Orange

Trichome Density: High

Score Details

Appearance:	5 / 5
High Quality:	5 / 5
Aroma:	15 / 15
Flavour:	13 / 15
Bud Quality:	30 / 30
High Potency:	26 / 30

Overall Score: 94%

Cultivar Ranking: 18th

Phenome OG Spike

Cultivar/Product Information

Type/Effect: Hybrid - Neutral
Legacy Name: Phenome OG Spike
Lineage: Phenome OG x Spike
Cannabinoids: 27.8% THC / <1% CBD
Terpenes: Myrcene, Caryophyllene, Humulene

First Impression

Review #405; January 16, 2021,

Phenome OG Spike by Qwest is an unreal cerebral blast, a head high so intense and potent that I'm struggling to write. A full-feeling head high has me experiencing waves of sensation through my skull and down my neck and spine. My eyes feel heavy but are wide open, and I'm wired. A euphoric rush of energy has me in a fantastic mood, but my stoned state has me doing little. A wild ride from Qwest that I won't soon forget, Phenome OG Spike is one kickass flower.

Observations

Aroma: Earthy, fresh, fruity, herbal, pungent, sour, sweet

Flavour: Earthy, floral, funky, grassy, herbal, spicy

Bud Colour: Light green

Pistil Colour: Brown/red

Trichome Density: High

Score Details

Appearance:	5 / 5
High Quality:	5 / 5
Aroma:	14 / 15
Flavour:	12 / 15
Bud Quality:	30 / 30
High Potency:	29 / 30

Overall Score: 95%

Cultivar Ranking: 14th

Pineapple Upside Down Cake

Cultivar/Product Information

Type/Effect:	Sativa Hybrid - Medium Heavy
Legacy Name:	Pineapple Upside Down Cake
Lineage:	Golden Pineapple x Trophy Wife
Cannabinoids:	22.1% THC / <1% CBD
Terpenes:	Caryophyllene, Bisabolol, Limonene

First Impression

Review #349; October 15, 2020,

A hazy forehead buzz is developing as I begin to intake Qwest's Pineapple Upside Down Cake. The taste is fantastic, sweet and fruity, almost creamy or cake-like, with its earthy and fresh notes. The high is building as I finish more of the bowl; hazy, not a thinking sativa. I wouldn't say I'm particularly motivated, given that this is a much more relaxed and mellow cultivar than I anticipated. This would pair nicely with a lazy afternoon, snacks, and mindless entertainment. An incredible, euphoric high, one I'll look forward to having again.

Observations

Aroma: Earthy, fresh, fruity, herbal, spicy, sweet

Flavour: Earthy, fresh, fruity, herbal, sweet

Bud Colour: Dark green/purple

Pistil Colour: Orange

Trichome Density: Medium-High

Score Details

Appearance:	5 / 5
High Quality:	5 / 5
Aroma:	13 / 15
Flavour:	14 / 15
Bud Quality:	30 / 30
High Potency:	26 / 30

Overall Score: 93%

Cultivar Ranking: 31st

Point Break

Cultivar/Product Information

Type/Effect: Indica Hybrid - Super Heavy
Legacy Name: Point Break
Lineage: Trophy Wife x Tropicana Cookies
Cannabinoids: 27.4% THC / <1% CBD
Terpenes: Caryophyllene, Bisabolol, Linalool

First Impression

Review #335; September 23, 2020,

Midway into my Volcano bags of Qwest's Point Break, I feel a very full-feeling high coming on, and it grows increasingly immense with every draw. Effect-wise, my entire body is numbed and chill, while my brain lies in a puddle on the floor, having melted inside my head from the monstrous, hitting-every-note high. I feel zoned-out and pleasant, content with doing nothing, given how stoned I am. The aroma and flavour are excellent, and this is some of the best fruity cannabis out there. Point Break nearly took me to my breaking point in a most amazing way.

Observations

Aroma: Earthy, fresh, fruity, herbal, orange, sour, sweet

Flavour: Earthy, fresh, fruity, herbal, orange, sour, sweet

Bud Colour: Dark green/purple

Pistil Colour: Brown/orange

Trichome Density: High

Score Details

Appearance:	5 / 5
High Quality:	5 / 5
Aroma:	15 / 15
Flavour:	14 / 15
Bud Quality:	30 / 30
High Potency:	29 / 30

Overall Score: 98%

Cultivar Ranking: 1st

Strawberry Cough

Cultivar/Product Information

Type/Effect: Sativa - Neutral
Legacy Name: Strawberry Cough
Lineage: Haze x Strawberry Fields
Cannabinoids: 21.2% THC / <1% CBD
Terpenes: Caryophyllene, Cymene

First Impression

Review #88; August 14, 2019.

I'm stoned off my ass this afternoon on Qwest's Strawberry Cough, watching cartoons while so high that I can't quite focus on them or this review for very long. My eyes dart around the room, looking at anything and everything. My mind races, my heart throbs, and my body melts. This is an impressive bud and a heady and potent sativa, not for the inexperienced with THC but an excellent product for the chronic connoisseur.

Observations

Aroma: Earthy, fruity, herbal, piney, sweet

Flavour: Berry, earthy, fruity, herbal, strawberry, sweet

Bud Colour: Light green

Pistil Colour: Brown/orange

Trichome Density: Medium-High

Score Details

Appearance:	5 / 5
High Quality:	5 / 5
Aroma:	14 / 15
Flavour:	13 / 15
Bud Quality:	30 / 30
High Potency:	26 / 30

Overall Score: 93%

Cultivar Ranking: 30th

Super Silver Skunk

Cultivar/Product Information

Type/Effect: Hybrid - Medium Light
Lineage: "Unknown Cultivar" x Super Silver Haze
Cannabinoids: 29.7% THC / <1% CBD
Terpenes: Caryophyllene, Myrcene, Limonene

First Impression

Review #399; January 7, 2021,

A lively cerebral haze, Super Silver Skunk by Qwest, has me feeling uplifted and inspired. My mind is aglow, and it feels alive. My eyes feel bright and open, and my mood is elevated. The high is strong cerebrally, with a slight buzz in my shoulders relative to the buzz in my head. One of the strongest but somehow still "light" cultivars I've had… I feel unreasonably high but still functional (to the extent that I could operate the microwave). However, I'm not overthinking, just experiencing the moment fully. Super Silver Skunk is a unique, partially unknown addition to the best of Qwest.

Observations

Aroma: Earthy, fresh, fruity, herbal, sweet, sweet candy

Flavour: Fresh, grassy, herbal, sweet, woody

Bud Colour: Light green

Pistil Colour: Orange

Trichome Density: High

Score Details

Appearance:	5 / 5
High Quality:	5 / 5
Aroma:	15 / 15
Flavour:	12 / 15
Bud Quality:	30 / 30
High Potency:	30 / 30

Overall Score: 97%

Cultivar Ranking: 5th

Wedding Breath

Cultivar/Product Information

Type/Effect: Indica Hybrid - Medium Heavy
Legacy Name: Wedding Breath
Lineage: Mendo Breath x Wedding Cake
Cannabinoids: 19.3% THC / <1% CBD

First Impression

Review #116; September 13, 2019,

On Qwest's Wedding Breath, I'm zoned out, stoned out of my mind, yet still able to write quickly and concisely without much pause. I'm super high, but I can think clearly when I'm not focused on the TV. One cannot overstate the quality of this bud: it is unreal, the best of the best with sticky and dense nugs.

Observations

Aroma: Diesel, earthy, piney, pungent

Flavour: Earthy, piney, pungent

Bud Colour: Dark green

Pistil Colour: Brown/orange

Trichome Density: High

Score Details

Appearance:	4 / 5
High Quality:	5 / 5
Aroma:	13 / 15
Flavour:	12 / 15
Bud Quality:	30 / 30
High Potency:	25 / 30

Overall Score: 89%

Cultivar Ranking: 77th

Wedding Cake

Cultivar/Product Information

Type/Effect: Indica - Super Heavy
Legacy Name: Wedding Cake
Lineage: Animal Mints x Triangle Kush
Cannabinoids: 26.2% THC / <1% CBD
Terpenes: Caryophyllene, Myrcene, Limonene

First Impression

Review #193; February 13, 2020,

Wedding Cake by Qwest, coming in at a hefty 26.2% THC, may be the most potent bud I've had on the recreational market to date. My body is melting, and my mind is miles away on Mars. Not as cerebrally out of control as other ultra-potent cultivars, but way more relaxing. I'm almost falling over trying to write this review, struggling to stand. Super enjoyable, supremely satisfying, and quality to rival the best around. This flower is unreal; Wedding Cake is a remarkable creation and achievement by Qwest.

Observations

Aroma: Diesel, earthy, piney, pungent, sweet

Flavour: Diesel, earthy, funky, piney, pungent

Bud Colour: Dark green

Pistil Colour: Brown/orange

Trichome Density: High

Score Details

Appearance:	5 / 5
High Quality:	5 / 5
Aroma:	14 / 15
Flavour:	13 / 15
Bud Quality:	30 / 30
High Potency:	30 / 30

Overall Score: 97%

Cultivar Ranking: 6th

Redecan

Overall Performance

Average Score: 80.20%

Brand Ranking: 39th Place

Brand Background

Beginning as a privately-owned, family-based operation, Redecan operates as a mid-sized cannabis producer. With over 30 years of agricultural experience under its belt, Redecan hopes to help consumers realize that "the best things in life are green."

Redecan cannabis is greenhouse-grown in the Niagara region of Ontario, utilizing proprietary growing methods.

Hexo Corp acquired Redecan in 2021.

Other Cultivars:	Black Cherry Punch, Lilac Diesel, Sour Diesel
Associated Brands:	48North, Hexo, Namaste, Up

Cultivar Selection

Charlees	76%
Cold Creek Kush	82%
God Bud	81%
Outlaw	77%
Wappa	85%

Charlees

Cultivar/Product Information

Type/Effect: Indica Hybrid - Neutral
Legacy Name: Amherst Sour Diesel
Lineage: Amherst Super Skunk x Chemdog
Cannabinoids: 17.1% THC / <1% CBD
Terpenes: Myrcene, Humulene, Caryophyllene

First Impression

Review #89; August 14, 2019,

Charlees by Redecan has me feeling nice and stoned but still clear-headed. It is an excellent option for the evenings-in when you want to hang out at home and waste some free time. I can think straight, but I'm relaxed, chilled out, and ready to get couch-locked. I'm going to go munch out, watch TV, and go to sleep.

Observations

Aroma: Herbal, minty, piney, sweet

Flavour: Cheese, funky, herbal, pungent, sour

Bud Colour: Dark green

Pistil Colour: Brown

Trichome Density: Medium

Score Details

Appearance:	4 / 5
High Quality:	5 / 5
Aroma:	12 / 15
Flavour:	10 / 15
Bud Quality:	24 / 30
High Potency:	21 / 30

Overall Score: 76%

Cultivar Ranking: 275th

Cold Creek Kush

Cultivar/Product Information

Type/Effect: Sativa Hybrid - Neutral
Legacy Name: Cold Creek Kush
Lineage: Chemdog x MK Ultra
Cannabinoids: 22.7% THC / <1% CBD
Terpenes: Myrcene, Ocimene, Caryophyllene

First Impression

Review #248; April 24, 2020,

The high from Redecan's Cold Creek Kush is potent and present mainly in the head and chest as an intense, pulsing, physical sensation. The high is quite dulling mentally, and I get a similar "I'm stupid" effect on this as I do on indica-oriented CCK's. But my eyes aren't heavy, and my mood isn't relaxed; I FEEL ALIVE, MAN! I'm ready to go, excited, but completely still physically because I'm baked beyond belief. This would pair perfectly with a 3D movie, or video game, though it may negatively affect your win rate.

Observations

Aroma: Fresh, grassy, herbal, sour, sweet

Flavour: Fresh, grassy, herbal, sour, sweet

Bud Colour: Light green

Pistil Colour: Orange/tan

Trichome Density: Medium-High

Score Details

Appearance:	5 / 5
High Quality:	5 / 5
Aroma:	13 / 15
Flavour:	11 / 15
Bud Quality:	24 / 30
High Potency:	24 / 30

Overall Score: 82%

Cultivar Ranking: 155th

God Bud

Cultivar/Product Information

Type/Effect: Indica Hybrid - Medium Light
Legacy Name: God Bud
Lineage: God x Hawaiian x Purple Skunk
Cannabinoids: 20.1% THC / <1% CBD
Terpenes: Myrcene, Farnesene, Caryophyllene

First Impression

Review #225; April 1, 2020,

God Bud by Redecan got me high; a crazy pleasant, super manageable, yet intense high. I felt like myself on this flower, but myself amplified 1000x. Have I ascended to the realm of the Gods? Nay. I'm just in a happy, creative mood, and I'm high! Have I mentioned that? Incredible effects all around, a great God Bud.

Observations

Aroma: Earthy, fruity, herbal, piney, sweet

Flavour: Earthy, fresh, piney, sweet

Bud Colour: Dull green

Pistil Colour: Orange/tan

Trichome Density: Medium

Score Details

Appearance:	4 / 5
High Quality:	5 / 5
Aroma:	13 / 15
Flavour:	13 / 15
Bud Quality:	24 / 30
High Potency:	22 / 30

Overall Score: 81%

Cultivar Ranking: 172nd

Outlaw

Cultivar/Product Information

Type/Effect: Sativa Hybrid - Light
Legacy Name: Outlaw Amnesia
Lineage: Amnesia x Super Haze
Cannabinoids: 20.9% THC / <1% CBD
Terpenes: Myrcene, Caryophyllene, Limonene

First Impression

Review #251; April 29, 2020,

The effects of Redecan's Outlaw are heady, uplifting, and focusing. I feel pretty concentrated on writing, enough to delay grabbing the next bag and continuing my session. The effects are light, just in the sense that this cultivar picks you up rather than puts you down. It's a clear, clean feeling high. Great for a day off outside in the sun or a morning in getting things done.

Observations

Aroma: Cheese, funky, herbal, sour, woody

Flavour: Funky, herbal, sour, woody

Bud Colour: Light green

Pistil Colour: Orange/tan

Trichome Density: Medium-High

Score Details

Appearance:	4 / 5
High Quality:	5 / 5
Aroma:	13 / 15
Flavour:	10 / 15
Bud Quality:	23 / 30
High Potency:	22 / 30

Overall Score: 77%

Cultivar Ranking: 256th

Wappa

Cultivar/Product Information

Type/Effect: Indica Hybrid - Medium Heavy
Legacy Name: Wappa
Lineage: "Unknown Cultivar" x Sweet Skunk
Cannabinoids: 21.6% THC / <1% CBD
Terpenes: Myrcene, Caryophyllene, Pinene

First Impression

Review #100; August 31, 2019,

I'm stoned out of my mind on Redecan's Wappa, about to eat a ton of apple pie: this night will be good. Heavy but heady and cerebral, with a strong body buzz, Wappa should please most consumers looking for something to enhance an evening. This is my favourite of Redecan's lineup of cultivars.

Observations

Aroma: Earthy, fruity, herbal, sweet

Flavour: Cheese, fresh, fruity, funky, grassy, herbal

Bud Colour: Dark green

Pistil Colour: Orange/tan

Trichome Density: Medium-High

Score Details

Appearance:	5 / 5
High Quality:	5 / 5
Aroma:	13 / 15
Flavour:	13 / 15
Bud Quality:	25 / 30
High Potency:	24 / 30

Overall Score: 85%

Cultivar Ranking: 115th

Reef

Overall Performance

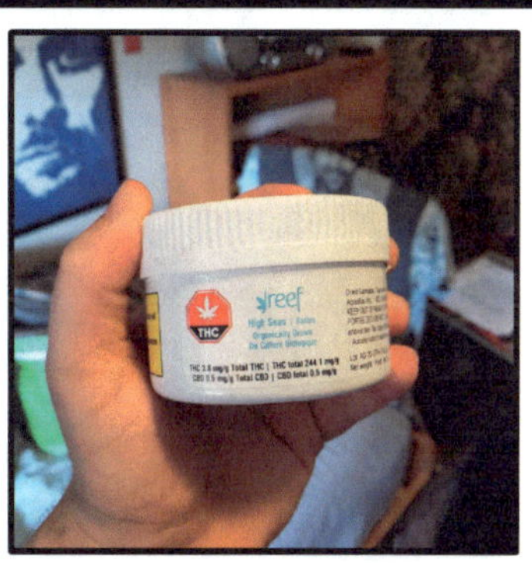

Average Score: 88.00%

Brand Ranking: 17th Place

Brand Background

Reef Organic is a premium cannabis cultivator located on the coast of the Atlantic Ocean. The name "Reef" was chosen both as a reference to its proximity to the ocean and a nod to the cannabis plant. Organic growing and ecological practices are essential to Reef: they respect the plant and the environment. They have managed to cut energy consumption by 50% and water consumption by 80% so far through facility design.

Cannabis for Reef products is grown in Nova Scotia utilizing a hybrid organic-aquaponic system. Reef employs aquaponics utilizing live Koi fish and then uses the nutrient-rich water from their tanks on cannabis plants grown in organic living soil.

Other Cultivars: Banana Daddy, Charlotte's Angel, Ebb & Flow, Queen Sang, Sky Cuddler Double Kush

Cultivar Selection

Coastal Kush	85%
High Seas	91%

Coastal Kush

Cultivar/Product Information

Type/Effect: Indica - Neutral
Legacy Name: Cold Creek Kush
Lineage: Chemdog x MK Ultra
Cannabinoids: 22.4% THC / <1% CBD
Terpenes: Myrcene, Limonene, Ocimene

First Impression

Review #417; February 11, 2021,

Reef's Coastal Kush feels like a rather heady indica, featuring plenty of cerebral stimulation and a state of relaxed bliss. I'm content and calm, still pretty collected as well. A mild full-body buzz relieves me of my fatigue and restores me anew. A wonderful, steady wave to ride, Coastal Kush is a great flower; my expectations of Reef were met for sure.

Observations

Aroma: Earthy, fresh, herbal, piney, sweet

Flavour: Earthy, fresh, funky, grassy, herbal

Bud Colour: Dull green

Pistil Colour: Orange

Trichome Density: Medium

Score Details

Appearance:	5 / 5
High Quality:	5 / 5
Aroma:	13 / 15
Flavour:	12 / 15
Bud Quality:	25 / 30
High Potency:	25 / 30

Overall Score: 85%

Cultivar Ranking: 117th

High Seas

Cultivar/Product Information

Type/Effect: Sativa - Medium Light
Legacy Name: Ghost Train Haze
Lineage: Ghost OG x Nevil's Wreck
Cannabinoids: 23.5% THC / <1% CBD
Terpenes: Myrcene, Limonene, Caryophyllene

First Impression

Review #320; August 26, 2020,

HIGH seas indeed Reef… I'm way up there - walking on sunshine - high on Reef's High Seas. My brain is buzzing on this vibrant, functional flower. Hazy still, I find myself pausing sometimes, but quickly I get back on track to the task at hand. My taste buds and olfactory receptors are satisfied fully by the rich terpene profile of this potent Ghost Train Haze. Easily the best version of the cultivar I've had on the recreational market, High Seas is an excellent first look at Reef.

Observations

Aroma: Cheese, citrusy, floral, fruity, herbal, pungent, sour

Flavour: Citrusy, floral, fruity, herbal, pungent, sour

Bud Colour: Dark green

Pistil Colour: Orange/red

Trichome Density: Medium

Score Details

Appearance:	4 / 5
High Quality:	5 / 5
Aroma:	14 / 15
Flavour:	13 / 15
Bud Quality:	28 / 30
High Potency:	27 / 30

Overall Score: 91%

Cultivar Ranking: 45th

Riff

Overall Performance

Average Score: 77.38%

Brand Ranking: 46th Place

Brand Background

Riff, a cannabis brand brought to market by Aphria, is driven by new ideas, focusing on creativity and collaboration. With these things in mind, they aim to push the boundaries of the industry in the same direction their cannabis will push their consumers: higher.

Riff cannabis is mass-produced via greenhouse grow in Leamington, Ontario.

Other Cultivars: Cryo Chronic, Gilded Grams, Hell Cat 33
Associated Brands: Broken Coast, Canaca, Good Supply, Grail, Marley Natural, Solei

Cultivar Selection

Blue Ninety Eight	72%
DT81	77%
Hawaii Heartbreak	83%
Raider Kush	80%
Subway Scientist	78%
Sunday Special	69%
Sweet Jersey 3	80%
Two-Tone Ban	80%

Blue Ninety Eight

Cultivar/Product Information

Type/Effect: Indica - Neutral
Legacy Name: Rockstar Kush
Lineage: Bubba Kush x Rockstar
Cannabinoids: 15.3% THC / <1% CBD
Terpenes: Caryophyllene, Limonene, Myrcene

First Impression

Review #166; December 24, 2019,

Ooooowwwiiieee (that's a Rick and Morty reference, folks), does Riff's Blue Ninety Eight have me in the right mood for my day off. I had this indica first thing in the morning, and it chilled me right out but got the wheels turning upstairs on overdrive. My mind is focused but going wild with creative ideas. I took a moment to admire some tunes, my appreciation of music heightened by the high from this flower. My appetite is also heightened, so I must go hunt for food in the kitchen now.

Observations

Aroma: Berry, diesel, earthy, pungent, sweet

Flavour: Diesel, earthy, pungent

Bud Colour: Green/tan

Pistil Colour: Brown/orange

Trichome Density: Low-Medium

Score Details

Appearance:	4 / 5
High Quality:	5 / 5
Aroma:	13 / 15
Flavour:	11 / 15
Bud Quality:	20 / 30
High Potency:	19 / 30

Overall Score: 72%

Cultivar Ranking: 318th

DT81

Cultivar/Product Information

Type/Effect: Sativa - Medium Light
Legacy Name: Super Lemon Haze
Lineage: Lemon Skunk x Super Silver Haze
Cannabinoids: 18.5% THC / <1% CBD
Terpenes: Terpinolene, Caryophyllene, Humulene

First Impression

Review #300; August 1, 2020,

I found myself staring intensely at the bushes across the street while reviewing Riff's DT81. I zoned out hard during the medium-heavy cerebral high. My forehead buzzes, and my brain is pulsing with physical sensation, racing with thoughts from the mostly heady experience. I'm uplifted and heightened mood-wise, almost antsy. A tremendous social high if you find those situations comfortable while sober. If you usually don't like socializing, well, don't do that on this flower (paranoia may ensue). This is also quite euphoric and inspiring, a very active-feeling high.

Observations

Aroma: Citrusy, fruity, herbal, piney, pungent, sour, sweet

Flavour: Grassy, herbal, sour, woody

Bud Colour: Light green

Pistil Colour: Brown/tan

Trichome Density: Medium

Score Details

Appearance:	4 / 5
High Quality:	5 / 5
Aroma:	14 / 15
Flavour:	11 / 15
Bud Quality:	22 / 30
High Potency:	21 / 30

Overall Score: 77%

Cultivar Ranking: 253rd

Hawaii Heartbreak

Cultivar/Product Information

Type/Effect: Indica - Heavy
Legacy Name: Headstash
Lineage: Biker Kush x (Cherry Pie x Girl Scout Cookies x KarmaRado OG)
Cannabinoids: 19.7% THC / <1% CBD
Terpenes: Limonene, Nerolidol, Caryophyllene

First Impression

Review #278; June 24, 2020,

If you're in the mood for a relaxing, heavy-eyed, stoned-all-over high, Hawaii Heartbreak from Riff might be for you. I can't think too well, and it's as though my mind has turned to sludge. My body is experiencing an intense physical sensation and is entirely relieved of all stress. I feel sleepy, baked, and pleasant - a great PM session option from Riff.

Observations

Aroma: Earthy, fresh, herbal, minty, piney, pungent

Flavour: Earthy, grassy, herbal, piney, pungent

Bud Colour: Dull green/tan

Pistil Colour: Orange

Trichome Density: Medium

Score Details

Appearance:	4 / 5
High Quality:	5 / 5
Aroma:	13 / 15
Flavour:	13 / 15
Bud Quality:	25 / 30
High Potency:	23 / 30

Overall Score: 83%

Cultivar Ranking: 146th

Raider Kush

Cultivar/Product Information

Type/Effect: Indica - Heavy
Legacy Name: Skywalker Kush
Lineage: Blueberry OG x Mazar
Cannabinoids: 20.1% THC / <1% CBD
Terpenes: Limonene, Caryophyllene, Myrcene

First Impression

Review #252; May 1, 2020,

Riff's Raider Kush will likely melt your body and mind in a super satisfying way. I'm almost rocking back and forth with the forceful pulsing sensation building within me. Headbanging to the music I'm listening to is proving difficult. I can barely move, as though I'm a sloth or something. Raider Kush has me super chill and relaxed physically, but my mind is empty; there are no thoughts when I pause, a common symptom of being baked.

Observations

Aroma: Earthy, fresh, grassy, herbal, pungent, sweet

Flavour: Earthy, grassy, herbal, pungent, sour

Bud Colour: Dull green

Pistil Colour: Brown/orange

Trichome Density: Medium

Score Details

Appearance:	4 / 5
High Quality:	5 / 5
Aroma:	13 / 15
Flavour:	12 / 15
Bud Quality:	22 / 30
High Potency:	24 / 30

Overall Score: 80%

Cultivar Ranking: 207th

Subway Scientist

Cultivar/Product Information

Type/Effect: Indica - Medium Heavy
Legacy Name: Granddaddy Purple
Lineage: Big Bud x Purple Urkle
Cannabinoids: 19.8% THC / <1% CBD
Terpenes: Caryophyllene, Myrcene, Humulene

First Impression

Review #64; May 23, 2019,

For a medium-high potency indica, Riff's Subway Scientist offers high relaxation, making for an excellent mid-evening high. A great pairing with a night at home or a night out with friends, Subway Scientist is enjoyable in most settings; not ideal for activity-heavy occasions, as you will want just to chill out and enjoy the bliss.

Observations

Aroma: Berry, cheese, earthy, funky, herbal, pungent, spicy

Flavour: Cheese, earthy, funky, herbal, sour, spicy

Bud Colour: Green/purple

Pistil Colour: Brown

Trichome Density: Low

Score Details

Appearance:	4 / 5
High Quality:	5 / 5
Aroma:	12 / 15
Flavour:	12 / 15
Bud Quality:	22 / 30
High Potency:	23 / 30

Overall Score: 78%

Cultivar Ranking: 249th

Sunday Special

Cultivar/Product Information

Type/Effect: Sativa Hybrid - Medium Light
Legacy Name: UK Cheese
Lineage: Skunk #1
Cannabinoids: 16.8% THC / <1% CBD
Terpenes: Myrcene, Pinene, Caryophyllene

First Impression

Review #353; October 21, 2020,

Riff's Sunday Special is a hazy and heady experience that offers a mellow high. Despite my overall mood being mellow, I can think quite quickly. I feel functional, though my squinting may suggest otherwise. I could see this as a worthy addition to a morning off. Whether accomplishing work around the home or lounging on the couch, it should perk you up and uplift your mood without making you feel too wired or intoxicated.

Observations

Aroma: Cheese, earthy, fruity, herbal, pungent, sweet, sour

Flavour: Cheese, earthy, funky, herbal, pungent

Bud Colour: Dark green

Pistil Colour: Brown/orange

Trichome Density: Low-Medium

Score Details

Appearance:	4 / 5
High Quality:	5 / 5
Aroma:	12 / 15
Flavour:	9 / 15
Bud Quality:	19 / 30
High Potency:	20 / 30

Overall Score: 69%

Cultivar Ranking: 357th

Sweet Jersey 3

Cultivar/Product Information

Type/Effect: Sativa Hybrid - Medium Heavy
Legacy Name: Jean Guy
Lineage: White Widow
Cannabinoids: 22.1% THC / <1% CBD
Terpenes: Caryophyllene, Limonene, Linalool

First Impression

Review #164; December 18, 2019.

A heady experience, Sweet Jersey 3 by Riff assaults the mind with its high THC potency, inducing an intense cerebral high, and waves of sensation in the head and shoulders. A perky and uplifting sativa, but too intense for one to be too helpful after consumption. It's a great sativa for getting stoned with a bunch of friends, though not for the first session of the day - it's powerful.

Observations

Aroma: Earthy, grassy, herbal, woody

Flavour: Cheese, earthy, herbal, woody

Bud Colour: Light green

Pistil Colour: Orange/tan

Trichome Density: Medium

Score Details

Appearance:	4 / 5
High Quality:	5 / 5
Aroma:	12 / 15
Flavour:	11 / 15
Bud Quality:	24 / 30
High Potency:	24 / 30

Overall Score: 80%

Cultivar Ranking: 218th

Two-Tone Ban

Cultivar/Product Information

Type/Effect: Hybrid - Medium Light
Legacy Name: Sour Kush
Lineage: OG Kush x Sour Diesel
Cannabinoids: 19% THC / <1% CBD
Terpenes: Myrcene, Limonene, Caryophyllene

First Impression

Review #165; December 22, 2019,

I got lost in the comments section of a Herb magazine article on Facebook, correcting people while stoned on Riff's Two-Tone Ban. You'll be super into whatever you're doing in the moment of your consumption of this flower. I'm zoned in, and I feel alive under the influence of this potent and peppy experience.

Observations

Aroma: Earthy, grassy, herbal, piney, sour, sweet

Flavour: Earthy, grassy, herbal, sour

Bud Colour: Light green

Pistil Colour: Orange

Trichome Density: Medium

Score Details

Appearance:	4 / 5
High Quality:	5 / 5
Aroma:	13 / 15
Flavour:	12 / 15
Bud Quality:	23 / 30
High Potency:	23 / 30

Overall Score: 80%

Cultivar Ranking: 203rd

Robinsons

Overall Performance

Average Score: 82.00%

Brand Ranking: 32nd Place

Brand Background

Robinsons story begins with Andrew Robinson and cannabis. Inspired by the plant, he set out to build a specialized team of professionals and establish Robinsons. The brand is "driven by a pursuit of excellence and precision," and such drive has produced great cannabis.

Located in the Annapolis Valley of Nova Scotia, Robinsons grows cannabis in a prime location bearing consistent temperatures and rainfall. Their cannabis is always produced in small batches and tended to by hand.

Cultivar Selection

GG#4	82%
Lemon Garlic OG	82%

GG#4

Cultivar/Product Information

Type/Effect:	Hybrid - Neutral
Legacy Name:	Original Glue
Lineage:	Chem's Sister x Chocolate Diesel x Sour Dubb
Cannabinoids:	18.9% THC / <1% CBD
Terpenes:	Limonene, Caryophyllene, Terpineol

First Impression

Review #371; November 23, 2020,

A lively euphoric rush, coupled with calming and soothing sensations, GG#4 by Robinsons is a wonderful time. It is a very full-feeling high, capturing the mind, body, and soul and elevating them to the heavens. An open-ended hybrid as far as activity pairing goes, I think I could enjoy anything under this flower's spell. Robinsons has grown a great glue, a grand introduction to the brand from an old favourite.

Observations

Aroma: Earthy, floral, fresh, herbal, pungent, sour

Flavour: Earthy, fresh, grassy, herbal, pungent

Bud Colour: Green

Pistil Colour: Brown/red

Trichome Density: Medium-High

Score Details

Appearance:	4 / 5
High Quality:	5 / 5
Aroma:	13 / 15
Flavour:	12 / 15
Bud Quality:	25 / 30
High Potency:	23 / 30

Overall Score: 82%

Cultivar Ranking: 150th

Lemon Garlic OG

Cultivar/Product Information

Type/Effect: Indica Hybrid - Medium Heavy
Legacy Name: Lemon Garlic OG
Lineage: OG Kush
Cannabinoids: 19.6% THC / <1% CBD
Terpenes: Caryophyllene, Limonene, Linalool

First Impression

Review #411; February 4, 2021,

A chill and laid-back experience, Lemon Garlic OG by Robinsons is a great way to kick off an evening. I found myself vibing pretty hard and dancing around my room to some early "A Tribe Called Quest"; the herb inspiring euphoria and a carefree attitude. A bit dry for premium flower, but certainly made up for by trichome presence: SO MUCH KIEF. Solid flower, and a unique cultivar, from Robinsons.

Observations

Aroma: Cheese, earthy, funky, herbal, sour, sweet

Flavour: Funky, grassy, herbal

Bud Colour: Light green

Pistil Colour: Brown/orange

Trichome Density: Medium-High

Score Details

Appearance:	4 / 5
High Quality:	5 / 5
Aroma:	13 / 15
Flavour:	12 / 15
Bud Quality:	26 / 30
High Potency:	22 / 30

Overall Score: 82%

Cultivar Ranking: 149th

Royal City Cannabis Co.

Overall Performance

Average Score: 82.40%

Brand Ranking: 29th Place

Brand Background

Royal City Cannabis Co. was founded in 2013 and is wholly owned by its employees. The folks at Royal City Cannabis Co. produce cannabis in small batches employing traditional cannabis cultivation practices backed up by the agricultural prowess of their community.

Cannabis for Royal City Cannabis Co. is grown in Guelph, Ontario.

Cultivar Selection

Dreamzicle	78%
Dukem	85%
Orange Hill Special	80%
Rockstar Tuna	88%
Royal Goddess	81%

Dreamzicle

Cultivar/Product Information

Type/Effect: Hybrid - Light
Legacy Name: Dreamzicle
Lineage: Blue Dream x Lemon Zkittles
Cannabinoids: 18.9% THC / <1% CBD
Terpenes: Pinene, Myrcene, Caryophyllene

First Impression

Review #410; February 2, 2021,

Royal City Cannabis Co.'s Dreamzicle is a middle-of-the-pack hybrid in strength and effect. Effect-wise, I feel calm in mood, but uplifted in spirit and quite clear-minded. I can still focus while high on this cultivar, so it's ideal for sessions where mental clarity is required. I wouldn't recommend this before bed, given that I'm wide awake on this bud, mentally alert, aware and alive. Just what I needed to take a second shot at the day after work.

Observations

Aroma: Fresh, fruity, herbal, sweet

Flavour: Fresh, herbal, woody

Bud Colour: Dark green

Pistil Colour: Brown

Trichome Density: Low-Medium

Score Details

Appearance:	4 / 5
High Quality:	5 / 5
Aroma:	12 / 15
Flavour:	11 / 15
Bud Quality:	24 / 30
High Potency:	22 / 30

Overall Score: 78%

Cultivar Ranking: 250th

Dukem

Cultivar/Product Information

Type/Effect: Sativa - Light
Legacy Name: Duke Nukem
Lineage: Chemmando x Chernobyl
Cannabinoids: 18.8% THC / <1% CBD
Terpenes: Ocimene, Farnesene, Caryophyllene

First Impression

Review #418; February 13, 2021,

I found myself belting out lyrics to Rush's Moving Pictures album (happy belated 40th birthday, you kickass album, you) while getting decently high off of Dukem from Royal City Cannabis Co. An excellent cultivar for elevating mood, energy, perception, and cognition. I barely feel impaired (though I am) relative to other recent clean and clear sativas. A social, active, upbeat high; the only time I wouldn't want this is right before a nap. I feel inspired to attack the day now, all thanks to Dukem.

Observations

Aroma: Floral, fresh, fruity, herbal, sweet, woody

Flavour: Funky, herbal, woody

Bud Colour: Dark green/purple

Pistil Colour: Brown/orange

Trichome Density: Medium-High

Score Details

Appearance:	5 / 5
High Quality:	5 / 5
Aroma:	14 / 15
Flavour:	11 / 15
Bud Quality:	28 / 30
High Potency:	22 / 30

Overall Score: 85%

Cultivar Ranking: 111th

Orange Hill Special

Cultivar/Product Information

Type/Effect: Sativa Hybrid - Medium Heavy
Legacy Name: Orange Hill Special
Lineage: California Orange x Orange Bud
Cannabinoids: 18.5% THC / <1% CBD
Terpenes: Terpinolene, Pinene, Caryophyllene

First Impression

Review #352; October 20, 2020,

Orange Hill Special by Royal City Cannabis Co. offers an elevating but hazy high that has uplifted my mood and energy, but rendered my brain periodically useless. I keep being able to write and think one second, and then the next, I'm as though I've been lobotomized, completely brain-slugged (a nod to Futurama). The high is quite intoxicating, a good mess-you-up sativa for afternoons to kill or for alleviating post-work fatigue.

Observations

Aroma: Chocolate, fresh, fruity, herbal, spicy, sweet, woody

Flavour: Fresh, funky, herbal, woody

Bud Colour: Dull green

Pistil Colour: Brown/red

Trichome Density: Medium

Score Details

Appearance:	5 / 5
High Quality:	5 / 5
Aroma:	13 / 15
Flavour:	10 / 15
Bud Quality:	25 / 30
High Potency:	22 / 30

Overall Score: 80%

Cultivar Ranking: 202nd

Rockstar Tuna

Cultivar/Product Information

Type/Effect:	Indica - Heavy
Legacy Name:	Rockstar Tuna
Lineage:	Rockstar x Tuna Kush
Cannabinoids:	17.9% THC / <1% CBD
Terpenes:	Caryophyllene, Limonene, Bisabolol

First Impression

Review #387; December 22, 2020,

My jar of Rockstar Tuna by Royal City Cannabis Co. came loaded with a gorgeous, massive, frosty, and "reminiscent of Broken Coast" nug. The high is very heavy-eyed and heavy-minded in effect; not overwhelmingly so, but super relaxing overall. I did find myself headbanging to a mix of metal music with what little energy I had, a suitable cultivar for jamming. Much stronger than expected and very impressive, Rockstar Tuna is a treat.

Observations

Aroma: Earthy, fresh, funky, grassy, herbal

Flavour: Earthy, fresh, funky, grassy, herbal, woody

Bud Colour: Dull green/brown

Pistil Colour: Brown

Trichome Density: High

Score Details

Appearance:	5 / 5
High Quality:	5 / 5
Aroma:	13 / 15
Flavour:	13 / 15
Bud Quality:	29 / 30
High Potency:	23 / 30

Overall Score: 88%

Cultivar Ranking: 84th

Royal Goddess

Cultivar/Product Information

Type/Effect: Indica Hybrid - Medium Light
Legacy Name: Royal Goddess
Lineage: Apple Jack x God Bud
Cannabinoids: 18.7% THC / <1% CBD
Terpenes: Myrcene, Caryophyllene, Farnesene

First Impression

Review #356; October 28, 2020,

Royal Goddess by Royal City Cannabis Co. is a fruity toke with a decent headband effect, chill effects, and a mellow vibe. Not overly relaxing or sedating, Royal Goddess is an indica for earlier rather than later in the day. Wake and bake sessions come to mind. My mind is clear, and I feel high and hazed from a great cultivar and experience.

Observations

Aroma: Berry, floral, fruity, herbal, sweet, woody

Flavour: Berry, floral, fresh, fruity, funky, herbal, sweet

Bud Colour: Dull green

Pistil Colour: Orange

Trichome Density: Medium

Score Details

Appearance:	4 / 5
High Quality:	5 / 5
Aroma:	14 / 15
Flavour:	12 / 15
Bud Quality:	24 / 30
High Potency:	22 / 30

Overall Score: 81%

Cultivar Ranking: 171st

Royal High

Royal High

Overall Performance

Average Score: 72.50%

Brand Ranking: 67th Place

Brand Background

A midrange-quality brand from the licensed producer United Greeneries, Royal High offers a variety of cannabis cultivars with moderate potency. Cannabis for the brand is created in small batches and selected by hand.

Royal High cannabis is grown on Vancouver Island, BC.

Other Cultivars:	CBD Tonic, Great White Shark, Mazar x GWX, Northern Lights, Serious Kush
Associated Brands:	18Twelve

Cultivar Selection

Liberty Haze	71%
Super Skunk	74%

Liberty Haze

Cultivar/Product Information

Type/Effect: Sativa - Super Light
Legacy Name: Liberty Haze
Lineage: Chemdog x G13
Cannabinoids: 11.9% THC / <1% CBD
Terpenes: Terpinolene, Caryophyllene

First Impression

Review #191; February 10, 2020,

There is a robust cerebral sensation present on this one, especially for its THC %, Liberty Haze by Royal High is more than I expected it to be. My mind is calm and chill, my thoughts come quickly, and I'm still in the driver's seat instead of the high. I could still accomplish something with my day after my half-hour with this flower. Enjoyable and functional.

Observations

Aroma: Citrusy, herbal, sour, woody

Flavour: Herbal, sour, woody

Bud Colour: Green

Pistil Colour: Brown/tan

Trichome Density: Medium

Score Details

Appearance:	4 / 5
High Quality:	5 / 5
Aroma:	12 / 15
Flavour:	12 / 15
Bud Quality:	22 / 30
High Potency:	16 / 30

Overall Score: 71%

Cultivar Ranking: 328th

Super Skunk

Cultivar/Product Information

Type/Effect: Indica Hybrid - Medium Heavy
Legacy Name: Super Skunk
Lineage: Afghani Indica x Skunk #1
Cannabinoids: 15.2% THC / <1% CBD
Terpenes: Caryophyllene, Myrcene, Pinene

First Impression

Review #109; September 9, 2019,

Super Skunk from Royal High is heavy and potent, especially surprising considering the medium THC level. A strong head buzz that relaxes and impairs can be expected, and a body sensation throughout the legs and torso. I'm blanking on what to write, my thoughts interrupted by the loss of focus brought on by this bud's effect profile - decent stuff.

Observations

Aroma: Fruity, herbal, pungent, spicy, sweet, woody

Flavour: Fruity, herbal, sweet, woody

Bud Colour: Dark green

Pistil Colour: Brown/orange

Trichome Density: Medium

Score Details

Appearance:	4 / 5
High Quality:	5 / 5
Aroma:	12 / 15
Flavour:	11 / 15
Bud Quality:	21 / 30
High Potency:	21 / 30

Overall Score: 74%

Cultivar Ranking: 298th

San Rafael '71

Overall Performance

Average Score: 82.50%

Brand Ranking: 27th Place

Brand Background

A brand offered by Aurora Cannabis, San Rafael '71 is well known for its unique varieties and flavours in the midrange cannabis category. Inspired by an old stoner story from the '70s in San Rafael, California, the brand is committed to a creative image backed up with consistent genetics and exclusive cultivars.

San Rafael '71 cannabis is grown in Ontario, Canada.

Other Cultivars: Driftwood Diesel, Farm Gas, Lemon Rocket, Sourdough Stonefruit Sunset

Associated Brands: AltaVie, Aurora, Whistler Cannabis Company

Cultivar Selection

Delahaze	86%
Great White Shark	87%
Island Sweet Skunk	78%
Pink Kush	84%
Purple Chitral	77%
Tangerine Dream	83%

Delahaze

Cultivar/Product Information

Type/Effect: Sativa - Medium Light
Legacy Name: Delahaze
Lineage: Lemon Skunk x Mango Haze
Cannabinoids: 22.8% THC / <1% CBD
Terpenes: Terpinolene, Myrcene, Pinene

First Impression

Review #40; April 24, 2019.

For a stimulating cerebral jolt, look for San Rafael '71's Delahaze. Whether you're taking on a day of housework, homework, or entertainment, Delahaze is the potent sativa to get you wired for the occasion. I feel energetic, motivated, and ready for anything. Excellent bud, gorgeous smell, fantastic high.

Observations

Aroma: Citrusy, herbal, sour

Flavour: Citrusy, fruity, herbal, mango, sour, sour candy, sweet

Bud Colour: Dull green

Pistil Colour: Brown/red

Trichome Density: Medium

Score Details

Appearance:	4 / 5
High Quality:	5 / 5
Aroma:	14 / 15
Flavour:	14 / 15
Bud Quality:	24 / 30
High Potency:	25 / 30

Overall Score: 86%

Cultivar Ranking: 98th

Great White Shark

Cultivar/Product Information

Type/Effect: Sativa Hybrid - Medium Light
Legacy Name: CBD Shark Shock
Lineage: Cannatonic x Shark Shock
Cannabinoids: 7% THC / 12.7% CBD
Terpenes: Myrcene, Pinene, Ocimene

First Impression

Review #16; April 13, 2019,

San Rafael '71's Great White Shark is a 2:1 ratio of CBD to THC, and with a hefty amount of both in the mix, this cultivar delivers an incredible high. A light head buzz that is focusing and motivating is accompanied by potent CBD relaxation of my body and mind. From walking the dog to watching viral videos, everything I do is accented with a particular 'goodness' after indulging in this cultivar. Thanks to Great White Shark, everything seems fantastic and certainly is.

Observations

Aroma: Citrusy, fruity, herbal, sweet

Flavour: Earthy, herbal, pungent, sweet

Bud Colour: Dark green

Pistil Colour: Brown/orange

Trichome Density: Low-Medium

Score Details

Appearance:	4 / 5
High Quality:	5 / 5
Aroma:	14 / 15
Flavour:	13 / 15
Bud Quality:	26 / 30
High Potency:	25 / 30

Overall Score: 87%

Cultivar Ranking: 89th

Island Sweet Skunk

Cultivar/Product Information

Type/Effect: Sativa - Medium Light
Legacy Name: Island Sweet Skunk
Lineage: Skunk #1 x Sweet Pink Grapefruit
Cannabinoids: 16.6% THC / <1% CBD
Terpenes: Myrcene, Terpinolene, Limonene

First Impression

Review #270; June 9, 2020,

My mood is amplified and alive, and my eyes are hazy and heavy; Island Sweet Skunk, by San Rafael '71, has given me the perfect post-work buzz to keep me productive rather than succumbing to laziness. My brain feels like it's vibrating. Creativity is up, the cultivar inspiring and imaginative in effect. This is a great way to make the best of the day, whether you're getting things done or being entirely useless. Uplifting, tasty, and unique, this hits all of the notes for a classic San Rafael 71 cultivar; a worthy addition to the line-up.

Observations

Aroma: Citrusy, fruity, herbal, pungent, sour

Flavour: Citrusy, herbal, sour

Bud Colour: Green

Pistil Colour: Orange

Trichome Density: Medium

Score Details

Appearance:	4 / 5
High Quality:	5 / 5
Aroma:	13 / 15
Flavour:	12 / 15
Bud Quality:	23 / 30
High Potency:	21 / 30

Overall Score: 78%

Cultivar Ranking: 245th

Pink Kush

Cultivar/Product Information

Type/Effect: Indica - Heavy
Legacy Name: Pink Kush
Lineage: OG Kush
Cannabinoids: 21.9% THC / <1% CBD
Terpenes: Limonene, Caryophyllene, Linalool

First Impression

Review #54; May 7, 2019,

I enjoy San Rafael '71's Pink Kush; it is one of my favourite nighttime buds, perfect to end the evening. The effects are strong and heavy in the body and mind; I'm undoubtedly stoned and ready for rest. Maybe some gaming first, but I fully expect to pass out from this potent indica flower during the gaming session. Not for the inexperienced, but a delight for those who can handle it.

Observations

Aroma: Earthy, herbal, minty, piney, pungent

Flavour: Earthy, funky, piney, pungent, spicy, woody

Bud Colour: Dark green/purple

Pistil Colour: Brown/orange

Trichome Density: Medium

Score Details

Appearance:	5 / 5
High Quality:	5 / 5
Aroma:	12 / 15
Flavour:	12 / 15
Bud Quality:	25 / 30
High Potency:	25 / 30

Overall Score: 84%

Cultivar Ranking: 130th

Purple Chitral

Cultivar/Product Information

Type/Effect: Indica - Medium Heavy
Lineage: Pakistani Kush x UK Cheese
Cannabinoids: 15% THC / <1% CBD
Terpenes: Myrcene, Pinene

First Impression

Review #4; April 4, 2019,

Purple Chitral is an excellent post-shift choice for early/mid-evening and unique addition to the San Rafael '71 bouquet. The bud itself is a gorgeous deep purple with a heavy frosting of trichomes. The smell is also distinctive: sweet and berry-like, but with a funky, almost cheesy overtone. There are few buds with more character than Purple Chitral. Mellow, light, and relaxing, it will not leave you wanting to end the day but will make you yearn to soak up the remaining hours instead.

Observations

Aroma: Berry, cheese, earthy, fruity, funky, pungent, sweet

Flavour: Berry, cheese, earthy, fruity, pungent, sweet

Bud Colour: Dark purple

Pistil Colour: Brown/red

Trichome Density: Medium-High

Score Details

Appearance:	4 / 5
High Quality:	5 / 5
Aroma:	13 / 15
Flavour:	13 / 15
Bud Quality:	23 / 30
High Potency:	19 / 30

Overall Score: 77%

Cultivar Ranking: 259th

Tangerine Dream

Cultivar/Product Information

Type/Effect: Sativa Hybrid - Neutral
Legacy Name: Tangerine Dream
Lineage: Afghani Indica x G13 x Nevil's A5 Haze
Cannabinoids: 14.5% THC / <1% CBD
Terpenes: Myrcene, Pinene, Caryophyllene

First Impression

Review #5; April 6, 2019,

Shockingly unique and beautiful is how I would begin to describe Tangerine Dream by San Rafael '71. Its appearance is gorgeous, and its scent is the sweetest orange-like smell I've found in cannabis. On top of that, the light sativa buzz offered by this gem is exceptionally calming instead of energizing, but far from sedating. It is motivating, however, and just genuinely great on all levels.

Observations

Aroma: Citrusy, floral, fruity, orange, sweet

Flavour: Citrusy, floral, fruity, orange, sweet

Bud Colour: Dark purple

Pistil Colour: Orange

Trichome Density: Medium

Score Details

Appearance:	5 / 5
High Quality:	5 / 5
Aroma:	15 / 15
Flavour:	15 / 15
Bud Quality:	25 / 30
High Potency:	18 / 30

Overall Score: 83%

Cultivar Ranking: 134th

Simply Bare

Overall Performance

Average Score: 88.60%

Brand Ranking: 16th Place

Brand Background

The goal at Simply Bare is one that many craft producers pursue: to produce the best organic cannabis in Canada. They have created a proprietary living soil blend sourced from all over BC, a cultivar collection of over 100 varieties, and a selection of growing practices and standards that produces cannabis that stands above much of the competition. Hang-dried and hand-packaged, Simply Bare's cannabis gets all of the extra care it deserves.

Cannabis from Simply Bare is grown in a greenhouse environment in Delta, BC.

Other Cultivars: Duct Tape, Gelato Cake, Lime Mi'jito, Sweet Bubba, White Rntz

Cultivar Selection

Cultivar	Score
Apple Toffee	84%
Blue Dream	90%
Creek Congo	88%
SFV OG Kush	90%
Sour Cookies	91%

Apple Toffee

Cultivar/Product Information

Type/Effect: Indica - Medium Heavy
Legacy Name: Apple Toffee
Lineage: Creme Brulee x Sour Apple
Cannabinoids: 18.9% THC / <1% CBD
Terpenes: Caryophyllene, Limonene, Farnesene

First Impression

Review #384; December 18, 2020,

I'm zonked and zoned out on Apple Toffee by Simply Bare. I just noticed my Volcano bag was empty and responded by turning on my Volcano's air switch with no bag attached (I'm definitely out in space now). The body effects of Apple Toffee are very relaxing and sedating, and my eyes are getting heavy. My mind feels heavy, and I'm slowed way down - a unique cultivar best enjoyed in the mid-to-late evening with snacks.

Observations

Aroma: Cheese, earthy, fruity, funky, herbal, sweet

Flavour: Earthy, fresh, grassy, herbal, sweet

Bud Colour: Dull green

Pistil Colour: Brown

Trichome Density: Medium

Score Details

Appearance:	4 / 5
High Quality:	5 / 5
Aroma:	13 / 15
Flavour:	11 / 15
Bud Quality:	27 / 30
High Potency:	24 / 30

Overall Score: 84%

Cultivar Ranking: 127th

Blue Dream

Cultivar/Product Information

Type/Effect: Sativa Hybrid - Medium Light
Legacy Name: Blue Dream
Lineage: Blueberry x Haze
Cannabinoids: 21.3% THC / <1% CBD
Terpenes: Myrcene, Caryophyllene, Ocimene

First Impression

Review #297; July 26, 2020,

A mellow haze envelops my mind, and a warm buzz comforts my head and body as Blue Dream by Simply Bare washes over me. Waves of sensation soothe me - the flower having both cerebral and physical effects is appreciated after a long workday. The head high is relatively clear-minded; though a bit hazy, I could still keep my eyes from squinting. My mood is elevated and active while still being mellow somehow. This is a lovely morning, afternoon, or after-work flower, fit to let you unwind and uplift.

Observations

Aroma: Berry, cheesy, fruity, funky, herbal, sour, sweet

Flavour: Berry, floral, fruity, grassy, herbal, sweet

Bud Colour: Green

Pistil Colour: Brown/red

Trichome Density: Medium

Score Details

Appearance:	4 / 5
High Quality:	5 / 5
Aroma:	15 / 15
Flavour:	13 / 15
Bud Quality:	29 / 30
High Potency:	24 / 30

Overall Score: 90%

Cultivar Ranking: 59th

Creek Congo

Cultivar/Product Information

Type/Effect:	Sativa Hybrid - Medium Light
Legacy Name:	Creek Congo
Lineage:	Red Congolese Sativa
Cannabinoids:	20% THC / <1% CBD
Terpenes:	Caryophyllene, Myrcene, Terpinolene

First Impression

Review #299; July 29, 2020,

I'm mellow in my mood but perked up in energy by Simply Bare's Creek Congo. My mind is alive with ideas and eyes bright, though red and hazed over. I feel this one at the back of my skull, creeping its way forward to my forehead - the headband effect is strong. A very cerebral cultivar, not much of a body component to the high, but this is made up for with mental sharpness and intensity. I feel uplifted and euphoric, motivated and creative, though not functional. I'm certainly stoned on another awesome option from Simply Bare.

Observations

Aroma: Citrusy, herbal, piney, pungent, sour, woody

Flavour: Citrusy, floral, herbal, sour, woody

Bud Colour: Dark green

Pistil Colour: Brown/red

Trichome Density: Medium

Score Details

Appearance:	4 / 5
High Quality:	5 / 5
Aroma:	14 / 15
Flavour:	12 / 15
Bud Quality:	29 / 30
High Potency:	24 / 30

Overall Score: 88%

Cultivar Ranking: 81st

SFV OG Kush

Cultivar/Product Information

Type/Effect: Indica - Heavy
Legacy Name: San Fernando Valley OG Kush
Lineage: OG Kush x SFV OG
Cannabinoids: 23.5% THC / <1% CBD
Terpenes: Limonene, Myrcene, Caryophyllene

First Impression

Review #291; July 20, 2020,

SFV OG Kush, my first Simply Bare product, is a heavy-eyed, lazy-minded indica perfect for evening consumption. I'm pretty zoned-out; my mood is absent, as is my mind - a potent flower in intensity and relaxing effect. This flower is exceptional in quality and high, and a great first look at Simply Bare.

Observations

Aroma: Cheese, earthy, funky, herbal, piney, pungent, sour

Flavour: Earthy, funky, herbal, piney, pungent

Bud Colour: Dull green

Pistil Colour: Orange

Trichome Density: Medium-High

Score Details

Appearance:	4 / 5
High Quality:	5 / 5
Aroma:	13 / 15
Flavour:	12 / 15
Bud Quality:	28 / 30
High Potency:	28 / 30

Overall Score: 90%

Cultivar Ranking: 69th

Sour Cookies

Cultivar/Product Information

Type/Effect: Sativa - Medium Light
Legacy Name: Sour Cookies
Lineage: Girl Scout Cookies x Sour Diesel
Cannabinoids: 21.7% THC / <1% CBD
Terpenes: Ocimene, Myrcene, Farnesene

First Impression

Review #292; July 21, 2020,

My mind is alive, and my spirits lifted while enjoying my experience on Sour Cookies by Simply Bare. I rambled off in text form to many friends about the creative, inspiring ideas I spontaneously came up with while getting hazy on this gorgeous flower. Super fun stuff, ideal for AM or whenever you want to feel euphoric and energized. Not physically much, but cerebrally it is damn potent. Offering mood elevation to the max, Sour Cookies is one flower I thoroughly enjoyed.

Observations

Aroma: Fruity, herbal, sweet, woody

Flavour: Earthy, fresh, funky, herbal, pungent, woody

Bud Colour: Dull green

Pistil Colour: Brown/orange

Trichome Density: Medium-High

Score Details

Appearance:	5 / 5
High Quality:	5 / 5
Aroma:	13 / 15
Flavour:	13 / 15
Bud Quality:	30 / 30
High Potency:	25 / 30

Overall Score: 91%

Cultivar Ranking: 49th

Skosha

Overall Performance

Average Score: 85.33%

Brand Ranking: 22nd Place

Brand Background

Skosha, Nova Scotia's first licensed producer of cannabis products, was created in 2014 by friends who were all passionate about quality homegrown cannabis. Utilizing their proprietary process, called PurePlant, Skosha produces flower at a high standard, free of any contaminants and never irradiated.

Skosha's cannabis is produced in Wentworth Valley, Nova Scotia.

Other Cultivars: Dartmouth Kush, Seagrass

Cultivar Selection

Lemon Dory	81%
Mirage	88%
Nor'Easter	87%

Lemon Dory

Cultivar/Product Information

Type/Effect: Sativa - Medium Light
Legacy Name: Lemon Nigerian
Lineage: Lemon OG Kush x Nigerian Hashplant
Cannabinoids: 15.9% THC / <1% CBD
Terpenes: Myrcene, Terpinolene, Caryophyllene

First Impression

Review #337; September 25, 2020,

Skosha's Lemon Dory provides a surprisingly potent cerebral buzz that is mellow, euphoric, and hazy. Were I not consuming alone, I feel I would be pretty social. I feel content just standing and doing nothing as I write; daydreaming while high is a favourite pastime. In the AM or afternoon, Lemon Dory would be a treat. Skosha's mid-range flower delivers above expectations, just as its premium offerings.

Observations

Aroma: Citrusy, fruity, lemon, pungent, sour, sweet

Flavour: Citrusy, grassy, herbal, lemon, sour

Bud Colour: Dark green

Pistil Colour: Brown/orange

Trichome Density: Low

Score Details

Appearance:	4 / 5
High Quality:	5 / 5
Aroma:	14 / 15
Flavour:	12 / 15
Bud Quality:	25 / 30
High Potency:	21 / 30

Overall Score: 81%

Cultivar Ranking: 166th

Mirage

Cultivar/Product Information

Type/Effect: Indica - Neutral
Lineage: God Bud x Harlequin
Cannabinoids: 24.7% THC / <1% CBD
Terpenes: Caryophyllene, Myrcene, Humulene

First Impression

Review #332; September 15, 2020,

Mirage from Skosha is a high potency, high quality, blissful option. A chill, relaxed experience that still leaves the mind intact. I'm able to think, write, and articulate still. I'm not zoned-out, stoned, baked, etc. I got groovy, dancing around to some Opeth in my room ("Sorceress" being the song). This cannabis option might be best shared with a partner - if you know what I'm saying. Overall, I feel lighthearted, silly, and jovial on this flower, and a strong sensation of relief is present in my body and mind. An excellent flower to reset and unwind with, very impressive.

Observations

Aroma: Earthy, fresh, fruity, herbal, sweet, woody

Flavour: Earthy, fresh, herbal, woody

Bud Colour: Dull green

Pistil Colour: Orange

Trichome Density: Medium-High

Score Details

Appearance:	5 / 5
High Quality:	5 / 5
Aroma:	13 / 15
Flavour:	11 / 15
Bud Quality:	28 / 30
High Potency:	26 / 30

Overall Score: 88%

Cultivar Ranking: 86th

Nor'Easter

Cultivar/Product Information

Type/Effect: Sativa - Medium Light
Legacy Name: White Shark
Lineage: Brazilian Sativa x South Indian Sativa x Super Skunk
Cannabinoids: 20.2% THC / <1% CBD
Terpenes: Nerolidol, Myrcene, Caryophyllene

First Impression

Review #330; September 11, 2020,

Skosha's Nor'Easter is a mellow body buzz and a chill, clear-headed high. It is a very full-feeling high - which is somewhat ironic, considering how empty my stomach is. I'm hungry but not compelled to eat; this cultivar is not particularly munchies-inducing. I'm pretty stoned, but I still feel somewhat uplifted and functional. An excellent afternoon enhancer, enjoy the cerebral euphoria.

Observations

Aroma: Earthy, fresh, fruity, herbal, sweet, woody

Flavour: Floral, fresh, grassy, herbal, sweet, woody

Bud Colour: Dull green

Pistil Colour: Brown/orange

Trichome Density: Medium-High

Score Details

Appearance:	4 / 5
High Quality:	5 / 5
Aroma:	14 / 15
Flavour:	12 / 15
Bud Quality:	28 / 30
High Potency:	24 / 30

Overall Score: 87%

Cultivar Ranking: 92nd

Solei

Overall Performance

Average Score: 74.00%

Brand Ranking: 61st Place

Brand Background

Solei, a cannabis brand brought to you by Aphria, offers a variety of cannabis options, each associated with a specific "moment" or "feeling." The brand is committed to sun-grown cannabis and sustainability, utilizing natural sunlight for its operations.

Solei cannabis is grown in Leamington, Ontario.

Other Cultivars:	Chocolate Cheesecake
Associated Brands:	Broken Coast, Canaca, Good Supply, Grail, Marley Natural, Riff

Cultivar Selection

Balance	74%
Free	73%
Gather	74%
Renew	70%
Sense	77%
Unplug	76%

Balance

Cultivar/Product Information

Type/Effect: Hybrid - Light
Legacy Name: CBD Nordle
Lineage: Cannatonic x Nordle
Cannabinoids: 6.2% THC / 11.2% CBD

First Impression

Review #6; April 6, 2019,

As a 1:2 THC:CBD cultivar, Balance by Solei helps you achieve balance. With relatively low THC, Balance has an excellent ratio and potency for morning use, as it won't get you too high. What it lacks in THC, it more than makes up for in CBD potency. The mellow, light, cerebral buzz is accompanied by body relaxation and a total sense of calm. It won't make you get up and go, but it won't couch-lock you either - Balance is very balanced in that sense.

Observations

Aroma: Chocolate, fresh, fruity, herbal, sweet

Flavour: Fruity, herbal, sweet

Bud Colour: Dark green

Pistil Colour: Brown/red

Trichome Density: Low

Score Details

Appearance:	3 / 5
High Quality:	5 / 5
Aroma:	13 / 15
Flavour:	11 / 15
Bud Quality:	20 / 30
High Potency:	22 / 30

Overall Score: 74%

Cultivar Ranking: 294th

Free

Cultivar/Product Information

Type/Effect: Sativa Hybrid - Super Light
Legacy Name: Treasure Island
Lineage: Cannatonic x Swiss Gold
Cannabinoids: <1% THC / 14% CBD

First Impression

Review #136; November 1, 2019.

It was a healthy start to an excellent day today with an 8-hour sleep (the first in months) and this bowl of Solei Free. A CBD-rich, low-THC flower, Free should give you a mild head buzz and a gentle experience that will enhance mood, focus, and awareness while leaving you feeling content and pleased. A solid option for those looking to enjoy cannabis without getting high.

Observations

Aroma: Chocolate, earthy, fresh, herbal, sour, sweet

Flavour: Fresh, funky, herbal, sweet

Bud Colour: Dark green

Pistil Colour: Brown/red

Trichome Density: Low

Score Details

Appearance:	4 / 5
High Quality:	5 / 5
Aroma:	12 / 15
Flavour:	12 / 15
Bud Quality:	20 / 30
High Potency:	20 / 30

Overall Score: 73%

Cultivar Ranking: 313th

Gather

Cultivar/Product Information

Type/Effect: Sativa - Medium Light
Legacy Name: Jack Herer
Lineage: Haze x (Northern Lights #5 x Shiva Skunk)
Cannabinoids: 20.3% THC / <1% CBD

First Impression

Review #33; April 21, 2019,

I got pretty trashed and watched sketch comedy on Gather by Solei. A full head high and headband effect is expected, same with a very social and focusing high. Gather is an excellent sativa bud and a superb option for anyone assuming they can handle the headiness.

Observations

Aroma: Cheesy, fruity, funky, herbal, sour

Flavour: Herbal, sour

Bud Colour: Dark green

Pistil Colour: Orange/tan

Trichome Density: Low-Medium

Score Details

Appearance:	4 / 5
High Quality:	5 / 5
Aroma:	11 / 15
Flavour:	10 / 15
Bud Quality:	21 / 30
High Potency:	23 / 30

Overall Score: 74%

Cultivar Ranking: 301st

Renew

Cultivar/Product Information

Type/Effect: Indica - Medium Heavy
Legacy Name: Alien Dawg
Lineage: Alien Technology x Chemdog
Cannabinoids: 20.1% THC / <1% CBD

First Impression

Review #22; April 16, 2019,

I'm pretty high on Renew by Solei. It does not feel too heavy mentally, but physically it melted me. I feel more like eating and watching TV than I do resting. My stomach won't quit, and I'm too hungry to write more - a decent addition to Solei's line.

Observations

Aroma: Earthy, herbal, spicy

Flavour: Earthy, herbal, spicy

Bud Colour: Green

Pistil Colour: Brown

Trichome Density: Low-Medium

Score Details

Appearance:	3 / 5
High Quality:	5 / 5
Aroma:	9 / 15
Flavour:	10 / 15
Bud Quality:	20 / 30
High Potency:	23 / 30

Overall Score: 70%

Cultivar Ranking: 354th

Sense

Cultivar/Product Information

Type/Effect: Hybrid - Neutral
Legacy Name: Sour Kush
Lineage: OG Kush x Sour Diesel
Cannabinoids: 20% THC / <1% CBD

First Impression

Review #60; May 15, 2019,

Solei's Sense packs a powerful punch with a head high that leaves you feeling relaxed, stoned, outgoing, and blissful. Great for an evening in or a day off with nothing to do or people to see. Somewhat social effects are present - you'll want to be able to speak, though you're going to sound baked - a solid, impairing option from Solei.

Observations

Aroma: Cheesy, fruity, funky, herbal, pungent, sweet

Flavour: Cheesy, funky, herbal, pungent, sour

Bud Colour: Dull green

Pistil Colour: Orange/tan

Trichome Density: Medium

Score Details

Appearance:	4 / 5
High Quality:	5 / 5
Aroma:	12 / 15
Flavour:	10 / 15
Bud Quality:	23 / 30
High Potency:	23 / 30

Overall Score: 77%

Cultivar Ranking: 262nd

Unplug

Cultivar/Product Information

Type/Effect: Indica Hybrid - Medium Heavy
Legacy Name: Rockstar Kush
Lineage: Bubba Kush x Rockstar
Cannabinoids: 19.3% THC / <1% CBD

First Impression

Review #3; April 3, 2019,

Mid-evening I enjoyed Solei's Unplug, and it made me do just that: Unplug. An enjoyable hybrid experience, but due to potency, likely best enjoyed later in the day. A great way to unwind and chill in the evening; all I want is to relax and play video games. Great stuff for anytime you want to decompress from Solei.

Observations

Aroma: Cheesy, earthy, fresh, funky, herbal, pungent, sour

Flavour: Cheesy, earthy, funky, pungent, sour

Bud Colour: Green

Pistil Colour: Orange/tan

Trichome Density: Medium

Score Details

Appearance:	4 / 5
High Quality:	5 / 5
Aroma:	12 / 15
Flavour:	11 / 15
Bud Quality:	22 / 30
High Potency:	22 / 30

Overall Score: 76%

Cultivar Ranking: 273rd

Spinach

Overall Performance

Average Score: 82.29%

Brand Ranking: 30th Place

Brand Background

Spinach is a cannabis brand centered around having fun with friends while consuming cannabis. Brought to you by Cronos Group, Spinach's cannabis lineup consists of a group of cannabis staples, with the variety covering a wide range of possible experiences.

Spinach cannabis is (likely) grown via greenhouse in Ontario.

Other Cultivars: Atomic Sour Grapefruit, Cocoa Bomba, GMO Cookies, Pineapple Paradise, Tangerine Twist, Wedding Cake

Associated Brands: Cove

Cultivar Selection

Cultivar	Score
Blueberry	81%
Blue Dream	80%
Dancehall	83%
Diesel	88%
Rockstar Kush	82%
Sensi Star	81%
White Widow	81%

Blueberry

Cultivar/Product Information

Type/Effect: Indica Hybrid - Medium Heavy
Legacy Name: Blueberry
Lineage: Afghani Indica x Purple Thai x Thai Sativa
Cannabinoids: 20.9% THC / <1% CBD
Terpenes: Myrcene, Limonene, Pinene

First Impression

Review #324; March 13, 2020,

In some creative daydream, I drifted away and was zoned out on Blueberry by Spinach. The high is heavy on the mind and the body; I feel this one everywhere. My mood is stoned but elevated, and reality becomes muted as I drift away again. Blueberry is great PM bud, for pre-snacking or pre-bedtime.

Observations

Aroma: Berry, earthy, fruity, herbal, sour, sweet

Flavour: Berry, fruity, funky, grassy, herbal, sour, sweet

Bud Colour: Dark green

Pistil Colour: Brown/orange

Trichome Density: Medium

Score Details

Appearance:	4 / 5
High Quality:	5 / 5
Aroma:	13 / 15
Flavour:	12 / 15
Bud Quality:	24 / 30
High Potency:	23 / 30

Overall Score: 81%

Cultivar Ranking: 212th

Blue Dream

Cultivar/Product Information

Type/Effect: Sativa - Medium Light
Legacy Name: Blue Dream
Lineage: Blueberry x Haze
Cannabinoids: 21.2% THC / <1% CBD
Terpenes: Pinene, Myrcene, Limonene

First Impression

Review #212; August 31, 2020,

Spinach's take on Blue Dream is much like other mid-range renditions of the genetic: hazy, mellow, relatively clear-headed, and uplifting. Not quite energizing, but certainly motivating in the sense that my mood has improved. I feel a slight headband effect, but not much else physically. It's a bit of a brain buzz too, now that I focus on it. It was a happy and chill experience, great for daytime, or morning sessions, to start the day right.

Observations

Aroma: Berry, earthy, fruity, funky, grassy, herbal, sour, sweet

Flavour: Berry, earthy, grassy, herbal, sweet

Bud Colour: Dull green

Pistil Colour: Orange/tan

Trichome Density: Medium

Score Details

Appearance:	4 / 5
High Quality:	5 / 5
Aroma:	12 / 15
Flavour:	11 / 15
Bud Quality:	25 / 30
High Potency:	23 / 30

Overall Score: 80%

Cultivar Ranking: 177th

Dancehall

Cultivar/Product Information

Type/Effect: Sativa - Light
Legacy Name: Dancehall
Lineage: Juanita la Lagrimosa x Kalijah
Cannabinoids: 6.2% THC / 9% CBD
Terpenes: Bisabolol, Pinene, Caryophyllene

First Impression

Review #400; January 8, 2021,

Within a couple of Volcano bags, I could feel Spinach's Dancehall in my eyes, head, and chest; the high is calm and serene. A welcome addition to my afternoon, Dancehall has mellowed my mood and brightened my perspective. The effects on the body and mind are light, and I could see getting a lot done after enjoying this functional cultivar. Hazy, but not lazy, I did find myself dancing around a bit during my experience. With an uplifting high and decent sensory qualities, Dancehall is a treat.

Observations

Aroma: Earthy, floral, fresh, fruity, herbal, spicy, sweet

Flavour: Earthy, floral, fresh, fruity, herbal, sweet

Bud Colour: Dark green/purple

Pistil Colour: Brown/orange

Trichome Density: Medium

Score Details

Appearance:	4 / 5
High Quality:	5 / 5
Aroma:	13 / 15
Flavour:	13 / 15
Bud Quality:	26 / 30
High Potency:	22 / 30

Overall Score: 83%

Cultivar Ranking: 141st

Diesel

Cultivar/Product Information

Type/Effect: Sativa Hybrid - Neutral
Legacy Name: Sour Diesel
Lineage: '91 Chemdog x Super Skunk
Cannabinoids: 22% THC / <1% CBD
Terpenes: Terpinolene, Limonene, Humulene

First Impression

Review #273; June 13, 2020,

Diesel is a heady and hazy hybrid experience brought to you by Spinach. My thoughts are still pretty usual, just coming more slowly. My body is chill, my mood is uplifted, and my mind is messed up. I feel Diesel throbbing in my forehead and pulsing through my chest and limbs; it is uniquely strong in the eyes, and I certainly look stoned. I feel stoned as well, stupid even. It lasted quite a bit longer in the Volcano than I expected, a welcome surprise. Diesel is potent, indeed.

Observations

Aroma: Citrusy, herbal, pungent, sour

Flavour: Citrusy, floral, herbal, pungent, sour

Bud Colour: Light green

Pistil Colour: Orange

Trichome Density: Medium-High

Score Details

Appearance:	5 / 5
High Quality:	5 / 5
Aroma:	14 / 15
Flavour:	13 / 15
Bud Quality:	26 / 30
High Potency:	25 / 30

Overall Score: 88%

Cultivar Ranking: 80th

Rockstar Kush

Cultivar/Product Information

Type/Effect: Indica - Heavy
Legacy Name: Rockstar Kush
Lineage: Bubba Kush x Rockstar
Cannabinoids: 21.5% THC / <1% CBD
Terpenes: Linalool, Humulene, Pinene

First Impression

Review #196; February 14, 2020,

Spinach's Rockstar Kush is an excellent rendition of the popular cultivar. It seems that my mind and body are fading away from me; the mellow and sedating high has taken hold of my consciousness. Waves of sensation wash over my head and chest as I struggle to keep my eyes open while writing this review. I'm comfortable just leaning into the hardwood of my desk, excited to see how a bed feels. I love my greens, especially Spinach.

Observations

Aroma: Berry, earthy, herbal, sour, sweet

Flavour: Fresh, funky, grassy, herbal, sweet

Bud Colour: Dull green

Pistil Colour: Brown/orange

Trichome Density: Medium-High

Score Details

Appearance:	5 / 5
High Quality:	5 / 5
Aroma:	13 / 15
Flavour:	11 / 15
Bud Quality:	24 / 30
High Potency:	24 / 30

Overall Score: 82%

Cultivar Ranking: 154th

Sensi Star

Cultivar/Product Information

Type/Effect: Indica - Heavy
Legacy Name: Sensi Star
Lineage: "Unknown Afghani"
Cannabinoids: 25% THC / <1% CBD
Terpenes: Myrcene, Limonene, Caryophyllene

First Impression

Review #304; August 5, 2020,

Spinach's Sensi Star is as potent as it was smooth in the Volcano: very easy on the throat and heavy on the mind and body. I feel relatively relaxed, both in mood and by physical sensations rippling through my head, chest, and limbs. My mind is active, and I can move without stumbling despite the relaxation. Spinach has a decent (and potent) take on this classic cultivar.

Observations

Aroma: Earthy, funky, herbal, minty, piney, pungent, sour

Flavour: Earthy, herbal, piney, pungent, woody

Bud Colour: Dark green

Pistil Colour: Brown/red

Trichome Density: Medium-High

Score Details

Appearance:	4 / 5
High Quality:	5 / 5
Aroma:	12 / 15
Flavour:	11 / 15
Bud Quality:	24 / 30
High Potency:	25 / 30

Overall Score: 81%

Cultivar Ranking: 190th

White Widow

Cultivar/Product Information

Type/Effect: Hybrid - Medium Heavy
Legacy Name: White Widow
Lineage: Brazilian Sativa x Indian Indica
Cannabinoids: 18.2% THC / <1% CBD
Terpenes: Myrcene, Limonene, Caryophyllene

First Impression

Review #144; November 24, 2019.

I'm stoned off my ass on Spinach's White Widow, an outstanding Sunday morning cultivar. I felt lazy before consuming, and now I still feel lazy, but also good about it, thanks to a healthy, Popeye-style serving of Spinach. Stimulating and stupefying, White Widow is perfect for downtime.

Observations

Aroma: Citrusy, grassy, herbal, sour

Flavour: Grassy, herbal, sour

Bud Colour: Light green

Pistil Colour: Orange/red

Trichome Density: Medium

Score Details

Appearance:	4 / 5
High Quality:	5 / 5
Aroma:	13 / 15
Flavour:	12 / 15
Bud Quality:	24 / 30
High Potency:	23 / 30

Overall Score: 81%

Cultivar Ranking: 178th

Strain Rec

Overall Performance

Average Score: 82.14%

Brand Ranking: 31st Place

Brand Background

Strain Rec is a cannabis brand focused mainly on sourcing and distributing quality cannabis rather than growing it. Cannabis sourced by Strain Rec is grown "to the highest available standards" and under strict quality controls.

Strain Rec is brought to you by High 12 Brands.

Associated Brands: Kingsway

Cultivar Selection

Cultivar	Score
24K Gold	82%
8 Ball Kush	81%
Candy Kush	81%
CVK Cookie	80%
Ice Cream Cake	90%
Raspberry Cough	79%
Strawberry Magic	82%

24K Gold

Cultivar/Product Information

Type/Effect: Indica Hybrid - Neutral
Legacy Name: 24K Gold
Lineage: Kosher Kush x Tangie
Cannabinoids: 22.4% THC / <1% CBD
Terpenes: Caryophyllene, Humulene, Bisabolol

First Impression

Review #388; December 23, 2020,

An uplifting to the mood but mellow to the mind high is what to expect from Strain Rec's 24K Gold. My body is relieved but not relaxed; I can still move around in a coordinated fashion, as evidenced just now as I dance around my room. My eyes feel like they look hazy; my mind is foggy for sure, but thinking isn't too tricky yet. As I delve further into the Volcano bowl, the high grows in power - the headband effect is enormous, my eyes are watery, and thinking is noticeably more challenging now. I think I know one thing for sure: I've enjoyed 24K Gold.

Observations

Aroma: Citrus, fresh, herbal, pungent, sour

Flavour: Fresh, herbal, woody

Bud Colour: Light green

Pistil Colour: Orange/tan

Trichome Density: Medium

Score Details

Appearance:	4 / 5
High Quality:	5 / 5
Aroma:	12 / 15
Flavour:	11 / 15
Bud Quality:	25 / 30
High Potency:	25 / 30

Overall Score: 82%

Cultivar Ranking: 161st

8 Ball Kush

Cultivar/Product Information

Type/Effect: Indica Hybrid - Heavy
Legacy Name: 8 Ball Kush
Lineage: Bubba Kush x King Kush
Cannabinoids: 23% THC / <1% CBD
Terpenes: Caryophyllene, Myrcene, Limonene

First Impression

Review #391; December 26, 2020,

I feel lazy and bogged down on 8 Ball Kush by Strain Rec - a pretty heavy experience that offers both relaxation and sedation. I feel like doing absolutely nothing meaningful. My mind is numb and empty, and the effects of the high soothe my body. A definite PM-only bud, but a solid one for sure. A KO if you're already tired and a great prep for naptime if you're not, 8 Ball Kush is a decent evening flower.

Observations

Aroma: Earthy, fresh, herbal, sour, spicy, woody

Flavour: Earthy, funky, grassy, herbal, spicy, woody

Bud Colour: Dark green

Pistil Colour: Brown/orange

Trichome Density: Medium

Score Details

Appearance:	4 / 5
High Quality:	5 / 5
Aroma:	12 / 15
Flavour:	11 / 15
Bud Quality:	25 / 30
High Potency:	24 / 30

Overall Score: 81%

Cultivar Ranking: 191st

Candy Kush

Cultivar/Product Information

Type/Effect: Indica Hybrid - Medium Heavy
Legacy Name: Candy Kush
Lineage: Blue Dream x OG Kush
Cannabinoids: 16.9% THC / <1% CBD
Terpenes: Caryophyllene, Pinene

First Impression

Review #357; October 28, 2020,

Strain Rec's Candy Kush is my first experience with a Blue Dream and OG Kush cross, and I hope it won't be my last… this high is chill, relaxed, and spacey. I'm alternating between a blissful, aware state and zoning out. My eyes and mind feel heavy, and my body is loose and relieved. I feel like cuddling some pillows and passing out right about now.

Observations

Aroma: Berry, earthy, fresh, fruity, pungent, sweet

Flavour: Berry, earthy, floral, funky, grassy, herbal, sweet

Bud Colour: Dull green

Pistil Colour: Orange/tan

Trichome Density: Medium

Score Details

Appearance:	4 / 5
High Quality:	5 / 5
Aroma:	14 / 15
Flavour:	13 / 15
Bud Quality:	25 / 30
High Potency:	20 / 30

Overall Score: 81%

Cultivar Ranking: 170th

CVK Cookie

Cultivar/Product Information

Type/Effect: Indica Hybrid - Heavy
Legacy Name: CVK Cookie
Lineage: Girl Scout Cookies x OG Kush
Cannabinoids: 21.8% THC / <1% CBD
Terpenes: Caryophyllene, Myrcene, Limonene

First Impression

Review #392; December 28, 2020,

A heavy head "stone" and a relaxed body are in store for consumers of CVK Cookie by Strain Rec. This is a cultivar best suited for evenings set aside to chill and waste. I find it difficult to find words to write and energy to expend. I can't see myself accomplishing much more than indulging in cartoons and music for the duration of the high. Thinking is tough, and I'm zoning out hard. It's time to relax a bit.

Observations

Aroma: Earthy, funky, grassy, herbal, sour, spicy

Flavour: Earthy, grassy, herbal, sweet, woody

Bud Colour: Dark green

Pistil Colour: Brown

Trichome Density: Medium

Score Details

Appearance:	4 / 5
High Quality:	5 / 5
Aroma:	12 / 15
Flavour:	11 / 15
Bud Quality:	24 / 30
High Potency:	24 / 30

Overall Score: 80%

Cultivar Ranking: 220th

Ice Cream Cake

Cultivar/Product Information

Type/Effect: Indica - Heavy
Legacy Name: Ice Cream Cake
Lineage: Gelato 33 x Wedding Cake
Cannabinoids: 21.3% THC / <1% CBD
Terpenes: Pinene, Ocimene, Caryophyllene

First Impression

Review #408; January 29, 2021,

Strain Rec's Ice Cream Cake is chill and vibey. My mood, body, and mind are relaxed by the potent high this flower provides. I could see consuming this right before bed as a KO punch or right before a meal to inspire munch(ing) (anything for a rhyme… gettin' all Dr. Seuss up in here). One of the most substantial 21% flower options I've experienced in a while, mad decent.

Observations

Aroma: Earthy, fresh, herbal, minty, piney, pungent

Flavour: Earthy, herbal, piney, pungent, spicy, woody

Bud Colour: Dull green/purple

Pistil Colour: Brown

Trichome Density: Medium-High

Score Details

Appearance:	5 / 5
High Quality:	5 / 5
Aroma:	14 / 15
Flavour:	13 / 15
Bud Quality:	27 / 30
High Potency:	26 / 30

Overall Score: 90%

Cultivar Ranking: 65th

Raspberry Cough

Cultivar/Product Information

Type/Effect: Sativa Hybrid - Medium Light
Legacy Name: Raspberry Cough
Lineage: Cambodian Sativa x ICE
Cannabinoids: 16.3% THC / <1% CBD
Terpenes: Pinene, Caryophyllene, Limonene

First Impression

Review #360; November 1, 2020,

Raspberry Cough by Strain Rec is a wicked good time and a hazy cerebral rush. The high is uplifting and clear-headed, quite functional overall, and I can think easily. My eyes' haziness comes into play; they feel heavy and partially shut, though I'm not tired still, just mellow. The aroma is to die for, fruity and sweet, especially when ground up. For a motivational, pleasant wake 'n bake, seek out Raspberry Cough.

Observations

Aroma: Floral, fresh, fruity, grassy, herbal, sweet, sour

Flavour: Floral, grassy, herbal

Bud Colour: Green

Pistil Colour: Orange

Trichome Density: Medium

Score Details

Appearance:	4 / 5
High Quality:	5 / 5
Aroma:	14 / 15
Flavour:	11 / 15
Bud Quality:	25 / 30
High Potency:	20 / 30

Overall Score: 79%

Cultivar Ranking: 226th

Strawberry Magic

Cultivar/Product Information

Type/Effect: Indica Hybrid - Neutral
Legacy Name: Strawberry Magic
Lineage: Original Glue x Strawberry Diesel
Cannabinoids: 22% THC / <1% CBD
Terpenes: Caryophyllene, Myrcene, Humulene

First Impression

Review #389; December 24, 2020,

I am quite cooked on Strawberry Magic by Strain Rec. This one is a brain-melter for sure; I find myself blanking in thought more often than not. I don't think I'm capable enough on this cultivar to accomplish much, but I feel immaculate, absolutely incredible as far as energy, mood, and perspective go. I could see this being a decent social cultivar, assuming you can remain focused enough on the conversation. Hazy eyes, a lazy body, and a brightened, heightened, enlightened mind are expected. Strawberry Magic has won me over with a powerful buzz and effects that are nothing short of "magical."

Observations

Aroma: Diesel, earthy, fruity, herbal, pungent, sweet

Flavour: Earthy, fresh, grassy, herbal, sweet

Bud Colour: Dark green

Pistil Colour: Brown/orange

Trichome Density: Medium

Score Details

Appearance:	4 / 5
High Quality:	5 / 5
Aroma:	13 / 15
Flavour:	11 / 15
Bud Quality:	24 / 30
High Potency:	25 / 30

Overall Score: 82%

Cultivar Ranking: 152nd

Sundial

Overall Performance

Average Score: 77.44%

Brand Ranking: 45th Place

Brand Background

Sundial is a cannabis brand with a broad product catalogue and a focus on consistency. Across the brand, cultivars are split into five main series - calm, ease, flow, lift, and spark - each with a specific goal in mind when it comes to the effects of the cultivars.

Sundial cannabis is grown in Olds, Alberta, where they attempt to scale a more craft-oriented grow-op. The facility features modular, cultivar-specific rooms, each with individual environmental controls.

Other Cultivars: Citrus Orchard, Wedding Cake
Associated Brands: Palmetto, Topleaf

Cultivar Selection

Berry Bliss	84%
Blue Nova	79%
Citrus Punch	75%
Daydream	72%
Lemon Riot	81%
Strawberry Twist	79%
Twilight	80%
Wild Indigo	76%
Zen Berry	71%

Berry Bliss

Cultivar/Product Information

Type/Effect: Indica Hybrid - Medium Light
Legacy Name: Voodoo Child
Lineage: Blue Lights x Purple Voodoo
Cannabinoids: 16% THC / <1% CBD
Terpenes: Ocimene, Caryophyllene, Humulene

First Impression

Review #179; January 12, 2020.

Sundial's Berry Bliss is relaxing, calming, and soothing to the body and mood, but mentally I'm alive and alert. With a medium-high potency and a unique, unreal smell and flavour, combined with pleasant effects, this is one of my favourites. Anyone who appreciates cannabis will appreciate the character, quality, and glorious high of Berry Bliss.

Observations

Aroma: Berry, fruity, sweet, sweet candy

Flavour: Berry, fruity, herbal, sweet

Bud Colour: Light green

Pistil Colour: Brown/red

Trichome Density: Medium

Score Details

Appearance:	4 / 5
High Quality:	5 / 5
Aroma:	15 / 15
Flavour:	15 / 15
Bud Quality:	24 / 30
High Potency:	21 / 30

Overall Score: 84%

Cultivar Ranking: 120th

Blue Nova

Cultivar/Product Information

Type/Effect: Sativa Hybrid - Medium Light
Legacy Name: Blue Dream
Lineage: Blueberry x Haze
Cannabinoids: 20.3% THC / <1% CBD
Terpenes: Myrcene, Pinene, Guaiol

First Impression

Review #398; January 4, 2021,

Blue Nova by Sundial has ignited my mind and creativity, and my head is alive with thoughts and ideas. My mood is relatively calm and mellow, but my energy and focus are way up; this is an active cultivar that still gets you stoned. Ideal for wake 'n bake sessions or afternoons off, Blue Nova is a functional and versatile high regardless of the activities you wish to partake in.

Observations

Aroma: Floral, fruity, herbal, pungent, sour, sweet

Flavour: Floral, funky, herbal, sweet

Bud Colour: Dark green

Pistil Colour: Orange

Trichome Density: Medium

Score Details

Appearance:	4 / 5
High Quality:	5 / 5
Aroma:	12 / 15
Flavour:	10 / 15
Bud Quality:	25 / 30
High Potency:	23 / 30

Overall Score: 79%

Cultivar Ranking: 241st

Citrus Punch

Cultivar/Product Information

Type/Effect: Sativa Hybrid - Neutral
Legacy Name: Agent Orange
Lineage: Jack the Ripper x Orange Skunk
Cannabinoids: 14.6% THC / <1% CBD
Terpenes: Myrcene, Caryophyllene, Humulene

First Impression

Review #126; October 9, 2019,

This sativa hybrid from Sundial, Citrus Punch, is a head-heavy, medium-intensity blast that elevates mood and energy. I don't feel sluggish or stoned, just pleasantly high and easily distracted by the TV - some decent stuff from Sundial.

Observations

Aroma: Herbal, sour, sweet

Flavour: Floral, fresh, herbal, sweet

Bud Colour: Dark green

Pistil Colour: Brown/orange

Trichome Density: Low-Medium

Score Details

Appearance:	4 / 5
High Quality:	5 / 5
Aroma:	11 / 15
Flavour:	11 / 15
Bud Quality:	24 / 30
High Potency:	20 / 30

Overall Score: 75%

Cultivar Ranking: 291st

Daydream

Cultivar/Product Information

Type/Effect: Sativa Hybrid - Medium Light
Legacy Name: Purple Chemdog
Lineage: Chemdog x Granddaddy Purps
Cannabinoids: 18.5% THC / <1% CBD
Terpenes: Myrcene, Caryophyllene, Terpinene

First Impression

Review #94; August 21, 2019,

A light haze envelops my mind as Daydream by Sundial takes hold of my consciousness. I'm clear-headed and focused on my review, but a nice cerebral buzz sits in the background. I feel content and in the moment - much unlike I'm daydreaming, which I find funny. Ideal for mornings or afternoons, for fans of sativas.

Observations

Aroma: Berry, cheese, earthy, funky, piney, sour, sweet

Flavour: Berry, cheese, earthy, funky, pungent

Bud Colour: Dark green/purple

Pistil Colour: Brown/orange

Trichome Density: Medium

Score Details

Appearance:	4 / 5
High Quality:	5 / 5
Aroma:	11 / 15
Flavour:	10 / 15
Bud Quality:	22 / 30
High Potency:	20 / 30

Overall Score: 72%

Cultivar Ranking: 332nd

Lemon Riot

Cultivar/Product Information

Type/Effect: Sativa Hybrid - Medium Light
Legacy Name: Raskal OG
Lineage: Fire Kush x San Fernando Valley OG Kush
Cannabinoids: 17% THC / <1% CBD
Terpenes: Myrcene, Pinene, Limonene

First Impression

Review #90; August 17, 2019,

Man, I'm baked. Lemon Riot from Sundial is a bit less of a riot than expected; I'm not too excited or energized, but I feel focused and very high. The high is mainly in the head, and the headband effect is substantial - my brain is pulsing, and my mind is sharp. Lemon Riot is a solid daytime option.

Observations

Aroma: Citrusy, earthy, herbal, sour, sweet

Flavour: Citrusy, herbal, sweet

Bud Colour: Dark green

Pistil Colour: Brown/orange

Trichome Density: Low-Medium

Score Details

Appearance:	4 / 5
High Quality:	5 / 5
Aroma:	13 / 15
Flavour:	13 / 15
Bud Quality:	24 / 30
High Potency:	22 / 30

Overall Score: 81%

Cultivar Ranking: 182nd

Strawberry Twist

Cultivar/Product Information

Type/Effect: Indica Hybrid - Medium Heavy
Legacy Name: Strawberry Banana
Lineage: Banana Kush x Strawberry Bubblegum
Cannabinoids: 18% THC / <1% CBD
Terpenes: Caryophyllene, Myrcene, Pinene

First Impression

Review #219; March 24, 2020,

Sundial's Strawberry Twist provides a hazy headband effect, mental and physical relief and relaxation, and a medium intensity high. Everything formerly on my mind is now gone; it's vacant. I can think and write clearly, but my ambition to do so is fading. I just want to sprawl out on the couch or cuddle with my cat. Very calm and comforting, though no yawns yet. A great addition to the Sundial line for a medium-light experience.

Observations

Aroma: Berry, earthy, floral, fruity, herbal, sweet

Flavour: Berry, earthy, floral, fruity, funky, herbal, sweet

Bud Colour: Green

Pistil Colour: Brown/orange

Trichome Density: Medium

Score Details

Appearance:	4 / 5
High Quality:	5 / 5
Aroma:	14 / 15
Flavour:	12 / 15
Bud Quality:	24 / 30
High Potency:	20 / 30

Overall Score: 79%

Cultivar Ranking: 227th

Twilight

Cultivar/Product Information

Type/Effect: Indica - Heavy
Legacy Name: Jager OG
Lineage: Hindu Kush x OG Kush x OG Kush
Cannabinoids: 20.4% THC / <1% CBD
Terpenes: Caryophyllene, Pinene, Myrcene

First Impression

Review #176; January 7, 2020,

Twilight by Sundial was enjoyed midday by me, so it's a good thing it's a day off, as I'm chilled right out. My mind and body are heavy, slow, and relaxed, making this excellent evening consumption material. I almost need a nap. I feel I need to melt into a couch now.

Observations

Aroma: Citrusy, fresh, herbal, pungent, sour

Flavour: Funky, herbal, pungent, sour, spicy, woody

Bud Colour: Green

Pistil Colour: Brown/orange

Trichome Density: Medium

Score Details

Appearance:	4 / 5
High Quality:	5 / 5
Aroma:	12 / 15
Flavour:	11 / 15
Bud Quality:	25 / 30
High Potency:	23 / 30

Overall Score: 80%

Cultivar Ranking: 219th

Wild Indigo

Cultivar/Product Information

Type/Effect: Indica Hybrid - Medium Heavy
Legacy Name: Blackberry Kush
Lineage: Afghani Indica x Blackberry
Cannabinoids: 17.9% THC / <1% CBD
Terpenes: Myrcene, Caryophyllene, Humulene

First Impression

Review #226; April 1, 2020,

I didn't feel too wild on Wild Indigo by Sundial; much more relaxed and yearning to go back to bed. A sense of calm washed over me upon completing my session. My eyes were heavy, not shut but getting there. The cerebral stimulation was enough to keep me awake and thinking of snacks. Notably, this cultivar induced some creativity, as evidenced in my Minecraft progress following this session.

Observations

Aroma: Berry, earthy, fruity, herbal, sweet

Flavour: Earthy, herbal, sweet

Bud Colour: Dark green/purple

Pistil Colour: Orange

Trichome Density: Medium

Score Details

Appearance:	4 / 5
High Quality:	5 / 5
Aroma:	13 / 15
Flavour:	10 / 15
Bud Quality:	24 / 30
High Potency:	20 / 30

Overall Score: 76%

Cultivar Ranking: 271st

Zen Berry

Cultivar/Product Information

Type/Effect: Indica Hybrid - Medium Light
Legacy Name: Shishkaberry
Lineage: "Unknown Afghani" x DJ Short Blueberry
Cannabinoids: 14.6% THC / <1% CBD
Terpenes: Myrcene, Caryophyllene, Pinene

First Impression

Review #18; April 14, 2019,

I got pretty zonked and zoned out on this one while watching some cartoons, a great start to my Sundial Zen Berry experience. The high is calm and mellow, ideal for the evening, as it makes me feel like resting for a bit. However, I also feel like munching out and watching cartoons, so I'd say this is an excellent multi-purpose indica.

Observations

Aroma: Berry, cheese, fruity, funky, pungent, sour, sweet

Flavour: Berry, earthy, fresh, fruity, sweet

Bud Colour: Dark green

Pistil Colour: Brown/orange

Trichome Density: Low-Medium

Score Details

Appearance:	4 / 5
High Quality:	5 / 5
Aroma:	12 / 15
Flavour:	10 / 15
Bud Quality:	22 / 30
High Potency:	18 / 30

Overall Score: 71%

Cultivar Ranking: 330th

Symbl

Overall Performance

Average Score: 68.43%

Brand Ranking: 72nd Place

Symbl

Brand Background

Symbl is a cannabis brand that caters to the curious and the creative. Their portfolio of cultivars covers a wide range of effect profiles, all designed to aid you in "exploring the unexpected."

Cannabis for Symbl is grown in Emblem's indoor facility in Paris, Ontario.

Other Cultivars: Super Sonic

Cultivar Selection

Bella Luna	63%
Daily Rind	66%
Dreamweaver	65%
Grape Royale	67%
Hoverboard	75%
Solar Power	68%
Wave Runner	75%

Bella Luna

Cultivar/Product Information

Type/Effect: Indica - Medium Light
Legacy Name: Conspiracy Kush
Lineage: Obama Kush x Space Queen
Cannabinoids: 9.4% THC / <1% CBD
Terpenes: Terpinolene, Caryophyllene, Limonene

First Impression

Review #65; May 30, 2019,

After a long day of work on two hours of sleep, Bella Luna from Symbl was precisely what I needed to start unwinding, chillaxing (if you will), and getting ready for bedtime. At only 9.4% THC, this one might surprise you, given that it feels as though it were more potent. I don't necessarily feel tired due to this cultivar either - it would be great anytime during the evening for consumption.

Observations

Aroma: Earthy, herbal, spicy

Flavour: Earthy, herbal, spicy

Bud Colour: Brown/green

Pistil Colour: Orange

Trichome Density: Medium

Score Details

Appearance:	4 / 5
High Quality:	5 / 5
Aroma:	11 / 15
Flavour:	10 / 15
Bud Quality:	19 / 30
High Potency:	14 / 30

Overall Score: 63%

Cultivar Ranking: 398th

Daily Rind

Cultivar/Product Information

Type/Effect: Indica Hybrid - Light
Legacy Name: Larry OG
Lineage: OG Kush x San Fernando Valley OG
Cannabinoids: 12.3% THC / <1% CBD
Terpenes: Caryophyllene, Limonene, Humulene

First Impression

Review #12; April 10, 2019,

Symbl's Daily Rind is an indica-dominant hybrid, which I largely ignored when picking my consumption time of 10am. A very light experience at this potency level, but I'm not complaining. This was an excellent way to start my daily grind. A perkier indica-dominant than most, I'm feeling relaxed but hardly tired. This helped me get ready for my day, for sure, and I feel more motivated than I did before consumption.

Observations

Aroma: Citrusy, herbal, pungent

Flavour: Citrusy, herbal, lemon, sour

Bud Colour: Light green

Pistil Colour: Orange

Trichome Density: Medium

Score Details

Appearance:	4 / 5
High Quality:	5 / 5
Aroma:	12 / 15
Flavour:	11 / 15
Bud Quality:	18 / 30
High Potency:	16 / 30

Overall Score: 66%

Cultivar Ranking: 384th

Dreamweaver

Cultivar/Product Information

Type/Effect: Indica - Medium Heavy
Legacy Name: MK Ultra
Lineage: G13 x OG Kush
Cannabinoids: 14.4% THC / <1% CBD
Terpenes: Caryophyllene, Pinene, Nerolidol

First Impression

Review #103; September 2, 2019,

Dreamweaver by Symbl has me ready to pass out and surprisingly stoned for a 14.4% THC cultivar. A medium potency but high-intensity indica, the high is foggy and cerebral; I can't think straight, and a heavy sensation is growing in my head, legs, and chest. The music I'm listening to has me distracted from writing - I lack focus on this bud, so I'd consider it a solid pick for accomplishing little.

Observations

Aroma: Cheese, chocolate, earthy, funky, herbal, skunk, sour, sweet

Flavour: Earthy, funky, herbal, spicy

Bud Colour: Dark green

Pistil Colour: Brown/orange

Trichome Density: Medium

Score Details

Appearance: 3 / 5
High Quality: 5 / 5
Aroma: 11 / 15
Flavour: 6 / 15
Bud Quality: 20 / 30
High Potency: 20 / 30

Overall Score: 65%

Cultivar Ranking: 391st

Grape Royale

Cultivar/Product Information

Type/Effect: Indica - Medium Heavy
Legacy Name: Royal Purple Kush
Lineage: Black Afghani x Bubba Kush
Cannabinoids: 15.8% THC / <1% CBD
Terpenes: Myrcene, Caryophyllene, Limonene

First Impression

Review #140; November 16, 2019,

A super relaxed high, Grape Royale (with cheese? - for Pulp Fiction fans) by Symbl is ideal for a night on the couch. Cerebrally stimulating enough to get you lost in the TV, but super chill. My body feels like I've been in a hot tub for a while: relaxed, rejuvenated, and refreshed. Grape Royale is suitable for all consumers as a manageable, night-time/free-time oriented high.

Observations

Aroma: Fresh, funky, grassy, herbal, sweet

Flavour: Fresh, funky, grassy, herbal, sweet

Bud Colour: Dull green

Pistil Colour: Brown/red

Trichome Density: Low-Medium

Score Details

Appearance:	4 / 5
High Quality:	5 / 5
Aroma:	9 / 15
Flavour:	9 / 15
Bud Quality:	22 / 30
High Potency:	18 / 30

Overall Score: 67%

Cultivar Ranking: 383rd

Hoverboard

Cultivar/Product Information

Type/Effect: Indica Hybrid - Medium Light
Legacy Name: Buddha's Sister
Lineage: Afghani Indica x Hawaiian Sativa x Reclining Buddha
Cannabinoids: 15.4% THC / <1% CBD
Terpenes: Terpinolene, Myrcene, Pinene

First Impression

Review #257; May 11, 2020,

Hoverboard, by Symbl, has a sharp aroma and flavour, coupled with a calm and mellow buzz that offers mental and physical escape. I feel serene, not too stoned, just right for the post-work hours when one wants to unwind.

Observations

Aroma: Citrusy, herbal, lemon, piney, pungent, sour, spicy

Flavour: Citrusy, herbal, lemon, pungent, sour

Bud Colour: Dull green

Pistil Colour: Brown/tan

Trichome Density: Medium

Score Details

Appearance:	4 / 5
High Quality:	5 / 5
Aroma:	13 / 15
Flavour:	12 / 15
Bud Quality:	23 / 30
High Potency:	18 / 30

Overall Score: 75%

Cultivar Ranking: 283rd

Solar Power

Cultivar/Product Information

Type/Effect: Indica Hybrid - Light
Legacy Name: Sour Kush
Lineage: OG Kush x Sour Diesel
Cannabinoids: 10.1% THC / <1% CBD
Terpenes: Pinene, Limonene, Nerolidol

First Impression

Review #68; June 4, 2019,

I'm certainly high but also high-functioning, thanks to Solar Power from Symbl. My mind is clear, my thoughts easily manageable, and my motor skills seem fine, as my writing is speedy and unimpaired. My mind is also relaxed, as is my body. Overall, a great, lighter-potency experience. This percentage is excellent for new consumers, those sensitive to THC, or anyone looking to get a little high rather than right stoned.

Observations

Aroma: Chocolate, earthy, herbal, sweet

Flavour: Earthy, herbal, woody

Bud Colour: Dull green

Pistil Colour: Brown/orange

Trichome Density: Medium

Score Details

Appearance:	4 / 5
High Quality:	5 / 5
Aroma:	11 / 15
Flavour:	10 / 15
Bud Quality:	23 / 30
High Potency:	15 / 30

Overall Score: 68%

Cultivar Ranking: 367th

Wave Runner

Cultivar/Product Information

Type/Effect: Sativa - Light
Legacy Name: Delahaze
Lineage: Lemon Skunk x Mango Haze
Cannabinoids: 14% THC / <1% CBD
Terpenes: Terpinolene, Pinene, Caryophyllene

First Impression

Review #111; September 11, 2019,

Wave Runner by Symbl has me feeling mellow, uplifted, and clear-minded. Everything feels right at this moment. I wish I were at the beach, baking in the sun on this flower, but I'll settle for my bedroom and some music; the jam session and this bud have my creative juices flowing. On top of the blissful high, this flower also tasted and smelled excellent, like sour candy. I would highly recommend this bud to anyone looking to spice up a morning or afternoon.

Observations

Aroma: Citrusy, fresh, herbal, sour, sour candy

Flavour: Citrusy, fresh, herbal, sour, sour candy

Bud Colour: Light green

Pistil Colour: Orange

Trichome Density: Medium

Score Details

Appearance:	4 / 5
High Quality:	5 / 5
Aroma:	14 / 15
Flavour:	12 / 15
Bud Quality:	22 / 30
High Potency:	18 / 30

Overall Score: 75%

Cultivar Ranking: 279th

Tantalus Labs

Overall Performance

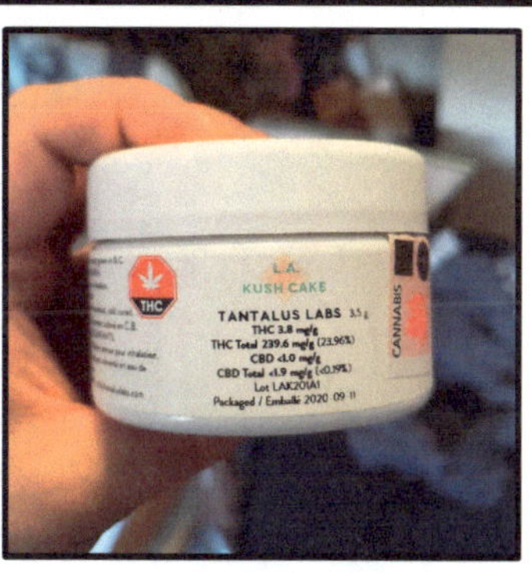

Average Score: 76.00%

Brand Ranking: 51st Place

Brand Background

Tantalus Labs focuses on producing quality flower products, utilizing small-batch practices, and sustainable methods. By mastering "elite genetics, pure inputs, and disciplined cultivation" - Tantalus' core principles - they aim to produce the highest quality of cannabis available.

Tantalus Labs grows its cannabis via a purpose-built greenhouse near Vancouver, BC, in the Fraser Valley.

Other Cultivars: Blackberry Cream, Black Diamond, More Cowbell, Orange Crasher, Petrocan, Slurri Crasher, Sunset Sherbert, Unicorn Poop, Wedding Crasher

Cultivar Selection

Blue Dream	70%
Harlequin	60%
LA Kush Cake	90%
Pacific OG	83%
Serratus	79%
Sky Pilot	74%

Blue Dream

Cultivar/Product Information

Type/Effect: Sativa - Light
Legacy Name: Blue Dream
Lineage: Blueberry x Haze
Cannabinoids: 11.5% THC / <1% CBD
Terpenes: Pinene, Caryophyllene, Myrcene

First Impression

Review #21; April 15 2019,

I enjoyed Tantalus Labs' Blue Dream over episodes of animated comedies. I find myself laughing more often than usual and getting distracted from my review process, which I attribute to both the high and the TV. I'm not too high, as this cultivar is light on THC, but the effects that accent the high are strong, indicating a potent terpene profile. This was a decent hazy option.

Observations

Aroma: Berry, herbal, pungent, sour, sweet

Flavour: Funky, herbal, sour, spicy

Bud Colour: Light green

Pistil Colour: Orange/tan

Trichome Density: Low-Medium

Score Details

Appearance:	4 / 5
High Quality:	5 / 5
Aroma:	12 / 15
Flavour:	12 / 15
Bud Quality:	21 / 30
High Potency:	16 / 30

Overall Score: 70%

Cultivar Ranking: 342nd

Harlequin

Cultivar/Product Information

Type/Effect:	Sativa Hybrid - Super Light
Legacy Name:	Harlequin
Lineage:	Colombian Gold x (Nepalese Indica x Swiss Sat. x Thai Sat.)
Cannabinoids:	3.5% THC / 7.5% CBD
Terpenes:	Pinene, Caryophyllene, Nerolidol

First Impression

Review #31; April 19, 2019,

Harlequin from Tantalus Labs provides a light THC buzz with a medium strength CBD high that will leave you relaxed and ready to take on the day. It is an excellent choice for those who want minimal THC and a great way to start their morning.

Observations

Aroma: Fresh, fruity, herbal, sweet

Flavour: Funky, herbal, pungent, spicy

Bud Colour: Dull brown/green

Pistil Colour: Brown/red

Trichome Density: Low-Medium

Score Details

Appearance:	4 / 5
High Quality:	5 / 5
Aroma:	12 / 15
Flavour:	10 / 15
Bud Quality:	17 / 30
High Potency:	12 / 30

Overall Score: 60%

Cultivar Ranking: 409th

LA Kush Cake

Cultivar/Product Information

Type/Effect: Hybrid - Heavy
Legacy Name: LA Kush Cake
Lineage: Kush Mints x Wedding Cake
Cannabinoids: 24% THC / <1% CBD
Terpenes: Caryophyllene, Limonene, Nerolidol

First Impression

Review #368; November 16, 2020.

Tantalus Labs' LA Kush Cake is a potent cultivar with a "f***-you-up" factor. I feel very empty-headed and slowed way down. The high is very relaxing, and I tend to zone out. I'm leaning super hard into my dresser while writing, as though it's comfortable - also because my legs are having a hard time supporting me under the spell of this intense high. A wonderful grow of a wondrous cultivar.

Observations

Aroma: Earthy, fresh, minty, piney, pungent, sweet

Flavour: Earthy, fresh, herbal, minty, piney, pungent, sweet

Bud Colour: Dull green

Pistil Colour: Brown/orange

Trichome Density: Medium

Score Details

Appearance:	4 / 5
High Quality:	5 / 5
Aroma:	14 / 15
Flavour:	13 / 15
Bud Quality:	28 / 30
High Potency:	26 / 30

Overall Score: 90%

Cultivar Ranking: 61st

Pacific OG

Cultivar/Product Information

Type/Effect: Sativa Hybrid - Medium Light
Legacy Name: Goji OG
Lineage: Nepali OG x Snow Lotus
Cannabinoids: 17.6% THC / <1% CBD
Terpenes: Myrcene, Linalool, Limonene

First Impression

Review #229; April 3, 2020,

Pacific OG had me lost in my phone for a half-hour before writing this review, so thank you, Tantalus Labs. A great morning or afternoon escape and a euphoric and peppy high. With decent sensory qualities and THC percentage, Tantalus has done well with this flower. I'm so ready for my day but too high to start it; I'll have to enjoy the ride.

Observations

Aroma: Berry, earthy, fruity, herbal, pungent, sweet

Flavour: Earthy, pungent, sweet

Bud Colour: Dull green

Pistil Colour: Orange

Trichome Density: Medium-High

Score Details

Appearance:	4 / 5
High Quality:	5 / 5
Aroma:	13 / 15
Flavour:	13 / 15
Bud Quality:	26 / 30
High Potency:	22 / 30

Overall Score: 83%

Cultivar Ranking: 144th

Serratus

Cultivar/Product Information

Type/Effect: Indica - Medium Heavy
Lineage: Afgooey x Blockhead x Sweet Tooth
Cannabinoids: 16.6% THC / <1% CBD
Terpenes: Pinene, Guaiol, Bisabolol

First Impression

Review #131; October 15, 2019,

Tantalus Labs has presented me with my favourite so far of their cultivars: Serratus. It is stupefying and satisfying, and oh boy, does it get you stoned. Despite the 16.6% THC, given how powerful this bud felt between the immense head-high and potent body-buzz, I had a tough time thinking - a solid zone-out pick.

Observations

Aroma: Citrusy, earthy, herbal, sour, sweet

Flavour: Earthy, sweet, woody

Bud Colour: Light green

Pistil Colour: Brown/orange

Trichome Density: Medium

Score Details

Appearance:	4 / 5
High Quality:	5 / 5
Aroma:	13 / 15
Flavour:	12 / 15
Bud Quality:	22 / 30
High Potency:	23 / 30

Overall Score: 79%

Cultivar Ranking: 230th

Sky Pilot

Cultivar/Product Information

Type/Effect: Indica Hybrid - Medium Light
Lineage: Blue Dream x Snow Lotus
Cannabinoids: 17.2% THC / <1% CBD
Terpenes: Myrcene, Linalool, Limonene

First Impression

Review #132; October 17, 2019,

A relaxing, chill, heady experience, Sky Pilot by Tantalus Labs is an excellent hybrid for any time you want to enjoy yourself and your free time. Not exceptionally motivating, but it certainly makes me want to indulge in the things I enjoy most when high. It is a superb medium-intensity option that should please old pros and new stoners alike.

Observations

Aroma: Earthy, herbal, piney, sweet

Flavour: Earthy, funky, grassy, herbal, sweet

Bud Colour: Dull green

Pistil Colour: Brown/orange

Trichome Density: Medium

Score Details

Appearance:	4 / 5
High Quality:	5 / 5
Aroma:	12 / 15
Flavour:	9 / 15
Bud Quality:	21 / 30
High Potency:	23 / 30

Overall Score: 74%

Cultivar Ranking: 296th

The Green Organic Dutchman

Overall Performance

Average Score: 77.25%

Brand Ranking: 47th Place

Brand Background

A premium organic producer of cannabis, The Green Organic Dutchman believes that "nature knows best." They utilize all-natural inputs for their plants, including rainwater, sunlight, and living soil. The brand is also committed to sustainable practices and attempts to minimize environmental impact. TGOD is certified by Pro-Cert, which ensures all of its cannabis growing methods follow those set out by the Organic Federation of Canada.

The Green Organic Dutchman's cannabis is grown in greenhouses in Valleyfield, Quebec.

Other Cultivars: Cherry Mints, Maple Kush, Sugar Bush, Wifi Mints

Cultivar Selection

GG#4	81%
Harmony	73%
Rockstar Tuna	76%
Unite	79%

GG#4

Cultivar/Product Information

Type/Effect: Indica Hybrid - Neutral
Legacy Name: Original Glue
Lineage: Chem's Sister x Chocolate Diesel x Sour Dubb
Cannabinoids: 19.9% THC / <1% CBD
Terpenes: Caryophyllene, Humulene, Myrcene

First Impression

Review #381; December 14, 2020,

I was coughing up a storm, pretty high as well, on GG#4 by The Green Organic Dutchman. Then I found myself profoundly distracted and intrigued by a science article on consciousness and quantum physics. This high got my mind going, but I was pretty relaxed overall despite some euphoria - an enjoyable time.

Observations

Aroma: Coffee, earthy, fresh, funky, pungent, woody

Flavour: Earthy, fresh, grassy, herbal

Bud Colour: Dark green

Pistil Colour: Brown/red

Trichome Density: Medium

Score Details

Appearance:	4 / 5
High Quality:	5 / 5
Aroma:	13 / 15
Flavour:	12 / 15
Bud Quality:	24 / 30
High Potency:	23 / 30

Overall Score: 81%

Cultivar Ranking: 181st

Harmony

Cultivar/Product Information

Type/Effect: Hybrid - Medium Light
Legacy Name: CBD Skunk Haze
Lineage: Cannatonic x Super Haze
Cannabinoids: 5.1% THC / 8.1% CBD
Terpenes: Farnesene, Caryophyllene, Terpinolene

First Impression

Review #194; February 13, 2020,

The effects of Harmony by The Green Organic Dutchman are calm and balanced. A light head buzz is present, as well as some body feels; the physical sensation and cerebral high work perfectly together. A great way to feel like you've just had a good nap and are waking up relaxed but refreshed. This may be my favourite rendition of CBD Skunk Haze on the market.

Observations

Aroma: Citrusy, fresh, herbal, sour, spicy, sweet

Flavour: Funky, herbal, sour, spicy, woody

Bud Colour: Dark green

Pistil Colour: Brown/red

Trichome Density: Low-Medium

Score Details

Appearance:	4 / 5
High Quality:	5 / 5
Aroma:	12 / 15
Flavour:	12 / 15
Bud Quality:	22 / 30
High Potency:	18 / 30

Overall Score: 73%

Cultivar Ranking: 314th

Rockstar Tuna

Cultivar/Product Information

Type/Effect: Indica - Medium Heavy
Legacy Name: Rockstar Tuna
Lineage: Rockstar x Tuna Kush
Cannabinoids: 19.3% THC / <1% CBD
Terpenes: Caryophyllene, Bisabolol, Humulene

First Impression

Review #370; November 20, 2020,

I found myself both relaxed and awakened by The Green Organic Dutchman's Rockstar Tuna. Stinky and flavourful, something I expected given the aroma. I was expecting a KO punch from this bud, but instead, I received a relaxing stoned effect with the cerebral activity of, say… a Pink Kush. A potent, mind-wandering time, pretty decent.

Observations

Aroma: Earthy, fresh, piney, pungent, sour

Flavour: Earthy, piney, pungent, spicy, woody

Bud Colour: Dark green

Pistil Colour: Brown

Trichome Density: Low-Medium

Score Details

Appearance:	4 / 5
High Quality:	5 / 5
Aroma:	12 / 15
Flavour:	12 / 15
Bud Quality:	21 / 30
High Potency:	22 / 30

Overall Score: 76%

Cultivar Ranking: 274th

Unite

Cultivar/Product Information

Type/Effect: Indica - Medium Heavy
Legacy Name: LA Confidential
Lineage: Afghani Indica x OG L.A. Affie
Cannabinoids: 17% THC / <1% CBD
Terpenes: Pinene, Myrcene, Caryophyllene

First Impression

Review #167; December 28, 2019,

Unite has me feeling mellow and calm; my first taste of the flower from The Green Organic Dutchman led to a very peaceful, serene indica high. The THC is doing wonders for my mood and focus, I was thinking a mile a minute before, but now I feel chill… my mind is on ice. The physical sensation is mild but strong enough to mirror in the body the experience of the mind. This is a Goldilocks cultivar: it's just right.

Observations

Aroma: Fresh, herbal, sour, sweet

Flavour: Earthy, funky, herbal, pungent, woody

Bud Colour: Dark green

Pistil Colour: Brown/red

Trichome Density: Low-Medium

Score Details

Appearance:	4 / 5
High Quality:	5 / 5
Aroma:	12 / 15
Flavour:	12 / 15
Bud Quality:	24 / 30
High Potency:	22 / 30

Overall Score: 79%

Cultivar Ranking: 239th

Thumbs Up Brand

Overall Performance

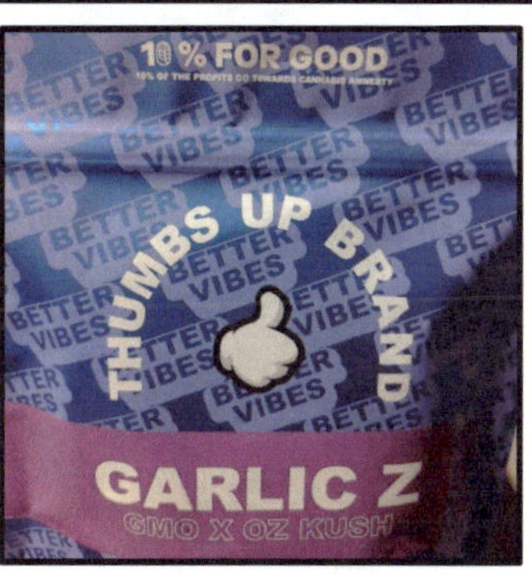

Average Score: 82.75%

Brand Ranking: 26th Place

Brand Background

Thumbs Up Brand, a cannabis brand brought to market by Trec Brands, features cannabis sourced from various growers. Typically with a mid-range price-point, THC above 20% (as a newer standard for the brand), and cultivars that feature distinct and robust terpene profiles, Thumbs Up Brand cannabis impresses me.

Cannabis for Thumbs Up Brand is sourced from various producers across Canada.

Other Cultivars: Mint Smash, Pink Cookies x Kush Mints, Snowbud x Afghan Kush
Associated Brands: Wink

Cultivar Selection

Cultivar	Score
Amnesia x Super Haze	84%
Garlic Z	82%
Strain Hunters' Lemon Skunk	84%
Strain Hunters' White Lemon	81%

Amnesia x Super Haze

Cultivar/Product Information

Type/Effect: Sativa - Light
Legacy Name: Outlaw Amnesia
Lineage: Amnesia x Super Haze
Cannabinoids: 24.7% THC / <1% CBD
Terpenes: Caryophyllene, Myrcene, Farnesene

First Impression

Review #412; February 6, 2021,

A light but high-intensity, clear-minded cerebral haze is in store for consumers of Amnesia x Super Haze by Thumbs Up Brand. A perfect, potent sativa pick that would be great anytime in the AM or afternoon. I feel euphoric, mellow, and uplifted. My creative juices are flowing, though I'm not thinking much. A very bright but calm sativa experience, though it may not be "calm" for those less experienced with the potency.

Observations

Aroma: Citrusy, fresh, herbal, lemon, sour

Flavour: Citrusy, grassy, herbal, sour

Bud Colour: Light green

Pistil Colour: Brown/orange

Trichome Density: Medium

Score Details

Appearance:	5 / 5
High Quality:	4 / 5
Aroma:	13 / 15
Flavour:	12 / 15
Bud Quality:	26 / 30
High Potency:	24 / 30

Overall Score: 84%

Cultivar Ranking: 124th

Garlic Z

Cultivar/Product Information

Type/Effect:	Indica - Heavy
Legacy Name:	Garlic Z
Lineage:	Garlic Cookies x OZ Kush
Cannabinoids:	20% THC / <1% CBD
Terpenes:	Caryophyllene, Myrcene, Limonene

First Impression

Review #386; December 20, 2020.

Garlic Z by Thumbs Up Brand is a lazy feeling high; it is super relaxed and heavy-eyed. I lack interest in doing much of anything and am pretty zoned out. Super dense buds with a light smell pre-grind, and like garlic post-grind, it was stinky, but in a good way. The high is detaching me from everything and dropping me off in the middle of nowhere - my mind is vacant, reality feels distant… maybe I'm falling asleep, or Garlic Z has some sort of spell on me. Incidentally, I'm drooling. This is a great cultivar for munching or getting right zonked.

Observations

Aroma: Earthy, funky, herbal, pungent, sour

Flavour: Earthy, funky, grassy, herbal, pungent, sour, woody

Bud Colour: Dull green

Pistil Colour: Brown/red

Trichome Density: Medium-High

Score Details

Appearance:	4 / 5
High Quality:	5 / 5
Aroma:	13 / 15
Flavour:	11 / 15
Bud Quality:	25 / 30
High Potency:	24 / 30

Overall Score: 82%

Cultivar Ranking: 157th

Strain Hunters' Lemon Skunk

Cultivar/Product Information

Type/Effect: Hybrid - Light
Legacy Name: Lemon Skunk
Lineage: Citral x Skunk
Cannabinoids: 19.5% THC / <1% CBD
Terpenes: Caryophyllene, Myrcene, Humulene

First Impression

Review #213; March 13, 2020,

I am coughing up a storm on the terpy wonder that is Strain Hunters' Lemon Skunk by Thumbs Up Brand. The smell and flavour are both distinctly Lemon Skunk, and I wasn't surprised the effects were meeting my expectations. Euphoric and clear, calm, but exciting. The effects are primarily heady, with only a mild body sensation. I found myself dancing around in my room on this flower - I think this Lemon Skunk deserves a thumbs up.

Observations

Aroma: Citrusy, diesel, earthy, fruity, herbal, sour, sweet

Flavour: Citrusy, diesel, fruity, herbal, sour, sweet, woody

Bud Colour: Green

Pistil Colour: Orange

Trichome Density: Low-Medium

Score Details

Appearance:	4 / 5
High Quality:	5 / 5
Aroma:	14 / 15
Flavour:	13 / 15
Bud Quality:	25 / 30
High Potency:	23 / 30

Overall Score: 84%

Cultivar Ranking: 122nd

Strain Hunters' White Lemon

Cultivar/Product Information

Type/Effect: Hybrid - Light
Legacy Name: White Lemon
Lineage: El Nino x Super Lemon Haze
Cannabinoids: 17.6% THC / <1% CBD
Terpenes: Caryophyllene, Terpinolene, Humulene

First Impression

Review #215; March 14, 2020,

Strain Hunters' White Lemon by Thumbs Up Brand is a soul-soothing, mind-melting (in a good, manageable way), citrusy wonder of a cultivar. Excellent quality and terpene profile, especially for its price category. I'm calm, focused, and honed in on what I'm doing. However, I'm also jovial and upbeat, alive with a creative flair. I have loved my experiences with Thumbs Up so far, and White Lemon is no exception.

Observations

Aroma: Citrusy, fruity, herbal, piney, pungent, sour

Flavour: Citrusy, herbal, pungent, sour, woody

Bud Colour: Dark green

Pistil Colour: Orange

Trichome Density: Low-Medium

Score Details

Appearance:	4 / 5
High Quality:	5 / 5
Aroma:	14 / 15
Flavour:	13 / 15
Bud Quality:	25 / 30
High Potency:	20 / 30

Overall Score: 81%

Cultivar Ranking: 167th

Tokyo Smoke

Overall Performance

Average Score: 66.25%

Brand Ranking: 74th Place

Brand Background

Tokyo Smoke, a cannabis brand owned by Canopy Growth, released a few cannabis products during 2019-2020 and has since transitioned into a primarily retail-oriented brand. The initial lineup featured intent-based naming, lining up your cannabis with the mood you were looking for it to inspire. It also featured some unique genetics.

Canopy Growth grew mid-grade, mass-produced cannabis in Ontario for the Tokyo Smoke brand.

Other Cultivars: Equalize
Associated Brands: 7Acres, DNA Genetics, Houseplant, LBS, Tweed, Van Der Pop

Cultivar Selection

Cultivar	Score
Ease	55%
Go	76%
Pause	63%
Rise	71%

Ease

Cultivar/Product Information

Type/Effect: Hybrid - Super Light
Legacy Name: CBD Therapy
Cannabinoids: <1% THC / 9.4% CBD
Terpenes: Caryophyllene, Limonene, Humulene

First Impression

Review #227; April 1, 2020,

Ease by Tokyo Smoke was just what I needed to take the edge off. A mellow calm overtakes me as I consume this flower, my mood improving as concerns fade. There's hardly a high or headband effect, nor physical sensation either, but a wellness factor is present that shouldn't be overlooked. Pleasant stuff, though low in potency.

Observations

Aroma: Floral, fresh, grassy, sweet

Flavour: Funky, grassy, herbal, woody

Bud Colour: Green/tan

Pistil Colour: Brown/orange

Trichome Density: Medium

Score Details

Appearance:	4 / 5
High Quality:	4 / 5
Aroma:	11 / 15
Flavour:	9 / 15
Bud Quality:	19 / 30
High Potency:	8 / 30

Overall Score: 55%

Cultivar Ranking: 417th

Go

Cultivar/Product Information

Type/Effect: Sativa Hybrid - Neutral
Legacy Name: Apple Pie
Lineage: Acapulco Gold x Highland Nepalese
Cannabinoids: 18% THC / <1% CBD
Terpenes: Myrcene, Pinene

First Impression

Review #149; December 1, 2019,

This is my first taste of Tokyo Smoke's Go, and I'll likely be inclined to ask for seconds in the future. The flavour is fresh, floral, and sweet, really great. The high is medium intensity for 18%, pretty relaxed for a sativa; not an energizing cultivar, but plenty of mood elevation. I feel fantastic, ready to Go (slow)!

Observations

Aroma: Floral, fresh, fruity, funky, grassy, sweet

Flavour: Floral, fresh, fruity, grassy, sweet

Bud Colour: Light green

Pistil Colour: Brown/tan

Trichome Density: Medium

Score Details

Appearance:	4 / 5
High Quality:	5 / 5
Aroma:	12 / 15
Flavour:	12 / 15
Bud Quality:	22 / 30
High Potency:	21 / 30

Overall Score: 76%

Cultivar Ranking: 278th

Pause

Cultivar/Product Information

Type/Effect: Indica Hybrid - Light
Legacy Name: Strawberry Banana
Lineage: Banana Kush x Bubblegum
Cannabinoids: 13% THC / <1% CBD
Terpenes: Limonene, Caryophyllene, Pinene

First Impression

Review #235; April 12, 2020,

The calm brought on by the high of Tokyo Smoke's Pause is blissful, except for the periods of coughing. A very fresh and floral cultivar, Pause offers a full-body sense of serenity and relief while bringing the mind to a crawl. A decent replacement for a dessert after dinner, though you'll likely want dessert as well.

Observations

Aroma: Floral, fresh, grassy, herbal, spicy, sweet

Flavour: Floral, fresh, herbal, sweet

Bud Colour: Dark green/orange

Pistil Colour: Orange/tan

Trichome Density: Low-Medium

Score Details

Appearance:	3 / 5
High Quality:	5 / 5
Aroma:	12 / 15
Flavour:	12 / 15
Bud Quality:	16 / 30
High Potency:	15 / 30

Overall Score: 63%

Cultivar Ranking: 397th

Rise

Cultivar/Product Information

Type/Effect:	Sativa Hybrid - Medium Light
Legacy Name:	Blue Dream
Lineage:	Blueberry x Haze
Cannabinoids:	16.3% THC / <1% CBD
Terpenes:	Limonene, Pinene, Caryophyllene

First Impression

Review #172; January 3, 2020,

While not the most potent 16% THC flower I've had, Tokyo Smoke's Rise was one of the most fun. Rise is aptly named as it is an ideal wake and bake cultivar. I found myself rocking out and dancing around in my bedroom the morning of its consumption. The high was uplifting and full of focus, very functional. Thought-provoking as well, but not the kind that will make you scared or paranoid.

Observations

Aroma: Floral, fresh, herbal, sweet

Flavour: Floral, fresh, funky, grassy, herbal, spicy

Bud Colour: Light green

Pistil Colour: Brown/red

Trichome Density: Low-Medium

Score Details

Appearance:	4 / 5
High Quality:	5 / 5
Aroma:	13 / 15
Flavour:	11 / 15
Bud Quality:	21 / 30
High Potency:	17 / 30

Overall Score: 71%

Cultivar Ranking: 327th

Topleaf

Overall Performance

Average Score: 86.30%

Brand Ranking: 20th Place

Brand Background

Topleaf was founded by a group of cannabis enthusiasts who asked: "what do we want to smoke?". That question would become Topleaf's guiding principle. Top Leaf as a brand reflects what its founders think the best in cannabis should be, with a product that aspires to rank best in class.

Cannabis for Topleaf is grown in small-batch, cultivar-specific grow rooms in Olds, Alberta.

Other Cultivars: LA Kush Cake
Associated Brands: Palmetto, Sundial

Cultivar Selection

Cultivar	Score
Blue Dream	86%
Bubba	91%
GSC	84%
Jager OG	84%
Northern Lights	84%
Oregon Golden Goat	85%
Pink Kush	86%
Purple Clementine	79%
Strawberry Cream	89%
Super Skunk	95%

Blue Dream

Cultivar/Product Information

Type/Effect: Sativa Hybrid - Medium Light
Legacy Name: Blue Dream
Lineage: Blueberry x Haze
Cannabinoids: 23% THC / <1% CBD
Terpenes: Myrcene, Pinene, Guaiol

First Impression

Review #181; January 27, 2020,

Clarity, focus, alertness, and calmness come to mind when I think about my experience with Topleaf's Blue Dream. I felt like starting my day after a bowl of this bud - my mood elevated, and my drive heightened. There is still a heaviness behind the eyes, but my mind is sharp, and I don't feel foggy. The high is strong but not overly so, making this a great AM cultivar for those looking for a sharp kick to brighten their mood. I feel serene, though quite hungry now. To the snacks!

Observations

Aroma: Fresh, grassy, herbal, sour, sweet

Flavour: Fresh, grassy, herbal, sour, sweet

Bud Colour: Light green

Pistil Colour: Orange

Trichome Density: Medium

Score Details

Appearance:	4 / 5
High Quality:	5 / 5
Aroma:	13 / 15
Flavour:	12 / 15
Bud Quality:	27 / 30
High Potency:	25 / 30

Overall Score: 86%

Cultivar Ranking: 104th

Bubba

Cultivar/Product Information

Type/Effect: Indica Hybrid - Super Heavy
Legacy Name: Death Bubba
Lineage: Bubba Kush x Death Star
Cannabinoids: 26.3% THC / <1% CBD
Terpenes: Caryophyllene, Myrcene, Humulene

First Impression

Review #265; May 25, 2020,

Topleaf's Bubba is a cerebral meltdown paired with physical bliss. I can't think too well, but I feel amazing. Zoned out, relaxed beyond belief, and craving snacks and bedtime. Heavy doesn't begin to describe the effects of this flower. I'm crazy stoned, and I love it. One for seasoned stoners only, newcomers beware the badass power of Bubba. Wonderful flower.

Observations

Aroma: Earthy, fresh, grassy, herbal, pungent, sour

Flavour: Earthy, fresh, grassy, herbal, sweet, woody

Bud Colour: Dull green

Pistil Colour: Orange/tan

Trichome Density: Medium-High

Score Details

Appearance:	5 / 5
High Quality:	5 / 5
Aroma:	13 / 15
Flavour:	12 / 15
Bud Quality:	28 / 30
High Potency:	28 / 30

Overall Score: 91%

Cultivar Ranking: 52nd

GSC

Cultivar/Product Information

Type/Effect: Hybrid - Medium Heavy
Legacy Name: Girl Scout Cookies
Lineage: Durban Poison x OG Kush
Cannabinoids: 21.5% THC / <1% CBD
Terpenes: Caryophyllene, Myrcene, Humulene

First Impression

Review #232; April 5, 2020,

I am pretty baked here, cooked up real good on GSC by Topleaf. Not exactly the high I was looking for this morning, but I'm enjoying getting messed up. The headband effect is super intense. Volcano bags remained milky and opaque with vapour for longer than typical - the high terpene and cannabinoid content apparent from both the visual and the stupefying cerebral blast. My eyes are heavy, and my mind and face are melting away, as is my attachment to reality. I love it.

Observations

Aroma: Cheese, diesel, earthy, funky, herbal, pungent, sour

Flavour: Floral, grassy, herbal, sour, woody

Bud Colour: Dull green

Pistil Colour: Orange

Trichome Density: Medium

Score Details

Appearance:	4 / 5
High Quality:	5 / 5
Aroma:	12 / 15
Flavour:	12 / 15
Bud Quality:	27 / 30
High Potency:	24 / 30

Overall Score: 84%

Cultivar Ranking: 133rd

Jager OG

Cultivar/Product Information

Type/Effect: Indica Hybrid - Heavy
Legacy Name: Jager OG
Lineage: Hindu Kush x OG Kush x OG Kush
Cannabinoids: 20% THC / <1% CBD
Terpenes: Myrcene, Pinene, Caryophyllene

First Impression

Review #183; February 3, 2020,

I'm pretty baked out of my mind, enjoying an evening bowl of Jager OG from Topleaf. A clear-headed, super-relaxing bud that feels just right before bed. Heavy, HEAVY flower, particularly in the eyes and body. Excellent quality from Topleaf. Now, time for rest.

Observations

Aroma: Fresh, herbal, sour, sweet

Flavour: Funky, grassy, herbal, sweet

Bud Colour: Dull green

Pistil Colour: Brown/red

Trichome Density: Medium

Score Details

Appearance:	4 / 5
High Quality:	5 / 5
Aroma:	13 / 15
Flavour:	11 / 15
Bud Quality:	27 / 30
High Potency:	24 / 30

Overall Score: 84%

Cultivar Ranking: 128th

Northern Lights

Cultivar/Product Information

Type/Effect: Indica Hybrid - Neutral
Legacy Name: Northern Lights
Lineage: Afghani Indica
Cannabinoids: 25% THC / <1% CBD
Terpenes: Myrcene, Caryophyllene, Humulene

First Impression

Review #416; February 10, 2021,

A physical relief and cerebral escape, Northern Lights by Topleaf is a euphoric delight. Certainly a strong high, but still manageable despite the THC. Not nearly as heavy as I would have assumed it may be. A great afternoon or after-work mood enhancer, Northern Lights met my expectations; well done, Top Leaf.

Observations

Aroma: Earthy, herbal, piney, pungent, sour, woody

Flavour: Earthy, fresh, grassy, herbal

Bud Colour: Dull green

Pistil Colour: Brown/tan

Trichome Density: Medium-High

Score Details

Appearance:	4 / 5
High Quality:	5 / 5
Aroma:	12 / 15
Flavour:	11 / 15
Bud Quality:	27 / 30
High Potency:	25 / 30

Overall Score: 84%

Cultivar Ranking: 131st

Oregon Golden Goat

Cultivar/Product Information

Type/Effect: Sativa Hybrid - Light
Legacy Name: Oregon Golden Goat
Lineage: Flo x Lemon Haze x Zelly's Gift
Cannabinoids: 20.3% THC / <1% CBD
Terpenes: Caryophyllene, Terpineol, Humulene

First Impression

Review #220; March 24, 2020,

My eyes are red and heavy, and I look how I feel - stoned and hazy - thanks to the powerful cerebral kick from Oregon Golden Goat by Topleaf. My body is tingling, a unique physical sensation present throughout my body and most in my head. My mind is alive and focused intensely on writing, creative flow aided by the Goat. Notably, this lasted forever in the Volcano, over ten bags! Euphoric, satisfying, and uplifting bud from Topleaf.

Observations

Aroma: Cheese, citrusy, diesel, herbal, minty, sour, woody

Flavour: Citrusy, funky, herbal, sour, woody

Bud Colour: Green

Pistil Colour: Orange

Trichome Density: Medium

Score Details

Appearance:	4 / 5
High Quality:	5 / 5
Aroma:	14 / 15
Flavour:	12 / 15
Bud Quality:	26 / 30
High Potency:	24 / 30

Overall Score: 85%

Cultivar Ranking: 112th

Pink Kush

Cultivar/Product Information

Type/Effect: Indica Hybrid - Heavy
Legacy Name: Pink Kush
Lineage: OG Kush
Cannabinoids: 25.4% THC / <1% CBD
Terpenes: Caryophyllene, Myrcene, Limonene

First Impression

Review #260; May 14, 2020,

Topleaf's Pink Kush packs a powerfully potent cerebral punch, so I can't think too straight. My eyes and body are heavy; I'm fully relaxed and ready to chill out and fade out. An intense flower, especially at this THC %, heavy stoners will find a friend in this cannabinoid-rich rendition of Pink Kush.

Observations

Aroma: Earthy, grassy, herbal, pungent, sour, woody

Flavour: Earthy, funky, grassy, herbal, piney, pungent

Bud Colour: Dark green/purple

Pistil Colour: Orange/tan

Trichome Density: Medium-High

Score Details

Appearance:	4 / 5
High Quality:	5 / 5
Aroma:	13 / 15
Flavour:	12 / 15
Bud Quality:	25 / 30
High Potency:	27 / 30

Overall Score: 86%

Cultivar Ranking: 108th

Purple Clementine

Cultivar/Product Information

Type/Effect: Sativa Hybrid - Neutral
Legacy Name: Mimosa
Lineage: Clementine x Purple Punch
Cannabinoids: 20.8% THC / <1% CBD
Terpenes: Ocimene, Caryophyllene, Limonene

First Impression

Review #409; February 1, 2021,

A mellow headband effect is what to expect from Topleaf's Purple Clementine. My mood is uplifted but calm; I feel clear-minded and can still think straight. After writing that last sentence, the zone-out was HARD for a while, so I'm not sure this is the most functional sativa I've had. I wouldn't like to do much on this bud, but socializing or creative endeavours sound great. Euphoric and enjoyable.

Observations

Aroma: Fresh, fruity, herbal, sweet, woody

Flavour: Fresh, grassy, herbal, sweet

Bud Colour: Dull green

Pistil Colour: Orange

Trichome Density: Medium

Score Details

Appearance:	4 / 5
High Quality:	5 / 5
Aroma:	12 / 15
Flavour:	11 / 15
Bud Quality:	25 / 30
High Potency:	22 / 30

Overall Score: 79%

Cultivar Ranking: 240th

Strawberry Cream

Cultivar/Product Information

Type/Effect: Indica Hybrid - Medium Heavy
Legacy Name: Voodoo Child
Lineage: Blue Lights x Purple Voodoo
Cannabinoids: 18.1% THC / <1% CBD
Terpenes: Ocimene, Caryophyllene, Humulene

First Impression

Review #170; December 31, 2019,

Strawberry Cream by Topleaf is a delight; a wonderfully sweet-smelling flower with a mellow and relaxed head buzz and chest sensation. Ideally consumed in a vaporizer, it tastes almost as unreal as it smells. I'd be down to sit and watch TV, but I don't need to do something so lazy… I don't feel overly inebriated. I can see myself being functional but fully stoned on this bud. Incredible aroma, one of the best, and a significant high, Strawberry Cream is a bud you must experience.

Observations

Aroma: Berry, fruity, strawberry, sweet, sweet candy

Flavour: Berry, fruity, herbal, sweet

Bud Colour: Dark green

Pistil Colour: Brown/red

Trichome Density: Medium

Score Details

Appearance:	4 / 5
High Quality:	5 / 5
Aroma:	15 / 15
Flavour:	15 / 15
Bud Quality:	27 / 30
High Potency:	23 / 30

Overall Score: 89%

Cultivar Ranking: 70th

Super Skunk

Cultivar/Product Information

Type/Effect:	Indica Hybrid - Super Heavy
Legacy Name:	Super Skunk
Lineage:	Afghani Indica x Skunk #1
Cannabinoids:	25.5% THC / <1% CBD
Terpenes:	Myrcene, Caryophyllene, Humulene

First Impression

Review #243; April 19, 2020

Topleaf has outdone past efforts with Super Skunk, their strongest flower yet. My room is filled with a thick vapour cloud. The high is intense both cerebrally and physically: speaking, thinking, writing, and focusing are difficult. I'm pretty inebriated; this is a fantastic "I wanna feel stupid" flower. The quality was perfect, and the aroma was so strong it seeped through my mail package, the Canada Post worker complained to me. A dank wonder.

Observations

Aroma: Earthy, herbal, pungent, sweet

Flavour: Earthy, floral, fresh, herbal, sweet, woody

Bud Colour: Green

Pistil Colour: Orange/tan

Trichome Density: High

Score Details

Appearance:	5 / 5
High Quality:	5 / 5
Aroma:	13 / 15
Flavour:	13 / 15
Bud Quality:	30 / 30
High Potency:	29 / 30

Overall Score: 95%

Cultivar Ranking: 16th

Tweed

Overall Performance

Average Score: 65.33%

Brand Ranking: 76th Place

Brand Background

The Tweed story begins with setting up in an abandoned Hershey's Chocolate factory in Smiths Falls, Ontario. It continues with several industry firsts, including the first brand to offer cannabis from coast to coast. Given their size and original mission statement of being "the largest cannabis brand in the world", one could assume the future for Tweed exists beyond just Canada.

Tweed cannabis is produced in Smiths Falls, Ontario.

Other Cultivars:	Royal Dankness, Powdered Doughnuts
Associated Brands:	7Acres, DNA Genetics, Houseplant, LBS, Tokyo Smoke, Van Der Pop

Cultivar Selection

Argyle	65%
Bakerstreet	66%
Balmoral	73%
Boaty McBoatface	45%
Donegal	75%
Herringbone	60%
Highlands	69%
Houndstooth	65%
Penelope	70%

Argyle

Cultivar/Product Information

Type/Effect: Indica Hybrid - Neutral
Legacy Name: CBD Nordle
Lineage: Cannatonic x Nordle
Cannabinoids: 6% THC / 6% CBD
Terpenes: Myrcene, Caryophyllene, Limonene

First Impression

Review #55; May 7, 2019,

Look no further than Argyle by Tweed for a mellow and relaxed balanced effect. The high is mild and light, though the headband effect is strong. This 1:1 has me feeling incredibly chill and rested, as though I had a nap; this cultivar is also very uplifting for the mind and allows you to unwind. I'm ready, thanks to Argyle, to begin & enjoy my evening.

Observations

Aroma: Earthy, fresh, fruity, spicy, sweet, woody

Flavour: Cheese, earthy, funky, pungent, sour, spicy, woody

Bud Colour: Dark green

Pistil Colour: Orange

Trichome Density: Low-Medium

Score Details

Appearance:	4 / 5
High Quality:	5 / 5
Aroma:	10 / 15
Flavour:	10 / 15
Bud Quality:	18 / 30
High Potency:	18 / 30

Overall Score: 65%

Cultivar Ranking: 392nd

Bakerstreet

Cultivar/Product Information

Type/Effect: Indica - Heavy
Legacy Name: Hindu Kush
Lineage: Hindu Kush
Cannabinoids: 20% THC / <1% CBD
Terpenes: Myrcene, Caryophyllene, Limonene

First Impression

Review #62; May 19, 2019,

I zoned out hard during my experience with Tweed's Bakerstreet. A high-THC nighttime indica, Bakerstreet delivers a decent head high coupled with a powerful body sensation for complete relaxation. This is a bud that might knock you out if you're not careful, but one you'll enjoy until you pass out.

Observations

Aroma: Earthy, herbal, pungent, sweet

Flavour: Earthy, herbal, spicy

Bud Colour: Light green

Pistil Colour: Brown

Trichome Density: Medium

Score Details

Appearance:	3 / 5
High Quality:	5 / 5
Aroma:	10 / 15
Flavour:	9 / 15
Bud Quality:	16 / 30
High Potency:	23 / 30

Overall Score: 66%

Cultivar Ranking: 387th

Balmoral

<u>Cultivar/Product Information</u>

Type/Effect: Hybrid - Medium Heavy
Legacy Name: UK Cheese
Lineage: Skunk #1
Cannabinoids: 23.7% THC / <1% CBD
Terpenes: Caryophyllene, Myrcene, Pinene

First Impression

Review #25; April 17, 2019.

I got pretty zoned out on this potent batch of Balmoral by Tweed. It is a heavy cerebral experience accompanied by a head and body sensation that will leave you feeling stoned. Likely best as a later-in-the-day hybrid, as the hefty amount of THC in this bud will leave you lazy and incapable. A potent addition to Tweed's line of products and a decent high.

Observations

Aroma: Cheese, fruity, funky, herbal, pungent, sour, sweet

Flavour: Cheese, funky, herbal, sour, spicy

Bud Colour: Dull green

Pistil Colour: Brown/red

Trichome Density: Medium

Score Details

Appearance:	3 / 5
High Quality:	5 / 5
Aroma:	12 / 15
Flavour:	12 / 15
Bud Quality:	17 / 30
High Potency:	24 / 30

Overall Score: 73%

Cultivar Ranking: 310th

Boaty McBoatface

Cultivar/Product Information

Type/Effect: Sativa Hybrid - Super Light
Legacy Name: CBD Medihaze
Lineage: "High CBD Cultivar" x (Nevil's Haze x Super Silver Haze)
Cannabinoids: 1.8% THC / 6% CBD
Terpenes: Bisabolol, Myrcene, Guaiol

First Impression

Review #47; April 30, 2019.

Tweed's Boaty McBoatface is not only the best-named cultivar on the market, but it is also exceptionally new-consumer friendly - a light, mellow and pleasant high. However, this batch may have been a bit too light for me as I am an experienced and regular consumer. I like to have >3.5% THC in my balanced cultivars, as anything below that is much too light to be apparent to my senses.

Observations

Aroma: Fresh, grassy, herbal, sweet

Flavour: Earthy, fresh, grassy, herbal, piney

Bud Colour: Green

Pistil Colour: Brown/red

Trichome Density: Low

Score Details

Appearance:	3 / 5
High Quality:	2 / 5
Aroma:	10 / 15
Flavour:	8 / 15
Bud Quality:	14 / 30
High Potency:	8 / 30

Overall Score: 45%

Cultivar Ranking: 420th

Donegal

Cultivar/Product Information

Type/Effect: Sativa - Medium Heavy
Legacy Name: Green Crack
Lineage: Afghani Indica x Skunk #1
Cannabinoids: 22% THC / <1% CBD
Terpenes: Pinene, Caryophyllene, Limonene

First Impression

Review #245; April 22, 2020,

Donegal by Tweed is heady, my mind is alive and well, but I'm stuck in place as soon as I sit down. Just as I'm physically stuck, writer's block is in full effect as my mind wanders from the task at hand to other things: the high has taken over. Enjoyable and potent, one of Tweed's better products.

Observations

Aroma: Fresh, herbal, sweet, woody

Flavour: Earthy, fresh, grassy, herbal, woody

Bud Colour: Dull green

Pistil Colour: Orange

Trichome Density: Medium

Score Details

Appearance:	4 / 5
High Quality:	5 / 5
Aroma:	12 / 15
Flavour:	10 / 15
Bud Quality:	21 / 30
High Potency:	23 / 30

Overall Score: 75%

Cultivar Ranking: 286th

Herringbone

Cultivar/Product Information

Type/Effect: Indica Hybrid - Medium Heavy
Legacy Name: Ken's Kush
Lineage: Granddaddy Purps x OG Kush x Sour Diesel
Cannabinoids: 11.6% THC / <1% CBD
Terpenes: Caryophyllene, Linalool, Santalene

First Impression

Review #61; May 15, 2019,

All I can think of to say about Tweed's Herringbone is: "this is the perfect afternoon bud." I'm high, but not stoned, not too in my head or stuck on the couch. I could do things, but Herringbone has me in the mood to chill and enjoy my spare time. A medium-intensity experience, though it feels more than 11.6%, Herringbone should be suitable for anyone at this potency, whether they are new to or experienced with cannabis. I was skeptical of the low THC, but I'm super impressed after trying it and would love to try a higher-potency version for comparison.

Observations

Aroma: Diesel, earthy, herbal, pungent, spicy, woody

Flavour: Earthy, piney, pungent, spicy, woody

Bud Colour: Brown/green

Pistil Colour: Brown/red

Trichome Density: Low-Medium

Score Details

Appearance:	3 / 5
High Quality:	5 / 5
Aroma:	10 / 15
Flavour:	10 / 15
Bud Quality:	16 / 30
High Potency:	16 / 30

Overall Score: 60%

Cultivar Ranking: 410th

Highlands

Cultivar/Product Information

Type/Effect: Indica - Medium Heavy
Legacy Name: Afghan Kush
Lineage: Afghani Indica
Cannabinoids: 21% THC / <1% CBD
Terpenes: Myrcene, Caryophyllene, Limonene

First Impression

Review #44; April 26, 2019,

Tweed's Highlands is a decent indica option that'll leave you chill, mellow, ready to rest, and zoned out. Classic kush, and a great end of the night bud.

Observations

Aroma: Earthy, fresh, grassy, herbal

Flavour: Earthy, herbal, spicy

Bud Colour: Dull green

Pistil Colour: Brown/red

Trichome Density: Low

Score Details

Appearance:	4 / 5
High Quality:	5 / 5
Aroma:	9 / 15
Flavour:	9 / 15
Bud Quality:	19 / 30
High Potency:	23 / 30

Overall Score: 69%

Cultivar Ranking: 363rd

Houndstooth

Cultivar/Product Information

Type/Effect: Sativa Hybrid - Light
Legacy Name: Candyland
Lineage: Granddaddy Purps x Platinum Bay GSC
Cannabinoids: 18% THC / <1% CBD
Terpenes: Myrcene, Pinene, Limonene

First Impression

Review #70; June 9, 2019.

Houndstooth by Tweed provides a lighter cerebral buzz than expected for its THC percentage, but the high is blissful and enjoyable nonetheless. The mind is left clear and relatively unimpaired compared to heavier sativas. It definitely could be a great bud to put you in a good mood before tackling some chores or munchies.

Observations

Aroma: Fresh, grassy, herbal, sweet

Flavour: Earthy, fresh, grassy, herbal, sour, spicy

Bud Colour: Dark green/purple

Pistil Colour: Brown

Trichome Density: Low-Medium

Score Details

Appearance:	3 / 5
High Quality:	5 / 5
Aroma:	12 / 15
Flavour:	11 / 15
Bud Quality:	15 / 30
High Potency:	19 / 30

Overall Score: 65%

Cultivar Ranking: 389th

Penelope

Cultivar/Product Information

Type/Effect: Hybrid - Light
Legacy Name: CBD Skunk Haze
Lineage: Cannatonic x Super Haze
Cannabinoids: 7.8% THC / 6.1% CBD
Terpenes: Pinene, Caryophyllene, Limonene

First Impression

Review #14; April 11, 2019,

This morning spent with Penelope was lovely, beginning with a bowl of this balanced cultivar and cartoons. I find myself laughing and enjoying the shows, the THC doing its job while a powerful body sensation develops… the CBD and THC are working in harmony. Indeed, a purchase-worthy balanced cultivar, as it boasts a THC and CBD % above 3%, my usual threshold for "feeling it" after a bowl.

Observations

Aroma: Fruity, herbal, minty, sweet

Flavour: Fresh, herbal, minty

Bud Colour: Dull green

Pistil Colour: Brown/orange

Trichome Density: Low-Medium

Score Details

Appearance:	4 / 5
High Quality:	5 / 5
Aroma:	10 / 15
Flavour:	11 / 15
Bud Quality:	19 / 30
High Potency:	21 / 30

Overall Score: 70%

Cultivar Ranking: 353rd

Up

Overall Performance

Average Score: 81.33%

Brand Ranking: 34th Place

Brand Background

Up cannabis, a brand initially brought to you by Newstrike Brands and The Tragically Hip, has seen two different product line-ups and a relaunch. After its purchase by Hexo in 2019, Up was largely taken off the market and later relaunched by Hexo with a 20% THC guarantee.

Up was initially produced out of two greenhouses in Ontario under Newstrike. Hexo Corp now produces flower for Up, somewhere among their 2 million square feet of growing space in Ontario and Quebec.

Other Cultivars: Gelato 29, Lemon Z, Ultra Sour
Associated Brands: 48North, Hexo, Namaste, Redecan

Cultivar Selection

Cold Creek Kush	82%
Ghost Train Haze	81%
Northern Berry	81%

Cold Creek Kush

Cultivar/Product Information

Type/Effect: Indica - Heavy
Legacy Name: Cold Creek Kush
Lineage: Chemdog x MK Ultra
Cannabinoids: 23.9% THC / <1% CBD
Terpenes: Pinene, Ocimene, Caryophyllene

First Impression

Review #325; August 31, 2020,

I was rocking out pretty hard to some Ihsahn while high on this potent Cold Creek Kush from Up. My girl Grace is back with a vengeance, ready to attack your mind and body with a relaxed but still f***-you-up kind of high. My body was comfortable and loose, and my head was vacant, devoid of thought entirely. I found myself trying to check if I was thinking or not, and when I tried to, I just froze mentally, and nothing occurred. I was undoubtedly stoned, immensely so. Welcome back Up!

Observations

Aroma: Earthy, floral, fresh, herbal, piney, pungent, sweet

Flavour: Earthy, grassy, herbal, piney, pungent

Bud Colour: Dark green

Pistil Colour: Brown/orange

Trichome Density: Low-Medium

Score Details

Appearance:	4 / 5
High Quality:	5 / 5
Aroma:	12 / 15
Flavour:	11 / 15
Bud Quality:	24 / 30
High Potency:	26 / 30

Overall Score: 82%

Cultivar Ranking: 159th

Ghost Train Haze

Cultivar/Product Information

Type/Effect: Sativa - Medium Heavy
Legacy Name: Ghost Train Haze
Lineage: Ghost OG x Nevil's Wreck
Cannabinoids: 21.3% THC / <1% CBD
Terpenes: Terpinolene, Pinene, Ocimene

First Impression

Review #373; November 27, 2020,

Ghost Train Haze by Up is a hazy, heady blast that should leave you amped up and somewhat zoned out. I have a lot of energy, but I can't let it out because I'm also pretty high and not too functional (my boy Eldo has grown up a bit percentage-wise). My mind is clear when it can focus, and I feel motivated and wired, but something about the haziness is distracting me. The headband effect on this flower is super intense, so I would not recommend large amounts to a beginner stoner. Up's comeback has made a great first impression, I'd say. Hopefully, it's only "up" from here.

Observations

Aroma: Cheese, citrusy, floral, funky, herbal, sour, woody

Flavour: Citrusy, floral, herbal, sour

Bud Colour: Dull green

Pistil Colour: Brown/orange

Trichome Density: Low-Medium

Score Details

Appearance:	4 / 5
High Quality:	5 / 5
Aroma:	12 / 15
Flavour:	12 / 15
Bud Quality:	24 / 30
High Potency:	24 / 30

Overall Score: 81%

Cultivar Ranking: 186th

Northern Berry

Cultivar/Product Information

Type/Effect: Indica - Heavy
Legacy Name: Northern Berry
Lineage: Blueberry x Northern Lights
Cannabinoids: 22.6% THC / <1% CBD
Terpenes: Caryophyllene, Myrcene, Humulene

First Impression

Review #407; January 18, 2021,

A heavy-hitting stoner's delight, Northern Berry by Up is a particularly excellent PM flower pick. My mind is pretty devoid of thought, and I'm STONED. I lack energy and motivation, but I'm super relaxed and chill. No worries here during this great escape before bedtime. My body is soothed by the endless waves of sensation provided by this tsunami of a high. I'm struggling to write more, thanks to Up.

Observations

Aroma: Berry, earthy, herbal, sour, sweet

Flavour: Berry, grassy, herbal, sweet, woody

Bud Colour: Dull green

Pistil Colour: Brown/orange

Trichome Density: Low-Medium

Score Details

Appearance:	4 / 5
High Quality:	5 / 5
Aroma:	12 / 15
Flavour:	11 / 15
Bud Quality:	24 / 30
High Potency:	25 / 30

Overall Score: 81%

Cultivar Ranking: 187th

Van Der Pop

Van Der Pop

Overall Performance

Average Score: 65.50%

Brand Ranking: 75th Place

Brand Background

Van Der Pop was an upscale, mid-high priced brand targeted toward the female demographic from Canopy Growth. The cultivar lineup features two products, one of which shares genetic lineage with Tweed's Balmoral.

It's hard to say precisely where cannabis for Van Der Pop was grown in Canada, given that Canopy Growth operates 7 million square feet of cultivation facility across the country.

Associated Brands: 7Acres, DNA Genetics, Houseplant, LBS, Tokyo Smoke, Tweed

Cultivar Selection

Cultivar	Score
Cloudburst	61%
Eclipse	70%

Cloudburst

Cultivar/Product Information

Type/Effect: Hybrid - Medium Light
Legacy Name: UK Cheese
Lineage: Skunk #1
Cannabinoids: 16.5% THC / <1% CBD

First Impression

Review #209; March 10, 2020,

Van Der Pop's Cloudburst provides a medium-intensity cerebral buzz that is only slightly cloudy. My thoughts and speech slowed only just so. The high is relaxed and mellow, with a go-with-the-flow vibe for a good casual session.

Observations

Aroma: Cheese, funky, grassy, herbal, pungent, sour, sweet

Flavour: Cheese, funky, grassy, herbal, sour, woody

Bud Colour: Green

Pistil Colour: Brown/red

Trichome Density: Low-Medium

Score Details

Appearance:	4 / 5
High Quality:	4 / 5
Aroma:	10 / 15
Flavour:	9 / 15
Bud Quality:	18 / 30
High Potency:	16 / 30

Overall Score: 61%

Cultivar Ranking: 406th

Eclipse

Cultivar/Product Information

Type/Effect:	Indica Hybrid - Medium Heavy
Legacy Name:	CBD Sweet 'n Sour Widow
Lineage:	Black Widow x Cannatonic
Cannabinoids:	5.4% THC / 8.7% CBD

First Impression

Review #155; December 7, 2019,

Van Der Pop's Eclipse is a mellow head buzz and a calm and relaxed body. The feeling is serene, and the senses are heightened by the THC, while the nerves are calmed and thoughts are slowed. I feel like this would make a great evening balanced cultivar for before bed, perhaps with a partner, given the mood provided by this flower.

Observations

Aroma: Floral, fresh, grassy, herbal, sweet

Flavour: Floral, fresh, grassy, herbal

Bud Colour: Dull green

Pistil Colour: Brown/orange

Trichome Density: Medium

Score Details

Appearance:	4 / 5
High Quality:	5 / 5
Aroma:	13 / 15
Flavour:	12 / 15
Bud Quality:	18 / 30
High Potency:	18 / 30

Overall Score: 70%

Cultivar Ranking: 340th

Vertical

Overall Performance

Average Score: 70.63%

Brand Ranking: 70th Place

Brand Background

Vertical's mission statement of "quality never compromised" is best shown through its work with Cold Creek Kush, their core cultivar, on the legal recreational market for three years. Through scientific research and innovation and intense quality control methods and standards, Vertical produces only a few focus cultivars at a time to help ensure the highest quality product.

Vertical cannabis is grown in small batches in specialized growing environments in Chatham, Ontario.

Other Cultivars: Strawberry Cake

Cultivar Selection

Banana Split	58%
Blissberry	67%
Cold Creek Kush	87%
Hifi 4G	81%
Kent County Kush	71%
Longwoods Leaf	68%
Maple City Monster	69%
Shishkaberry	64%

Banana Split

Cultivar/Product Information

Type/Effect: Sativa Hybrid - Super Light
Legacy Name: Banana Split
Lineage: Banana Sherbert x Tangie
Cannabinoids: 9.1% THC / <1% CBD

First Impression

Review #142; November 19, 2019,

I'm coming up with some great ideas at the moment, inspired by Vertical's Banana Split. A mild THC buzz on this flower feels low-mid intensity, but the creative juices are flowing. I feel motivated, elevated, and excited about my day. This may not satisfy those looking to get good and stoned, but anyone looking for a light THC and terpene experience may find a good one in Banana Split.

Observations

Aroma: Earthy, herbal, piney, sweet

Flavour: Earthy, herbal

Bud Colour: Dark green/purple

Pistil Colour: Orange

Trichome Density: Low-Medium

Score Details

Appearance:	4 / 5
High Quality:	5 / 5
Aroma:	8 / 15
Flavour:	8 / 15
Bud Quality:	21 / 30
High Potency:	12 / 30

Overall Score: 58%

Cultivar Ranking: 415th

Blissberry

Cultivar/Product Information

Type/Effect: Indica Hybrid - Light
Legacy Name: Blissberry
Lineage: Shishkaberry
Cannabinoids: 13.3% THC / <1% CBD

First Impression

Review #139; November 12, 2019,

Vertical's Blissberry is aptly named. I don't feel crazy high or stoned, just calm and relaxed, ready for a day at home. Not the sort of indica to make you pass out, just the one to elevate your mood and get you prepared to chill. A great midday cultivar or a good pick for the early evening, the light high from Blissberry is super enjoyable.

Observations

Aroma: Berry, earthy, herbal, sweet

Flavour: Berry, earthy, funky, sweet

Bud Colour: Dark green

Pistil Colour: Brown/red

Trichome Density: Low

Score Details

Appearance:	4 / 5
High Quality:	5 / 5
Aroma:	10 / 15
Flavour:	10 / 15
Bud Quality:	22 / 30
High Potency:	16 / 30

Overall Score: 67%

Cultivar Ranking: 382nd

Cold Creek Kush

Cultivar/Product Information

Type/Effect: Indica - Heavy
Legacy Name: Cold Creek Kush
Lineage: Chemdog x MK Ultra
Cannabinoids: 20.2% THC / <1% CBD
Terpenes: Myrcene, Ocimene, Caryophyllene

First Impression

Review #51; May 6, 2019,

I’m pretty baked after a bowl of this dank, fresh, dense bud from Vertical; their Cold Creek Kush is quite potent. The head high is relaxing, and the body high is powerful and present everywhere. The quality of the high is remarkable. I’m stoned, no doubt about it. Probably best for experienced consumers. New consumers, beware - this one is deadly powerful.

Observations

Aroma: Fresh, grassy, herbal, piney, sweet

Flavour: Fresh, herbal, piney

Bud Colour: Dark green

Pistil Colour: Orange/tan

Trichome Density: Medium-High

Score Details

Appearance:	5 / 5
High Quality:	5 / 5
Aroma:	14 / 15
Flavour:	12 / 15
Bud Quality:	26 / 30
High Potency:	25 / 30

Overall Score: 87%

Cultivar Ranking: 88th

Hifi 4G

Cultivar/Product Information

Type/Effect: Hybrid - Medium Heavy
Legacy Name: Hifi 4G
Lineage: Glueberry OG x Wifi OG
Cannabinoids: 20.3% THC / <1% CBD
Terpenes: Limonene, Caryophyllene, Nerolidol

First Impression

Review #401; January 10, 2021,

My eyes are half shut already, only halfway through my experience with Vertical's Hifi 4G. Dense, aromatic, quality flower with a high that is immobilizing, chill, and relaxed. I don't feel like getting up to much other than some tunes and some snacks. I could see this as an excellent post-work crash or reset option. I've never used the word "vibey" before, but I'm certainly vibey between the Hifi 4G and A Tribe Called Quest. I'm also pretty stoned.

Observations

Aroma: Floral, fruity, herbal, sour, spicy, sweet

Flavour: Floral, funky, grassy, herbal, woody

Bud Colour: Green/tan

Pistil Colour: Brown/orange

Trichome Density: Low-Medium

Score Details

Appearance:	4 / 5
High Quality:	5 / 5
Aroma:	12 / 15
Flavour:	10 / 15
Bud Quality:	26 / 30
High Potency:	24 / 30

Overall Score: 81%

Cultivar Ranking: 185th

Kent County Kush

Cultivar/Product Information

Type/Effect: Indica - Neutral
Legacy Name: Kent County Kush
Lineage: "Unknown Cultivar" x Blueberry
Cannabinoids: 17.7% THC / <1% CBD
Terpenes: Pinene, Caryophyllene, Limonene

First Impression

Review #56; May 8, 2019,

Kent County Kush from Vertical is an indica that is ideal for late evening consumption when you want to unwind and zone out. A note on flavour: started fresh, sweet, and mango-like, ended cheesy and woody. The high is potent in both the body and mind; my head and chest are experiencing the bulk of the body sensation, and the high is relatively clear but very relaxing. Kent County Kush is another potent kush option from Vertical worth trying.

Observations

Aroma: Cheese, fruity, funky, herbal, minty, piney, sour, sweet

Flavour: Cheese, floral, fresh, funky, herbal, mango, sweet, woody

Bud Colour: Dark green

Pistil Colour: Brown/orange

Trichome Density: Medium

Score Details

Appearance:	4 / 5
High Quality:	5 / 5
Aroma:	11 / 15
Flavour:	11 / 15
Bud Quality:	18 / 30
High Potency:	22 / 30

Overall Score: 71%

Cultivar Ranking: 332nd

Longwoods Leaf

Cultivar/Product Information

Type/Effect: Indica Hybrid - Medium Light
Cannabinoids: 14.5% THC / <1% CBD

First Impression

Review #148; November 28, 2019,

Longwoods Leaf by Vertical has left me calm and content, with a medium-intensity cerebral buzz and a light body sensation in the chest. It's relaxing, hardly tiring, though it may get you there in the evening if you're already tired. Great longevity in the Volcano, tons of terpenes are there to amplify that 14.5% THC. A lighter indica, great for anyone without too many plans.

Observations

Aroma: Earthy, herbal, minty, piney, sour, sweet

Flavour: Cheese, earthy, funky, herbal, sweet

Bud Colour: Dull green

Pistil Colour: Orange/tan

Trichome Density: Low-Medium

Score Details

Appearance:	4 / 5
High Quality:	5 / 5
Aroma:	12 / 15
Flavour:	11 / 15
Bud Quality:	19 / 30
High Potency:	17 / 30

Overall Score: 68%

Cultivar Ranking: 365th

Maple City Monster

Cultivar/Product Information

Type/Effect: Hybrid - Medium Heavy
Cannabinoids: 15.8% THC / <1% CBD

First Impression

Review #138; November 11, 2019,

Maple City Monster by Vertical is a monster of a high for a <16% THC cultivar. I feel super stoned, and I can't think straight. The terpene profile is intense, providing an experience much more powerful than I had imagined. The smell and flavour are intense and potent, super impressive. The nugs weren't much to look at, but they delivered a unique, robust, and relaxed high.

Observations

Aroma: Earthy, herbal, minty, piney, pungent, sour, spicy

Flavour: Earthy, herbal, pungent, sour, spicy

Bud Colour: Dark brown/green

Pistil Colour: Brown/orange

Trichome Density: Medium

Score Details

Appearance:	2 / 5
High Quality:	5 / 5
Aroma:	13 / 15
Flavour:	12 / 15
Bud Quality:	16 / 30
High Potency:	21 / 30

Overall Score: 69%

Cultivar Ranking: 355th

Shishkaberry

Cultivar/Product Information

Type/Effect: Indica Hybrid - Light
Legacy Name: Shishkaberry
Lineage: "Unknown Afghani" x DJ Short Blueberry
Cannabinoids: 11.5% THC / <1% CBD

First Impression

Review #106; September 4, 2019,

A lighter indica, and a mild-medium intensity high, is what to expect from Shishkaberry by Vertical. Just a nice, pleasant high, not strong at all, but enough to elevate the mood, lift the spirits, and relax the body, mind and soul. Real chill, "I wanna jam to some tunes" kind of material here. An indica for any time, given that I don't feel tired, and anyone, given the approachable 11.5% THC%.

Observations

Aroma: Berry, earthy, fresh, fruity, herbal, sweet

Flavour: Earthy, herbal, woody

Bud Colour: Dark green/purple

Pistil Colour: Brown/orange

Trichome Density: Low-Medium

Score Details

Appearance:	4 / 5
High Quality:	5 / 5
Aroma:	12 / 15
Flavour:	9 / 15
Bud Quality:	20 / 30
High Potency:	14 / 30

Overall Score: 64%

Cultivar Ranking: 395th

Viridis

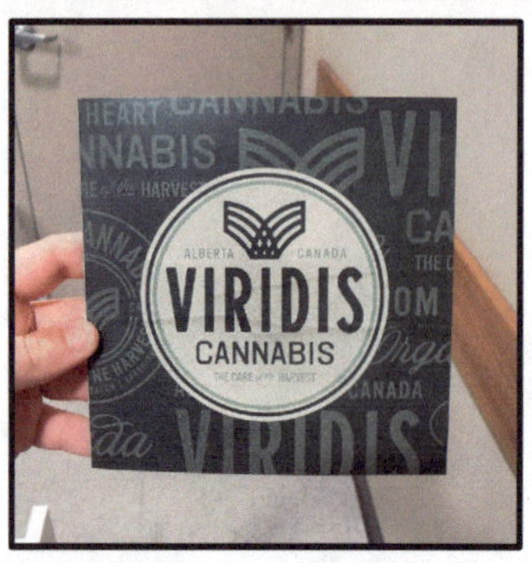

Overall Performance

Average Score: 80.50%

Brand Ranking: 38th Place

Brand Background

Viridis is a craft cannabis producer taking a balanced approach to growing, mixing in both traditional practices and modern methods. Notably, Viridis grows in soil versus the hydroponic setup many producers have. They cite this as one of the reasons their cannabis quality comes out on the higher end of the spectrum for products on the market.

Small-batch and hand-harvested Viridis cannabis is produced indoors in Edmonton, Alberta.

Other Cultivars: Bruce Banner, Chocolope, GSC

Cultivar Selection

Blue Dream	76%
Durban Spice	83%
Northern Lights	81%
White Widow	82%

Blue Dream

Cultivar/Product Information

Type/Effect: Sativa - Light
Legacy Name: Blue Dream
Lineage: Blueberry x Haze
Cannabinoids: 13.3% THC / 2% CBD
Terpenes: Linalool, Pinene, Caryophyllene

First Impression

Review #202; February 28, 2020,

A more comforting high than anticipated, Blue Dream by Viridis is a hazy way to ease yourself into your day. Most of the physical sensation is in the forehead but is accompanied by a light and mellow body buzz. My mind is calm, and my thoughts are slowed and focused; this high is cool and satisfying - a solid mid-range option for the low to moderate frequency consumer and a great first look at Viridis.

Observations

Aroma: Berry, floral, fresh, fruity, herbal, sweet

Flavour: Berry, floral, fruity, herbal, sweet

Bud Colour: Green

Pistil Colour: Brown/red

Trichome Density: Medium

Score Details

Appearance:	4 / 5
High Quality:	5 / 5
Aroma:	13 / 15
Flavour:	12 / 15
Bud Quality:	25 / 30
High Potency:	17 / 30

Overall Score: 76%

Cultivar Ranking: 270th

Durban Spice

Cultivar/Product Information

Type/Effect: Sativa - Light
Legacy Name: Durban Poison
Lineage: African Sativa
Cannabinoids: 20.5% THC / <1% CBD
Terpenes: Terpinolene, Humulene, Geraniol

First Impression

Review #403; January 13, 2021,

I wrote this review inspired by the uplifting nature of Durban Spice. It was a very bright experience, except for my eyes; while they weren't too squinty, they felt heavy and hazy. The haze shrouded my mind, as my brain was buzzing with muddled thoughts. As I delved deeper into the Volcano bowl, serene euphoria developed to replace the haze, introducing a more mellow experience. I was still super motivated and energized; the high was active despite the mellowness.

Observations

Aroma: Citrusy, floral, herbal, pungent, sour, spicy

Flavour: Citrusy, floral, grassy, herbal, sour, spicy

Bud Colour: Green

Pistil Colour: Orange/tan

Trichome Density: Medium

Score Details

Appearance:	4 / 5
High Quality:	5 / 5
Aroma:	13 / 15
Flavour:	11 / 15
Bud Quality:	25 / 30
High Potency:	25 / 30

Overall Score: 83%

Cultivar Ranking: 139th

Northern Lights

Cultivar/Product Information

Type/Effect: Indica - Medium Heavy
Legacy Name: Northern Lights
Lineage: Afghani Indica
Cannabinoids: 15.4% THC / <1% CBD
Terpenes: Myrcene, Pinene, Limonene

First Impression

Review #206; March 3, 2020,

I got real dark and heavy in my room today for this review of Northern Lights by Viridis as I was headbanging to some "Wolves in the Throne Room". I got super into it. The high is euphoric, cerebral, and very relaxed but clear-minded - I wrote with relative ease. A stronger feeling experience than a typical 15.4% flower, and very tasty with its excellent profile.

Observations

Aroma: Berry, diesel, earthy, piney, pungent, sweet

Flavour: Berry, diesel, earthy, funky, pungent, sweet

Bud Colour: Green

Pistil Colour: Brown/orange

Trichome Density: Medium

Score Details

Appearance:	4 / 5
High Quality:	5 / 5
Aroma:	14 / 15
Flavour:	12 / 15
Bud Quality:	26 / 30
High Potency:	20 / 30

Overall Score: 81%

Cultivar Ranking: 169th

White Widow

Cultivar/Product Information

Type/Effect: Hybrid - Neutral
Legacy Name: White Widow
Lineage: Brazilian Sativa x Indian Indica
Cannabinoids: 21.9% THC / <1% CBD
Terpenes: Pinene, Caryophyllene, Humulene

First Impression

Review #218; March 20, 2020,

I got stoned and watched many music videos on White Widow by Viridis. The high is hazy and cerebral, mild-medium physically, but with a strong headband effect. I feel awake but not very focused. I'm pretty baked. Viridis aims to please, and they have with White Widow.

Observations

Aroma: Earthy, grassy, herbal, minty, piney, sweet

Flavour: Earthy, funky, grassy, herbal, sweet

Bud Colour: Green

Pistil Colour: Orange

Trichome Density: Medium

Score Details

Appearance:	4 / 5
High Quality:	5 / 5
Aroma:	13 / 15
Flavour:	11 / 15
Bud Quality:	25 / 30
High Potency:	24 / 30

Overall Score: 82%

Cultivar Ranking: 151st

Weed Me

Overall Performance

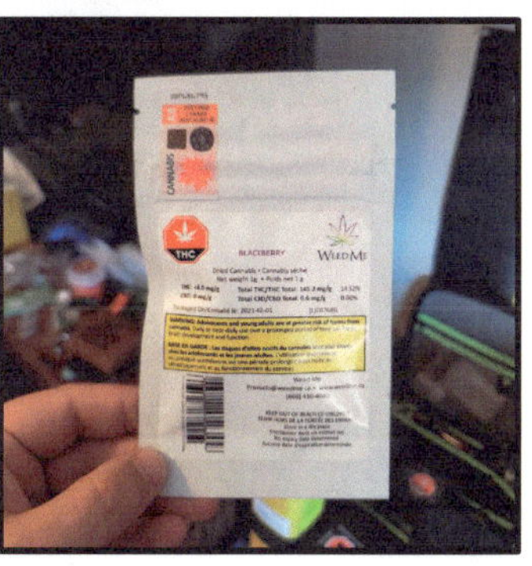

Average Score: 78.80%

Brand Ranking: 42nd Place

Brand Background

Weed Me is a cannabis brand founded on bonds created by a love of cannabis and a passion for what it can do to change lives. The company was founded in 2016 with the goal in mind of providing Canadians with quality premium cannabis at an affordable price.

Cannabis for Weed Me is grown in a 20,000-square-foot tiered indoor facility in Pickering, Ontario. Automated systems monitor the environmental conditions of grow spaces, where Weed Me's plants are grown in rockwool under LED lighting. Nugs are machine-trimmed and hand-polished.

Other Cultivars:	Blue Iguana, Garlic Jelly, Ice Cream Cake, Lemon Z, Mandarin Cookie, Powdered Doughnuts, Slurricane, Wedding Cake

Cultivar Selection

Blackberry Gum	70%
Cindy Jack	71%
Grandpa's Stash	81%
Melon Gum	85%
Tutti Frutti	87%

Blackberry Gum

Cultivar/Product Information

Type/Effect: Indica - Medium Heavy
Legacy Name: Blackberry Gum
Lineage: Blueberry x Bubblegum
Cannabinoids: 14.9% THC / <1% CBD
Terpenes: Myrcene, Caryophyllene, Limonene

First Impression

Review #223; March 29, 2020,

A chill, hazy, heavy-eyes high is what I experienced from Weed Me's Blackberry. While stoned, I find it hard to write; my mind is vacant, and nothing comes to me but a desire to nap and eat. I feel like a zombie who also happens to be " walkin' on sunshine,"... so I'm feeling great but dead.

Observations

Aroma: Berry, earthy, herbal, piney, sweet

Flavour: Earthy, herbal, pungent

Bud Colour: Dark green

Pistil Colour: Orange/tan

Trichome Density: Low-Medium

Score Details

Appearance:	3 / 5
High Quality:	5 / 5
Aroma:	12 / 15
Flavour:	10 / 15
Bud Quality:	22 / 30
High Potency:	18 / 30

Overall Score: 70%

Cultivar Ranking: 343rd

Cindy Jack

Cultivar/Product Information

Type/Effect:	Sativa Hybrid - Medium Light
Legacy Name:	Cindy Jack
Lineage:	Cinderella 99 x Jack Herer
Cannabinoids:	20% THC / <1% CBD
Terpenes:	Myrcene, Pinene, Caryophyllene

First Impression

Review #184; February 3, 2020,

A clean and clear cerebral high is what's to be expected from Weed Me's Cindy Jack. My head is experiencing a sensation as though it were slightly pressurized, but it's pleasant and calming, at least compared to the pace of my thoughts and heartbeat. Serene, stimulating and satisfying, Cindy Jack is a significant functional high once the initial rush is settled into. Perky and enjoyable, but perhaps not for those prone to bad times when consuming high-potency, high-intensity sativas.

Observations

Aroma: Citrusy, earthy, fruity, mango, sweet

Flavour: Fresh, funky, grassy, herbal, piney, sweet

Bud Colour: Dull green

Pistil Colour: Orange

Trichome Density: Low-Medium

Score Details

Appearance:	3 / 5
High Quality:	5 / 5
Aroma:	13 / 15
Flavour:	10 / 15
Bud Quality:	20 / 30
High Potency:	20 / 30

Overall Score: 71%

Cultivar Ranking: 325th

Grandpa's Stash

Cultivar/Product Information

Type/Effect:	Hybrid - Heavy
Legacy Name:	Grandpa's Stash
Lineage:	'70 Afghan Kush x '92 OG Kush x '94 Super Skunk
Cannabinoids:	20.2% THC / <1% CBD
Terpenes:	Caryophyllene, Myrcene, Limonene

First Impression

Review #284; July 6, 2020,

Look no further than Weed Me's Grandpa's Stash for a heavy cultivar. What this high lacks in functionality, it makes up for in sedation. My body is super relaxed, as are my mood and eyelids. I'm pretty zoned out, baked, stoned, etc. I certainly feel sleepy; this high would pair well with the end of an evening. My mind, relatively vacant, keeps fading out and away from writing. It is time for rest.

Observations

Aroma: Earthy, fresh, herbal, pungent, sour

Flavour: Earthy, fresh, herbal, piney, pungent

Bud Colour: Dark green

Pistil Colour: Orange

Trichome Density: Low-Medium

Score Details

Appearance:	4 / 5
High Quality:	5 / 5
Aroma:	13 / 15
Flavour:	11 / 15
Bud Quality:	25 / 30
High Potency:	23 / 30

Overall Score: 81%

Cultivar Ranking: 183rd

Melon Gum

Cultivar/Product Information

Type/Effect: Indica Hybrid - Medium Heavy
Legacy Name: Melon Gum
Lineage: Bubblegum x Lavender
Cannabinoids: 20.7% THC / <1% CBD
Terpenes: Myrcene, Caryophyllene, Pinene

First Impression

Review #358; October 31, 2020,

Calm and chill, both cerebrally and physically, Melon Gum by Weed Me is a beautiful way to spend an afternoon or morning off work. A euphoric bliss washed over me, growing stronger with each bag. As I got deeper into the bowl, it became more relaxing and spacey, and I started zoning out more. Overall a great hybrid; while not as fruity tasting as I had hoped, the high certainly delivers.

Observations

Aroma: Floral, fresh, herbal, sour, sweet

Flavour: Funky, grassy, herbal, sour, sweet

Bud Colour: Dull green

Pistil Colour: Orange

Trichome Density: Medium-High

Score Details

Appearance:	4 / 5
High Quality:	5 / 5
Aroma:	13 / 15
Flavour:	12 / 15
Bud Quality:	27 / 30
High Potency:	24 / 30

Overall Score: 85%

Cultivar Ranking: 116th

Tutti Frutti

Cultivar/Product Information

Type/Effect: Hybrid - Light
Legacy Name: Tutti Frutti
Lineage: Blue Haze x Diesel Ryder x Green Haze x Sour Diesel x Thai Sativa
Cannabinoids: 20.2% THC / <1% CBD
Terpenes: Myrcene, Pinene, Caryophyllene

First Impression

Review #308; August 12, 2020,

A social, aware, and active high, Tutti Frutti by Weed Me is a pleasure to vaporize and a euphoric blast. I was texting tons of friends rapidly throughout my session with this flower, my mind alive and mood outgoing. The flavours and aroma are fantastic: sweet and fruity, with fresh herbal notes. An excellent cultivar for fans of Tangerine Dream, Sour Tangie, Mimosa, and anything orange-like. A joy to consume and experience, ideal for mornings, a pre-brunch joint, or an afternoon adventure.

Observations

Aroma: Citrusy, fruity, herbal, orange, sweet, sweet candy

Flavour: Citrusy, floral, fresh, fruity, herbal, orange, sweet

Bud Colour: Dull green

Pistil Colour: Brown/tan

Trichome Density: Medium

Score Details

Appearance:	4 / 5
High Quality:	5 / 5
Aroma:	14 / 15
Flavour:	13 / 15
Bud Quality:	27 / 30
High Potency:	24 / 30

Overall Score: 87%

Cultivar Ranking: 90th

Whistler Cannabis Company

Overall Performance

Average Score: 92.00%

Brand Ranking: 4th Place

Brand Background

As Canada's first FVOPA-certified organic cannabis producer, Whistler Cannabis Company grows some of the finest bud in the land. Whistler uses a living soil medium to produce small-batch premium flower, both for the medical and recreational markets.

Whistler Cannabis Company grows their cannabis in (you guessed it) Whistler, BC.

Other Cultivars: Deja Glue, Sour Jack
Associated Brands: AltaVie, Aurora, San Rafael '71

Cultivar Selection

Cultivar	Score
Bubba Kush	95%
Chocolope	90%
Rockstar	91%
SSC	92%

Bubba Kush

Cultivar/Product Information

Type/Effect: Indica - Super Heavy
Legacy Name: Bubba Kush
Lineage: Northern Lights x Triangle Kush
Cannabinoids: 23.3% THC / <1% CBD
Terpenes: Limonene, Caryophyllene, Myrcene

First Impression

Review #153; December 4, 2019,

Bubba Kush by Whistler Cannabis Company is as potent as can be due to its rich cannabinoid and terpene content. It knocked me apart. I can barely stand and speak. I'm ready to munch out and pass out, relaxed in body and mind, by the power of this spectacular and intense flower. Unreal stuff, as usual, from Whistler Cannabis Company.

Observations

Aroma: Chocolate, earthy, pungent, sour, spice, sweet

Flavour: Diesel, earthy, funky, grassy, herbal, pungent, sour

Bud Colour: Dark green/purple

Pistil Colour: Orange/tan

Trichome Density: High

Score Details

Appearance:	5 / 5
High Quality:	5 / 5
Aroma:	14 / 15
Flavour:	12 / 15
Bud Quality:	30 / 30
High Potency:	29 / 30

Overall Score: 95%

Cultivar Ranking: 13th

Chocolope

Cultivar/Product Information

Type/Effect: Sativa - Light
Legacy Name: Chocolope
Lineage: Cannalope Haze x Chocolate Thai
Cannabinoids: 14.6% THC / <1% CBD
Terpenes: Terpinolene, Limonene, Ocimene

First Impression

Review #135; October 31, 2019,

Packing quite a kick for a 14.6% THC flower, Chocolope from Whistler Cannabis Company is potent… the most powerful feeling bud I've ever had below 15% THC. It is super hazy in taste and effect. Heady as well, I'm super high and focused, elevated in energy, spirit, and creativity. This is a fun, happy and social high, super creative and mind-opening. An excellent experience and expert grow.

Observations

Aroma: Citrusy, earthy, herbal, sour, sour candy, sweet

Flavour: Fresh, herbal, piney, sour, sweet

Bud Colour: Dark green

Pistil Colour: Brown/orange

Trichome Density: Medium-High

Score Details

Appearance:	4 / 5
High Quality:	5 / 5
Aroma:	15 / 15
Flavour:	14 / 15
Bud Quality:	29 / 30
High Potency:	23 / 30

Overall Score: 90%

Cultivar Ranking: 58th

Rockstar

Cultivar/Product Information

Type/Effect: Indica - Heavy
Legacy Name: Rockstar
Lineage: Rock Bud x Sensi Star
Cannabinoids: 20.8% THC / <1% CBD
Terpenes: Myrcene, Limonene, Nerolidol

First Impression

Review #146; November 27, 2019,

Whistler Cannabis Company makes some of the best bud on the market, and their Rockstar is both literally and figuratively a rock-star cultivar. It's heavy on the body and mind, with a full-on stoned effect throughout the experience. Based on the increased intensity and pungent aroma, the terpene content is high, from what I can tell. This is great night-in material, pretty incapacitating and super-strong; be careful with this one - it is not for beginners. Pros and aficionados will be pleased with this and any other Whistler offering.

Observations

Aroma: Earthy, fresh, herbal, minty, piney, pungent

Flavour: Earthy, minty, piney, pungent

Bud Colour: Dark green/purple

Pistil Colour: Brown/orange

Trichome Density: Medium-High

Score Details

Appearance:	4 / 5
High Quality:	5 / 5
Aroma:	14 / 15
Flavour:	13 / 15
Bud Quality:	29 / 30
High Potency:	26 / 30

Overall Score: 91%

Cultivar Ranking: 48th

SSC

Cultivar/Product Information

Type/Effect: Hybrid - Neutral
Legacy Name: Strawberry Short Cookies
Lineage: SinMint Cookies x White Strawberry
Cannabinoids: 18.9% THC / <1% CBD
Terpenes: Limonene, Caryophyllene, Humulene

First Impression

Review #127; October 9, 2019,

SSC by Whistler Cannabis Company is a treat; a tremendous head-high coupled with a body buzz, all from a high-quality, sensory-pleasing bud. The flower looks and smells gorgeous and is of the highest quality; dense but spongy and moist, with a frosting of trichomes - cannabis excellence.

Observations

Aroma: Earthy, fruity, herbal, minty, piney, sweet

Flavour: Earthy, herbal, spicy

Bud Colour: Dull green/purple

Pistil Colour: Brown/orange

Trichome Density: Medium-High

Score Details

Appearance:	5 / 5
High Quality:	5 / 5
Aroma:	15 / 15
Flavour:	12 / 15
Bud Quality:	30 / 30
High Potency:	25 / 30

Overall Score: 92%

Cultivar Ranking: 34th

Wink

Overall Performance

Average Score: 86.33%

Brand Ranking: 19th Place

Brand Background

Wink, another cannabis brand brought to market by Trec Brands, sources high-grade cannabis from other producers. Typically with a mid to high price-point, high THC, and cultivars that feature unique terpene profiles, Wink cannabis is meant to be something special.

Cannabis for Wink is sourced from various producers across Canada.

Other Cultivars: Animal Face Cookies, Blue Sherbet, Dairy Cream, Granola Funk, Mango Sapphire, Purple Punch x GSC, Rntz Muffins, Slurmintz, Titanimal

Associated Brands: Thumbs Up

Cultivar Selection

Mmmosa	86%
Strain Hunters' Super Lemon Haze	80%
Wedding Cake	93%

Mmmosa

Cultivar/Product Information

Type/Effect: Sativa Hybrid - Light
Legacy Name: Mimosa
Lineage: Clementine x Purple Punch
Cannabinoids: 21.4% THC / <1% CBD
Terpenes: Pinene, Caryophyllene, Myrcene

First Impression

Review #346; October 10, 2020,

A mellow, uplifting, and social high, Mmmosa by Wink is an excellent addition to any morning off, afternoon in, or post-work evening. Depending on your choice of consumption time, it'll mellow out your morning, enhance your afternoon, or liven up your evening. Consuming this rather late and tired, I was awakened by the high and put into a focused, clear-headed, calm state. I was also bursting with the urge to talk and laugh, revealing that this would be a great cultivar for get-togethers - an impressive flower and high.

Observations

Aroma: Floral, fresh, fruity, herbal, orange, sweet, sweet candy

Flavour: Floral, fresh, fruity, herbal, orange, sweet, woody

Bud Colour: Dull green

Pistil Colour: Brown

Trichome Density: Medium

Score Details

Appearance:	4 / 5
High Quality:	5 / 5
Aroma:	14 / 15
Flavour:	14 / 15
Bud Quality:	26 / 30
High Potency:	23 / 30

Overall Score: 86%

Cultivar Ranking: 100th

Strain Hunters' Super Lemon Haze

Cultivar/Product Information

Type/Effect: Sativa Hybrid - Light
Legacy Name: Lemon Skunk
Lineage: Lemon Skunk x Super Silver Haze
Cannabinoids: 13.4% THC / <1% CBD
Terpenes: Terpinolene, Caryophyllene, Ocimene

First Impression

Review #221; March 25, 2020,

A very cerebral and "alive" high is what you should expect from Wink's Strain Hunters' Super Lemon Haze. My mind is experiencing increased alertness and awareness, not necessarily focus. I'm easily distracted, but not for too long. A high that perks you up, one that keeps the eyes open rather than half-shut. Anything I touch is supremely comfortable due to enhanced tactile senses from the high. The terpene profile is excellent, and the smell and flavour are both distinctly hazy and citrusy. This is lovely flower in quality, effect, and enjoyability.

Observations

Aroma: Citrusy, herbal, lemon, sour, sour candy, sweet

Flavour: Citrusy, herbal, pungent, sour, woody

Bud Colour: Green

Pistil Colour: Brown/orange

Trichome Density: Medium

Score Details

Appearance:	4 / 5
High Quality:	5 / 5
Aroma:	14 / 15
Flavour:	13 / 15
Bud Quality:	26 / 30
High Potency:	18 / 30

Overall Score: 80%

Cultivar Ranking: 193rd

Wedding Cake

Cultivar/Product Information

Type/Effect: Indica - Medium Heavy
Legacy Name: Wedding Cake
Lineage: Cherry Pie x Girl Scout Cookies
Cannabinoids: 24.2% THC / <1% CBD
Terpenes: Caryophyllene, Nerolidol, Pinene

First Impression

Review #396; January 1, 2021,

Wink's Wedding Cake is messing me up, and I'm barely halfway finished with my bags - this one is not for the uninitiated with cannabis. The aroma of this particular cake is heavenly, as is the high. Contrary to my expectations, I am super relaxed and mellow but still aware and present, not zoned out too bad. The physical sensations from the high are far-reaching: every part of my body feels stoned. I fear I look too stoned due to the immense headband effect. Wedding Cake is certainly worth a celebration, given the massive high it provides.

Observations

Aroma: Cherry, earthy, floral, fruity, pungent, sweet

Flavour: Earthy, floral, herbal, sweet, woody

Bud Colour: Dark green

Pistil Colour: Brown/red

Trichome Density: Medium-High

Score Details

Appearance:	5 / 5
High Quality:	5 / 5
Aroma:	15 / 15
Flavour:	12 / 15
Bud Quality:	29 / 30
High Potency:	27 / 30

Overall Score: 93%

Cultivar Ranking: 23rd

Cultivar Rankings

Top 50 Overall Score

1. Qwest - Point Break (98%)
2. Qwest - Kush Mints (98%)
3. Qwest - MAC1 (97%)
4. Citizen Stash - MAC1 (97%)
5. Qwest - Super Silver Skunk (97%)
6. Qwest - Wedding Cake (97%)
7. Qwest - Forbidden Fruit (96%)
8. Boaz - Green Kraken (96%)
9. Boaz - Zour Apples (96%)
10. Citizen Stash - SAGE n' Sour (96%)
11. Qwest - Ice Cream Cake (96%)
12. Natural History - LA Kush Cake (95%)
13. Whistler Cannabis Company - Bubba Kush (95%)
14. Qwest - Phenome OG Spike (95%)
15. 7Acres - Island Pink Kush (95%)
16. Topleaf - Super Skunk (95%)
17. Good Buds - Sapphire OG (94%)
18. Qwest - Original Glue (94%)
19. Qwest - Goji OG (94%)
20. Broken Coast - Sonora (94%)
21. Good Buds - Salty God (93%)
22. Qwest - Gelato #33 (93%)
23. Wink - Wedding Cake (93%)
24. Citizen Stash - Stonewall (93%)
25. Haven St. - Noisy Neighbour (93%)

Cultivar Rankings

Top 50 Overall Score

26. Broken Coast - Quadra (93%)
27. Broken Coast - Gabriola (93%)
28. Artisan Batch - Meat Breath (93%)
29. Ignite - GG4 (93%)
30. Qwest - Strawberry Cough (93%)
31. Qwest - Pineapple Upside Down Cake (93%)
32. Qwest - JB Cookies (93%)
33. Joi Botanicals - Cake Crasher #1 (92%)
34. Whistler Cannabis Company - SSC (92%)
35. Natural History - Zour Apples (92%)
36. Broken Coast - Ruxton (92%)
37. Broken Coast - Denman (92%)
38. Qwest - Gelato #41 (92%)
39. Qwest - Oregon Lemons (92%)
40. Qwest - Kalifornia (92%)
41. Natural History - Mandarin Cookies (92%)
42. Highland Grow - White Lightning (92%)
43. Qwest - Death Bubba (92%)
44. Natural History - Fruit Cake (91%)
45. Reef - High Seas (91%)
46. Abba Medix - Sage 'n Sour (91%)
47. Broken Coast - Savary (91%)
48. Whistler Cannabis Company - Rockstar (91%)
49. Simply Bare - Sour Cookies (91%)
50. Broken Coast - Saturna (91%)

Top 20 Bud Quality

1. Citizen Stash - MAC1
2. Qwest - MAC1
3. Artisan Batch - Meat Breath
4. Qwest - Ice Cream Cake
5. Topleaf - Super Skunk
6. Boaz - Zour Apples
7. Qwest - Point Break
8. Broken Coast - Quadra
9. Qwest - Kalifornia
10. Broken Coast - Gabriola
11. Whistler Cannabis Company - Bubba Kush
12. Boaz - Green Kraken
13. Qwest - Wedding Cake
14. Qwest - Forbidden Fruit
15. Habitat - Cake
16. Qwest - JB Cookies
17. Broken Coast - Keats
18. Qwest - Goji OG
19. Simply Bare - Sour Cookies
20. Qwest - Phenome OG Spike

Top 20 High Potency

1. Qwest - Kush Mints
2. Qwest - MAC1
3. Citizen Stash - MAC1
4. 7Acres - Island Pink Kush
5. Qwest - Wedding Cake
6. Citizen Stash - SAGE n' Sour
7. Qwest - Super Silver Skunk
8. Qwest - Point Break
9. Boaz - Green Kraken
10. Whistler Cannabis Company - Bubba Kush
11. Topleaf - Super Skunk
12. Qwest - Ice Cream Cake
13. Qwest - JB Cookies
14. Qwest - Phenome OG Spike
15. Broken Coast - Sonora
16. Natural History - LA Kush Cake
17. Qwest - Death Bubba
18. Topleaf - Bubba
19. Natural History - Mandarin Cookies
20. 18Twelve - 8 Ball Kush

Top 20 Aroma

1. Qwest - Forbidden Fruit
2. Topleaf - Strawberry Cream
3. Good Buds - Sapphire OG
4. Good Buds - Mango Taffie
5. San Rafael '71 - Tangerine Dream
6. Qwest - Point Break
7. Qwest - MAC1
8. Citizen Stash - MAC1
9. Joi Botanicals - Cake Crasher #1
10. Boaz - Zour Apples

11. Whistler Cannabis Company - Chocolope
12. 7Acres - Jack Haze
13. Qwest - Black Lime Reserve
14. Good Buds - Salty God
15. Boaz - Green Kraken
16. Wink - Wedding Cake
17. Ogen - Gas Berries #112
18. Haven St. - Noisy Neighbour
19. Ness - Lemon Berry
20. Simply Bare - Blue Dream

Top 20 Flavour

1. Qwest - Forbidden Fruit
2. Topleaf - Strawberry Cream
3. Good Buds - Mango Taffie
4. San Rafael '71 - Tangerine Dream
5. Haven St. - Noisy Neighbour
6. Citizen Stash - Stonewall
7. Sundial - Berry Bliss
8. Namaste - Ultra Sour
9. Good Buds - Salty God
10. Abba Medix - Sage 'n Sour
11. San Rafael '71 - Delahaze
12. Qwest - Point Break
13. Joi Botanicals - Cake Crasher #1
14. Ignite - Tropicana Cookies
15. Qwest - Pineapple Upside Down Cake
16. Whistler Cannabis Company - Chocolope
17. Qwest - Black Lime Reserve
18. Ignite - GG4
19. Color - Pedro's Sweet Sativa
20. Ness - Lemon Berry

Top 20 Appearance

1. Citizen Stash - MAC1
2. Qwest - MAC1
3. Artisan Batch - Meat Breath
4. Qwest - JB Cookies
5. Qwest - Forbidden Fruit
6. Qwest - Kalifornia
7. Habitat - Cake
8. Topleaf - Super Skunk
9. Boaz - Zour Apples
10. Qwest - Super Silver Skunk
11. Boaz - Green Kraken
12. Citizen Stash - Sunset Sherbet
13. Good Buds - Sapphire OG
14. San Rafael '71 - Tangerine Dream
15. Color - White Shark
16. Broken Coast - Keats
17. Thumbs Up Brand - Amnesia x Super Haze
18. Spinach - Diesel
19. Abba Medix - Sage 'n Sour
20. Skosha - Mirage

Top 20 High Quality

1. Qwest - Kush Mints
2. Qwest - Point Break
3. Qwest - MAC1
4. Citizen Stash - MAC1
5. Qwest - Wedding Cake
6. Qwest - Super Silver Skunk
7. Qwest - Forbidden Fruit
8. Boaz - Green Kraken
9. Qwest - Ice Cream Cake
10. Boaz - Zour Apples
11. Citizen Stash - SAGE n' Sour
12. Haven St. - Noisy Neighbour
13. 7Acres - Island Pink Kush
14. Natural History - LA Kush Cake
15. Whistler Cannabis Company - Bubba Kush
16. Good Buds - Sapphire OG
17. Topleaf - Super Skunk
18. Joi Botanicals - Cake Crasher #1
19. Kolab - Ice Cream Cake
20. Broken Coast - Sonora

My Top 10 THC Sativas

1. Qwest - Goji OG
2. Good Buds - Mango Taffie
3. Citizen Stash - SAGE n' Sour
4. 7Acres - Jack Haze
5. Qwest - Strawberry Cough
6. Whistler Cannabis Company - Chocolope
7. Reef - High Seas
8. San Rafael '71 - Delahaze
9. Thumbs Up Brand - Amnesia x Super Haze
10. Emerald Health - Jack the Ripper

My Top 10 THC Sativa Hybrids

1. Boaz - Green Kraken
2. Boaz - Zour Apples
3. Spinach - Diesel
4. Natural History - Mandarin Cookies
5. Ogen - Lemon Z #42
6. Haven St. - Noisy Neighbour
7. Northern Harvest - Strawberry Ice
8. San Rafael '71 - Tangerine Dream
9. Namaste - Citrique
10. Delta 9 - Lemon Meringue

My Top 10 THC Hybrids

1. Citizen Stash - MAC1
2. Qwest - MAC1
3. Joi Botanicals - Cake Crasher #1
4. Natural History - Fruit Cake
5. Whistler Cannabis Company - SSC
6. Qwest - Gelato #33
7. Qwest - Super Silver Skunk

8. Weed Me - Tutti Frutti
9. Natural History - Crescendo
10. Delta 9 - Space Cake

My Top 10 THC Indica Hybrids

1. Topleaf - Strawberry Cream
2. Qwest - Forbidden Fruit
3. Artisan Batch - Meat Breath
4. Qwest - Point Break
5. Qwest - Original Glue
6. Qwest - Ice Cream Cake
7. Ogen - Gas Berries #112
8. Qwest - Black Lime Reserve
9. Robinsons - Lemon Garlic OG
10. Color - Blueberry Seagal

My Top 10 THC Indicas

1. Qwest - Wedding Cake
2. Broken Coast - Quadra
3. Good Buds - Sapphire OG
4. Kolab - Ice Cream Cake
5. Broken Coast - Gabriola
6. Good Buds - Salty God
7. Vertical - Cold Creek Kush
8. Natural History - LA Kush Cake
9. Fireside - Wappa
10. Whistler Cannabis Company - Bubba Kush

My Top 10 THC Cultivars

1. Topleaf - Strawberry Cream
2. Boaz - Green Kraken
3. Qwest - Wedding Cake
4. Citizen Stash - MAC1
5. Qwest - MAC1
6. Qwest - Forbidden Fruit
7. Broken Coast - Quadra
8. Qwest - Goji OG
9. Boaz - Zour Apples
10. Good Buds - Sapphire OG

My Top 5 THC:CBD Balanced Cultivars

1. San Rafael '71 - Great White Shark
2. Color - Mango Haze
3. Spinach - Dancehall
4. Natural History - ACDC Cookies
5. Kiwi - Cali-O

My Top 3 CBD Cultivars

1. Pure Sunfarms - Pure Sun CBD
2. Canaca - Great North CBD
3. Flowr - Intergalactic Princess

A - Ca

Autoflower - A characteristic of the Ruderalis species of cannabis that causes the flowering phase of the plant's growth cycle to begin without a light cycle change

Bag (Volcano) - A thin, plastic bag connected to a valve piece that allows for it to be filled with cannabis vapour by a Storz and Bickel Volcano vaporizer and inhaled from

Baked - A state of highness of greater potency than being "high," but lesser potency than being "stoned;" number 3 of 5 on the Highness Scale

Balanced Cultivar - A cultivar that has a balanced cannabinoid ratio featuring a mix of both THC and CBD

Balanced Hybrid - A cultivar that has both sativa and indica genetic lineage, typically at or near a 50/50 split

Blunt - A large amount of milled cannabis flower wrapped in the leaf of a tobacco plant (traditionally) or hemp plant to be smoked

Bowl (Volcano) - A round metal bottom and top piece in a plastic housing that threads together; to be filled with milled flower and vaporized with a Storz and Bickel Volcano vaporizer

Burn-Out - A characteristic of a high that causes the effects to become more heavy toward the end of the duration of the high

Buzzed - A state of highness of greater potency than being sober but lesser potency than being "high;" number 1 of 5 on the Highness Scale

Calyx - A part of cannabis flower anatomy that forms the bulk of the bud's structure and houses the female reproductive parts

Cannabidiol (CBD) - A non-intoxicating cannabinoid that is calming, relieving, and renowned for its therapeutic effects and wide variety of applications

Cannabigerol (CBG) - A non-intoxicating cannabinoid with therapeutic effects; its cannabinoid acid is the precursor for other cannabinoid acids

Cannabinol (CBN) - A slightly-intoxicating cannabinoid with sedating effects; its cannabinoid acid is formed when THCA is exposed to air or light for extended periods of time

Cannabinoids - A large group of compounds that are found principally in the cannabis plant

Cannabinoid Acids - A precursor to cannabinoids that will become a cannabinoid in the presence of heat (ie. THCA, CBDA, CBGA, CBNA, etc.)

Cannabis Species - A term that describes a particular species of a cannabis plant, either indica, hybrid, sativa, or ruderalis

Cannabis Tolerance - A reduced perceived potency of cannabis over time and with routine consumption that is typically experienced by frequent cannabis consumers

Cannon - A large joint, typically 1g or more

Chronic - 1. A stoner who is more often high than not

2. A slang word for cannabis

Cola - A cluster of buds that is found at the top of a cannabis plant and on a main stem that typically has higher cannabinoid and terpene percentages than the rest of the buds on the plant

Couch-Lock - A characteristic of a high that causes the consumer to become seated still for extended periods of time, often unwilling to move due to excessive comfort or highness

Cr - F

Craft - A variety of cannabis product that is grown in smaller batches and under increased scrutiny and care, often with higher quality and potency as a result

Cultivar - A variety of cannabis with distinct genetic makeup and characteristics from other varieties that is often categorized by genotype and producer (brand) on the recreational market

Decarboxylation - A process that involves heating up a cannabinolic acid in order to turn it into a cannabinoid, such as THC, for consumption

Dried Flower - A fully cured and dried cannabis flower that is ready for consumption; often just called "cannabis flower," "flower," "buds," or "nugs"

Effect - A defining characteristic of a high that is not related to the intensity of the high (uplifting, relaxing, energetic, calming, etc.)

Eighth - A 3.5g unit of cannabis flower

Endocannabinoid System - A body system composed of receptors whose function involves interaction with cannabinoids and restoration of homeostasis

Entourage Effect - A resultant effect from consuming cannabinoids and terpenes together that is often different or greater in effect than if the same cannabinoids and terpenes were each consumed separately

Environmental Conditions - A combination of factors, including humidity, temperature, growing medium, etc., that affect the phenotype of a cultivar as it grows

FUBAR - A state of highness of greater potency than being "stoned;" a "f***ed-up-beyond-all-recognition" experience that is often overwhelming and is a contender for the highest experience the consumer has had; number 5 of 5 on the Highness Scale

Genotype - A particular genetic makeup that defines a cannabis plant

Half-Ounce - A 14g unit of cannabis flower; sometimes found in 15g amounts as well on the recreational market

Half-Quarter - An alternative term for a 3.5g unit of cannabis flower

Headband Effect - A physical sensation experienced in the forehead during a cannabis high

Heavy - An effect profile that may feel lazy, distracting, sedating, relaxing, spacey, chill, blissful, stupefied or zoned-out

High - A state of highness of greater potency than being "buzzed," but lesser potency than being "baked;" number 2 of 5 on the Highness Scale

Highness Scale - A scale that describes the potency of a given high; ranges from sober to buzzed, high, baked, stoned, and finally, FUBAR

Hit - A draw from a cannabis consumption device; synonyms include chop, hoot, puff, riff, rip, toke, etc.

Hybrid - A type of cannabis that is a genetic mix of either sativas, indicas, or ruderalis species

Indica - A type of cannabis species originating in regions such as the middle east and northern Africa

Intensity - A defining characteristic of a high that describes the magnitude of the high (how powerful does the high feel?)

Joint - An amount of milled cannabis flower wrapped in a rolling paper for the purpose of being smoked

Landrace - A type of cannabis species that is native to a particular region, typically with 100% sativa, indica, or ruderalis genetics

Legacy Name - A name for a particular type of cannabis variety that originates from pre-legalization times

Licensed Producer - A company that is fully licensed to produce cannabis within Canada

Lid - An alternative term for a 28g unit of cannabis flower

Light - An effect profile that may feel active, social, focusing, motivating, uplifting, mellow, calm, euphoric, inspiring, or zoned-in

Lineage - The genetic history of a cannabis plant, often expressed as a cross of parent cultivars (ie. "OG Kush x Sour Diesel")

Milled Flower - A fully cured and dried cannabis flower that is ready for consumption and pre-milled for convenience

Munchies - A phenomenon experienced by cannabis consumers that causes profound hunger or cravings for food while high

Neutral - An effect profile that neither feels light nor heavy

Ounce - A 28g unit of cannabis flower

Parent Cultivar - A direct genetic predecessor of a given variety of cannabis

Phenotype - A particular set of expressed traits that exist as a response to a cannabis plant's environment and define its characteristics

Pistil - A part of cannabis flower anatomy that acts as a reproductive organ by collecting pollen; a tiny, hair-like structure that extends from a cannabis flower's surface

Potency - A defining characteristic of a high that takes both effect and intensity into consideration; the total entourage effect is considered when judging potency

Pre-Roll - A prepared cannabis flower product that is ready to smoke in joint form

Premium - A price category of cannabis flower product that is often expensive but boasts higher quality, as well as cannabinoid and terpene content

Psychoactive - A characteristic of cannabis flower, often due to THC content, that produces intoxicating effects in consumers

Quality - A defining characteristic of cannabis flower that takes into consideration appearance, moisture content, trichome coverage, bud density, bud size, and bud trim

Quarter - A 7g unit of cannabis flower

Roach - A resinous remnant of a joint once smoked; the remaining bud and resin at the end of a joint before the filter (if any)

Ruderalis - A type of cannabis species originating in regions such as Asia and Russia

Sativa - A type of cannabis species originating in regions such as Africa and South America

Smoking - A method of cannabis consumption that involves combustion of the plant material to produce a smoke that is consumed via inhalation

Sober - A state lacking intoxication; number 0 of 5 on the Highness Scale

Spliff - A joint that combines both cannabis and tobacco

Stoned - A state of highness of greater potency than being "baked," but lesser potency than being "FUBAR;" number 4 of 5 on the Highness Scale

Stoner - A daily, ritualistic cannabis consumer

Strain - An alternative term for cultivar that is less scientifically accurate

Su - Z

Sugar Leaf - A part of cannabis flower anatomy that serves to make food for the plant via photosynthesis; small leaves extending from the cannabis flower that are often removed during trimming

Terpenes - A group of naturally occurring organic aromatic molecules produced by cannabis and other plants that are responsible for cannabis' aroma and flavour, as well as some of its effects

Tetrahydrocannabinol (THC) - A cannabinoid that is psychoactive in effect when consumed; the compound most responsible for the high experienced by cannabis consumers

Tolerance Break - A pause in cannabis consumption for a desired length of time to reduce an individual's cannabis tolerance

Trichome - A part of cannabis flower anatomy that consists of tiny clear or white resin glands that are principally composed of cannabinoids and terpenes

Type - An alternative term for cannabis species

Vaporizing - A method of cannabis consumption that involves heating up the plant material to pre-combustion temperatures to boil off the cannabinoids and terpenes into a vapour that is consumed via inhalation

Volcano - A desktop cannabis vaporizer produced by Storz and Bickel, renowned for being the top of its class

Wake 'n Bake - A cannabis consumption session that takes place immediately or shortly after waking up for the day

Whole Flower - An alternative term for dried flower; a description used for pre-rolls that signifies that they are made of entire milled buds rather than lower grade product

"I inhaled frequently,
that was the point."

- Barack Obama (2006)

About the Author

Dylan Bruck

Dylan Bruck has dedicated most of his free time in the past decade to exploring cannabis through consumption, experimentation, and appreciation. He currently operates as Cannabis Education and Procurement Specialist at Plantlife Cannabis.

"It all began one fateful night in 12th grade… Aided by my best friend and my sister, I took my first bong toke. I got so high I briefly thought I was Rush frontman Geddy Lee…" and the rest is history.

Graduating in 2014 as class valedictorian, most of Dylan's peers knew nothing of his passion for cannabis. That passion would grow over the years to come, and peak around October 17, 2018 - legalization day for cannabis in Canada.

Dylan saw an opportunity for a career he was passionate about. Quickly, an interview was lined up with Plantlife Cannabis, and he was hired soon after.

Between April 2019 and February 2021, Dylan worked tirelessly, moving up from budtender to district manager, as well as writing over 420 cannabis reviews. Over the next two years, with the goal in sight, Dylan created his first book: The Budtender's Guide to the Galaxy.

Manufactured by Amazon.ca
Bolton, ON